THE COURSE OF HUMAN LIFE

Authors

James F. T. Bugental
Charlotte Bühler
Bernice T. Eiduson
Rudolf Ekstein
Robert Friedman
John L. Fuller
Herbert Goldenberg
Althea J. Horner
Arthur L. Kovacs
Fred Massarik
Marianne Marschak
William H. McWhinney
Mortimer M. Meyer
Jean Livermore Sanville
Everett L. Shostrom
Tommy M. Tomlinson
Melvin Wallace
Edith Weisskopf-Joelson

THE COURSE of HUMAN LIFE

A Study of Goals in the Humanistic Perspective

Charlotte Bühler
Fred Massarik

Editors

Springer Publishing Company, Inc., New York

SPRINGER PUBLISHING COMPANY, INC.
200 Park Avenue South, New York, New York 10003

Library of Congress Catalog Card Number: 68-23550

Printed in U.S.A.

Preface

While the dynamic and emotional aspects of motivation, particularly in their pathology, have emerged as major interests of psychology, the topic of goals has, until recently, remained relatively unexplored. In spite of the availability of individual inquiries, the complexity of the goal setting process and its significance for the course of human life has not received requisite attention. This book attempts to remedy this lack by enlisting the joint efforts of eighteen authors in examining goal setting from a variety of viewpoints, and within the broad context of life's course. The theory that all goal setting must be understood as it relates to the course of life as a whole is presented as a basic hypothesis.

The book is focused on the interplay of the principal codeterminants of goal setting. The structure of human life itself (Part I) and the genetic base (Part II) set a framework within which other factors unfold. Early emotional dynamics (Part III) provide initial specificity to the choice of goals and to the manner in which the process of their establishment is to go forward at later stages. The role of the self begins to take shape, and the degree of the personality's health or malaise is gradually revealed.

Already operative at the earliest moments of life but becoming still more explicit in youth and adulthood, socio-cultural factors (Part IV) come to exert their impact. Noteworthy among these are forces that relate to pervasive cultural, institutional, and class influence and those having to do with small-group behavior. Invariably, education and vocation both affect and are affected by goals as considered important by significant persons and reference groups in the individual's personal world.

Ultimately, there remains the need for an integrating system to lend significance to the process of human striving (Part V). Here, the authors consider the function of the integrating self, and the roles of time, meaning, and values in transforming daily existence into life's fulfillment or failure.

Concern with the person's goal setting as a procedure contributing to his eventual fulfillment (based largely on self-realization) or failure represents the book's humanistic orientation. The authors were willing to take this view into account even though some of them adhere to other theoretic persuasions. Their statements of alternate positions in the present context should serve to place the issues in an appropriately broad perspective.

Beyond the primary task of examining how goal setting proceeds during the course of human life, this volume serves an additional purpose: to lay the groundwork for a psychotherapeutic approach that does justice to the person's outlook and to his reflections on the totality of life. This consideration of what life should add up to is not an essential one in the traditional psychotherapies. Examples are given which indicate the motivational power of these reflections. The book hopes to provide a starting point for psychotherapeutic approaches that are more effectively geared to the important human concerns with life's wholeness and ultimate significance.

Many friends were interested in this book and furthered its production through their comments. Above all, Dr. Gordon W. Allport and Dr. Abraham H. Maslow encouraged the senior editor to bring her earlier studies on the course of human life into the frame of present-day American psychology.

Dr. Zoltan Gross, Dr. Georgene Seward, and Dr. Hedda Bolgar assisted at various points with comments and suggestions. Last but not least, the collaborators were helpful in furthering and integrating the book's basic intention. To all these the editors extend their thanks.

CHARLOTTE BÜHLER
FRED MASSARIK

Los Angeles, California

Authors

* Charlotte Bühler, Ph. D., *University of Southern California, Los Angeles, Calif.*

J. F. T. Bugental, Ph.D., *Psychological Service Associates, Los Angeles, Calif.*

Bernice T. Eiduson, Ph.D., *Reiss-Davis Child Study Center, Los Angeles, Calif.*

Rudolf Ekstein, Ph.D., *Los Angeles Psychoanalytic Society and Reiss-Davis Child Study Center, Los Angeles, Calif.*

Robert Friedman, Ph.D., *Educational Psychologist in Private Practice, Los Angeles, Calif.*

John L. Fuller, Ph.D., *The Jackson Laboratory, Bar Harbor, Maine*

Herbert Goldenberg, Ph.D., *California State College at Los Angeles*

Althea J. Horner, Ph.D., *Clinical Psychologist in Private Practice, Arcadia, Calif.*

Arthur L. Kovacs, Ph.D., *Western Psychological Center, Los Angeles, Calif.*

William H. McWhinney, Ph.D., *University of California, Los Angeles, Calif.*

Marianne Marschak, Ph.D., *Research Psychologist, Los Angeles, Calif.*

Fred Massarik, Ph.D., *University of California, Los Angeles, Calif.*

Mortimer M. Meyer, Ph.D., *Reiss-Davis Child Study Center, Los Angeles, Calif.*

Jean Livermore Sanville, M.S.S., *Social Worker in Private Practice, Los Angeles, Calif.*

Everett L. Shostrom, Ph.D., *Institute of Therapeutic Psychology, Santa Ana, Calif.*

T. M. Tomlinson, Ph.D., *Office of Economic Opportunity, Washington, D.C.*

Melvin Wallace, Ph.D., *Rohrer, Hibler and Replogle, Los Angeles, Calif.*

Edith Weisskopf-Joelson, Ph.D., *University of Georgia, Athens, Georgia*

* The spellings *Bühler* and *Buhler* are used interchangeably, with the former now preferred.

Contents

Introduction

Charlotte Bühler

The Course of Human Life and Its Goal Aspects

The course of human life can be viewed as a whole composed of a multitude of events and processes which an individual experiences between his birth and his death. Although psychologists usually study these events and processes in relation to certain phases and aspects of a person's life, this study will focus on the course of a life in its entirety. The succession of significant occurrences that make up life is what biographers, clinicians, and others call a person's history, but it is only under certain circumstances that these various occurrences are seen as a whole of life: for instance, when a life is being reviewed by the individual himself or by another.

Both instances require that a large number of events which have taken place over a long period of time be collected and considered together. One who embarks on such an undertaking usually does so in order to understand and evaluate a person's life. Such an understanding and evaluation also may serve to guide, direct, or interpret that life in the light of practical, historical, philosophical, or religious considerations.

To understand the manifestations and data of a person's life it is necessary to know the interrelatedness of events. This interrelatedness of events is the result of their structural properties and of the motives and purposes that affect the continuity of individual development. By development we mean a succession of events that occurs in a recognizable order or pattern and conveys a certain direction and unity. And it is this process of development that we are looking for when we study a person's history.

An effective person has a direction aimed toward certain results, and these results are as eagerly hoped for and expected during the midst of life as they are toward the end. However, they mean different things to different people and are therefore variously conceived of as being happiness or success, possessions or accomplishments, belonging of participating, self-improvement or self-development. Humanistic psychologists have agreed more or less on the concept of self-realization, introduced by C. Jung, K. Horney, and E. Fromm, or self-actualization, as suggested by K. Goldstein and A. Maslow. I myself recommend the concept of self-fulfillment as the one which covers more completely all of the things to which people actually aspire.

To live a goal-directed life means to have the desire, or even the feeling of obligation, to see one's life culminating in certain results. Ideally, these results would represent a fulfillment of the aims toward which a person is striving with a determination that governs him throughout his life. People who live in this way always seem to know where they are going and to hold only themselves responsible for their fate. Others, however, seem to be more "outer-directed" than "inner-directed," to use David Riesman's expression. They, too, are seeking fulfillment and want to have something to show for life, but they feel that it is external circumstances that determine their development. Since it is their belief that much in life depends on luck, they are convinced that misfortune and lack of opportunity have prevented them from succeeding.

Attempts at self-inspection often lead to self-evaluation, and evaluation has been previously mentioned as the second of two reasons why one may want to view his or somebody else's life in its entirety. It is a process in which the results are related to goals. Some people also evaluate their future prospects in the hope of accomplishing what they have not as yet attained. They may feel that they are "on the way up" or "on the way down" as far as additional accomplishments are concerned, or that they had better start to think about the final result.

Many people never think of their lives as a whole or conceive of them as a continuous period of development. They live what might be called a segmented life. They live in expectation of certain happy events to be brought about by some miracle that is about to happen. A stroke of luck, they feel, such as winning the Irish sweepstakes or succeeding in the perfect crime, will make it possible for them to live "happily ever after."

Others regard their lives in terms of certain decisive occurrences, perhaps of the kind that A. Maslow (1962) has described as "peak experiences," unique and deeply fulfilling. They also may tell themselves that what they want to get out of life is excitement or intoxication, gambling, sexual perversion, or even crime. Then there are those who admit that they live only for the day, or from day to day, or that they are merely "existing or vegetating—not really living at all."

People who seem, consciously or unconsciously, to be incapable of conceiving of life as a whole may be involved in too severe a struggle for their livelihood to indulge in thoughts of the future. Or they may be too confused or too unaccustomed to thinking things through, being able only to react to a given situation and to follow the beaten path. Some also rush off in various directions without ever stopping long enough to assess themselves.

However, because most people have been brought up within the framework of particular religious and/or moral philosophies, they have been taught to assume that only they are responsible for their lives and the eventual accountability. This is difficult to forget, despite the conscious efforts some people make not to concern themselves with any goals beyond the here and now of their existence.

Not infrequently people become deadlocked within themselves. This may be because of failures, disappointments, losses, or unforgettable tragedies, in the face of which the striving for goals seems hopeless and senseless. Such individuals have lost their faith in the possibility of ever achieving their goals, and their lives seem to be falling apart. It is this kind of situation which we often encounter in psychotherapy and which is the opposite of the integrated striving of one who functions as a whole, self-possessed and with confidence in his goals.

The understanding and evaluation of life histories also can serve, as mentioned before, as a basis for guidance, redirection, and interpretation of life in a large context.

Educational guidance and therapeutic redirection originally grew out of theoretical considerations of socially and culturally acceptable and effective ways of living. Recently, however, we have found that guidance and redirection become more effective and realistic when we understand the factors that determine a person's actions. These factors are numerous, and only lately have we learned to appreciate their great complexity.

In this book, then, we will attempt to investigate the goal structure of human life in its varying forms and how this structure appears from a theoretical as well as a developmental and clinical viewpoint. We will study some of the basic conditions and processes of the individual's self-directed drive toward his goals, and the modes by which he builds his life. In addition, we will discuss these subjects in as wide a frame of reference as possible, including biological, genetic, dynamic, social, and socio-cultural considerations.

Basic Determinants of Goal Setting

As we are going to deal with the goal aspects of life, a word should be said about the difference between goals and needs. Both are motivational concepts, but each represents a different aspect of motivation.

The common denominator of most definitions of need is the belief that it results from deficiencies in the organism. These deficiencies cause tensions which, in turn, initiate processes. The inherent aim of these processes is to relieve the pressures of the need and/or to satisfy it. This inherent aim may or may not also be the goal. It becomes the goal if by his action the individual strives for the satisfaction of the need as an end, that is, if, besides the urge, he also has the intent.

Let us clarify this with an example. A hungry person who prepares himself a meal experiences the urge to satisfy his hunger. He may or may not have an aim other than this urge. He may want to fill himself up so as not to be hungry for several hours, or he may want to eat just enough so as not to spoil his appetite for an early dinner invitation.

This leaves the question of how these intents occur. There is no doubt that in purposeful actions the anticipated end appears in an image based on a previous perceptual experience. There are, however, stages of actions, specifically in creative work, where the urge seems to contain an aim directed toward an end which is not yet clearly defined. This is true particularly in the early stages of creative development. A young person, for instance, may feel an urge to write or the desire to help others without knowing specifically how or why. The initial urge is part of a process that, once achieved, will then be identified as having been the inherent goal.

The definition of goals and their position in the system varies with different theories. In psychoanalysis goals appear on the ego level. Heinz Hartmann (1964), for instance, while being aware of the variety of levels on which goal-directed actions can be controlled and organized, concludes that all goal direction is determined by perceptions, however undeveloped they may be at the beginning. He quotes Freud as having shown "how the partial replacement of merely reactive motor outlet, and of instinctual breakthrough, by directed and organized action is an important part of ego development and an essential step in replacing the pleasure principle by the reality principle" (p. 39).

Accordingly, the goal lies in the "outer world" toward which the child feels himself driven "in perception and activity" if his wants "exceed a certain degree without being satisfied, and if they can no longer be satisfied by fantasy either . . ." (p. 39).

In other words, in psychoanalytic theory the goal-directed ego action replaces the original pursuit of a satisfaction, after it has proven to be unsuccessful, with a blind drive.

A different concept of goals is advanced by Kurt Goldstein (1939). Goldstein holds that the drives of a healthy organism are never mere reactions tending only to rid the organism of frustrations and tensions. Instead, he sees all action as resulting from a need to actualize or realize potentialities. He incorporates the action goal in the need, which means that he considers the urge itself to be goal-directed even before any perception has taken place. He sees goals as being certain definite ends which the organism is set to bring about.

The question, however, remains as to what exactly these inherent goals encompass. Goldstein's examples refer primarily to such formal characteristics of action as striving for perfection or for orderly performance. He also considers the act of coping with danger as an inherent goal of the healthy person who is out "to conquer the world."

In 1954, I developed the theory, based on observations of infants, that we assume "a principle which represents the living being's *expansiveness and creativity,* implying an active outgoing force, directivity, intent with positive anticipation, preparedness to cope . . ." (p. 640). The accomplishment of something, somehow, somewhere, is the inherent goal of the activity drive in this conceptualization.

Individual aptitudes and talents may add a specific flavor to this need to become active. We can observe unspecific as well as specific tendencies toward activity in young children who, while still crawling, may explore, hit or move things. A little later they may want to build or paint, sing or talk, and may try to accomplish something with varying degrees of vigor, individuality and talent by whatever means are available to them.

For the followers of this theory, then, these inherent activity tendencies constitute the first contributory determinants of the individual's goal-setting drive. I consider them to be structural, as they belong to the primary, i.e., congenital human equipment. At best they initiate the activation of the individual's intent, that is, the direction and purpose of his innermost self. This does not preclude the fact that their actualization and characteristics are largely codetermined by environmental influences. Perceptions, emotional reactions, and evaluations play decisive roles in the individual's goal-setting process. Nor does it preclude the fact that the individual must learn to incorporate many other goals in his inventory, goals which his environment either forces upon him or persuades him to pursue, and the intents that he eventually uses to substitute for or add to his original objectives.

Several collaborators of this book see the human goal development primarily in psychoanalytic terms. They prefer Hartmann's theory of goal setting to Goldstein's theory, and they think of the individual's goal development largely in terms of his ego development without considering the action of an underlying self. (These differences will be discussed in Parts III and V of this book.) But neither these nor other occasional differences of opinion seemed serious enough to endanger our collaboration. On the contrary, it appeared to us that the hypothetical nature of the theoretical concepts would serve us well in a collaborative venture and that our differences could add a new dimension of interest to the study, particularly since the theoretical bias that determined the selection of the material will be explained.

Factors Contributing to Goal Setting

The functioning of the individual from the beginning to the end of his life is determined by a multitude of factors. The biological and psychophysical life-cycle structures may be considered the first determinant of the potentialities and limitations of his goal-setting process.

At birth the individual begins a life cycle which leads him from phases of growth, including a limited period of reproduction, to phases of decline, and ultimately, to death. This cycle is characterized by a sequence of ages as well as of growth and decline. Inherent in its structure also is a psychophysical system which activates behavior, experience, and performance. The development of this system is determined by three factors: 1) the sequential order of growth and decline involving unfolding, maturing, and aging; 2) the influence of individual endowment on the tempo and certain only partially known congenital qualities of the individual life process, and 3) the role the environment plays in furthering or hindering the use of potentialities.

The process which results from these three interacting determinants is called development. Development is an irreversible process and is unique with each and every individual. As I have observed in my earlier studies on the course of human life (1933), and as J. E. Birren has stated as recently as 1964, the relationship between the structurally determined process of maturing and aging and the psychophysically determined process of development has not yet been sufficiently clarified to allow a valid comparison.

The two processes are not independent of each other either; there is always an approximate relationship. Average curves, therefore, charting the increase and decrease of functions, interests, attitudes, aptitudes, etc., can be and have been established (Pressey and Kuhlen, 1957; Solberg and Zubeck, 1954).

The moment a person is conceived, he is activated by a unique genetic setup. As we have learned recently, the probability of two unrelated individuals having the same genotype is practically zero, and even for related individuals it is extremely slight (J. Hirsch, 1954). This unique equipment then may be considered to be the second determinant, remembering that from the very beginning clashes with the environment affect behavior.

Such environmental clashes experienced by the infant in his physical and emotional surroundings of the mother-child relationship soon develop into an ever-increasing multitude of impressions and influences. They open up a world of stimuli, information, and satisfactions as well as frustrations, and affect the developing perceptual, intellectual, emotional, motivational, and behavioral systems of the growing individual.

A fourth factor in the development of a psychophysical system, with sometimes an indirect but usually forceful impact on the individual's goal-setting process, is the social system and cultural ideology of which he is a member and exponent. This system and ideology are strong codeterminants of his group behavior and his social roles, of his opportunities and limitations, of his values and beliefs. It is only recently that we have learned to distinguish their influences from those exerted by the closer environment and the emotional and intellectual climate.

A fifth factor is the integrative system of the personality which unifies more or less successfully the impulses that the various subsystems contribute to goal setting. This system obviously is the final determinant of a person's goal-setting efforts, but there is still a great deal of speculation as to exactly how such personality integration is accomplished. Allport (1961) identifies integration as a "hierarchical organization" of the personality which, however, is at no time perfect. Furthermore, he believes that integration is accomplished on different personality levels by different kinds of operations. On the other hand, Thomas M. French (1952) hypothesizes a specific "integrative mechanism" and also assumes a quantitatively varying "integrative capacity." Both theories suggest that integration may be an inner-directed process, the roots of which I would assume to be in the "core-self" of the genetic setup. Other concepts of the integrative process will be discussed subsequently by some of the other authors.

In order to understand the structure and development of the goal-setting drive, we will have to examine each contributory determinant separately.

The first determinant is the biological and psychophysical life-cycle structure. It shows human development as being a sequence of certain progressive steps of behavior, inner experiences, and performance during which phases of goal setting become apparent. The main problem here is to determine or hypothesize the extent to which the growth and decline of abilities and aptitudes, as well as changes in motivation, is structurally determined.

The second determinant is the individual's unique endowment. It is still the most problematic of the known factors. The question of primary tendencies so far has remained unanswered, and the influence of innate tendencies and traits on development is as yet undetermined. Modern research on heredity, however, has produced a certain number of new and reliable findings, and modern infant psychology, too, has provided us with evidence of individual behavior characteristics observed at the very beginning of infancy. Recent studies of creativity and intelligence have further afforded us some extremely interesting and penetrating insights into the structure of different individual endowments.

The third determinant, the individual's clash with his environment, has been most intensively researched. A study dealing with the dynamics of individual motivation under the impact of gratifications, frustrations, and demands, presents in a wealth of psychoanalytically oriented case studies most of what is known about goal setting. Less information in terms of depth understanding is available on how education and training of the developing individual influence his aims, so that we are still working on a rather superficial level in this area.

The fourth determinant, socio-cultural membership, has been the subject of some recent empirical studies. Social psychology has assembled an enormous body of information on group behavior and social roles, and empirical procedures have disclosed the ways in which, within certain subcultural groups, value and belief patterns are being transmitted from parents to children. It will be interesting to examine our individual case studies to learn to what extent these group determinants intertwine with an individual's dynamic determinants.

The fifth factor, the integrative system, has not been studied in relation to the subsystems previously mentioned. T. M. French has done some pioneering work on integration, but his investigations are oriented toward a different set of problems. Our work in this area, therefore, will necessarily have to be mainly exploratory.

Problems of Methodology

A study of life goals encounters several methodological problems. The first is the sheer mass of material involved in the examination of a complete life history. The second results from the multitude of factors that codetermine the process of goal setting. To consider these methodological problems properly requires not only a study of several different scientific resources but also an integration of different kinds of data obtained by varying methods. What complicates the process is the necessity for dealing with statistical observations and interview data on the one hand, and long-range views and detailed studies conducted over a short period of time, on the other.

I would suggest, therefore, that we use two separate approaches: the macroscopic and the microscopic. The macroscopic approach will be applied when we consider the course of life as a whole, and view primarily its major outlines and aspects. The microscopic approach will be used to examine in detail individual behavior at specific moments in certain phases of development. But it is only through a combination of both of these approaches that we can hope to master this plentiful and complex material.

Obviously, each approach implies a different technique and focus and therefore proceeds from a different rationale. To study life in its entirety, the investigator needs an orientation and a readiness to perceive unifying factors and consistent trends. To examine specific aspects of a person's life presupposes a step-by-step process and an ability to build a whole from separate pieces.

The orientation in Part I of this book will be a global one, and we will use macroscopic techniques, particularly in the presentation of the biographical material. Biographical data will be discussed in terms of events and of their influence on behavior, and as they can be traced in inner experiences, in productions or in other traceable effects. This procedure enables us to depict the general structure of a person's life and to present it in a schematic diagram of up-and-down movements.

While we realize that all events have their own histories and backgrounds, we will deal with them in this part of the book only insofar as they contribute to the general structure of the life cycle. We will use two biographies as examples: one of an average middle-class individual and the other of an outstanding personality.

Part I also contains the results of group studies, another macroscopic approach to investigation. These same group studies also will be referred to in Parts II and IV, particularly as they relate to the problems of natural gifts and talents and to the influences of socio-cultural factors on the individual.

Microscopic approaches to psychological problems are many and complex. They form the basis for studies using experimental and observational techniques, for longitudinal studies, and for interviews and clinical case reports of various levels of depth. Parts II and III utilize all these methods except for the longitudinal studies. Part V, too, insofar as it is not purely theoretical, shows the advantages of this approach. Theoretical considerations, of course, play an essential role in this book; they appear in all sections and culminate in Part V.

References

Allport, G. W. *Pattern and growth in personality,* New York: Holt, Rinehart and Winston, 1956, 1961.

Birren, J. E. *Relations of development and aging.* Springfield, Ill.: Charles C. Thomas, 1964.

Buhler, C. The reality principle, *Amer. Psychother,* 1954, *VIII*: 4, 626-647.

Buhler, C. *Der menschliche Lebenslauf als psychologisches Problem. (The course of human life as a psychological problem).* Leipzig: S. Hirzel, 1933.

French, M. T. *The integration of behavior.* Chicago: University of Chicago Press, 1952-55.

Goldstein, K. *The organism.* New York: American Book Co., 1939.

Hartmann, H. *Essays on ego psychology.* New York: International Universities Press, 1964.

Hirsch, J. Behavior genetics and individuality understood, *Science,* 1963, *142*: 3598.

Maslow, A. *Toward a psychology of being.* New York: D. van Nostrand, 1962.

Maslow, A. *Religious values and peak experiences.* Columbus: Ohio State University Press, 1964.

Pressey, S. L., and Kuhlen, R. G. *Psychological development through the life span.* New York: Harper Bros., 1957.

Zubek, J. P., and Solberg, P. A. *Human development.* New York: McGraw-Hill, 1954.

I The Structure of Human Life as Codeterminant of Goal Setting

Goal setting in human life is most generally believed to be codetermined by what the authors of this book call the structure of human life. The individual's life is a product of nature and it begins as a relatively independent entity; it sustains itself for a limited time by means of various processes and stops when these fail. Life itself is divided into successive steps called ages, which are characterized by certain phenomena which appear, develop, end or are transformed.

These biologically conditioned expansions and restrictions of human existence are reflected in the up and down, as well as in the increase and decrease of functions, aptitudes, and productions. But just how many of these changes and the ensuing processes and operations are the result of the structure of life as such, and how many of the multitude of other factors, has never been sufficiently clarified.

Thus an attempt is being made in Part I of this book to ascertain the extent to which an individual's goal-setting drive is determined by the biological factors of birth and death as well as of growth and decline. In the first two chapters, Charlotte Buhler lists the ten basic properties of life, among them goal orientation, and describes the development of the goal-setting drive. In the third chapter, C. Buhler and H. Goldenberg discuss the structural aspects and the various phases of an individual's history, particularly as they relate to the biological processes of growth and decline. A. Horner, in Chapter 4, presents a complex biography which demonstrates the general characteristics of the structure of human life and also indicates the psychologically conditioned deviations from the schematic pattern.

Chapter 1

The General Structure of the Human Life Cycle

Charlotte Bühler

Some Basic Concepts and Assumptions

This book starts with the assumption that the individual's course of life has a definite basic structure and that this structure is evident in his biological life cycle as well as in his psychophysical development. By structure we mean an organized system with certain consistent properties and potentialities. It is also a basic assumption that the life-cycle structure codetermines the goals the human being sets for himself.

The subsequent discussion will describe ten basic properties of the life cycle and will relate them briefly to the characteristics of the goal-setting process.

Properties Reflecting the Organization of Life

First, each life cycle belongs to one individual. This means that within the narrow confines of a single organism the individual harbors a complex system with relatively independent subsystems, all of which participate in the major events of the life cycle in some interrelated way. These events take place within certain predetermined categories, and the course of action is codetermined in varying degrees by external and internal factors.

Initially there is the growth and decline of the organism, a process to which every individual is subjected and over which he has little influence. Then there is the maturational order in which the functions of the psychophysical system develop, a sequence whose speed and quality can be influenced by learning and also by the impact of emotional experiences.

There are abilities and aptitudes, motives and goals, all of which contribute to the development of personality. The relative freedom of individual exploitation of these gifts and aims depends on what use the individual makes of himself and his circumstances.

The outcome of these partially directed but partially uncontrollable processes is, then, the person's life history as measured by the events of his life, the evolution of his behavior, his inner experiences, and his accomplishments. The life history contains the whole of the individual as he emerges in his given time and space. In the end, of course, this life cycle terminates, and what remains are evidences of life in the stream of history.

The second property of the life cycle is its limited duration; death ends the physical life cycle. However, in man's hopes, beliefs, and religious dogmas, he has long speculated about the continued existence of his soul. We know that a person may live on in the memory of his friends. If he has lived an outstanding public life, he may even go down in the annals of history. Some try to perpetuate their existence by beneficial bequests, as well as by the accomplishments and influence they may leave behind. Some believe in an afterlife for which they try to prepare themselves. We know there have been certain periods in history when considerations of life after death seemed more important to people than life itself.

A third property of the life cycle is individual development according to a "ground plan," as defined by S. Brody (1945). The ground plan manifests itself in the orderly sequence of organ formation and in the unfolding of the growth and decline processes. These processes vary with environmental circumstances depending on time limits and actual characteristics, but their general development seems to be permanently set.

It is a development in which a process of progression is followed by a period of "stationary growth," which, in turn, is followed by a period of decline. The middle period, also called "the prime of life," is a zone, the width of which, according to Brody, "varies with the particular index of aging employed." In human beings, reproductive activities begin shortly before the growth period ends, and stop before or during the period of decline.

This ground plan results in a phasic organization of the life cycle which may be called its fourth property.

The organization of a three-phasic process can best be described as 1) a growth period from birth until the organism is fully developed; 2) a stationary growth period during which the organism's power to maintain itself and develop is equal to the forces of decline; and 3) a last period of decline. Furthermore, it is characterized by the lack of reproductive ability in the initial stages, the presence of this reproductive ability in the middle phase, and in the last phase—although with differences between the sexes—by the loss of this ability.

If both categories, growth and reproduction, are used, the life cycle then can be described as having five biological phases:

1. A period of progressive growth without reproductive ability.
2. A period of progressive growth with the onset of reproductive ability.
3. A period of reproductive ability and stationary growth.
4. A period of beginning decline and loss of reproductive ability by the female.
5. A period of further decline, following loss of reproductive ability in one or both sexes.

Chronologically, these periods could be shown, roughly and schematically, as ages 0–15; 15–25; 25–45 (50); 45(50)–65 (70), and 65(70) to the end (C. Buhler, 1933).

Whether these phases have any parallel in the psychological organization of life, and to what degree, is a much debated question. The main arguments against describing the life cycle in terms of psychological phases have been that 1) psychological development is continuous and lacks distinct steps, and 2) there is no exact parallel between biological and psychological development.

Both arguments, of course, are correct, but only partially so. I do not think, therefore, that they eliminate the necessity for phase divisions. The assumption of a parallel raises some interesting questions about human productivity and creativity.

Earlier studies of human productivity, as carried out by E. Frenkel and E. Brunswik (in C. Buhler, 1933 and 1961; E. Frenkel, 1936), indicate that there is a kind of productivity which in its rise and fall follows closely the organism's curve of growth and decline. It is not surprising to find that it includes all activities in which physical ability plays the major role, such as sports and activities involving manual labor.

On the other hand, Frenkel and Brunswik established extremely late culminations in certain other categories of productivity where systematic thinking and long experience were the essential requirements, as, for instance, in philosophy and statesmanship. This type of late culmination seems to result from a slow developmental process, differing from the physical, and largely independent of biological factors and outlasting the ability of reproduction.

Both types of production curves and culminations have been confirmed subsequently, especially by H. Lehman (1953). Strangely enough, Lehman emphasizes only that middle-age peak in a person's thirties, which he derived by combining all his data. This statistical procedure, however, obscures the fact that two different factors are at work in human productivity and creativity. I have tentatively called these factors vitality and mentality. The latter's relative independence of physical processes seems to be the main reason that psychological development does not parallel biological development.

Not only in productivity, but also in motivation and goals do we expect a certain age relatedness. We speak of premature and immature behavior and attitudes when people act in ways that do not seem appropriate for their ages (although society's standards change in these respects).

Society, more than the individual, assigns roles according to age. For instance, there are definite age requirements for entrance into or retirement from certain occupations; age is an important factor in our own society as well as in others. And because this holds true for societies all over the world, it must be explained ultimately by the developmental changes of human attributes and aptitudes with which society interacts. These changes do occur. And no matter how slowly they evolve, they bring about new directions.

Because many different roles begin and end during a person's lifetime, phases may be distinguished from a variety of viewpoints. It seems arbitrary to decide on specific turning points. Yet, if we see the human being not simply by himself but as a member of society, we find that practically everywhere society assigns differing roles to the child, the youth, the young adult, the middle-aged, and the aged. These changing roles go hand in hand with changing abilities and aptitudes, functions and interests, motives and goals, and accompany the changing relationships with other individuals and groups.

This succession, then, of normally irreversible phases with definite directions is called development, and it represents the fifth property of the life cycle. Human beings, like other multicellular organisms, grow from an initial form into a final mold, and their functions develop through an interwoven process of maturation and learning. The various stages of this development represent an irreversible sequence, with one exception which will be discussed below. Generally speaking, all development is oriented toward structurally and psychologically anticipated goals.

Biologists frequently limit the use of the term "development" to the period of progressive growth which begins with birth and ends with maturity, and they speak of the period following maturity as "aging." "Aging," says J. E. Birren (1959), "may be defined as beginning at the point in time when the forces of growth of the organism in size, form and function have arrived at a relatively steady state" (p. 13).

Psychologists, however, extend the term "development" to the whole of life. Anybody who thinks in terms of "self-realization" or "fulfillment" must assume that the individual develops more or less steadily all through life. This assumption seems particularly valid in view of the previously discussed fact that certain aspects of a person's psychological development take place independently of the biological part of his nature. In other words, his creative mentality may still allow him to be mentally productive and to unfold new personality trends at an age when his physical self may already have deteriorated. By the same token, such a personality, because of its relative independence from biological processes, may react to the environment in such a way as to hamper individual development or even cause it to regress.

Properties Reflecting the Dynamics of the Life Cycle

While it lasts, life is a continuous process, and the individual is continually active, a characteristic which may be called the sixth property of the life cycle. There is immense variety in these activities, and they occur partly within the individual and partly in relation to the outside world. They form a complex pattern involving different subsystems as well as the whole individual, and they constitute the basis for the continuing changes brought about by the developmentally changing potentials and environmental opportunities and demands.

There are quantitative and qualitative changes. Quantitative changes are brought about by an increase and decrease of physical and mental capabilities and are the result of changing abilities and aptitudes. Generally speaking, most abilities and aptitudes increase and improve throughout a person's childhood and youth and decline at varying points in middle age. Qualitative changes in activities and objectives are mostly the consequences of changes in motives and goals as they occur during a lifetime.

This brings us to the seventh property of the life cycle: the pressure of needs exerted on the individual throughout his life. These needs are instrumental in propelling him into action, and inasmuch as intents are inherent in these needs, they also give him direction.

There is, however, a wide gap between the intents inherent in basic needs and the complex goals pursued by the mature mind in which the need aspect is partly replaced by one of values and beliefs. (The human ability to detach intents of value from need pressures will be treated as a separate property.)

With this discussion we leave the area of factual description and enter the realm of speculative thinking.

It is generally acknowledged that man, like all other living beings, is never in complete balance and that this partial or total imbalance is the cause of development. But there are two viewpoints as to what this development represents. Some believe it is a continuous drive to establish and maintain such an equilibrium or homeostasis, while others contend that there is a second aspect, that of "creating a change toward producing new potentialities." This latter formulation grew out of the 1956 Interdisciplinary Conference in Chicago which reconsidered the whole concept of homeostasis, and established "maintenance" and "change" as being two equally basic tendencies in life. According to J. E. P. Toman (1956), change takes the form of production and adaptation.

Following these ideas, I came to the conclusion (1959a) that maintenance also takes place in two ways: by the restitution of deficiencies, and the upholding of the complex system's internal order. I furthermore hypothesized that there are four basic tendencies that work toward what I call the fulfillment of life: need satisfaction, self-limiting adaptation, creative expansion, and upholding of internal order. Need satisfaction and upholding of order involve principles of stability, while self-limiting adaptation and creative expansion involve principles of change. Human beings go through life changing and creating change, satisfying needs, adapting themselves to given circumstances, and upholding internal order. The different tendencies determine, with changing predominance, the utilization of a person's inner and outer potentials, and the availability as well as management of these determine the attainable fulfillment.

These tendencies, it is assumed, are present at birth, since from the very beginning an infant has to adapt himself in order to satisfy his needs and to extend himself and coordinate his behavior, if only to a small degree. And obviously, the newborn's drive is directed primarily toward need satisfaction.

Thus, normatively speaking, we find fluctuating degrees of predominance in the various stages. The growing child develops his self-limiting adaptation during the learning process, the adolescent and adult move into a widened world during a period of predominant creative expansion, the adult begins to assess his past and himself in the climacteric age, probably because he wants to restore his inner order, and the old person either regresses to need-satisfying tendencies or continues

to follow his previous adaptive or creative drives. One aspect of fulfillment is believed to be the experience of having used these basic tendencies toward the most complete realization of one's own potential.

Freud developed the theory that life's basic tendency is to establish a condition of homeostasis. He, too, was the first to relate time motives to development, if not to the whole of the life cycle. His well-konwn theory holds that at the beginning of life, drive alone—the id—pursues that satisfaction which the ego and superego later try to capture indirectly by taking reality and society into consideration.

While Freud concerned himself mostly with the establishment of these early motivating factors, followers of his, notably Erik Erikson (1959), have studied the development of motives during the entire life cycle. Erikson's theory of phases of life sees development primarily in terms of ego changes.

In formulating my basic theory, I have decided not to use the Freudian triad as the fundamental parameter of personality tendencies. I reached this decision because Freud's system leaves no room for the fundamental role of creativity, for a primarily "positive" reality, anticipated and accepted as an opportunity rather than as a hindrance, and for a conscience that is rooted in the self instead of in social rules. (For a more detailed discussion, see C. Buhler, 1954 and 1959.)

For those of us with similar convictions, Freud's important theoretical and clinical contributions lie in the context of that behavior pathology within which it originated. He has demonstrated that the defenses and repressions which deter the individual from pursuing the development of his potential are the result of a negative frustrating reality and of social pressures with which the individual cannot cope. These factors, as well as the overwhelmingly important role of the negative unconscious directives, will receive due consideration within the larger framework of the normally self-fulfilling personality.

I conceive of this normally self-fulfilling personality as one that is able to work out defenses and repressions while at the same time pursuing the realization of potentialities by means of the four basic tendencies. I further hypothesize that this normal personality is directed by a core system which organizes, selects, and integrates the multitude of motivational trends, i.e., the self.

Psychoanalysis has attributed this organizing and guiding role to the ego, and modern ego psychology, too, has emphasized this integrative function of the ego. But since the ego is only a manifestation of the individual's reality interests, it is hard to see how it can do justice to the personality as a whole with its sometimes reality-transcendent orientation and its subconscious depths.

It is to Karen Horney's great credit that she emphasized the "self" as a "whole" person as against Freud's subdivided personality. Horney's "real self" is inborn, while Carl Jung's self is achieved. However, this real self and its workings were not clearly defined, a fact which Ruth Munroe (1955) termed a weakness of the nonlibidinal schools, together with their lack of concern for the genetic process. Only Harry Stack Sullivan concerned himself with developments, but, as Munroe says, the nature of the self-realizing self remained obscure.

My definition of the self and my assumptions about its development (1962) are as follows: the motivational parameters of need satisfaction, self-limiting adaptation, creative expansion, upholding of internal order, as well as those of the id, ego, and super ego represent vectors with certain inherent ends and potential goals. Unconsciously or consciously, the individual decides which of the various directions is to predominate at a given time, and then selects the goal that will most effectively satisfy the corresponding need structure. Thus, even if ends are considered inherent in the structure, they become goals only after they have been selected and become the focal point. As a chosen goal, the end represents a value which may be factual or normative.

Properties Reflecting the Goal Orientation of Life

The eighth property of the life cycle can be found in the supposition that a human being's activities are always goal-directed.

Despite the assumption, held by some, that there exists a purely tension-releasing id at the beginning of life, and in later stages of regression, it can hardly be denied that normally most of life is lived in the pursuit of numerous goals, partly conscious, partly unconscious, short-range and long-range, related and unrelated.

More important is the difference of opinion regarding the nature of goal setting where, according to one definition, the goal or, more precisely, the intent of a pursuit is inherent in the urge (Goldstein), and, according to the other, the drive is merely a "reactive outlet" (Freud). The latter theory, which has been elaborated by H. Hartmann (1964), holds that any anticipation of the future as incorporated in an intention toward a goal is "one of the most important achievements of early ego development" (p. 40).

In the first theory, intents are seen as inherent in the basic tendencies of human beings, as belonging to the individual's genetic setup and to his self, and conceived of as a core system.

The second theory presupposes perceptual awareness and a certain degree of ego development for a person to move toward goals in the outer world. These goals, then, are largely determined by how the individual experiences his environment, i.e., by the influence of reality and society on his life.

As long as an individual's self-system operates and consciously or unconsciously directs him, he is constantly made aware of his intrinsic, authentic being (Bugental). According to Freud's theory, ego, on the other hand, operates by means of identification which, as we know from therapy, may distort, repress, or destroy an individual's genuineness. The ego may pursue ambitions or false values, and it is in fact the agent most frequently responsible for a person's defecting from his true self or "real self" (Horney). Even when perceiving and thinking without any bias, the personality that lets itself be guided solely by considerations on the ego level will be lacking in depth because its self-direction does not come from the core of its system.

Gordon Allport (1961) also sees the self, "this awesome enigma," as a "kind of core in our being." "And yet it is not a constant core. Sometimes the core expands and seems to take command of all our behavior and consciousness; sometimes it seems to go completely offstage, leaving us with no awareness whatsoever of self" (p. 110). In this formulation, the self appears as an active agent on the one hand, and an object of our awareness on the other.

In Gardner Murphy's presentation (1957), the self, although the perceiver as well as the perceived, is more the object than the subject of integrative functions. He defines the ego as "the system of activities, organized around the self" (1947, p. 523), and sees the integrative activities as ego functions.

His studies have led him to believe that there are three human natures. The first consists of "our organic make-up, our capacities, our cravings, our need to use the equipment with which life supplies us." The second is "full of acquired tastes, cultural needs, insatiable new demands upon the environment." And the third is "the insatiable craving to understand, hoping to be realized in a world of science and arts; and no longer limited to an elite few, but demanded by common men and women everywhere" (p. 243). All three natures may be in conflict with each other, but ideally they would form a hierarchial organization, culminating in the "integration in terms of a stable concept of self" (p. 57).

There is, however, as we have said before, a wide gap between the intents inherent in basic needs and the complex goals which the mature human mind pursues. While a few basic motivational directives develop very early in life, intents are established only gradually, and new and different interests may be pursued all through life. There are innumerable goals from which the individual can choose with some measure of freedom.

As yet we do not have any inventories of the goals an individual may set for himself. Nor do we know what part the self plays in its directive role. From biographical as well as from clinical studies, I have gained the impression that the self is concerned with ultimate purposes.

Ultimate purposes are not pursued by everyone, perhaps not even by many. But in therapy as well as in accounts of life histories, we do encounter people who ask: "What am I living for?" "What am I here for?" These questions are raised frequently by the same person who asks "Who am I?" These people often seem to feel that they should discover or provide for themselves an ultimate purpose in life, something they refer to as the "meaning of life."

I have used the term *"intentionality"* (1933) to describe this phenomenon of people wanting "to live for something," which then becomes for them life's meaning. I have defined "intention" as the pursuit of an objective and "intentionality" as an essential characteristic of those who give to their lives an ultimate purpose. This ultimate purpose often is something they choose to believe in or think they ought to believe in. They themselves determine to be active in the direction of this purpose and sometimes even to dedicate their lives to it. My descriptive term for a life that is directed toward the fulfillment of an ultimate purpose is "self-determination."

The concept of "meaningful" living was recently revived by Viktor E. Frankl (1955), and that of intentionality reintroduced by Rollo May (1964), who also defines it as a directedness toward purposeful, meaningful living, emphasizing the "will" and "decision" necessary to live this way.

Both V. E. Frankl and R. May feel that living for a purpose with meaning is the presupposition for reaching fulfillment.

This subject of the meaningfulness of life, however, is still very controversial. Existentially speaking, we know nothing about what is meaningful. Paul Tillich (1952) holds that we cannot liberate ourselves from the anxiety of meaninglessness, and therefore sees only one solution: to have the courage to be oneself despite the doubts one may suffer about the meaning of existence.

A. Maslow (1964) sees the meaningfulness of life in experiences "which are worthwhile in themselves," such as the peak experiences he describes as containing "universality and eternity." These are experiences which are "detached from human concerns," "ego-transcending," and in which "the world is accepted." Meaningfulness of life in this conceptualization is not derived from the pursuit and fulfillment of an ultimate purpose.

A definition of meaningfulness that supports this kind of inner-determined fulfillment was proposed by K. Buhler in 1929, when he characterized as meaningful anything that functions as a contributory constituent to a teleological whole, for instance, the way a word belongs to a sentence or a mechanical part to the whole machine. This definition seems to fit in well with present-day thinking about personally essential experiences and thereby the realization of one's most essential being.

Many people today consider the realization of their full potential as a meaningful purpose and as their contribution to life. Meaningfulness here is seen from within the individual, while the other definitions relate it to purposes outside the individual.

This kind of general thinking and overall awareness of one's own self, however, is only accessible to relatively few people. How do the others conceive of themselves and of their life goals?

Most people who do not think in theoretical and abstract terms, if they are above the living-from-day-to-day level, have some general directives for their self-concepts and their strivings. Frequently these are derived from cultural traditions and from what their environment, school, and church have taught them. We know more today about the codetermining roles which biographical, genetic, dynamic, and socio-cultural factors play in inducing the goal choices of an individual, and we also are beginning to know more about certain clusters of goals that would appear to go together.

Studies such as McClelland's (1953) in which the achievement motive is shown in association with other goals derived from environmental dynamic impacts, and studies like Strodtbeck's (1958) in which traditional clusters of goals are shown in different cultural groups, give us new insights into the context in which determining values and principles are formed.

A recent experimental research study of life goals, which I conducted in collaboration with W. Coleman and W. H. McWhinney (in prep.), shows that people with an average traditional Western education are conscious of a great many of their strivings. Our study also shows that only a minority of people has goal patterns that appear to be adequate, effective, and leading to integration. The majority has ideas of goals that seem to be worthless, inappropriate, unrealistic, or internally contradictory.

These findings were generally confirmed by observations made during clinical interviews. I am often struck by the incompatibility of a patient's ideals on the one hand and his selfish and shrewd methods to exploit people on the other, by the contradiction of his ambitions and his laziness. Patients, of course, are not necessarily characteristic of people in general. However, most patients referred to in this context are mild neurotics who often function quite well in their occupations, but their problems and conflicts hamper their personal relationships and personal happiness.

How all of this ties in with personal inclinations and environmental influences, with ideas and cultural traditions, remains to be shown, though some of the internal contradictions of our aspirations have been lucidly described by Crane Brinton in his "History of Western Morals" (1959). We still are unable to fathom how all these directives work in the individual, but an attempt to assemble data about our present sources of information is being made in this book.

We consider the dualism of human purposes the ninth property of the life cycle.

We have previously mentioned that an individual from an early age on is able to choose goals, and this, of course, means that he can prefer one goal over another. In his first choice of toys, for example, a baby may, if left to himself, grab what appeals to him most at the moment; he pursues a factual value. Soon, however, he learns that there are other reasons for choosing a specific action, when, for example, his mother tells him that a good boy does as he is told. In learning that he can be "good" or "bad," he begins to realize that there are values other than immediate preferences, and thus he becomes aware of normative values. From this moment on, he experiences the kinds of conflicts that accompany us all our lives.

At the beginning it is usually in terms of "good" and "bad" that the individual subjects himself to society. But he soon discovers that there are many choices among actions, choices whose outcomes may be good or bad for him in ways that have nothing whatever to do with rules and orders. He may find out that he has chosen a friend who was bad for him because the friend proved to be disloyal, or good for him because he sustained him. He may discover later that his educational, occupational, social, and marital choices were right or wrong, or good or bad, for his own development and fulfillment. He learns that he lives constantly with a polarity of goals and that he always must be making choices and decisions. When discussing the kind of value that persists throughout a person's life, we shall refer to it as fulfillment value.

Fulfillment, of course, means different things to different people. Much depends on the structure of an individual's basic tendencies and on what he has learned and absorbed from his environment. While one person conceives of fulfillment in terms of comfort and ease, another may feel fulfilled only if he has been able to accomplish certain things in this world. A predominant tendency toward need satisfaction plays a role in the one case, and a predominant tendency toward creative expansion in the other. However, environmental factors also exert their influence in both cases. The polarity between comfort and accomplishment seems to me most decisive as far as life goals are concerned.

Because of the dualism of human nature, many people experience a conflict between these two goals, and few seem to be able to harmonize them satisfactorily. Both goals are observable in the early as well as late stages of life, although at the very beginning and again at the very end there is a predominant need for comfort. Accomplishment, on the other hand, seems to belong to that middle period of life in which the individual is, normatively speaking, creatively expansive.

However, the choice between either comfort or accomplishment as a predominant goal seems to be not so much developmentally conditioned as it is a consequence of individual personality structure and environmental givens.

It is interesting to note in this connection that D. McClelland's studies (1953) also emphasize achievement as a general motive. He ends his well-known investigations on "The Achievement Motive" by asking: "Does this mean that we have found a motive 'common to all men' which is not simply a physiological need?" (p. 332). I think achievement is indeed common to all men, and that it has a biological foundation in the basic tendencies toward productivity.

I should like to refer once more to the Chicago Interdisciplinary Conference in which J. E. P. Toman defined "creating change toward producing new potentialities" as a tendency of the organism equally as basic as that toward maintenance. Either alternating or in a pattern in which one or the other tendency predominates, these seem to be two basic directives which people follow in their drives to fulfillment.

One of the reasons for the dualistic conflict between comfort and accomplishment as predominant goals is the fact that we always live in the future as well as in the present and never without the aftereffects of the past. This lifelong simultaneous orientation to present, past, and future is the tenth property of the life cycle.

The evidence of this triple orientation is noticeable in our actions, our inner life and in the things we create. As shown in Chapter 3, a listing or diagram of a person's activities indicates his concern with the present, past, and future. This concern becomes even more evident when we conduct a study of a person's inner experiences, which always relate to his present, past, and future, although to varying degrees. The same is true of an individual's creations. These include, first of all, his children who, to many people, are not only part of their present lives but also of the future. The relationships a person creates, his work record, and his other actions accompany him from the past into the present and on into the future. Much of what a person hopes to accomplish is planned with the future in mind.

It probably is true that the person who lives more in the present than in the future has a greater interest in comfort than in accomplishment. However, there are those who work hard for the accomplishment of future comfort, and others who enjoy accomplishing things on a day to day basis. "Function pleasure" (K. Buhler) and the creative pleasure of accomplishment reward their efforts. Those who work primarily for the future anticipate satisfaction with "hope" (Th. French). They often find satisfaction in an easier life, in future recognition, or in creating something that will survive them and do them honor.

Developmentally speaking, children normally live in the present. Depending on his maturity, the adolescent begins to take the future into account. If his childhood was unhappy, if it did not allow him to develop a sufficient zest for living, he may fall prey to "brooding over the past," a characteristic of neurotic development. The healthy adult considers the past and the future alike. In other words, he tries to learn from the past in order to decide in the present what will benefit his future, regardless of the direction in which his goals lie.

E. Shostrom (1963) recently obtained more detailed information on this subject. The standardization studies conducted in conjunction with his "Personal Orientation Inventory" show that the self-actualizing person lives in the present "with the past memories serving as significant learning experiences and with future goals tied to the here-and-now activity." (See Chapter 20.)

Events which influence a person's life are part of his history. They act as a counteragent to his own dispositions and may either support or impair his goals.

The incidence and role of such events will be examined in the subsequent life histories insofar as their influence can be traced in actions, inner experiences, and/or productions.

References

Allport, G. *Pattern and growth in personality.* New York: Holt, Rinehart and Winston, 1961.

Birren, J. E. *Handbook of aging and the individual.* University of Chicago Press, 1959.

Brody, S. *Bioenergetics and growth.* New York: Reinhold Publishing Corp., 1943.

Bugental, J. F. T. *The search for authenticity.* New York: Holt, Rinehart and Winston, 1961.

Buhler, C. *Kindheit und Jugend (Childhood and adolescence)* Leipzig, Germany: S. Hirzel, 1928. 3rd ed., 1931. Reprinted by Göttingen: Verlag für Psychologie, 1967.

Buhler, C. *Der menschliche Lebenslauf als psychologisches Problem (The human course of life as a psychological problem).* Leipzig: S. Hirzel. 1933, 2nd ed., Göttingöen: Hogrefe, 1959.

Buhler, C. Theoretical observations about life's basic tendencies. *Amer. J. Psychother,* 1959, *13*: 3, 501-581.

Buhler, C. Meaningful living in the mature years. In R. W. Kleemeier (ed.), *Aging and leisure.* New York: Oxford University Press, 1961.

Buhler, C. Genetic aspects of the self, Mon., New York Acad. Sciences, 1962.

Buhler, C., and Coleman, W. Life goal inventory, Mimeographed ed., 1964.

Buhler, K. *Die geistige Entwicklung des Kindes (The mental development of the child).* Jena: G. Fischer, 1918.

Buhler, K. *Die Krise der Psychologie.* Jena, 1929. Transl. *The crisis of psychology.* Cambridge, Mass.: Schenkman, in press.

Erikson, E. Identity and the life cycle, *Psychological Issues,* 1959, New York: International Universities Press, *1*:1.

French, T. M. *The integration of behavior, 3.* University of Chicago Press, 1952-55.

Frenkel, E. Studies in biographical psychology, *Character and personality,* 5: 1, 1-35.

Frankl, V. E. *The doctor and the soul.* New York: A. A. Knopf, 1955.

Hartmann, H. *Essays on ego psychology.* New York: International Universities Press, 1964, p. 40.

Lehman, H. C. *Age and achievement.* Princeton University Press, 1953.

Maslow, A. Religious values.

May R. Will, decision and responsibility. New Haven Conference, 1964.

McClelland, D. C. *et. al. The achievement motive.* New York: Appleton-Century-Crofts, 1953, p. 332.

Munroe, R. L. *Schools of psychoanalytic thought.* New York: Henry Holt & Co., 1955.

Murphy, G. *Human potentialities.* New York: Basic Books, 1957, p. 57; p. 243.

Murphy, G. *Personality.* New York: Harper Bros., 1947, p. 523.

Strodtbeck, F. L. Family interaction, values, and achievement. In D. C. McClelland, A. L. Baldwin, U. Bronfenbrenner, and F. L. Strodtbeck, *Talent and society.* Princeton: D. van Nostrand, 1958.

Tillich, P. *The courage to be.* New Haven: Yale University Press, 1952.

Toman, J. E. P. In Grinker, R. R. (ed.), *Toward a unified theory of human behavior.* New York: Basic Books, 1954.

Chapter 2

The Developmental Structure of Goal Setting in Group and Individual Studies

Charlotte Bühler

The previous chapter discussed the structure of the life cycle with respect to its organizational and dynamic properties. This chapter examines the questions of whether and/or how actual data reflect the structural aspects of goal setting and attempts to determine the kinds of data that may be related to the structure of life rather than to individual genetic or environmental factors.

Psychological data may be obtained through group or individual studies by a variety of techniques. The findings help to establish norms and statistical distributions and to develop descriptive or interpretative reports and biographical histories.

Normative studies, strictly speaking, are concerned with the development of intelligence or the development of behavior, specifically in childhood. They show maturational sequences and a certain age-relatedness of various functions and thus seem to relate to the structural aspects of development. They also disclose the beginnings of new functions but are not geared to the problem of categorizing intents.

DEVELOPMENTAL STUDIES

Beginning and Earliest Development of Intent

Several theoretical analyses of observational studies have concentrated on investigating the beginning and the earliest development of intent. The controversy surrounding the infant's first signs of interest is caused by the fact that all theory in this area is based on interpretation.

The diversity of interpretations that characterizes the older literature on the subject is, in turn, the result of two opposing theories. The American hypothesis, proposed by the disciples of behaviorism and psychoanalysis, is that all behavior has to be understood in terms of stimulus reactions. The European position subscribed to particularly by the developmental psychologists, however, is that the individual has some primary initiative.

The latter point of view was never accepted by its opponents because it never was believed to be satisfactorily proven. The European child psychologists saw initiative in the category of the so-called "spontaneous" movements which differed from mass activity and reactions to stimuli. They also thought they noticed selective perception from the very first days on. Evidence for this was found in the newborn's behavior during feeding. According to Ripin and Hetzer's observations (1930), the 4- or 5-day-old begins to eliminate movements hindering his feeding, and some infants of 5 to 7 days make active movements to recapture the lost nipple or try to find it with head turned and mouth open.

Other Viennese studies, as reported in C. Buhler (1931), showed the selectiveness of responses to different sensory stimuli. B. Löwenfeld (1927) found that only in the first month does a baby respond to different sounds with unspecific mass movements; between the second and third month he turns with intense interest in the direction of the sounds he hears and responds with different behavior to the different sounds. The same is true of responses to color and light stimuli about a month later (1929). Active imitation of sounds to which the baby listened intently were reported by both Buhler (1931) and Piaget (1951).

In 1959, Schachtel, by using primarily F. Stirniman's (1940) observations, stated that the newborn already "does not wish merely to abolish external stimuli, but also turns toward them and wants to prolong contact with them" (p. 117 ff). This turning toward as well as away from stimuli is observable from at least the first 10 to 14 days on (Buhler and Hetzer, 1930; Ripin and Hetzer, 1930). It is confirmed by F. Stirniman (1940), who observed head-turning toward thermal, tactile, gustatory, auditory—and a little later—visual stimuli. Schachtel is of the opinion that this is a selective movement and concludes "that the infant is born with the capacity to perceive a variety of sensory qualities, in the autocentric mode to be sure, but also that some of these are felt as pleasurable and attractive before there has been any experience of satiation" (p. 131). His opinion is "that the active turning toward the objects and the wish to expand the boundaries and variety of his world in the encounter with an increasing number and variety of objects is stronger in the healthy infant and child than the wish to remain in the narrow confines of the familiar. . . . The embeddedness principle yields to the transcendence principle of openness toward the world and of self-realization which takes place in the encounter with the world" (p. 157).

The thus established selectivity of the individual's perception, the persistence of which has been gradually acknowledged, forces us to assume the existence of a primary individuality, even a singularity of personality. In this sense Tinbergen (1955) speaks of an "innate perceptual pattern" and Hilgard (1951) of the "pursuit of innate preferences."

Apart from preferences, this individuality also seems to entail an individual degree of sensitivity. Hypersensitivity is one of the most generally acknowledged inborn characteristics, and the vulnerability of the hypersensitive child is one of the conditions which are apt to induce neurotic development.

On the basis of refined experiments, American child psychologists have come close to accepting the European position. According to B. Eiduson's survey, needs for stimulation and arousal are being acknowledged as primary. There is also a recognition of selective "discriminating behavior from birth" which until the 1930's or 1940's was largely ignored in American child psychology "because of the theoretical understanding of the infant as a passive recipient of stimuli impinging on him from within himself and from the world without" (Ch. 7). Generally speaking the infant is now acknowledged to be an "active seeker of experience."

The vehicle for this is that primary activity which Preyer has called "spontaneous." B. Eiduson discusses in Chapter 7 studies by Lashley and others describing the constancy, rhythmicity, and automaticity of the brain's activity. According to this research, the brain is itself an active, orienting, and directing organ, made up of components which themselves are active, orienting, and directive.

The resulting primary activity was described by M. Fries (1937; 1953) in terms of five activity levels, starting with a very passive and ending with an overactive behavior.

The question of how activity levels relate to exploratory and manipulative behavior, on the one hand, and to aggressive or passive behavior, on the other, is as yet unanswered. In terms of goal-directed behavior this is an important question. While we recognize that curiosity and exploration exist early in life, as do consistency and individuality of behavior, we do not know precisely how these characteristics relate to the different activity levels. Nor are we sure to what degree curiosity and explorative behavior represent the roots of a later preference for adventure over familiar situations. Is this where creativity or noncreativity, interest or disinterest in discovering and doing something new, originate?

The relationship between activity level and aggression also has not been clearly established. The ambiguity in the use of the word "aggression" still crops up in many discussions.

Aggressiveness, when defined as an active going-ahead and a tackling of reality and its problems, seems to be the opposite of passivity and to be related to activity levels. L. W. Sontag 1950) sees this aggressiveness and passivity as representing the infant's earliest approaches to working out the basic problem of dependency versus independence. This theory implies an important assumption: namely, that the natural tendency to be passive or aggressive predisposes the baby already early in life to two fundamentally opposed human relationships, the acceptance of dependency and the struggle for independence. Of course, passivity and aggression are not the sole determinants of dependent or independent behavior, nor are passivity and aggressiveness completely unalterable. But within limits, Sontag's theory, supported by experimental evidence from the Fels Institute's research projects, appears to be sound. Kagan and Moss (1962) pursued this Fels Institute research study on a longitudinal range from infancy into adulthood and found that the continuity of the previously mentioned traits was later influenced by the individual's sex-role standard.

However, neither these studies nor other data reported by Eiduson allow us to draw definite conclusions about the relative contribution of native or experiential factors to dependency or independence tendencies.

Aggression, in the sense of hurting someone, is usually assumed to be secondary, and Freudian theory relates its development to the severity of toilet training. It well may be asked whether this trait perhaps is not rooted in those early defense reactions which Buhler and Hetzer (1930) observed even in the first months of life (p. 138).

The activity degrees implying possible tendencies toward dependency or independence, aggressiveness or passivity, as well as the selective approach to and withdrawal from stimuli, seem to indicate an early expression of the expansive or adaptive tendencies which I have assumed to be in operation from the beginning of life.

Coordinative endeavors which may be considered the forerunners of organizational and integrative tendencies can be observed equally early. They occur in the feeding situation (Ripin and Hetzer, 1930), where the infant after only a few feedings begins to coordinate his movements. The fact of his intentional behavior development when he tries to focus on getting hold of his bottle was established by Rubinow and Frankl (1934), whose study shows the infant as being active and organizing his behavior in a basic situation of need satisfaction.

Reactions to care and contact

The satisfaction of psychophysical needs is recognized to be a basic goal from the very beginning of a person's life. However, this satisfaction seems to be beneficial only if it is brought about in what R. Spitz

(1965) calls the right "emotional climate." This climate depends on the type of personal care the mother or her substitute gives to the infant, who subconsciously wants to receive his psychophysical need satisfactions in an atmosphere of love and care. I do not see how this can be interpretated other than that the infant has a need for and an unconscious intent toward human closeness.

Although I disagree with Spitz's (1965) conclusion that the infant's ability to establish objects is developed only within the framework of the mother-child relationship, this relationship is indeed an important one for the infant's optimal development. As Ripin and Hetzer (1930) showed, the infant's learning to adjust to the feeding situation begins in the first days of his life and, as a matter of fact, some of the Viennese infants studied had been put out for adoption and cared for by nurses. Thus, although the infant can establish objects as long as he has the ability to coordinate, organize, and integrate his own experiences, the relationship with others who care about him seems to be of fundamental importance for his full development.

As mentioned before, an infant 3 to 6 weeks old responds with a smile to another person's smile and initiates sounds. Piaget (1951) observed, as I did, a behavior which can only be described as resulting in "strenuous efforts" to imitate sounds and mouth movements. Here we find rudimentary stages of understanding and of identification. An active interest in contact is displayed from as early as 5 to 6 months on, when two infants are placed together (C. Buhler, 1927). One infant touches the other, they smile at each other, and, when they are 6 or 8 months old, may even exchange toys. Again, a number of the subjects who were observed in these situations were infants who in their first days had been placed in the Viennese placement home in which Spitz also conducted many of his observations.

Thus, while I cannot agree with the theory that the mother's care is the *sine qua non* for the baby's finding his way into the world of objects, I do agree that to establish contacts with responding persons is part of the infant's most basic needs and goals.

Beginning Self-Realization

The fourth behavior contributing to goal setting becomes conscious in the experience of "I want." And the resulting conflicts with his experiences of "I must" and "I want" make the 2- to 4-year-old child ask "Who am I?"—a question that sometimes can plague an individual far into his adulthood or even all through his life. "Will," "conscience," and "identity" are being established in these experiences.

In his first "I want to" behavior, the child is quite arbitrary regarding his objective, and may say "Yes" and "No" in close succession to the same offer or request. He is trying to see how it feels to make choices and decisions of his own and, if his environment permits, to discover himself as a person in his own right.

This then is the period when the autonomous ego is established, when the child begins to discover his own self and the possibility of giving himself a direction of his own. Erikson speaks of the happenings of this period as being the "battle for autonomy."

But recent clinical studies show how very individually different children experience this period. There are some who, while having tantrums and resisting their own environment, do not really establish goals of their own. They fight submission but in the end remain just as dependent on their environment as before. All they want is the opposite of what their environment dictates.

Some of my patients who are now in their thirties or forties or even older, remember that all they ever wanted to do was the opposite of what was suggested to them. Clearly, this is the beginning of a completely neurotic self-determination. Unfortunately, space does not allow me to illustrate this point with case histories. But there are children who are set on a neurotic love relationship with a parent and do not want autonomy but want possessive domination.

This neurotic outcome of the battle for autonomy notwithstanding, there are also healthy solutions. Depending partly on the specific environment and partly on the child, the healthy outcome may be voluntary submission and identification with adult goals.

The child with a creative potential begins his first attempts toward self-realization when he is between 2 and 4 years old. A more or less creative little girl may already have ideas of how to set up her identity; she may feel, as I have shown in a previous publication (1962), that she does not want to be like her mother but rather like her aunt whom she admires, or that she wants to do things like the "lady next door," who can teach her something she wants to know.

These tentative early goals show us the beginning of the child's conscious attempts to identify with certain persons and objectives in the humanistic perspective of values of which the child has become aware. These first goals may have to do with attitudes or with moral considerations. "Is he a good boy or is he a bad boy?" asks Peter, 2, in talking thoughtfully to himself. "No, he is a bad boy," he concludes with a certain glee. Peter is too young to even think of himself as "I," but he already conceives of a moral goal for himself. All this, of course, is partly play, but it is astonishing how many valid and lasting decisions are being made in this period.

Besides evaluation and identification, there is, however, something more to be noted. As vascillating in their directives as these children's self-expressions may be, there definitely is a degree of intentionality in them. They are not sure exactly what they want or what they should do with themselves, but they know vaguely that there is something to be realized in some distant future.

If we now look at the young adolescents whom Getzels and Jackson examined, we find a fully established self-awareness, and dependently conforming or independently self-responsible identities. In their excellent study of creativity and intelligence (1962), we meet adolescents in their high school years who have very clear ideas about themselves.

There is the noncreative girl with a high IQ who has a positive image of her family. She states in her autobiography that she has "internalized" her mother's ideals and is "very close to her" (p. 163). And then there is John who declares: "If I could achieve one thing during my lifetime, I would want it to be independence." His equally original sister, Joan, says that although she thinks of her parents as being pleasant enough, she has no intention of identifying with them. Asked whether she would like to be like her mother, she merely asserts: "When they try to get me to be like my mother, I . . . tell them that I am me. And that is that." (p. 191).

These identity concepts go along with elaborate self-evaluations, and the beginnings of certain features of long-range goal setting become noticeable.

The cases of this study also will serve as examples for the next factor that determines goal setting: a person's potentialities in terms of abilities and aptitudes.

Mastery

The experience in the area of mastery begins with "I can" or "I cannot." I agree with Lois Murphy (1962) that the "I can" or "I cannot" concept belongs to the earliest experiences of infancy. The 4- to 5-month-old baby who swings his rattle with good control as against the one who hits himself or loses his grip, and the 1½-year-old who puts one block on top of the other in a way that makes them stay as against the child whose tower always tumbles before it is finished, have no conscious awareness of being able or unable to master their material, but semi-consciously experience their first success or failure. Proof of this are the happy smiles of the one and the unhappy rages of the other. Observations of the despair and helplessness of failing children have thus far only been made in an incidental way. They usually are children with birth injuries or childhood schizophrenia, children who are uncoordinated and unintegrated.

Experiences in coping and mastery contribute essentially to the establishment of a child's personality, as L. Murphy showed in her extensive observations in "The Widening World of Childhood" (1962). During that period already we can distinguish between the more adaptively and the more creatively coping individual, a difference which becomes very pronounced in adolescence when the first distinctive characteristics of life goals become noticeable.

In the well-known studies of Getzels and Jackson of creative versus highly intelligent, noncreative high-school students, great pains were taken to establish all the relevant variables that could codetermine the subject's behavior. The findings show us the creative and the high-achievement, although noncreative, type in connection with different motivational patterns. The noncreative students, moving toward conventional standards and conforming with what is expected of them, show themselves as being in dependency relationships with their environment. The creative group, on the other hand, which moves away from models provided by teachers and seeks careers that do not conform with what is expected of them show themselves as being in independence relationships with their environment.

There are further related results regarding the social and moral orientation of these two groups. While both groups participate in activities that are expected and approved of by the social order, the adaptive, noncreative group tends to be more what one usually calls socially "adjusted." They are "insiders"; they seem "to prefer social interaction to individual achievement, to seek experiences that are immediately enjoyable as against those that promise more remote gratification, to find more satisfaction in experiencing with others than in asserting their own autonomy, to be willing to sacrifice moral commitment in the interest of inter-personal harmony" (p. 159).

The highly creative students show the reverse of these trends. They tend to be outsiders and stand up individualistically for highly moral principles.

While these findings are suggestive of different innate tendencies in these two groups, Getzels and Jackson did not neglect the possible role of environmental influence, "irrespective of the possible role of genetic factors" (p. 61).

The findings in this direction show that the high IQ family "is one in which individual divergence is limited and risks minimized, and the overall impression of the high creativity family is that it is one in which individual divergence is permitted and risks are accepted" (p. 76).

The cautious conclusion that can be drawn from these findings is that in his eventual goal structure and goal development, an individual's inherent tendencies to be more creative and independent or more noncreative and dependent are codetermined by the goals and values of his environment. These enhance the "openness to experiences" and the willingness to take risks which were found in the creative child as, on the other hand, they encourage the orientation toward security and success which were found in the noncreative child.

The question of how the child who is not as creative and adaptive as his family expects fares under these influences has not as yet been answered in correspondingly thorough studies.

Beginning Comprehensive Intentionality toward Life as a Whole

Constructiveness and destructiveness

From the beginning the infant is exposed to the impact of his environment. Parents, siblings, peers, and others contribute to the child's goal setting through information, guidance, and social relationships. These factors may be conditioned not only by the previously mentioned feelings of dependency and independence, but as well by love and fear, frustration and hostility, security and insecurity, the feeling of belonging or being a loner, of rivalry and jealousy, and an attitude of submission or domination, of cooperation and opposition, friendships and crushes, and many other sensations.

Apart from the impressions the child receives from his environment, he becomes increasingly aware of how his elders and his peers manage themselves and their affairs. He begins to interpret their intents, their selfishness, or their kindness. In responding to and coping with parents, elders, and others, with their demands, rebuffs, and beatings, the 8- to 12-year-old child develops ideas, methods, and directions of his own. He becomes an essentially constructive person if he handles himself and his social relationships in the direction of goals that benefit him and others, as compared to an essentially destructive person, who is full of hostilities and whose mind is set on damaging others or himself.

In introducing the concepts of constructiveness and destructiveness, I want to emphasize that I think of them as complex motivational patterns. Constructiveness is not a simple entity, such as activity, but rather a complex unit to be likened to achievement. It may contain an instinctual element of building, but as understood here, constructiveness as well as destructiveness are developed through a person's interaction with his environment. Probably everybody harbors both constructive and destructive attitudes, but as is the case with achievement, constructiveness or destructiveness may under certain circumstances be all pervasive.

Studies of constructiveness or destructiveness as basic attitudes of life are not as yet available. Fritz Redl and David Wineman's (1951) studies, *Children Who Hate,* describe and analyze an all-pervasive destructiveness of a group of preadolescent youngsters and probably represent the best that has been done in this field.

Constructiveness can be defined as the basic orientation of one who tries to work things out in a beneficial way for himself and others. "Beneficial" may mean a result that pleases, educates, or contributes to any kind of growth and development. The opposite orientation is that of one who harbors hostility and tries to damage others or himself. Such damage may be consciously or unconsciously planned and may range from preventing the happiness and success of others or himself to actually trying to injure, ruin, or eliminate others or himself.

Harmful aggression with a destructive intent may be observed even in nursery school children. As a basic attitude of malevolence, it seems to dominate from about 8 to 10 or 12 years on, the period when some of the conflicts between children and their parents culminate.

Criminal adolescents and adults often show evidence of a predominant orientation toward destructiveness.

Achievement motivation

In the 8- to 12-year period, all foregoing experiences of being able to master things and situations and to overcome failures converge to generate an attitude toward a concept of achievement. The idea of achievement as a goal has by then become more or less clearly established in the child's mind, but many different factors have contributed to how he conceives of it.

In the studies conducted by D. McClelland and his collaborators (1953), the enormous influence of the parental attitude toward achievement has not only been established but also been analyzed in its various characteristics.

Children establish achievement styles, which often remain the same all through life. They establish a certain style of working, of dependency or independence in goal setting, of orientation toward success or failure and, particularly, they develop an attitude toward values and beliefs. Evidence accumulated by the McClelland group, by Getzels and Jackson, Eiduson, and Goertzel and Goertzel (1962), demonstrates that attitudes toward achievement are consistent and almost always to be linked to beliefs and values.

Beliefs and values

In this same period when the child begins to have an overview of his various personal relationships as well as his competence in life, he also begins to consolidate his beliefs and values. The constructive or destructive attitudes which he starts to build are the results of experiences and evaluations which now crystallize in opinions and convictions. Eight- to 12-year-old children are known to debate with others or themselves such issues as honesty, fairness, popularity, power, the importance of being an accomplished person, or just being the best in everything.

With these beliefs and values, the growing child establishes his own ordering principles. As is the case with some other goal-determining principles, namely, need satisfaction, self-limiting adaptation, and creative expansion, the ordering principle, too, is noticeable from the time the infant makes his first attempts at coordination and organization. I consider all of these principles as basic tendencies and like to refer to the ordering principle as the tendency to uphold the internal order. (C. Buhler, 1959).

Love and other committing relationships

As mentioned previously, the infant's need satisfaction depends on care given within the framework of a warm human relationship. In the first few months of life, an infant not only responds to the emotional climate which the adult creates, but actually strains toward a contact and understanding.

The adolescent discovers and aspires to two new goals of human relationship: intimacy and commitment. Healthy intimacy and commitment may be defined as voluntarily chosen bonds. Although they represent a voluntary reduction of independence, the free-choice element distinguishes them from involuntary dependency.

Intimacy and commitment in a sex and love relationship, if shared by both partners, develop the relationship beyond merely functional enjoyment to the ecstatic experience of a unity. To achieve this goal is one of the most, if not *the* most, essential aims of the maturing person.

Maslow describes this feeling of unity as being among the individual's peak experiences, and psychoanalysis recognizes in this new step the development of object relations, which it terms the development of genitality. "Genitality," says Erikson (1959), "is the potential capacity to develop orgastic potency in relation to a loved partner of the opposite sex" (p. 96).

Development in this area is, as we all know, full of problems and perils for the majority of youths. The degree to which they want to allow themselves the pleasure of sexual excitement is one problem. The finding of and commitment to a love partner is another, and the accomplishment of self-dedication through intercourse is a third. And what is perhaps the most difficult to decide is the extent to which they should concern themselves with these questions as against the pursuit of other goals such as achievement and dedication to the group. The pursuit of sexual and other pleasurable excitements often conflicts with the adolescent's other goals of life.

Integration

We have observed that all during childhood and adolescence the development of goal setting increases and proceeds in various directions. Several factors have a decisive influence on this development. The complexity of the goal-setting process is extraordinary, and the integrative task required tremendous.

Very little research has been done so far on this question of integration. Thomas French (1952) has devoted a comprehensive study to it but has concentrated primarily on the factor of hope as an integrating principle.

Hope undoubtedly is of fundamental importance in holding a person together and keeping him going, but it seems to me that the varying role that values and beliefs play in the organization of our goals is possibly more important. G. Allport (1961) also sees a hierarchy of values as the organizing principles of the self.

But what determines that hierarchy of values?

In the first instance, we must think of it as changing in time and being determined by age. A second determinant obviously is the genetic factor about which we know least of all. Undoubtedly, a person's dispositions, his gifts and aptitudes, as well as his deficiencies, are codetermining in the hierarchy of values and thus the structure of his goal-setting endeavors. Environmental influences form the third determinant.

Emotional dynamics at present is the best known of all factors that influence a person. However, as far as goal setting is concerned, we are limited to recent clinical studies for relevant information regarding the environmental impact. The same is true of the influence of socio-cultural factors on goal setting, a subject which recent social psychological studies (e.g., F. L. Strodtbeck, 1958) have explored.

Despite our increasing knowledge in these areas, the how and why of the integrating procedure which an individual uses to evaluate and order the codeterminants of his goal-setting attempts are still largely unknown. Much of it, of course, may take place in the unconscious.

How does it happen that in one case a mother's ambition, in another the cultural prejudice acquired in a group, plays the decisive role in a person's beliefs and wants? To say one factor is stronger than the other explains nothing, although clearly it is the individual who reacts more strongly to one than to the other factor. And what determines his choices and decisions? A discussion of these problems is contained in subsequent chapters of this book.

Little has been done to investigate integration in its early stages. A. Weil (1956), who specializes in the study of childhood schizophrenia, concludes that the unevenness of these children's maturational patterning, apart from their peculiarities, is the reason their development lacks integration at all times. She considers this their basic pathology. And, indeed, the inability of integration seems part of the basic pathology of schizophrenia at any age.

But does this mean that an even and regular maturation progress is a guarantee of successful integration? It seems to me that we know far too little about people's inner organization, how they arrive at decisions between preferences, and what ultimate needs they have other than the more visible or pressing ones. Few people know themselves in this respect. Most subjects or patients whom I ask what they ultimately want to do or what is important to them, usually give such vague answers as "I wish I knew myself."

Direction, purpose, and meaning

The problem of integration includes, in a way, direction, purpose, and meaning, because it seems that we integrate ourselves with certain goals in mind. These goals may be close or far away, short-term or long-term. But whatever they are, they have an influence on the way an individual organizes his behavior. The integrative process of the person who wants the "here and now" will undoubtedly differ from the person who has a long-range plan. B. Eiduson's study of "Scientists" (1962) shows how people absorb and integrate a variety of determining factors into a specific way of life with specific goals and purposes. By using tests and interviews, she describes the development and personalities of

40 scientists. All of these men, she observes, "whose early determining factors show a great variety, seem to have in common that their excellent intellectual abilities lead them to early concentration on intellectual interests, and they all turn away from their families during adolescence or when starting college" (p. 66), and want to get ahead on their own. It is interesting to note that the independence factor which previously we found to be associated with creative abilities also becomes apparent here. Furthermore, as Eiduson (1962) states in summarizing her findings, these scientists all have "a great diversity of sources that fed the investment in the intellectual" (p. 89). Yet they all are men whose life goals, to an extraordinary degree, are identified with and related to their creative research.

From this and other investigations it appears that the creative person finds it easier to set directions and goals for himself than does the noncreative individual. In addition, these goals lead the creative person in a rather natural way to transcend himself, considered by Frankl (1966) as well as Maslow (1964) to be a specifically human accomplishment. It becomes increasingly evident that in dedicating himself to a self-transcending goal, a person feels his life to be meaningful. But for the goal to be meaningful and at the same time to fulfill a basic existential human need, it must be chosen in accordance with a person's best potentialities.

This concept of meaningfulness, which has a long history of definition, has occupied many thinkers. Worth mentioning are the works of Brentano and Husserl, W. Dilthey, E. Spranger, K. Buhler, the existentialistically oriented writings of Paul Tillich and V. Frankl, as well as my own. The concept seems to refer to the development of an existential quality of life which I think is best characterized by two definitions: one by K. Buhler (1927), who defines "meaningful" as something that is a contributory constituent to a teleological whole; and the other by P. Tillich (1952), whose discourse on the despair of meaningfulness calls for an act of faith by which to accept oneself in a meaningful act.

As for creative work, it usually enhances a person's enthusiasm for life and his self-esteem, and helps him to find more quickly his identity and to establish himself as a person in his own right. For this reason, too, the humanistic psychologist is interested in awakening and increasing people's creative potential. H. Otto (1962) has started systematic work with older persons in this direction, and schools and parents are becoming increasingly aware of the fundamental importance of creativity, a factor which, as Guilford (1950) observed, psychologists and educators had nearly forgotten.

However, not everybody is primarily creative. What about the direction of people who are primarily noncreative?

Getzels and Jackson's previously mentioned studies demonstrated how easy it was for the noncreative youngsters, who were essentially healthy and non-neurotic, to follow their families' and teachers' guidance and ideas in regard to their futures. In other words, they allowed their elders to help them find their direction in life.

A mutually satisfactory development under these circumstances, however, depends not only on the willingness and adaptability of the child but perhaps even more on the wisdom and adequate understanding of his adult environment.

End Goals in Adolescence

In the second decade of life, we observe the appearance of certain motivational trends which seem to extend further into the future. They include a constructive or destructive attitude toward life; a motivation toward and a style of achievement; beliefs and values; opinions and convictions relating to life as a whole; love and other committing relationships; an integration of influential factors, as well as a beginning concern for direction, purpose, and meaning of life. Do we also find attempts to establish end goals of life?

To actually live with a direction and purpose means to live with some definite goals in mind. How do the goals established in adolescence relate to the whole of life? Exceptionally gifted individuals, as, for instance, the scientists in Eiduson's study, often have clear plans and goals at a fairly early age. Generally speaking, however, adolescents have only vague and tentative life goals.

If young people are planning at all, their definite goals seem to be short termed; longer-term goals usually are quite uncertain. Young people think of success and failure, and a thoughtful adolescent may speak of the fulfillment he hopes to find. But the idea that life could be experienced as fulfillment or failure hardly ever occurs to them.

L. Rosenmayer (1963) asked about 2,000 Austrian youths between 15 and 17 years about their life plans and found that only about two-thirds of them had long-range goals. These could be divided into four groups: two larger groups who saw occupational success and/or the foundation of a good family as their main goal; and two smaller groups, one of whom mentioned material, social, or political accomplishments as their ultimate goal, and the other character or ideal values. The majority saw occupational success in terms of the security it brings, and only a few identified it with special achievement. The idea of contributing to humanity, society or a smaller group thereof, occurred to only about 5 percent of the sample.

While this is a beginning, there is still a great need for a systematic investigation using depth exploration of adolescents' long-range goal-setting practices.

Judging from individual and group therapy with adolescents, their attitudes toward the future are open-ended. They are mostly preoccupied with preliminary goals, such as training, exams, temporary jobs, the solutions of acute relationship problems, etc. It is a minority who tries to take on definite commitments, such as a marriage or a career project for life. There is little enthusiasm to discuss ultimate concerns, but many an adolescent evinces considerable interest in social issues and, to a lesser degree, in adventure.

Time quotes Buell Gallagher, president of the City College of New York, as saying that "the New Lefter today rejects ideologies—he's issue-oriented, not ideology-oriented" (Jan. 6, 1967, p. 21). This seems to be true of a great many youths of today who are willing to dedicate time to Head Start work or to other issues concerning society and their role in it. Fulfillment and failure of life is not yet their concern. It is the exceptional youth who asks what life is all about.

In spite of this apparent absence of intentionality to encompass life as a whole, developments in later phases of life seem to justify our assumption that some unconscious directivity is taking place.

The two biographies presented in Chapters 3 and 4, as well as interview studies with older people to be reported elsewhere, reveal that the more the individual progresses in years, the greater is his tendency to view life as an entirety. Even those people who never before seemed to have considered this matter suddenly become aware of certain threads which lead through their whole lives. They see themselves as successes or failures, and in reviewing their lives, begin to feel that from this or that particular time they were actually directed toward certain results. Not infrequently this is a belated realization of what they have tried to do or to be all along.

Self-Determination Phases and Goals of Life

My five-phase theory of self-determination in regard to a person's life goals was first conceived in connection with some biographical studies (1933). A survey of 200 biographies led to the hypothesis of a normative model of the course of life. In terms of goal development the first phase, childhood, seemed to be a time when life goals were hardly ever visualized, and this period, age 0 to 15, was called the phase before the self-determination to life goals sets in. The second phase, that of adolescence, roughly between age 15 to 25, was one of tentative, programmatic self-determination. Only in the third phase, that of middle adulthood, between 25 and 45 years of age, was a more specified and definite self-determination the rule.

The fourth phase, later adulthood, roughly from age 45 to 60 or 65, was defined as a period of self-assessment and a review of past activities, with a reorientation for the future.

The fifth phase, representing the older and old age, the years after 65, was conceived of as a period when an individual experiences life as fulfillment, resignation, or failure.

Our introduction summarized the more recent data of child and adolescent psychology and essentially confirmed the theory of the first two phases. It also showed goal setting being gradually established during the first two decades of life.

The two biographies presented in the third and fourth chapters show two different time schedules, as related to the theoretical model. The life of Bill Roberts, representative of what might be called an average life history, shows a regular self-determination curve which corresponds in age distribution to the figures of the theoretical model. The biography of Clarence Darrow also contains all five phases but in a somewhat deviating age distribution. Darrow was slow in clarifying for himself what he felt to be his specific goals in life. We find a self-realizing development of his occupation as well as a truly congenial marriage in the fourth phase of adulthood, a period in which the average person usually has just passed or reached the peak of his accomplishments and begins to assess them in retrospect. Darrow reached his peak unusually late.

Bill Roberts' life history shows a beginning decline somewhere in the fourth phase of his life. Life statistics indicate a steep increase of morbidity and mortality in this climacteric age, besides a declining vitality.

Healthy and strong individuals may, however—similar to Darrow—begin to set themselves new goals or renew their efforts on previously set goals after having evaluated themselves and their lives.

Depending on health and on the results of the foregoing self-assessment, the last phase of life may be lived in a number of different ways. In fact, there appear to be a greater variety of living styles in the fifth phase than in any other.

The majority of people probably appreciate retirement and rest.

Some are partly removed from life through serious illnesses, and others through depression in the wake of a total disappointment. Some, however, seem to keep going strong until the very end.

These stages of self-determination represent, if not a psychological parallel, a certain relationship with the underlying biological structure of life, which we discussed in Chapter 1. We present it here in a schematical model (Figure 1) which suggests that the individual's growth

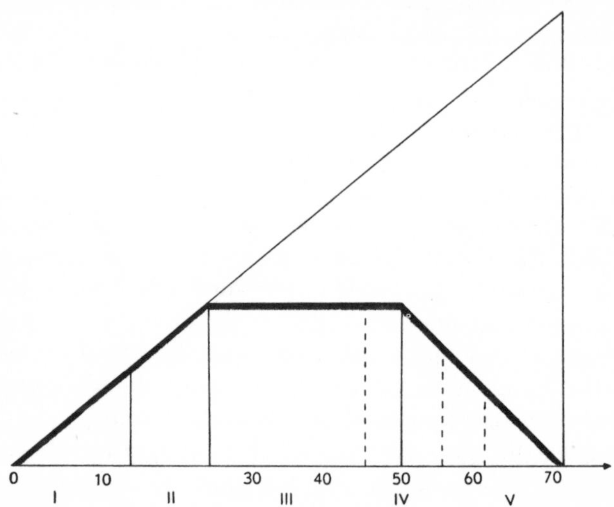

Figure 1. Schematical Model Showing the Underlying Biological Process of Growth, Reproduction and Decline.

The straight line represents the years from 0 to 70 +, with subdivisions of decades. The heavy line represents the curve of accelerated growth from birth to a maximum about 25 years, of relative stability between about 25 to about 50 years of age, of decline from approximately 50 years to the end. These phases are still essentially applicable, even though modern medicine has increased longevity.

The diagonal line represents schematically the onset and continuous growth of reproductive products.

The vertical full and dotted lines represent at 15 the mean age of beginning of reproductivity, which may occur any time between 10 and 20 years of age; at 25 the latest end of accelerated growth; at 45 to 55 to 60 the end of reproductivity, varying between individuals and both sexes; at 50 to 60 the beginning of decline.

The Roman figures I to V represent schematically conceived five phases of life: I: Period of accelerated growth before reproductivity sets in; II: Period of continuing of accelerated growth with beginning ability to reproduce; III: Period of relative stability between accelerated growth and decline, period of reproductivity; IV: Period of loss of reproductivity, at least for the female sex, and beginning decline; V: Period after reproductivity and of decline.

and expansion is gradually taken over by his products. As they increase and grow, the individual declines and is increasingly restricted in his activities until he dies. But part of him lives on in his products.

This factual process of beginning, expanding, reproducing, restricting and ending, is interpreted in the human being's self-determination process in two ways. First, he conceives of producing and reproducing as goals; second, he interprets his whole life process as having one imminent—if not transcendent—goal, namely, to complete it in a manner that impresses him as fulfillment by realizing potentials of development and productivity.

In the previous chapter we introduced four basic tendencies that implement the individual's striving toward fulfillment. We assumed that predominance among them varies but also that a certain developmental predominance has to be established. While need satisfaction and self-limiting adaptation predominate before the self-determination for goals sets in, creative expansion begins to take over when the individual develops his tentative and later more definite self-determination. The tendency toward upholding and re-establishing the internal order leads all other factors when self-assessment begins to prevail.

The self-determination model, the expansion-restriction model, and the four-basic-tendencies model represent a triad of assumptions about the structure of the life cycle. Their usefulness will be indicated in two biographies, in Chapters 3 and 4, and in some related statistical material.

However, we must realize that none of these models is a clean-cut reflection of structural data of development. While all three keep close to the maturational sequence of basic functions, abilities, and aptitudes as determined by structure, they also operate with concepts of life which are culturally determined. The idea of the "becoming" as such, of intentionality, and of self-realization are those of the Western civilization.

Actually, only a few of these model sequences are structurally conditioned. It is the expansion and restriction of the radius of action, together with the rise and fall of productivity and reproduction, which reflect the biological life cycle. The sequence of basic rational order is also reflected in certain behavioral sequences. The goal direction toward fulfillment, however, and the different phases of self-realization are the result of the person's intentionality and interpretation of life.

In using the developmental models as well as empirical studies for the disclosure of structural contributions to goal setting, we are limited to the establishment of the rise and decline of motives, functions, and productions, including their age relatedness and sequential order, and to the attainment of inherent pursuits of satisfaction or accomplishment.

STATISTICAL STUDIES ON LIFE GOALS

There are relatively few statistical studies of life goals and of such aspects of adult life as self-determination and self-actualization, but statistical questionnaire studies relevant to other life data are available. Most of these deal with functions and performances of various sorts rather than with goals.

S. L. Pressey and R. G. Kuhlen (1957) tried to evaluate a number of statistical studies that were concerned with the change in motivation during the life span. But the problem in this area is that there is no established system of categories. Particularly lacking is a clear distinction between developmentally and circumstantially conditioned aspects of goals and of their changes. This constitutes one of the main difficulties of this kind of studies. An individual change of interests through the years is only in part developmentally conditioned; the degree to which comfort and achievement seem the most desirable goals is not at all developmentally determined.

If we learn from a study on adolescents' goals (M. Brown and V. Martin, 1941) that 54 percent of the goals named by high school students could be classified as long-term, we know that high school students are capable of thinking in these terms, but we do not know that this percentage is representative of this age group.

Somewhat more pertinent conclusions can be drawn from a study by R. G. Kuhlen and G. H. Johnson (1952) of changes in goals of public school teachers which shows certain developmentally conditioned trends. Foremost among single as well as married women between 20 and 25 is the interest in marriage, a home, and a "housewife's" life. The wish to get into different jobs or to get a better education culminates in the earlier part of adult life, i.e., for men between the ages of 25 and 30 and for single as well as married women between 30 and 35. The desire to stay in the same job culminates later, around 40 for women, and 45 plus for men. (See Figure 2.)

These figures might be interpreted in the sense that in the first half of life wishes prevail which indicate striving for self-development and self-improvement, both in private life as well as in vocational achievement. At around 40, self-assessments take place which often lead to redirections. In the second half of life the tendency to stay in the same job prevails, to be superceded only by the wish for retirement which increases steadily from the forties on. These data compare favorably with the previously mentioned Viennese biographical studies (C. Buhler, 1933; E. Frenkel, 1936).

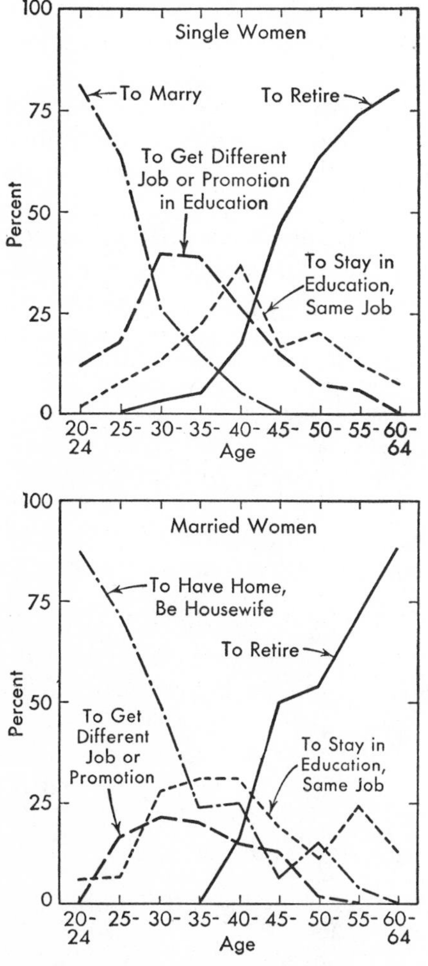

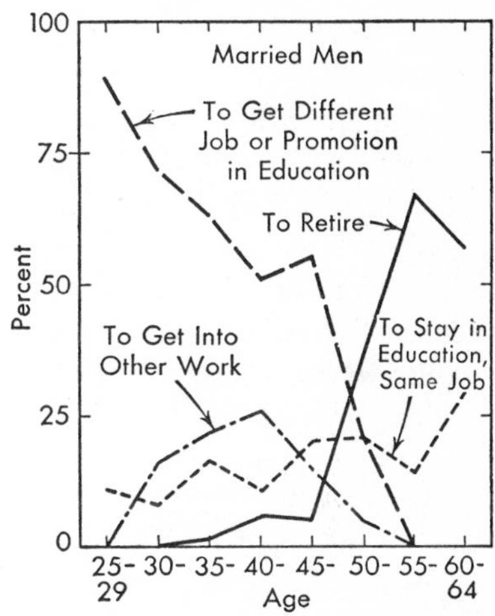

Figure 2. Changes in goals with increasing adult age as reflected in the responses of public school teachers to the question, "What would you most like to be doing ten years from now?" (From R. G. Kuhlen and G. H. Johnson, Change in Goals with Increasing Adult Age. *J. Consult. Psychol.*, 1952, 16, 1–4. Reproduced with permission of the American Psychological Association.)

Most of the statistical studies concerned with human development concentrate on objective data of behavior and performances. In as much as conclusions about motivation may be derived from them, the assumption would be that what people do and are able to do, must at least to some extent also be what they want to do. The question is, of course, to what extent.

The Viennese biographical studies showed a parallel between the trends of behavioral moves and productions on the one hand, and corresponding wishes, plans, and satisfactions, on the other hand. The latter could be studied in some detail in cases where much documentary material was available. It would be desirable to examine these parallels in greater depth with long-range case studies.

But maybe we can hypothesize that what a person can do best at a certain time is something he normally would want to do and derive satisfaction from, provided he operates within the accepted patterns of his culture and of his time.

Work activities and leisure activities are two main areas in modern civilization where abilities and aptitudes find their utilization and realization. Marriage and family are two other areas of life which offer fulfillment for the most basic personal needs. How is the development in these areas related to the structural pattern of the life cycle?

A great many data have been assembled about the rise and decline of physical abilities, mental abilities, and aptitudes. The general trend rises for physical and mental abilities until a person is about 20, with the prime being reached between 20 and 35 for physical and 20 and 45 for mental abilities, and the decline beginning between 45 and 50 and increasing rapidly.

Correspondingly, we find participation in the labor force increasing from about 17 to 40 or 45, after which time first a moderate, then a rapid decrease takes place. "At ages 65 to 69, only about half of all men are in the labor force, while among men aged 70 and over, approximately a fourth are working or seeking work" (M. S. Gordon, 1961, p. 17). The work curve of single women has recently shown a pattern not dissimilar to that of men, while that of married women declines earlier (M. S. Gordon, 1961).

Notable accomplishments were found to culminate in the early thirties; eminent leadership, however, between 50 and 65 or 70 (H. C. Lehman, 1942, 1953). Our biographical studies (C. Buhler, 1933) showed that certain creative activities peaked at an early, middle, and late age. I hypothesized the predominance of what I called "vitality" in the early and "mentality" in the late peak performances. (See also Chapters 1 and 3.)

The age-related predominance of these factors is also reflected in the choice of certain leisure activities. Take sports, culminating between 20 and 40 (H. C. Lehman, 1953), as against an interest in more thoughtful reading, such as public affairs (W. Schramm and D. M. White, 1949), or listening to religious programs (P. F. Lazarsfeld and P. L. Kendall, 1948) culminating between 40 and 60 +, while socially less demanding hobbies and resting belong to old-age leisure activities. The great bulk of leisure activities, however, is correlated with personality and environment factors rather than with age.

The only positive age correlation which Havighurst (1961) found is that of expansion and constriction of interests and activities. This finding corresponds well to the previously mentioned biographical findings along these lines, and with our statement about expansion and restriction as two basic parameters of development.

Havighurst places the beginning of marriage and family life among the developmental tasks of early adulthood, i.e., the twenties. According to U.S. law persons have to have reached the statutory age of 18 before they can obtain a marriage license. However, marriages at younger ages do take place, not only here but in cultures in which the young couple remains part of an extended family and where the responsibility of sustaining themselves and raising children in a house of their own does not rest on them alone. Thus the beginning of marriage in early adulthood is more culturally than structurally conditioned. The psychological as well as educational maturity needed to meet the demands of a committing relationship, of providing a living, running a home, and sustaining and raising a family are presupposed in our culture.

If, in spite of increasing difficulties in these areas, the median marriage age has considerably declined in the last half century, the reasons lie partly in a changed attitude toward the desirability of earlier sex satisfaction in socially acceptable forms. If, besides the age drop of males from 26.1 to 22.6 years and of females from 22.0 to 20.0 years, the age difference between the sexes has been decreasing, it may be the result of the trend toward companionship marriages (Burgess, Locke and Thomas, 1963).

Evelyn Mills Duvall (1962), using a variety of resources, gives some representative figures for the husband's and the wife's median ages at selected stages of the life cycle of the family in the United States. In comparing trends between 1890 and the present, it appears that today's family, if it stays together, can look forward to a span of about thirty years with, and another of fifteen years or so without, children. This then places the period in which marriage and family life have their greatest fulfillment value between the early twenties and early fifties, after which time the couple may still sustain their union for another fifteen years.

How do these figures relate to people's satisfactions and to the experience of progressive self-realization?

The assumption of people's pursuing their self-realization and finding satisfaction as they proceed from one phase to another has not yet been studied with stringent procedures. What answers there are are based on the case-study method.

The measurement of life satisfactions meets with considerable difficulties. A recently developed instrument by B. L. Neugarten, R. J. Havighurst, and S. S. Tobin (1961) has thus far not proved satisfactory, except for the oldest age group.

Statistical studies of basic satisfactions in life center mostly on the question of what a person's happiest period in life was. In two major studies (J. T. Landis, 1942; M. Morgan, 1937), the years between 25 and 45 are named as the best by about half the cases. The years beyond 60 seem to contribute least to the experience of happiness.

These data were collected prior to World War II and could be obsolete if they depended on certain conditions of life which have since changed. They have, however, at least in part, been confirmed by a recent German research study by U. Lehr (1964). Lehr found that men and women experienced the years from 20 to 40 as the "happiest" period of life. Strangely enough the next "happiest" period for men proved to be between 60 and 70, years which the women did not mention. The "unhappiest" times, according to the German study, are the two crisis periods of adolescence and climacterium (for women between 40 and 50, and for men between 50 and 60).

These statements about "happiness" reflect, of course, only partly the experience of and reactions to goal attainments. Lehr's analysis of her data permits some conclusions, although unfortunately the age arrangement obscures the kind of information one would wish to obtain. The peak of satisfaction regarding occupation, social success, marital and family life falls, as would be expected, into the middle of life (20 to 50). Twenty-one percent of the men and 34 percent of the women in the sample considered the years between 30 and 50 to be the peak of life and the period during which they felt the greatest expansion. The most unsatisfactory experiences of this period have to do with occupational difficulties and marital problems. Satisfaction about being able to form one's life—the statement which comes closest to any observation about the progress of self-realization—is expressed by the 20- to 30-year age group.

Unfortunately, the decades from 30 to 50 and from 50 to 70 are lumped together in this study so that the effect of the decisive breaking points in the climacteric forties and at the retirement age of 65 is obscured. It seems strange and may be a reflection more of cultural than developmental factors that among the satisfactions that Lehr's 50- to 70-year age group emphasized were the serenity obtained by retiring from obligations and the retrospective enjoyment of having lived a good life. It appears extremely early to think that way if the years from 50 to 65 are included. There is also relatively little dissatisfaction about the end of the career. Illnesses represent the bulk of the complaints. About 20 percent of the group name the loss of beloved ones, increasing loneliness, emptiness of their lives, and awareness of the approaching end among their unhappy experiences.

Some of the predominantly satisfied people appear to be what in my terminology I would call "fulfilled." The same seems to apply to some of the cases in the study by B. L. Neugarten and associates (1964). Regrettably, neither Lehr nor Neugarten employ concepts relating to self-realization.

Neugarten, however, is one of the first researchers to make a valid attempt to distinguish truly developmental data from changes of other origins. In her penetrating summary of eight empirical studies of her own and ten of her collaborators she comes to a number of enlightening and new conclusions.

The main insight obtained through her interpretation of the accumulated data is that what she calls intrapsychic personality phenomena are more age-conditioned than they are socio-adaptional. Her assumption is that "the former may lie closer to biological than to social determinants of behavior" (p. 196).

This seems a plausible argument, and would lead one to expect some revealing data regarding the progress of self-realization. Yet the goal-directed and purposive personality qualities were not found to be age dependent.

The question is, of course, which aspect of goal direction one studies. If it is that of adjustment and coping, it may indeed be more a function of personality than of age. But age dependency of goal setting lies in other directions, as we have indicated in the foregoing considerations.

The intrapsychic changes established in these studies of mostly 40- to 70-year-old individuals point essentially to two directions: changes of outlook, and changes of functions.

A person's outlook generally changes toward a greater "inward orientation." And this increased preoccupation with the inner life with increasing age is measurable by the midforties in this sample of well-functioning adults, well before the social losses of aging have occurred and well before the decrease in social interaction described by Cumming and Henry (1961) or in competency of performance in adult social roles described by Havighurst (1957). These findings, furthermore, argue against the implication that increased interiority and increased eccentricity of behavior in the aged follow a thinning of social interaction and a lessening of normative controls over behavior (Neugarten, p. 194).

The changes of function lie in the direction of "a certain *reduction* in the complexity of the personality" (p. 198) and a "decreased efficiency of certain cognitive processes" (p. 193).

Neugarten concludes that the well-adjusted aging individual seems capable of maintaining the continuity of his personality by using different strategies of coping, by increasing his inner circulation, and by decreasing his emotional investments in persons and objects of his environment.

If it were possible to assemble similarly specified data about the progress of self-realization in the corresponding period, the total pattern of human development would be immensely clarified.

References

Allport, G. *Pattern and growth in personality*. New York: Harper, 1961.

Buhler, C. Theoretical observations about life's basic tendencies, *Amer. J. Psychother.*, 1959, *13*: 3, 561-581.

Buhler, C. *Values in psychotherapy*. New York: Free Press, 1962.

Buhler, C. Die ersten sozialen Verhaltungsweisen des Kindes (The first social behavior of the infant). *Quellen und Studien zur Jugendkunde,* 1927, 5, Jena: G. Fischer.

Buhler, C. Der menschliche Lebenslauf als psychologisches Problem. Leipzig: S. Hirzel, 1933. 2nd ed. Göttingen: Verlag für Psychologie, 1959.

Buhler, C. *Kindheit und Jugend (Childhood and adolescence),* Leipzig: S. Hirzel, 3rd ed., 1931.

Buhler, C., and Hetzer, H. *The first year of life,* New York: John Day, 1930.

Buhler, K. *Die Krise der Psychologie*. Jena: G. Fischer, 1927.

Burgess, E. W., Locke, H. J., and Thomas, M. M. *The family,* 3rd ed. New York: American Book Co., 1963.

Brown, M., and Martin, V. The University High School study of adolescents characteristics of high school students, *Univ. High Sch. J.*, 1941, *19,* 177-219.

Cumming, E., and Henry, W. E. *Growing old,* New York: Basic Books, 1961.

Duvall, E. M. *Family development,* Philadelphia: J. B. Lippincott, 2nd ed., 1962.

Eiduson, B. *Scientists,* New York: Basic Books, 1962.

Erikson, E. Identity and the life cycle, *Psychol. Issues*. New York: International Universities Press, 1959, *1*:1.

Frankl, L. Development of object constancy: stages in the recognition of the baby's feeding bottle, *Humanistic Psychol.*, Fall, 1963, *III*.

Frankl. V. Self-transcendence as a human phenomenon. *J. Humanistic Psychol.*, 1966, *6*: 2, 97-106.

Frenkel, E. Studies in biographical psychology, *Character and Personality,* 1936, *5,* 1-34.

Getzels, J., and Jackson, P. *Creativity and intelligence, explorations with gifted students*. New York: John Wiley & Sons, 1962.

Goertzel, V., and Goertzel, M. *Cradles of eminence.* Boston: Little, Brown & Co., 1962.
Guilford, J. P. *Fields of psychology.* New York: D. van Nostrand, 1950.
Havighurst, R. J. *Developmental tasks and education.* New York: Longmans, Green & Co., 2nd ed., 1952.
Havighurst, R. J. The nature and value of meaningful free-time activity. In R. W. Kleemeier (ed.) *Aging and Leisure,* New York: Oxford University Press, 1961.
Havighurst, R. J. The social competence of middle-aged people, *Gen. Psych. Mon.,* 1957, *56,* 297-375.
Hilgard, E. The role of learning in perception. In R. R. Blake and G. V. Ramsey (eds.), *Perception.* New York: Ronald, 1951.
Kagan, J., and Moss, H. A. *Birth to maturity.* New York: John Wiley & Sons, 1962.
Kuhlen, R. G., and Johnson, G. H. Change in goals with increasing adult age, *J. Consult. Psychol.,* 1952, *16,* 1-4.
Landis, J. T. What is the happiest period of life? *School and Society,* 1942, *55,* 643-645.
Lazarsfeld, P. F., and Kendall, P. L. *Radio listening in America.* Englewood Cliffs, N.J.: Prentice-Hall, 1948.
Lehman, H. C. *Age and achievement.* Princeton University Press, 1953.
Lehr, U. Positive and negative Einstellung zu einzelnen Lebensaltern (Positive and negative attitude to different ages), *Vita Humana,* 1964, *7,* 201-227.
Maslow, A. *Religions, values, and peak-experiences.* Columbus: Ohio State University Press, 1964.
McClelland, D., Atkinson, W., Clark, R., and Lowell, E. *The achievement motive.* New York: Appleton-Century-Crofts, 1953.
Morgan, M. The attitudes and adjustments of recipients of old age assistance in upstate and metropolitan New York, *Archives of Psychol.,* 1937, *30*: 214, 131.
Murphy, L. *The widening world of childhood.* New York: Basic Books, 1962.
Neugarten B. L., Havighurst, R. J., and Tobin, S. S. The measurement of life satisfactions, *J. Geront.,* 1961, *16,* 134-143.
Neugarten, B. L. and Assoc. *Personality in middle and late life.* New York: Atherton Press, 1964.
Otto, H. The personal resource development research—the multiple strength perception effect. *Proceedings of Utah Acad. Sci., Arts, & Letters, 38,* 1961-62.
Pressey, S. L., and Kuhlen, R. G. *Psychological development through the life span,* New York: Harper Bros., 1957.
Piaget, J. *The origins of intelligence in children,* New York: International Universities Press, 1952.
Piaget, J. *Play, dreams and imitation in childhood.* New York: W. W. Norton, 1951.
Redl, F., and Wineman, D. *Children who hate, the disorganization and breakdown of behavior controls,* Glencoe, Ill.: Free Press of Glencoe, 1951.
Ripin, R., and Hetzer, H. Frühestes Lernen des Säuglings in der Ernährungssituation (Earliest learning of the newborn in the feeding situation), *Zeitschr. f. Psychol.* 118, 1930.
Rosenmayr, L. *Lebensziele in der Pubertät* Bd. II österr. Inst. f. Jgdkde. Wien, 1963.
Rubinow, O., and Frankl, L. Die erste Dingaufassung beim Säugling (The first object awareness of infants), *Zeitschr. f. Psychol.* 133, 1934.
Schachtel, E. G. *Metamorphosis,* New York: Basic Books, 1959.
Schramm, W., and White, D. M. Age, education, economic status: factors in newspaper reading, *Journalism Quart.,* 1949, *26,* 148-159.
Sontag, L. The genetics of differences in psychosomatic patterns in childhood, *Amer. J. Orthopsychiat.,* 1950, *20,* 3.
Spitz, R. A. Genèse des premières relations objectales (Genesis of the first object relationships), *Revue Française de Psychoanalyse,* Paris, 1954.
Spitz, R. A., and Cobliner, G. *The first year of life. A psychoanalytic study of normal and deviant development of object relations.* New York: International Universities Press, 1965.

Stirnimann, F. *Psychologie des neugeborenen Kindes* (*Psychology of the newborn infant*). Zürich: Rascher, 1940.
Strodtbeck, F., McClelland, D., *et al. Talent and society,* Princeton, N.J.: Van Nostrand, 1958.
Tillich, P. *The courage to be.* New Haven: Yale University Press, 1952.
Time. Twenty-five and under, Jan. 6, 1967, 89.
Tinbergen, N. *The study of instinct.* Oxford: Clarendon Press, 1955.
Weil, A. Some evidences of deviational development in infancy and early childhood, *11, Psychoanalytic Study of the Child,* New York: International Universities Press, 1956.

Chapter 3

Structural Aspects of the Individual's History

Charlotte Bühler and Herbert Goldenberg

The Uniqueness of the Individual

Modern genetics tells us that the individual is unique. As P. B. Medawar (1957, p. 185), one of the leading authorities on the uniqueness of the individual, says: "The texture of human diversity is almost infinitely close-woven."

Psychologists, however, although long aware of "individual differences" (W. Stern, 1900), continued to be more interested in group data. They felt that especially in studies of development, it was not only important but necessary to establish community factors before establishing individuality. Because of the great advances in science and psychology we are in a better position today to study individuality, but we also are better able to realize how difficult it is to arrive at truly valid conclusions about individual traits of personality or development.

Unfortunately, science gives us little encouragement to make definitive statements about the heredity of traits or behavioral trends. John Fuller, in "Genetics and Goal Setting" (Chapter 5), concludes that while "all characteristics of an organism, including its behavior, are related to its genotype," psychologists "will find no correspondence between protein molecules and forms of behavior." The only general orientation available, he says, is that "given a particular genotype, an individual has restrictions upon possible courses of development."

Our present inability to trace heredity in behavior would not necessarily prevent a hypothesizing of innate trends. But here we are hindered by our knowledge that innate and environmental factors interact from the moment of conception on, so that the individuality of each person may have to be explained by "the multiplicity of overlapping groups with which the individual may be behaviorally identified" (Anastasi and Foley, 1954, p. 618).

These complexities notwithstanding, modern research has been trying to find new techniques of extrapolating traits which seem to have originated in the individual himself. A recent investigation by Thomas, Chess, Birch, Hertzig, and Korn (1963) has tackled the problem of behavior individuality in childhood by a longitudinal study of young infants. With the cooperation of parents, nine behavioral traits were listed in which varying degrees of consistency were established. The traits listed were: 1) activity level, 2) rhythmicity, 3) approach or withdrawal, 4) adaptability, 5) intensity of reaction, 6) threshold of responsiveness, 7) quality of mood, 8) distractability, and 9) attention span and persistence. The most consistent traits were mood, intensity, adaptivity, and approach to a new stimulus. The authors display much care in drawing theoretical conclusions from their observations. Besides the "genetic familial" factor, they have listed "prenatal, paranatal, and early life experience" as possibly being responsible for the individual differences in the behavioral style they established.

Adaptivity and approach to new stimuli, which correspond to our basic tendencies of self-limiting adaptation and creative expansion, according to this group's findings, would be among the most consistent behavioral traits, either innate or having been established very early.

Another way to study early individuality of behavior is to examine an individual's "coping style," i.e., the way in which he handles his problems. [The concept of a "style" of life was introduced by Alfred Adler (1929) who used it to designate the uniqueness of the individual.]

Katherine Wolf (1955) and associates conducted longitudinal studies of individualization following birth. Wolf's purpose was to delineate behavioral patterns at birth and immediately thereafter which would have predictive value for later responses and personality development. Her findings led her to suggest that every developmental step, from the very first days of life, represents a genetic or constitutionally based "individual solution." Each infant, for example, quickly develops a personalized way of solving problems or of coping with danger, and the variations in the tension-reduction techniques of infants are great.

Escalona and Heider (1959), also utilizing longitudinal studies, correlated observations of a group of infants of 8 months and younger, with the characteristics of preschool children. The authors noted that specific behavior underwent continual changes, but that there was an inherent continuity in a child's behavioral style and in his pattern of adaptation. The child's behavior between 3 and 6 years showed "consistency of everything a person is and does at any age and in all sets of circumstances." In particular, the authors found that it was easier to predict the more formal aspects of behavior, such as *how* a child would move, think, speak, and play, than it was to forecast *what* it would be likely to do, think, say, or play.

In a continuation of their Menninger Clinic research studies, Lois Murphy (1962) reported on the great individuality of coping styles by describing her observations of a group of nursery school children. She found the experiential and behavioral complexity at this age is already so pronounced that each of these children appeared as a different and unique personality. The coping styles, while individually different, could be grouped according to certain basic determinants, some of which Murphy considers to be constitutional. Among the significant determinants are sensitivity degrees, autonomic reactivity, drive, and developmental balance.

Murphy did not elaborate on the difference between "adaptive" and "creative" coping, and yet it is this difference that is indicative of the ultimate goals that children seem to have at nursery school age. It is natural for them to want to master situations and to solve certain problems; some do it by adapting themselves to their environment, others by trying to change it. They also may pursue such other goals as self-gratification or believing that what they do is "right" or "good." It would be interesting to examine the individuality of goal patterns in terms of these basic tendencies.

Studies have shown that the individualization of a person's behavioral structure increases the longer he lives. With advancing age, says Shock (1963), individuals become less and less similar. B. Neugarten (1964) demonstrated that the growing individualization is enhanced by an increasing "interiorization"; Shneidman's (1963) quote of Noyes aptly sums this up: "As we grow older, we grow more like ourselves."

This then makes an individual's life and biography unique, and it is this uniqueness as well as complexity that make it difficult to use biographical materials in a demonstration of general developmental trends. Yet we cannot understand man's behavior and striving unless we consider his complete life cycle, and techniques for a comparative study of biographies will of necessity have to be developed.

Structural Aspects of the Individual Biography

Biographies are particularly useful for the study of human lives because they represent the whole life, including its termination. They are less suitable, however, for dynamic or other individual investigations where case studies offer more opportunity for in-depth investigations. One of the problems in presenting life histories, especially when it comes to abstracting general principles, is the mass of the material.

In an effort to see a person's life in its total structure, C. Buhler (1933) devised a technique by which the data of a person's life history could be divided into three categories: external events and activities, inner experiences, and physical as well as mental productions. All three categories are integral parts of an individual's life cycle, and their distribution over the course of a life is indicative of its structure. To make this distribution visible, major "dimensions" were established which signify different behavioral areas of life. Using some sample cases, E. Brunswik, E. Frenkel, and C. Buhler (1933) also categorized different kinds of inner experiences and creative productions, a procedure which permitted them to see the structural aspects of life histories more distinctly.

What follows is an application of Buhler's technique to the life history of a 67-year-old traffic manager who was interviewed in his retirement years. It first describes the external events and activities of his life and then shows and interprets the structure of his work output and inner experiences.

> Bill Roberts and his wife live in a nicely kept suburban house of their own, with a backyard full of blooming roses and a well-cared-for car in the garage. Bill takes pride in his home, paints it regularly outside and inside, and makes most of the repairs on it himself. He and his wife visit with their neighbors and with family members. They are very proud of their two sons and two daughters, all of whom are married and have enriched their parents' lives with nine grandchildren. The Roberts present a typical, settled American middle-class family in secure circumstances.
>
> Bill comes from old pioneer stock. His father's as well as his mother's ancestors immigrated in 1775 and settled in Kentucky as farmers, grocery store owners, railroad and post office men, ministers, and school teachers. Originally his father's family came from England, his mother's from Ireland; there are also Pennsylvania Dutch and French among his ancestors.
>
> He had seven brothers and sisters; he is the second child and eldest son. He grew up and went to school in a small Kentucky town where his father owned a grocery store and some farm land. When Bill was 14 years old, his father died unexpectedly, his mother remarried, and Bill

no longer felt happy at home. He then moved to Cleveland where he lived with relatives and worked in a factory.

From his 17th to his 20th year, Bill was in the army and after his discharge worked for a while as a railroad clerk in Cincinnati. During this time he fell deeply in love. He went "steady" and wanted to marry the girl, but her family's and her own religious convictions clashed with his. They were strict Catholics, while he came from a Presbyterian family. He refused to change his religion. Instead, he decided to return to his high school love, a girl from his home town. "There is nothing sweeter and more adorable than Southern women," he says. He was 26 when he married.

Six months later he was drafted and sent to England and France where he spent a year as a "doughboy." "I loved Europe and what I saw of it," he admits, "but I was dazed from the whole affair." His first son was born when he was abroad. During that time, too, his mother died; the old family farm was sold and the proceeds were divided among the children. Finding the situation thus changed upon his return, Bill and his wife decided to move to the West Coast where he got a job in the traffic department of a big trucking company in San Francisco. For three years he went to school in order to qualify for the position of assistant manager.

Three more children arrived in short intervals and seemed to have given their parents much real joy and relatively little trouble. Bill says he always loved children, and his family life was happy. "We were a closely knit family and we still are." During the depression it became difficult to support the family, and Bill had to accept many odd jobs to make ends meet. Then for a few years he was back again as traffic manager, but the company had to sell out. When he was let go he was paid extra money, and he decided to use this for a three-month vacation trip through the United States for him and his family. He was then 48.

On their return Bill found a good job in a Los Angeles trucking firm, and the family moved and bought a better home. But shortly thereafter, when he was 49 years old, Bill had to have a serious kidney operation.

He returned to his job after the surgery but soon felt that he needed to leave it because of his health and establish a business of his own. He took his savings and, at age 53, bought himself a grocery store. Eleven years later he retired and turned the store over to his youngest son.

Bill has pursued many interests during his life and seems never to have been lacking for something to do with his free time. He and his wife are religious people, although not fanatics, and often attend the Presbyterian church to which they belong and where their children went to Sunday School.

In his middle fifties, Bill joined the Masons, feeling that he wanted to devote his energies to doing good on a larger scale since his own family was now taken care of. With his lodge work and his wife's activities in the women's club, they try to be "an asset to the community."

Politically, Bill has strong convictions and "votes and talks a lot" in favor of the Democratic party, thus breaking an old Republican family tradition.

The couple does not entertain much. They visit their children and other relatives, belong to a canasta club, and used to belong to a folk-dancing club.

For recreation, Bill goes on fishing and hunting trips, and for many years took along one of his boys. Once, between jobs and after his illness, he and the family took a long trip through the United States which they considered most educational. Bill likes to swim, play some golf, go to the movies, watch ball games on TV, listen to music, and enjoys playing the piano, which he does by ear. He reads popular magazines, occasionally a book, keeps himself informed about current events, and follows the stock market. He and his wife love art and are proud owners of three original paintings.

For a hobby, Bill works (as mentioned before) in the yard, paints his house, and repairs almost everything himself. He also makes toys for his grandchildren and, if necessary, repairs their bicycles.

During the war and when he gave up his managerial job, he received several decorations which he cherishes.

When speaking of his life as a whole, Bill says, "We have tried to live a clean and religious life always. We always were in good health, and good food came always first. We were blessed with a wonderful family, all healthy and normal children. We are proud of our children, they all made a place for themselves, were successful, and are happily married, except for one. People warned us not to move to the Wild West, but ever since we are in California we always had wonderful neighbors, that is a big asset."

The biography of Bill Roberts was chosen as a model of an average middle-class life history in Western civilization. It has a simple structure, typical of many. Bill lives at a steady pace, with a good ability to adapt himself to difficult circumstances, with enough resourcefulness to find new solutions, and with sufficient courage and determination to steer away from trouble and unconquerable difficulties. He married a good woman, raised a family with whom he has always felt close, does an adequate job in using his abilities to best advantage, and has an unusually wide range of leisure activities and interests that he pursues and shares with his wife.

When presenting a person's life history schematically, one has to make a somewhat arbitrary decision about which data to include and which to omit. The selection usually depends on the purpose.

The purpose of this chapter is to show what might be called the most basic data of a person's life history because they reveal the structure of the life cycle. Although one might debate the inclusion of one or another "dimension," as C. Buhler calls these data, the reader probably will agree that most of the dimensions included here are basic. The following then is a schematic rendering of Bill Roberts' life, presented to make the basic dimensions of this life history "visible."

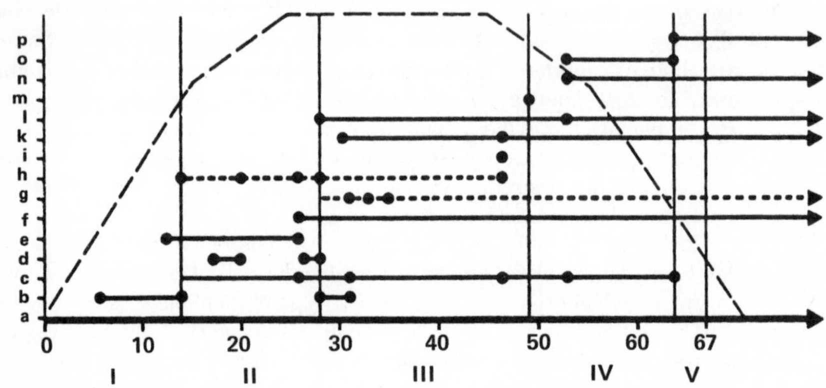

Schematic Presentation of Bill Roberts' Life History

a. Time dimensions in ages
b. Education
c. Career
d. Service in army
e. Dating
f. Marriage
g. Children
h. Changes of domiciles
i. Extended trip
k. Home ownership
l. Church and ofgarnizational memberships
m. Illness
n. Children on their own
o. Departure from job and beginning of own business
p. Retirement
– – – Biological life cycle

Line a refers to Bill's age up to the interview, which took place when he was 67 years old. Lines b to f refer to the main events and activity areas of Bill's life.

The broken line above the data represents the schematic growth and decline curve which we introduced in Chapter 1.

The following findings emerged when we compared Roberts' life with the models presented in the preceding chapters.

Using first the expansion-restriction model, we find a gain in new dimensions until Bill is about 30 and the family acquires its first home. This is followed by a fairly stationary period in which the family grows and Bill's jobs improve. At 46, Bill experiences what he himself considers the peak in his life, when he and the family take a trip through the United States. Bill's serious kidney operation at 49 marks the beginning of his relatively early descent. After a short return to work, he decides he is no longer strong enough to hold a full-time job. He buys a grocery store with the family's savings and works part time, with his wife assisting him. At 64 he retires completely.

Second, using the self-determination model, we find that Bill's period of tentative self-determination starts relatively early, i.e., at 14 when he leaves his parents' home. The phase of his definite self-determination begins with his marriage at age 26, and it unfolds more fully two years later when he settles down in a steady job and at a place where he intends to remain. He then starts his family and buys a home.

The phase of self-assessment and reorientation begins when Bill is 49 and, following his kidney operation, he decides he can no longer cope with his office job and turns to running his own grocery store with his wife's help. But at 64, Bill feels he is not strong enough to share the responsibility of the store and he retires.

While Bill Roberts' biography exemplifies the phasic structure of events and activities during a life cycle, the available data on his inner experiences and his work do not lend themselves to quantitative treatment.

Viennese Life-History Studies

In the life-history studies which the senior author of this chapter pursued in Vienna (1933), assisted by Egon Brunswik, Else Frenkel (Brunswik), Paul Lazarsfeld, and a number of students, an effort was made to find ways and means to make the history of a person's inner experiences and his productions visible.

The development of inner experiences relating to the goals of life was traced through documents of various kinds, such as correspondence, diaries, reported conversations, and other items. We found that we could fit such experiences into the five phases of self-determination as they relate to goals and their fulfillment. Statements about plans, projects, programs, hopes, preparations, and experimental attitudes were considered signs of preliminary self-determination, which were expected to culminate in the adolescent years (15–25).

Statements concerning attainment of definite satisfaction in terms of occupation, of love and a companionable relationship, such as marriage, or of success in any other area of life, were considered signs of definite self-determination, usually culminating in the middle of life (25–45).

Statements indicative of a self-evaluating attitude, i.e., a person took his past successes and failures into account when he made decisions for the future, were interpreted as signs of self-assessment, which usually reached a peak in the climacteric age (45–65).

Extensive studies were conducted by E. Brunswik and E. Frenkel Brunswik to implement a quantitative, schematic presentation of individual creative output or production. This task was comparatively easy when it involved merely the counting of such production units as inventions, stage appearances, or works of art. It became more difficult when speeches, legal briefs, or medical activities were involved, and it was impossible when it concerned the activities of, for example, a teacher or a nurse.

Frenkel and Brunswik (in C. Buhler, 1933) succeeded, however, in producing discriminative quantitative accounts of the various forms of human productivity, reminiscent of the various kinds of music a musician composes during his life time. They worked out methods by which they could make visible the achievements of inventors, businessmen, and statesmen, as well as techniques which demonstrated documented and material successes. Their research, based on a study of about 200 biographies, led them to conclude that a person's productive capacity, if examined quantitatively, may culminate at different periods of his life.

There is an early culmination, characteristic not only of the laborer, the athlete, and the sportsman, but also of certain artists and musicians. Jenny Lind is an example of this kind of early rise and decline, having reached her peak when she was in her middle twenties.

There is a middle-age culmination, which appears to be the usual pattern in most careers. Such highly creative people as Edison, Nansen, Liszt, Verdi, Feuerbach, and Lessing are outstanding examples. Their peaks occurred, quantitatively and often also qualitatively, when they were in their mid-thirties.

There also is a late culmination characteristic of accomplishments based on experiences and/or long, systematic planning. The most outstanding example of long-term, systematic planning is the philosopher, I. Kant, who made his greatest contributions when he was in his sixties and seventies. Typical members in this category are statesmen; Bismarck's and Cavour's careers culminated late in life as have those of some of our leading statesmen.

Harvey Lehman (1953), although insisting emphatically that the middle of life is the peak period of a person's creative work, has compiled very interesting data on late-age peaks which seem typical for certain positions requiring high responsibility, experience, and wisdom. His survey includes industrial executives, members of Parliament, popes, and other religious leaders. An example of new creative endeavor which started and culminated late is the case of W. von Humboldt's linguistic research, which was begun when he was in his fifties and brought to a peak when he was 62.

There is still a fourth group of individuals, those whose productivity is distributed irregularly over their life span or who have several productive peaks. Some well-known examples of this category are Schopenhauer, Descartes, Richard Wagner, and the inventor W. von Siemens.

In trying to explain very early and very late culminations, C. Buhler hypothesized that in the former certain physical aptitudes predominated and in the latter specific mental aptitudes. Both types of aptitudes seem to be more or less in balance in those who reach the peak of their productivity in the middle of their lives, and in those who are productive at various periods of their lives.

The Brunswik and Frenkel study stopped abruptly with the end of the Viennese School of Psychology. Summaries of the results have been published by C. Buhler (1933, 1959, 1961) and E. Frenkel (1936).

References

Adler, Alfred. *The science of living.* New York: Greenberg, 1929.

Anastasi, A., and Foley, Jr., J. P. *Differential psychology.* New York: Macmillan, 1954.

Buhler, C. *The human course of life as a psychological problem.* Leipzig: S. Hirzel, 1933.

Escalona, S., and Heider, G. *Prediction and outcome.* New York: Basic Books, 1959.

Frenkel, E. Studies in biographical psychology, *Character and Personality,* 5: 1, 1-35.

Lehman, H. C. *Age and achievement.* Princeton University Press, 1953.

Medawar, P. B. *The uniqueness of the individual.* New York: Basic Books, 1957.

Murphy, L. and Assoc. *The widening world of childhood–paths toward mastery.* New York: Basic Books, 1962.

Shneidman, C. Orientation toward death: a vital aspect of the study of lives. Chapter 9 in Robert W. White (ed.), *The study of lives,* New York: Atherton, 1963.

Shock, N. W. (ed.) *Problems of aging.* New York: J. Macy Jr. Foundation, 1951.

Stern, W. *Uber Psychologie der individuellen Differenzen (About the psychology of individual differences).* Leipzig: Barth, 1900.

Thomas, A., Birch, H. G., Chess, S., Hertzig, M. E., and Korn, S. *Behavioral individuality in early childhood.* New York: New York University Press, 1963.

Wolf, K. Problems of early infancy. *Amer. Psychoanalyt. Assn.,* 1955, *III.*

Chapter 4

The Evolution of Goals in the Life of Clarence Darrow

Althea J. Horner

". . . I am satisfied that life is a serious burden, which no thinking humane person would wantonly inflict on someone else" (Darrow, 1932).* When Clarence Darrow, toward the end of his days, came to this weary conclusion, he was expressing the ambivalence that so many people experience when they view their lives, either in prospect or in retrospect. Because of the tremendous idealism which originally permeated his concept of man, Darrow became increasingly cynical the more he came to know man as he actually is. Darrow protested this discrepancy bitterly, and his protests comprise the bulk of his productive output.

As his physical and emotional strength ebbed and flowed through the various stages of his life, so did his involvement with the demands the world made upon his talents. When we look back on Darrow's life and his involvement with the world, we cannot help but wonder what the factors were that led him to choose one path over another; why should he at one point give up a lucrative law practice to spend several years fighting for as unpopular a cause as that of unionized labor, and why should he at another point respond to the many requests for his help by saying: "I cannot go about the country opening jail doors, I wish I could. Sometimes I write a letter in reply to some victim of fate, saying how helpless I am and how impossible it is to do anything toward mercy and understanding in a crazy world . . ." (p. 434).

What happens in the course of a person's life—of a Darrow or of anybody else—that leads him first to rush headlong toward his ideals and goals but ultimately to realize, with a kind of passive resignation, that his goals cannot be reached but only be approached, and that the time has come for him to slow down and turn his goals over to those who succeed him?

* Reprinted with permission. From Clarence Darrow, *The Story of My Life*. New York: Charles Scribner's Sons. Excerpts from this book which appear in this chapter are reprinted with permission.

C. Buhler (1933, 1961) sees in this changing course of events, attitudes, and accomplishments an orderly progression of phases, a theoretical framework which we can use in an attempt to understand the complexity of life.

Let us use this framework to examine the course of Clarence Darrow's life. According to Buhler, there are several stages through which the individual passes before he arrives at what she calls "self-determination to fulfillment," or decides what his life's goals are:

Age	Stage
0–15	Prior to self-determination
15–25	Experimental or preparatory self-determination
25–45	Definite and specific self-determination toward goals and fulfillments
45–65	Self-assessment of obtained results
65 and up	Experience of fulfillment or failure, with the remaining years spent in either continuance of previous activities or a return to the need-satisfying orientation of childhood.

Theoretically the events of a man's life, the formation and changes of his attitudes, and his products or achievements should show some kind of correlation or parallel to these evolutionary steps in goal development. Was this actually so in the case of Darrow? He himself was keenly aware of the changes that come with age. As he says in his autobiography:

> The young man's reflections of unfolding life concern the future—the great, broad, tempestuous sea on whose hither shore he stands eagerly waiting to learn of other lands and climes. The reactions and recollections of the old concern the stormy journey drawing to a close; he no longer builds castles or plans conquests of the unknown; he recalls the tempests and tumults encountered on the way and babbles of the passengers and crew that one by one dropped silently into the icy depths. No longer does the aging transient yearn for new adventures or unexplored highways. His greatest ambition is to find some snug harbor where he can doze and dream the fleeting days away (p. 5).

Clarence Darrow was born on April 18, 1857, in the small town of

Kinsman, Ohio. Kinsman could hardly be called a cradle of great men, being typically narrow and provincial in its activities and attitudes. To understand how a Clarence Darrow came from its midst we will have to consider the role his father played. According to the son, his father always had been a visionary and a dreamer, a man who had graduated from a theological seminary only to find he had lost his faith and come to question and distrust orthodoxy. "My father was the village infidel, and gradually came to glory in his reputation," wrote the younger Darrow. His mother, who died when he was quite young, was the source of stability in practical matters and, as he observed: "Through my mother's good sense my father was able to give his children a glimpse into the realm of idea and ideals in which he himself really lived." The children admired their father, loved him, and identified with him. The last words that Clarence Darrow wrote before his death describe their feeling toward him: "The fact that my father was a heretic always put him on the defensive, and we children thought it was only right and loyal that we should defend his cause." There can be little doubt that Darrow's relationship with his father had a deep and far-reaching effect on the formation of the son's personality, and on the set of values that came to dominate his life. Clarence Darrow found the fulfillment of his professional and public life in the service of these values rather than in his personal life. His autobiography contains one short paragraph about each of his two wives, and barely mentions his son Paul. Stone (1941), however, tells us that Darrow was proud and fond of his son, and that, when he sent him off to Dartmouth University somewhat against his will, he gave him two pieces of advice: "Never get into a poker game unless there is a limit," and, "If you ever get into difficulty of any kind, you had better tell me, because I don't think you can get into anything I haven't been in." According to the autobiography, Paul took on greater importance when Darrow, in his final years, traded his work for the satisfactions of family life.

In his autobiography Darrow, like Buhler, chose to treat the first fifteen years of his life as a unit, commenting, "The memory pictures of the first fifteen years of life that drift back to me now are a medley of all sorts of things, mainly play and school." He tells us that never was there a time when he did not like to go to school, and that his one unalloyed joy in life was baseball. "I am not at all sure about the lessons that I learned at school," he adds, "but I do know that we got a great deal of fun between the study hours, and I have always been glad that I took all the play I could as it came along" (p. 18). So Darrow's life during the stage preceding self-determination was occupied with the day to day present, with learning and playing, and with the enjoyment of just being alive.

In 1873, at the age of 16, and after several years of schooling which he felt to be totally irrelevant to life, Darrow was forced to, as he put it, abandon school and begin his education. He decided that he was not fond of manual labor and that he was destined for better things. This is the point at which he began to search for his goals. He tried teaching and began to study law. "I am not sure what influenced me to make this choice. I know that I never intended to work with my hands, and no doubt I was attracted by the show of the legal profession." He began to show an interest in public life, and admits that he "enjoyed the way the pettifoggers abused each other, and as I grew toward maturity I developed a desire to be a lawyer, too." He enrolled in the University of Michigan's law department for one year after which, for financial reasons, he decided to continue his studies on his own. As was the custom in those days, he worked in a law office in Youngstown, Ohio, until, in 1878, he was admitted to the Ohio bar.

Although the pattern of Darrow's life phases follows the sequence described by Buhler, he would probably disagree with the term "self-determination." Darrow had a strong deterministic view of human behavior, and applied it equally to the kinds of choices made by criminals and those which shaped his own life. He noted:

> Believing that the law of cause and effect reached through every part of the universe—believing that men and women do what was set down for them to do and what was indestructibly woven through the whole warp and woof of life, I come but to one conclusion—no one deserved either praise or blame. In my defense of men and women I have sought to bring courts and juries to understand the philosophy which I think is largely responsible for what success I have had . . . (p. 425).

And, as he remarked subsequently:

> Often it seems strange that of the infinite patterns that have been presented by Nature seemingly for our choice we did not select some other scheme. But no act was induced by choice; each one was the result of what went before, and if we look at life in its entirety we understand that we could have gone no other way (p. 446).

Darrow was almost completely unaware of how his values determined his choices.

> My sympathies always went out to the weak, the suffering, and the poor. Realizing their sorrows I tried to relieve them in order that I myself might be relieved. I had a thoroughly independent, perhaps individual way of looking at things, and was never influenced by the view of others unless I could be convinced that they were nearly right. I had little respect for the opinion of the crowd. My instinct was to doubt the majority view. My father had directed my thought and reading. He had taught me to question rather than accept. He never thought that the fear of God was the beginning of wisdom. I have always felt that doubt was the beginning of wisdom and the fear of God was the end of wisdom. (p. 32).

His value structure rejected adaptation and conventional success. His opinion of success was that "to some—perhaps to most—it means 'money.' I never cared much for it nor tried to get much of it or ever had a great deal, but still most of my life I have had what I needed. To some, success means political preferment; this I never wanted." In other words, he rejected having power as well.

Although he attributed the course his life took to the demands of fate, Darrow did make choices based not only on his rejection of certain values, but also on his overwhelming concern for the right of the individual and his distrust of organized society, be it management, religious reformers, or what he called the "greatest enemy that ever confronted man—public opinion . . . I could never be convinced that any institution was wholly good or wholly evil. This feeling has prevented me from obeying orders or being a bitter partisan on any question. Instinctively I lean toward the integrity of the individual unit, and am impatient with any interference with personal freedom . . . (p. 55).

The second stage of Darrow's life—that of experimental or preparatory self-determination—found him teaching, studying, and setting up a small rural law practice in the town of Andover. His first marriage in 1878, although it lasted nineteen years, must be considered part of this preparatory stage. He had married Jessie Ohl, whose parents were friends and neighbors of his family, when he was 21, and all he tells us is that his son Paul was born of this marriage, and that he and Jessie were divorced in 1897, without bitterness, still having confidence in and respecting one another. Stone, from whom we learn a little more, reports that Darrow was attracted to Jessie because she was pretty and a good dancer, that he had previously not gone out with girls, and that they both had simple tastes and were apparently well suited to each other.

After a year or two in Chicago, Stone goes on, Darrow realized "that the choice of his youth was not the choice of his maturity." Jessie no longer fitted into his expanding world of people, interests, and activities. They had increasingly less and less in common. "There was almost no point at which their minds could touch, no common ground on which they could be companionable."

Darrow's dissatisfaction with the limitations of life in a small Ohio town led him to a choice which he claims to be an accident of fate. He had made up his mind to buy a home in the small town of Ashtabula, but when the wife of the owner refused to sign the deed, Darrow answered, barely controlling his temper, "All right, I don't believe I want your house because—because—I'm going to move away from here" (p. 39). Darrow always felt that the woman's whim had shaped his future, neglecting to credit the energy within him that was seeking a broader outlet for his talents and a larger stage for him to stand upon. He was already 31 years old, but he still had some experimenting to do.

Darrow moved to Chicago and gradually narrowed down his activities, realizing after a brief trial involvement that politics was not for him. In 1896, at the age of 39, he ran for Congress but was defeated.

> I really felt relief when I learned of my defeat. I did not want to be in political life. I realized what sacrifices of independence went with office seeking . . . (p. 93). It is hard enough to maintain an independent stand and freely express one's self without being handicapped by the desire for office or money. Most people who follow a political career grow to be cowards and slaves; for that matter, so do men who sell prunes . . . (p. 33).

He now turned his attention to law.

Darrow had formed a close friendship with John Altgeld who had become governor of Illinois in 1892. Altgeld won his everlasting admiration for an act that took great courage (ensuring, as it did, his political demise), namely to pardon the anarchists that had been convicted of murder as the result of the Haymarket Square uprising. Darrow made Altgeld, a former judge, his law partner for the last six months of the judge's life. Altgeld's dedication to what he thought right was a source of great inspiration to Darrow, second only to that provided by his father in his earlier years. He spoke with great emotion at his friend's funeral, exclaiming, " . . . your brave words will speak for the poor, the oppressed, the captive and the weak, and your devoted life inspire countless souls to do and dare in the holy cause for which you lived and died."

The decision to forego politics was temporarily revoked when in 1902 Darrow ran for and won a two-year term in the state legislature. But this experience merely reinforced his former opinion, and he retired permanently from the political arena at the age of 47.

In 1903 Darrow married Ruby Hamerstrom with whom he lived happily and companionably until the end of his life. Again, he devoted only a short paragraph of his autobiography to this relationship, talking about it in a rather detached way. He tells how Ruby traveled everywhere with him, "relieving me of all responsibility and exertion in arranging for everything in the way of transportation and hotel accommodations, baggage, communications, engagements, and the countless inevitable details. I really could not have made these journeys without her assistance and constant care" (p. 126). Stone gives us a more personal account. He describes how Darrow, after his first marriage, was involved in a love affair with a Miss X who was followed by others, and how he enthusiastically espoused the case of free love. Rather than experimenting during adolescence or early adulthood, as one might expect, Darrow did his experimenting in his forties, after a marriage which was the result of his youthful lack of goal direction and before a second marriage which was an expression of his final formulation of goals. Stone reports that Darrow particularly enjoyed his relationships with social workers, because he could engage them in intelligent conversation before feeling amorous. He was attracted to women "who were vividly aware of their times and the important movements within it." Ruby Hamerstrom was just such a woman.

Although Darrow was now 46 years old, the legal achievements which made him famous were still to come. It was not until twenty-two years later, when he was presented with the challenge of the Loeb-Leopold murder trial, that he began to lose some of the driving force for which he was known. But his dominant value in life, despite the waning physical vigor, still drove him on.

> I knew of no good reason for refusing, but I was sixty-eight years old, and very weary. I had grown tired of standing in the lean and lonely front line facing the greatest enemy that ever confronted man—public opinion. But I went in, to do what I could for sanity and humanity against the wave of hatred and malice that, as ever, was masquerading under its usual nom de plume: "Justice" (p. 232).

A year later he volunteered his services in the Scopes trial. His legal adversary was William Jennings Bryan, whom he had met earlier in Chicago and for whom he had little use. Here again, Darrow was motivated by his belief in his values and convictions. "My object, and my only object, was to focus the attention of the country on the programme of Mr. Bryan and the other fundamentalists in America. I knew that education was in danger from the source that always hampered it—religious fanaticism" (p. 249).

It was at this point that Darrow was ready for a change. His goal, his main purpose in life, was still to fight for the liberty of the individual but he shifted the arena in which to fight the battle. After 50 years of practicing law, he officially retired and devoted his energies to speaking and writing, with the liberty of the individual his foremost concern.

However, Darrow was called back into legal service for two more major cases, one of them the defense of eleven Negroes in Detroit who had been charged with murder. As he recalled it:

> I made the usual excuses that I was tired, and growing old, and was not physically or mentally fit. I knew that I would go when I was making the excuses (p. 302).

But eventually he did make a move toward retirement:

> I had stood with the hunted for many years. I had fought against hatred, passion, and vengeance to save liberty and life, and I was weary, and timorous of the crowd. It was hard to longer brace myself for the fray. I wanted to rest and play, and not to be harassed and worried in the few years left through which I might cling to life. I did not want longer to fight in a courthouse all day and study and contrive far into the night, and be back in the courtroom at ten in the morning after a troublous sleep. I wanted to get up when I wished and stay at home all day if I wished, and read some of the books in my library that I had always intended to enjoy but could not, and work crossword puzzles whenever tired or bored. So I determined to close my office door and call it my day's work. Or a life work. Loafing and dreaming looked calm and restful and alluring to my tired nerves and mind. I was seventy-two years old, and it was high time that I should begin to stroll peacefully toward the end of the trail, which, at best, must be but a little way beyond (p. 333).

And so, at the age of 72, Darrow entered the phase of self-assessment, all the while continuing to write and speak. This culminated when he was 75 and when his autobiography was published. Reviewing his life he noted:

> I cannot appraise myself, and will scarcely try. Sometimes I think that I have occupied too much space in the public eye; and that it is due to no merit or demerit of my own, but purely to chance. Then again, I think that whatever I have done is due to a degree of ability that I cannot estimate or understand. As a lawyer I cannot appraise myself. I know only one way this can be tested, and that is my results. Under this test I believe that few lawyers have accomplished more in court than I have . . . (p. 425).
>
> If I have been charitable in my judgments of my fellow man; if I have tried to help him as best I could; if I have done my utmost to truly understand him, I know why I have taken this course—I could not help it. I could have had no comfort or peace of mind if I had acted any other way. . . . I have done it more or less involuntarily as a part of my being, without choice, and without stopping to weigh which were most deserving or worth saving. If I had paused, I should probably still be wondering and doing nothing. I claim no credit, and want no praise (p. 450).

Physically and mentally weary, Darrow's world became smaller and more concerned with the ordinary pleasures of life. Buhler maintains that in the final phase of his life a person often returns to the need-satisfying orientation of his childhood. This theory seems to have been borne out by Darrow.

> I rarely go out, except for a short walk. My son Paul and his wife and three daughters live a block away, and often I go to see them, or some of them come to my home; it is surprising how strong the tendrils bind one to those they love and to habitual haunts. An automobile ride in the evening or a game of cards or just a visit with my son and his family at the end of the day has grown all-sufficient for my social needs, and it is an effort to do more than that . . . (p. 433).

There were moments when his former vitality returned, as, for instance, when he admitted that he "would like to produce a screen-picture showing the cause of crime and the treatment that probably would remove it from the world. . . ."

But, accepting the limitations of strength and time, he added realistically, ". . . I cannot expect too much of the short time that is left of my life, and perhaps this dream is among the ones that will not come true" (p. 424).

But for men like Darrow, there are always dreams of tomorrow, and he concluded his autobiography in this hopeful note: "Still, even old men have more extensive visions, and all my hopes are not limited by the day or night. . . ." And remembering a beautiful trip abroad, he mused, "Yes, I may go again, and once more I may see the beloved Mediterranean, . . . I may, . . . I may . . ." (p. 453).

In retrospect, then, we see in Darrow's life the slow development of both personal and professional goals. Stability and the height of productivity were reached when he was about 47 years old. The peak of productivity lasted until he was 63, when the decline of his physical vigor dictated a diminishing of his professional activity. At 72 Darrow began to assess his life and the degree to which he had succeeded in fulfilling what was for him the most important and meaningful parameter of his life: his concern for the liberty of the individual. This concern which channeled his energies into specific work goals originated in his youth under the strong influence of the values of his father, as he lived and expressed them. He identified closely with his father who had opposed the culture around him. Darrow's goals and his belief in his values were more important to him than love and family needs. Only at the very end of his life, when his vitality was nearly exhausted, did he begin to consider the physical and emotional comforts of home and family. He disavowed conventional success as well as power, and found fulfillment through his dedicated fight for the individual's liberty.

The flow of Darrow's literary output paralleled his legal activities to some degree. Both reached their heights between age 43 and 63, the period which can be described as his peak years. As his legal activities declined his literary output increased as though to take up the slack left by his gradual withdrawal from the practice of law. In the final eight years of his life, both areas of productivity declined sharply, paralleling the rapid decline in physical vigor which came with his advanced age.

When we examine the pattern of Darrow's life, we notice that the course and distribution of his productive activity follow that of individuals for whom the most important factor is mentality rather than biological or physical vitality, a distinction first made by C. Buhler (1933). The lives of mentality-oriented individuals culminate later, and their rate of development is slower. The early culminators are those

COMPARISON OF LIFE STAGES AS SEEN BY BUHLER AND LIVED BY DARROW

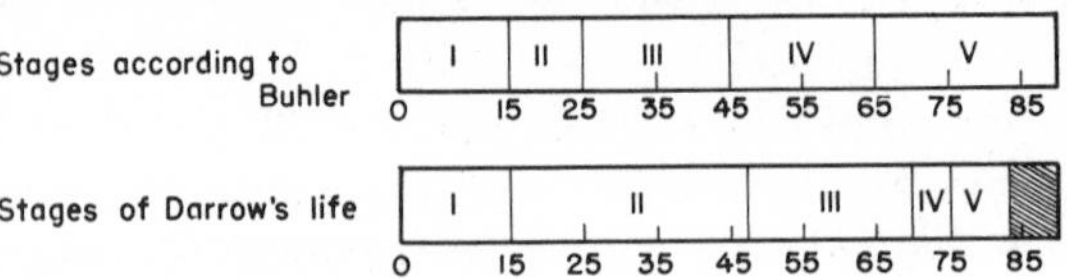

Figure 1. Comparison of Life Stages.

I. Prior to self-determination.

II. Experimental or preparatory self-determination.

III. Definite and specific self-determination toward goals and fulfillments.

IV. Self-assessment of obtained results.

V. Return to need-satisfaction orientation of childhood and/or a continuance of previous activities.

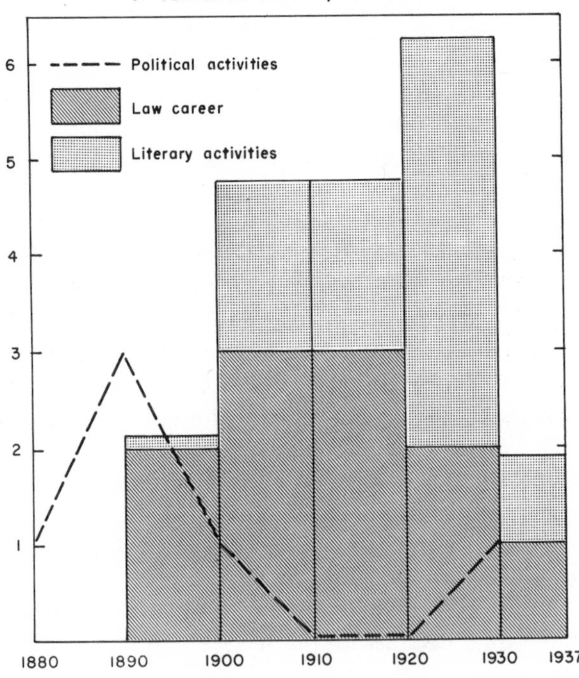

Figure 2. Accomplishments and Productions.

Political activities were determined by the number of offices held during a ten-year period.

Law career was determined by the number of cases of nationwide interest which Darrow defended during each ten-year period.

Literary activities were determined by the number of publications written by Darrow during each ten-year period.

(Adapted from McNally, 1941.)

for whom physical vitality is most essential, such as athletes, ball players, and others. Businessmen and inventors have a more symmetrical curve of development, with the culmination of productivity coming in the middle years of life. Statesmen, on the other hand, for whom wisdom is an essential factor, reach their peak much later in life. According to Frenkel (1936), "We can say that the more vitality needed for the type of accomplishment, the earlier the culmination point for this work; whereas the more systematically integrated experience involved, the later the high point of production is reached. This applies to both the quantitative and qualitative culmination points" (p. 28). Darrow himself was painfully aware of the conflict between his still-to-come mental culmination and his physical decline. Such conflict often is the result of the different developmental rates of the physical and mental faculties.

Figure 1 shows a comparison between the stages of Darrow's development and the "average" course of life as described by Buhler, and Figure 2 a schematic presentation of Darrow's accomplishments and productions.

References

Buhler, C. *Der menschliche Lebenslauf als psychologisches Problem.* Leipzig: S. Hirzel, 1933. 2nd ed. Göttingen: Verlag für Psychologie, 1959.

Buhler, C. Meaningful living in the mature years. In *Aging and Leisure,* R. W. Kleemeier (ed.), New York: Oxford University Press, 1961.

Darrow, C. *The story of my life.* New York: Scribner, 1932.

Frenkel, E. Studies in biographical psychology, *Character and Personality,* 1936, 5, 1-34.

McNally, G. A. The life of Clarence Darrow, a psychobiographical study. Unpublished paper, 1941.

Stone, I. *Clarence Darrow for the defense.* New York: Doubleday, 1941.

II The Genetic Factor as Codeterminant of Goal Setting

The question to which degree and in what way goal setting is codetermined by the genetic factor is most problematic.

In strict scientific terms, the presently available biological knowledge about heredity does not yield much information that would be applicable to the psychological description of behavior. The reason is, as John Fuller shows in Chapter 5, that "the relationship between genes and behavior is noncongruent" and that the "psychologists do not have a natural unit of behavior comparable to the gene. . . . Fragmenting the psychological phenotype into subunits will bring one no closer to the gene, if the subunits are defined in psychological terms which involve organismic functioning."

Although "at present genetics provides only a general orientation to the problem of variation in goal setting," Fuller sees some merit in the discussion of C. Buhler's four basic tendencies as possibly genetically given. He also points to defects and talents as areas in which the role of heredity continues to command attention.

The theory of the four basic tendencies as primary givens is presented by C. Buhler in Chapter 6 with a discussion of their earliest functioning. M. Marschak contributes concrete exemplification from a number of cases she investigated. Some observations from a nursery school were contributed by N. Dilworth.

These tendencies are considered givens in the same sense that Freud thought of id, ego, and superego as genetically given substructures of the persoality. Psychoanalytic theoreticians, as, for example, L. S. Kubie (1952) or H. Hartmann (1964), are aware of the problem of establishing the genetic characteristics of these components of personality on the one hand, and, on the other, the manner in which and the extent to which they are modifiable.

A "strong" and a "weak" ego can hardly be thought of other than in terms of at least partially structural determinants. Yet the analyst speaks of ego strengthening. The discussion of ego strength leaves us, as Hartmann (1964, p. 140) admits, with some confusion.

Correspondingly, we are not yet in the position to determine the extent to which the four basic tendencies are to be considered genetic and modifiable.

The theory of four basic tendencies conceptualizes the basic organization of the personality in terms different from Freud's theory. This new theory as discussed in the original study about the subject (Buhler, 1959) and also in the first chapter of this book was needed because Freud's system offers no room for the fundamental role of creativity, nor for a primarily as "positive" experienced reality, nor for a conscience that has its roots in the self rather than in social demands.

The triad of id, ego, superego will be used within the framework of the Freudian system of personality analysis. The chapter ends with a discussion of an application of the concept of the four basic tendencies to a Life Goal Questionnaire, in preparation by C. Buhler and W. Coleman.

Bernice Eiduson presents in Chapter 7 an extremely carefully documented review of what may be stated according to present-day information about goal-setting behavior in infancy. As far as primary needs are concerned, all recent research agrees that the infant is active, orienting, directive, and selective from the start. While the long-lasting controversy regarding the nature-nurture issue is no longer meaningful, current knowledge favors the assumption of primary individual differences.

The new data confirm essentially the position held by C. Buhler that the individual starts life with spontaneity, initiative, and direction, and with a selective responsiveness to the world. B. Eiduson, however, cautions the reader regarding the conclusiveness of presently available behavioral data.

In Chapter 8, Althea Horner discusses the contribution of genetic factors to an individual's creativity. In using some of the criteria of probably primary trends which B. Eiduson had assembled, A. Horner applies them to the case of two brothers raised in the same family. She then scans and discusses theoretically the literature concerned with creative behavior, and concludes that creativity resides "initially within the biological givens of the newborn child." But if it is to become "an important determinant in the choice of goals throughout the various stages of the life cycle," it needs the enhancement of parental values.

Chapter 5

Genetics and Goal Setting

John L. Fuller[1]

The ability to set goals as distinguished from simply responding to them is a peculiarly human ability. All the issues discussed in this book presuppose a human genotype and thus, in a broad sense, involve heredity. The question with which I shall deal here concerns the possibility that variability in goal setting might be ascribable in part to differences in heredity. In other words, I should like to ask, for instance, whether we can blame "bad" genes for a person's failure to direct his activities toward a consistent and realistic objective.

Human variation springs from many sources among which genes are only one, and some time ago it seemed as though students of psychological individuality were either hereditarians or environmentalists, each having harsh words to say about the opposite camp. Happily this apposition has softened, although we are still far from fully understanding the relationship between heredity and behavior. Some people wonder why genetics has not provided us with precise information on the inheritance of capacities and personality traits. Fifty years ago, in the surge of effort which followed the rediscovery of Mendel's work, many studies were undertaken to demonstrate genetic transmission of artistic skills or traits (Fuller and Thompson, 1960). But these studies do not stand up to modern criticism for they imply an isomorphism between genes and complex forms of behavior which is not validated by a more rigorous analysis. Behavior is influenced by genetic variation but there is no universal congruence between actions and genes.

The lack of congruence creates difficulties for geneticists who are interested in behavior. Mendel's success derived from his decision to study unit characters (e.g., tall vs. short plants, green vs. yellow seeds), each related specifically to a corresponding factor now called "gene." The concept of phenotype has been broadened to include not only visible characteristics, distinguishable by ordinary observation, but details of

[1] This chapter was written while the author held a special fellowship from the United Health Foundation.

molecular structure accessible only through biochemical and biophysical techniques. Such traits, as long as they show congruence with hereditary units, are well suited for genetic analysis.

Once we extend the concept of phenotype to morphological and psychological characteristics which cannot be classified into two or three distinct classes, we are forced to adopt statistical models. These models, as we shall see, have been useful but they do not lead to the isolation and characterization of genetic units. Rather, since these phenotypes are influenced by both heredity and environment, we seek to partition the variance between the two sources, usually specifying neither in any detail. Quantitative genetics provides us with estimates of how much heredity contributes to variation but tells us little about how it operates. We shall consider these two problems separately.

Quantitative Genetics

The hereditarian idea that a given gene strictly determines a given phenotype is still being reinforced by teachers of genetics who find their best examples in characters which stand in one-to-one correspondence with genes. In the elementary genetics class probability plays a part in the distribution of genes from parent to offspring but not in the expression of a gene in the phenotype. Organismic functions such as growth and adaptive behavior depend upon the synchronization of many genetic processes which are difficult to identify separately. When a character is regulated by many controls, each with a small effect, it is commonly found that a normal distribution results, with a majority near the middle and a smaller number at the extremes. Traits showing multiple factor variation may also be strongly affected by single gene substitutions which interfere seriously with development. Thus the distribution of IQ scores in the general population is bell-shaped and consistent with multiple factor regulation, but there is an excess of very low scores, largely attributable to rare genes producing mental defect.

Quantitative genetics combines the Mendelian laws of gene distribution with the probability laws of large numbers and thus provides a method for dealing with multiple factor heredity. A key concept in this area is heritability, i.e., the proportion of total variance attributable to genes whose effects on a trait combine additively. The probability that two individuals have genes in common is calculated from their degree of relationship. The degree of correspondence between similarity in phenotype and in genotype leads to an estimate of heritability. The methods are most accurate when applied to pure-breeding animals and plants raised under standard experimental conditions, but with suitable assumptions they can be applied to man. Twin and family studies provide the most direct evidence for the heritability of psychological differences in man.

Family and Twin Studies

No special training is needed to recognize family resemblance in physical and psychological traits. However, since families share more than genes this does not prove biological inheritance. Investigators experimenting with animals have been able to separate environmental and hereditary factors according to plan, but when it comes to man, one must interpret nature's experiments. Comparisons between one-egg (identical) and two-egg (fraternal) twins have been widely used in psychology and psychiatry. One-egg pairs are more alike on measures of intelligence, personality, and psychiatric risk. An excellent selection of papers in this area, particularly those dealing with intelligence, has been compiled by Jenkins and Patterson (1961). Critical summaries have been prepared by Anastasi (1958), and Fuller and Thompson (1960). Criticisms of twin studies generally have centered on the argument that identical co-twins have more common experiences than fraternals; hence their greater similarity does not prove that genes are responsible. Family studies often involve comparison between natural and foster children, and it may be that the quality of the family relationship is consistently different for the two kinds of family members. These arguments must be taken seriously, but the better studies have attempted to control for such possibilities and to correct for their influence.

The comparison of one-egg co-twins who have been reared apart provides a good indication of the power of the social environment to mold individuality, for none of the differences between such co-twins can be attributed to heredity. A fairly large series of separated twins has been observed in Britain by Shields (1962). The twins were evaluated by a combination of clinical and psychometric methods with emphasis on the former. Naturally data of this kind are complicated and personal judgment must enter into the interpretation. In some cases the separated co-twins lived in similar socio-economic conditions where the critical influences could have been as alike in different families as they are to different children in the same family. In other cases the diversity of environment was close to a maximum for British society. After weighing all factors Shields concluded that heredity played a major role in shaping personality, though he refrained from quantification of its influence.

The twin method is actually a special case of the family correlation method which is used in genetics for the study of quantitative inheritance. Cattell and his colleagues (1955) have used a wide range of family relationships (twins, ordinary siblings, adopted children) to estimate the heritability of personality factors as measured by psychometric tests. Cattell argues that a factor derived from a table of intercorrelations among test responses is based on the operation of a common cause upon the correlated items. He had anticipated finding a rather clear separation between the factors based upon biological relationship and those founded in common experience. Actually the factors were typically mixed, though the proportion of genetic variance fluctuated widely.

Shields and Cattell are almost antithetic in their approach to the problems of genetics and personality; the former relies on case histories and interviews, the latter on elaborate psychometric techniques. It is remarkable that both have come to similar conclusions regarding the importance of heredity. They agree that individuality develops from an interplay of genetic and environmental factors. One can find statements that one-fourth, one-half, or even more of the total variance of a score is genetic, though the generality of these estimates has not been confirmed and their accuracy is not high. But the chief limitation of the biometric approach is not imprecision or lack of generality; it is the tendency to lump all pertinent variables into only two classes, heredity and environment. This is not an essential limitation and Cattell has suggested cross-cultural surveys which would help to define the critical influences in the social milieu. However, the practical difficulties of such surveys are staggering. More direct approaches to the investigation of genetic processes in behavior are found in experimental animal genetics and in developmental studies of human and animal infants.

Experimental Behavior Genetics

The animal experimenter has at hand pure lines of great variety. He can also breed selectively on the basis of behavior, set up complex mating systems, cross-foster offspring at various ages, and otherwise regulate the lives of his subjects. Several general conclusions have emerged from the published research in this area (Fuller and Thompson, 1960). It is possible, for example, to change the frequency of occurrence of many forms of behavior through selection. Rats and mice have been bred to make many or few errors in mazes, to be aggressive or peaceful, to freeze or explore in an open field, to prefer alcohol to water or vice versa, and to be resistant or susceptible to sound-induced convulsions. Selection is not merely a laboratory phenomenon, for domestic species such as dogs and poultry demonstrate striking breed differences in temperament and aptitudes. Given a genetically variable population at the start one can be as confident of success in selecting for behavioral criteria as one can be for structural criteria. Even insect geotaxis, supposedly highly stereotyped, can be altered by selection (Erlenmeyer-Kimling, Hirsch, and Weiss, 1962). Selection, of course, produces no new behavior but sorts out genes into separate lines and imposes order on pre-existing variation. Following selection, however, previously rare phenotypes may become common, thus producing novel effects in the population.

Experimenters have also found that genetically distinct lines of animals, developed for such purposes as disease resistance or large body size, behave differently (Fuller and Thompson, 1960). It is not certain that the genes producing the behavioral differences are the same as those responsible for the physical differences. Most selected lines are at least partially inbred and inbreeding results in the fixation of genes of all types. An association between excessive emotionality and high cancer incidence may mean nothing more than the chance fixation of two independent groups of genes in one line, though a relationship through body chemistry is a possibility which can be tested. Whatever the mechanisms, it is certain that strains which are genetically similar tend to be alike in behavior; distantly related strains are unlike in behavior. It is not possible to state whether genetically induced variation in behavior is quantitatively more or less important in the so-called higher species, but it is certainly as prominent in the dog with a well-developed cerebral cortex as it is in the mouse with a primitive one.

The influence of heredity on producing behavioral individuality does not diminish as animals age. In dogs, breed differences often become more sharply defined as psychological development proceeds (Scott and Fuller, 1965). In some way the genotype exercises control over the incorporation of experience. There is no logical reason to exclude man from the pervasive effects of heredity upon behavior because of his convoluted brain or his long period of maturation. A long childhood actually may provide an opportunity to amplify the phenotypic effects of genetic variability.

Developmental Processes

Many psychologists are concerned with the origins of individuality. Usually they must rely upon retrospective methods and seek to explain a person's present directions through his past history. Aside from problems associated with accuracy and completeness of recall there are those of interpretation. It is easy to find "causes" in the past, especially if one has a theory at hand, but validation of a theory by prediction is more difficult.

Geneticists also start with diverse phenotypes and trace them back to earlier and earlier stages of development, often even into prenatal life, seeking to discover a primary physiological deviation from which an entire syndrome may emerge. This method has been highly successful with the hemoglobin diseases, each of which has been shown to result from a small change in one or another portion of the hemoglobin molecule. Such conditions have been called molecular diseases. Some forms of mental deficiency have been found to be consequences of metabolic errors, fundamentally molecular in origin, and it is hoped that psychotic disorders might be similarly explained, although efforts in this area have been unsuccessful.

Analagous methods can be used to trace the expression of multiple genetic differences which underlie behavioral variation among pure breeds and strains of animals. Scott and Fuller (1965) observed puppies from birth, when they were relatively more immature than a human newborn, until they were 1 year old. Well-defined breed differences, which appeared when the puppies were 3 or 4 weeks old, became more pronounced as the puppies matured. The earliest differences were found in autonomic responses (e.g., cardio-acceleration when disturbed), and in the ease with which overt activity could be inhibited. Correlations between test scores from early and late puppyhood were usually low, a finding similar to that reported for intelligence tests of children. Knowledge of the breed of a dog was often a better predictor of its test performance than knowledge of its scores on earlier tests of apparently similar content.

The logic of longitudinal studies of children is similar to that of the dog study, except that the degree of experimental control is necessarily much less rigid. The best procedure, perhaps, is to select children from a specific geographical and socio-economic background and to follow their individual characteristics over a period of years. From protocols of child behavior obtained in interviews with parents, Thomas et al. (1963) abstracted nine formal attributes, each applicable to a great variety of particular responses. The results were analyzed to determine whether children had a characteristic style of behaving which was reasonably stable. During the first two years of life the children were highly consistent in mood, intensity of response, adaptability, and approach tendencies as rated on three-point scales; the consistency of rhythmicity of behavior and of persistence was moderate. The children varied most in threshold of arousal, distractibility, and activity level, though even in these categories there was evidence for stable individual patterns. Rutter et al. (1963) separately analyzed data from the siblings and a few twins who were included in the sample, and reported greater similarity in one-egg than in two-egg twins. The size of their sample, however, was too small to allow definite conclusions. It may be significant that the greatest evidence of genetic effects was found in attributes which were somewhat unstable, and hence presumably especially subject to environmental modification. In experiments with dogs, Fuller (1964) found that behavior scores most affected by isolation during early life were also most variable between breeds. Some behavioral systems may be particularly sensitive both to changes in genes and changes in experience.

To sort out the environmental and genetic factors in a real life history is an unrealistic objective. In a very extensive investigation of identical schizophrenic Genain quadruplets, Rosenthal (1963) was unable to judge the relative importance of heredity in inducing the mental disorder. While at first glance the concordance of the quadruplets seemed to be positive proof of a powerful genetic determinism, a strong case would also be made for restrictive family environment as an etiological factor. Rosenthal seems to favor a diathesis-stress theory for schizophrenia, a viewpoint which I share. Superior performance may, in fact, be explicable by an inverse diathesis-challenge model in which individuals become superior only when superable barriers are present.

It appears that though all infants have essentially the same behavioral repertoire, each shows from birth a characteristic style of response. Child-rearing practices and specific experience undoubtedly contribute to the development of individuality, but the process is an interaction. A mother cannot rear an intensely active child and a passive one in the same manner. The world is not simply impressed upon a child; he approaches it or withdraws, attends or is distracted.

It is unlikely that the search for causes of individuality, at least in the so-called normal range, will lead to an identifiable gene. We will have to be satisfied with discovering in the infant prognostic signs of a physiological or psychological nature, representative of forces which impose some degree of direction upon continued maturation and differentiation of behavior. Our knowledge of how these forces are related to genes is at present based on conjecture, but enough is known of the nature of gene action to provide some guidelines.

Genetic Information and the Regulation of Phenotype

The key problem of behavior genetics is the conversion of genetic information to psychological events. Genes which influence behavior are transmitted like all other genes and their distribution from parent to offspring holds few mysteries. The primary action of genes and their chemical nature is increasingly being revealed through a combination of genetic and biochemical methods, although the coordination of many genes to produce an organism with adaptive properties is not yet understood. Much of our information about the nature of gene action comes from a study of the colon bacillus, an organism so simple that it has no proper behavior. A brief digression on inheritance in this microbe may help to frame the questions which psychologists should ask of genetics.

Although details of grammar and vocabulary are incomplete, the basic language by which genetic information is transmitted from generation to generation has been deciphered (see Maddox, 1964, for a nontechnical account). The code consists of variations in the order of four nitrogenous bases, adenine, guanine, thymidine, and cytosine incorporated into molecules of deoxyribonucleic acid (DNA). Sequences of three bases specify particular aminoacids, and a series of such sequences determines the order of aminoacids in a protein chain which may have secondary and tertiary twists to form globular structures. A change of one base in a triad leads to substitution of a different aminoacid in the chain with consequences which may be severe or benign, depending upon the amount of functional disruption the substitution causes.

A bacillus does not necessarily utilize all the genetic information it possesses. For example, the enzyme which digests milk sugar is synthesized only when that sugar is present in the immediate environment, though the specifications for its construction are normally present. In this case it has been shown that special genes turn the synthesizing process on or off, depending on the amount of milk sugar in the culture medium. We can distinguish, then, between structural genes which specify the molecular arrangement of parts of an organism, and regulator genes which control the activation of synthesis and are responsive to the environment. The extension of this concept to multicellular organisms is difficult because of technical barriers. Obviously some regulatory mechanisms exist, for the diverse cellular elements, neurons, epithelia, muscle fibers, and others utilize different portions of the information coded in their DNA's.

DNA molecules are replicated at every cell division so that the accuracy of transmitted information is conserved. The assemblage of amino-acids into proteins is delegated to a related group of molecules, the ribonucleic acids (RNA's). The RNA's of spleen, liver, and kidney are chemically different, but the corresponding DNA's are similar if not identical (McCarthy and Hoyer, 1964). We must assume that the transcription of messages from DNA to RNA is selective within each type of cell, though the manner in which it is accomplished in an orderly fashion is unknown. Once differentiated, cells can interact by electrical or chemical means and induce activation or inhibition of one another as seen in classical physiology.

The language of DNA seems remote from the discourse of psychology, particularly from such organismic concepts as goal direction. Yet genetic effects upon individuality can be mediated only through cellular mechanisms, and all theories of psychological genetics must recognize that inherited differences are due to variations in protein structure or in the timing of interrelated syntheses.

DNA's are stable substances but they do mutate, and mutations which are not lost through natural selection remain in the gene pool. The capacity for variation that is built into the genetic code is truly incomprehensible; the actual amount of variation is so great that we can be reasonably sure that no two human beings, except one-egg twins, have been or ever will be alike in genotype. How can genotypic differences which are expressed in protein synthesis also appear as determinants of behavioral variations?

Genes and Behavior: Implications Of Noncongruence

I have described the relationship between genes and behavior as noncongruent, and would now like to examine the implications of this term. A map of a city and the city itself are congruent, for instance, because one can match any location in the city with a point on the map. In a similar way proteins are congruent with DNA molecules and mutant genes with linkage maps of chromosomes. But as one moves from primary gene products to phenotypes arising from interactions between these products, the congruence with the original map is blurred. Yet all the characteristics of an organism, including its behavior, are related to its genotype.

The relationship of the pattern of a man's life to his genes is like that of a nation's history to its geographical features and natural resources. History is not independent of climate, mineral and agricultural resources, riverways, harbors, and mountain ranges, but we could scarcely write a nation's history from even the most encyclopedic catalog of such characteristics. Social tradition, the inventiveness of a few scientists, and the oratorical skill of a single political or religious leader influence the course of a nation in a way not predictable from geography. But natural resources do impose restrictions. A head of state cannot increase wheat yield by oratory; a scientist may have the know-how but is limited by conditions of temperature, rainfall, and soil. Of course, the failure of geographical features to completely determine history does not mean that they are unimportant to the historical analyst. On the contrary, much of history is made understandable by the knowledge of such matters.

Returning to the relationship between genetic and psychological systems, it is clear that psychologists of all persuasions will find no correspondence between protein molecules and forms of behavior. The most suitable behavioral unit for the geneticist is the phenotypic change produced by the substitution of a single gene. The behavioral effects of such a change may ramify widely and certainly need not be confined to one act or one trait. The untreated phenylketonuriac or galactosemic does not show a deficiency in only one aspect of intelligence, he displays a syndrome of effects which are related through dependence upon chemistry but do not necessarily share common psychological characteristics.

The relationship of genetic informational deficits (or duplications) to psychological conditions is clearer for mental defect than for special talents. Just as a flaw in a single part of a complicated machine can impair or even stop its function, so can the failure of a critical gene-controlled synthesis cause development to go seriously awry. It has not been possible to recognize genes which, when substituted for their more common variants, produce a genius. In a strict sense it is unlikely that such genes exist, for so many functions must be coordinated in advanced human skills that no one can be singled out as the critical one.

Despite the practical and logical difficulties of research in this area, the role of heredity in shaping human talents continues to command attention. Many people find it hard to believe that outstanding artistic and musical skills, for example, are simply the result of exposing a normal child to a particularly stimulating environment. I share this disbelief even though genes for artistic talent have not been identified. We need more developmental studies of the creative process in children which will illuminate the possible role of hereditary variation. Is there, for example, a general creative talent which is channeled through any appropriate outlet which is provided? Or, we may ask, are creative aptitudes more dependent upon specific sensory modalities or response systems? I suspect the latter but more proof is needed. Prospective rather than retrospective studies are essential.

Psychologists do not have a natural unit of behavior comparable to the gene, but a series of actions directed toward a goal is perhaps the most generally useful unit for analysis. Goal-directed sequences may extend over seconds or years, the shorter sequences being imbedded in the longer ones or sometimes interrupting them. Potentially a behavioral unit of this kind could be affected by any of numerous gene substitutions but is congruent with no single gene. Fragmenting the psychological phenotype into subunits brings us no closer to the gene, if the subunits are defined in psychological terms which involve organismic functioning.

It follows, therefore, that the analysis of the gene-behavior relationship in terms of processes must be undertaken by stages. It is essential to do more than classify and enumerate goal-seeking actions. The behavior of an individual must be characterized by attributes which are common to many actions. Given such a set of attributes it is necessary to determine how each attribute is related to physiological parameters as, for example, neurological and endocrinological characteristics. Finally, physiological variation will have to be explained in terms of cell functions controlled by RNA and DNA. This type of reductionist analysis will not appeal to everyone, and indeed the fulfillment of such a scheme lies in the remote future. The chief value, perhaps, of outlining the procedure is to point out how much is being omitted when one studies the genetics of behavior as a quantitative problem and ascertains that trait A has a heritability of 0.2 and trait B one of 0.5.

The major contribution psychologists could make is to develop a system (or systems) of behavioral classification which yields units of high heritability. If we had such units the more fundamental studies of development would most likely be more successful. It is important to describe behavior in terms which have generality across ages and conditions. Cattell's (1955) personality factors, Eysenck and Prell's (1951) neuroticism and extroversion factors, Gottesman's (1963) factors derived from the MMPI, and Thomas' (1963) formal attributes of behavior represent attempts to define and classify behavior for genetic analysis. The systems are quite unlike and need to be independently validated. Other systems of behavioral units are possible and it might be profitable to look at ethology and neurophysiology for suggestions. Hays (1962) has presented a hypothesis particularly pertinent to goal-setting behavior. He believes that inherited differences in performance may reflect a more fundamental difference in capacity for reinforcement. For example, novelty may be relatively more rewarding to one individual, social contacts to another, and freedom from discomfort or access to well-flavored food to still others. This agrees with the findings of Scott and Fuller (1965), who learned that many of the behavioral differences among five breeds of dogs they were studying were based on motivational factors. It is interesting to note that the kinds of motivational differences that can be distinguished in dogs can be related to three of Buhler's (Chapter 1) four basic tendencies, i.e., food to need satisfaction, socialization to adaptation, and novelty to creative expansion. Her fourth category, maintenance of internal order, could possibly be related to susceptibility to conflict.

Genetics and Goal Setting

At present genetics can do no more than provide a general orientation to the problem of variation in goal setting. Failure to establish realistic goals and to direct one's life toward their achievement is not attributable to faulty genes the way that phenylketonuria is. Rather, given a particular genotype, an individual may have restrictions on the possible courses of his development. He has many potential capabilities but does not have an infinite variety. Genetic information that has been transmitted from his parents may never be manifested in his phenotype because it is not being evoked. On the other hand, he will never be able to synthesize a gene product without the appropriate DNA, no matter what his environment may be.

In dealing with psychological phenotypes it is difficult to differentiate between a situation in which a trait is poorly developed because some genes are missing and one in which a trait failed to develop because it was not properly evoked. Helping individuals under these circumstances becomes a matter of treating symptoms or proximate causes. It is conceivable that compensating for genetic deficiencies at a cellular level may have favorable psychological effects, but we really do not know. Future progress will depend upon the collaboration of developmental psychologists and behavioral geneticists, upon hypothesizing and experimenting, and upon comparisons between man and animals. Since we know how difficult the task is, we can begin to frame our questions in terms of genetic processes. Genetics, indeed, may become the discipline that unifies the study of organic and experimental determinants of behavior.

References

Anastasi, A. *Differential Psychology*. 3rd ed. New York: Macmillan, 1958.

Cattell, R. B., Blewett, D. B., and Beloff, J. R. The inheritance of personality, *Amer. J. Hum. Genet.*, 1955, *7*, 112-146.

Erlenmeyer-Kimling, L., Hirsch, J., and Weiss, J. M. Studies in experimental behavior genetics: III. Selection and hybridization analysis of individual differences in the sign of geotaxis. *J. Comp. Physiol. Psychol.*, 1962, *55*, 722-731.

Eysenck, J., and Prell, H. J. The inheritance of neuroticism: an experimental study, *J. Ment. Sci.*, 1951, *97*, 441-465.

Fuller, J. L. Effects of experiential deprivation upon behavior in animals. *Proc. 3rd. Wor. Cong. Psychiat. Montreal, 1961*. 1964, *3*, 223-227.

Fuller, J. L., and Thompson, W. R. *Behavior genetics*. New York: John Wiley & Sons, 1960.

Gottesman, I. I. Heritability of personality; a demonstration, *Psychol.* Mon., 77:9, 1-21. (Whole No. 572).

Gruber, H. E. *Contemporary approaches to creative thinking*. New York: Atherton, 1962.

Hays, K. J. Genes, drives and intellect, *Psychol. Rept.*, 1962, *10*, 299-342.

Jenkins, J. J., and Patterson, D. G. (eds.). *Studies in individual differences*. New York: Appleton-Century-Crofts, 1961.

Maddox, J. *Revolution in biology*. New York: Macmillan, 1964.

McCarthy, B. J., and Hoyer, B. H. Identity of DNA and diversity of messenger RNA molecules in normal mouse tissues, *Proc. Nat. Acad. Sci.*, 1964, *52*, 915-922.

Rosenthal, D. (ed.). *The Genain quadruplets: a case study and theoretical analysis of heredity and environment in schizophrenia*. New York: Basic Books, 1963.

Rutter, M., Korn, S., and Birch, H. G. Genetic and environmental factors in the development of "primary reaction patterns," *Brit. J. Clin. Soc. Psychol.*, 1963, *2*, 161-173.

Scott, J. P., and Fuller, J. L. *Genetics and the social behavior of the dog*. Chicago: University of Chicago Press, 1965.

Shields, J. *Monozygotic twins brought up apart and brought up together; an investigation into the genetic and environmental causes of variation in personality*. London: Oxford University Press, 1962.

Thomas, A., Chess, S., Birch, H. G., Hertzig, M. E., and Korn, S. *Behavioral individuality in early childhood*. New York: New York University Press, 1963.

Chapter 6

Basic Tendencies of Human Life

Charlotte Bühler and Marianne Marschak

Theoretical Considerations

The theory that human life is determined by a number of basic tendencies was developed after a critical study of the theoretical thinking on motivation. Present thinking on this subject is still largely dominated by the Freudian notion that a person's basic striving is directed toward the achievement of homeostasis. Joseph Wilder in an article on Basimetric Approach to Psychiatry in the *American Handbook of Psychiatry* states as recently as 1966 that "psychoanalysts are increasingly using the concept of homeostasis" (p. 337). It is curious that in the same volume L. von Bertalanffy (pp. 705–741) presents the opposite point of view, similar to that taken here by C. Buhler. The analytic point of view, criticized by Bertalanffy as it is by C. Buhler, is that if an individual is motivated to withstand tension and move in the direction of self-discipline and accomplishments, he does so only because of the pressures of reality and society.

In contradistinction to this conceptualization, K. Goldstein held as early as 1939 that it is only the sick organism who constantly strives toward relaxation, whereas the healthy individual enjoys a certain amount of tension as part of an attempt to accomplish his main goal, self-actualization.

C. Buhler (1959) later developed the theory that in the course of self-fulfilling self-actualization even the newborn demonstrates adaptive, creative, and coordinative tendencies, in addition to those toward need satisfaction, long before reality and society force such goals upon him. She presented the view (1954, 1959) that homeostasis was not a goal in itself but merely a favorable condition of functioning. She stated that the organism's goal, because of its built-in energy, was to be active and productive in a reality which is assumed to allow for accomplishments.

Evidence of a certain degree of primary adaptiveness can be seen in the manner in which the newborn, from his second or third meal on, eliminates actions that hinder the procedure of feeding (Ripin and

Hetzer, 1930). One cannot possibly call this an enforcement by reality, since the baby's being fed does not depend on cooperation. It is as unenforced as a plant's turning toward the light to improve its conditions for survival.

There are, of course, higher degrees of adaptation which are enforced, for instance, when an individual is prevented from getting a satisfaction he craves.

Primary creativeness, i.e., when the individual engages in an activity which results in the discovery of new potentials, is observable from about the infant's second week of life. The playful finger movements which the baby watches and "experiments" with constitute one example; another is his strenuous effort to imitate the sounds an adult makes in talking to the child (C. Buhler, 1928; J. Piaget, 1951). Yet another is his attempts toward what we consider to be ordering or integrating processes. None of these activities originates as a consequence of any outside pressure, be it that of reality or of society. They are autonomous, even if later in their development a pressuring environment enhances productivity and ordering.

In view of these observations and considerations, C. Buhler theorized that need satisfaction, self-limiting adaptation, creative expansion, and instituting as well as upholding internal order, are basic tendencies of the human being. Their implicit ultimate intent is self-development, the establishment of contacts, the mastering of reality, and the fulfillment of life through an integrated actualization of the individual's potentials.

The tendency to need satisfaction is broadly conceived of as the pursuit of any kind of tension-reducing satisfiers, be they physical, emotional or intellectual, while the other basic tendencies are tension-upholding.

Self-limiting adaptation is defined as being a person's tendency to adapt his own behavior to that of others and to the given circumstances. The desire to belong and to participate requires self-restraint.

Creative expansion is defined as being the tendency to advance in the world and to change it creatively through actions or through physical or mental productivity. This concept includes aggressive as well as leadership behavior which an individual uses to extend his influence and productions of any kind, such as the production of offspring, the manufacture of a product, the establishment of a business, or the creation of technical, scientific, or artistic products.

Upholding the internal order is the most complex of the concepts. It is assumed to comprise different ordering principles which work toward the unity of personality and behavior. These principles are first found in the coordination of movements; a little later in the organization of activities; still later in the operation of such integrating principles as goals, ideals, and those self-assessments which fall under the heading of what generally is called "conscience."

All these tendencies, noticeable in different degrees in all infants that are not defective, must be considered indispensable not only for full and successful development but also for survival. If one or the other of them is missing, personality defects ensue; and the disproportionate functioning, it is hypothesized, may result in neurotic developments. Normal limits, within which the proportionate participation of these tendencies may vary, have not been definitely established. However, observational as well as clinical and questionnaire data indicate that the degree to which one or the other develops varies from individual to individual.

The early and autonomous appearance of these tendencies forces us to assume that they are innate in kind as well as in gradation. But, as is the case with any other disposition, be it emotionality, intelligence, or talent, we must also assume that they can be influenced and molded by the environment.

An originally seemingly adaptive baby, therefore, may be roused to stubborn opposition by an environment's excessive demands or insensible treatment. Or an active baby, who started out exploring his environment with curiosity indicating creativity, may have his spirits dampened by the deprivation of all stimulation and the opportunity to expand. The depressed infants whom R. Spitz (1945) discussed are those who were impaired in adaptive as well as creative self-expression.

In psychotherapy we sometimes notice radical changes in the structure of an individual's basic tendencies. Persons who, under the influence of a given environment, have become completely unadaptive or uncreative may in a different atmosphere be restored to a healthier, more genuine expression of their basic tendencies. Previously unadaptive individuals, for instance, who were expelled from their countries by the Nazis were found to be able to change to an unexpected adaptivity.

While the predominance of one or the other of the basic tendencies is assumed to be individually different, a certain sequential predominance is hypothesized during a person's development. Infants are predominantly need-satisfying. Self-limiting adaptation predominates during the later childhood years and creative expansion is pre-eminent in adolescence and adulthood. The tendency toward upholding order prevails during the climacteric age, together with that period's concern for self-assessment. The period of old age finds many individuals regressing to infantile need satisfaction, while others try to accept in self-limiting adaptation the restrictions which are forced upon them. Some persons are able to continue their creatively expansive activities. Others dwell on their past in an ordering process of reminiscing and of assessments of their lives. Examples of these individual and developmental predominances follow.

Psychological Observations on the Behavior of Children

Nancy Dilworth and Marianne Marschak collected about 100 examples of behavioral situations in which 1½- to 4½-year-old children made statements about wishes and goals. N. Dilworth made her notations during nursery school sessions, while M. Marschak acquired her material by observing the mothers at home.

Their observations show that children of this age group express wishes and goals in the direction of all four basic tendencies; need satisfaction, however, still predominates, and there is rarely any expression of order-upholding needs.

Typical expressions of desires for need satisfaction are the statements by three 4-year-olds. Dana: "I want to have lunch with grandma." Johnny: "Let's not like Edmond. I want to be your friend today." Mark: "Tie my shoe."

> Marschak contributes a more complex observation. Julie, 1½, has been carrying her security blanket with her from the time she could move around. She used to pick it up from her bed in the morning and drag it along to the breakfast room. One morning she left the blanket in the crib. She was helped down from her highchair after breakfast and went to "discover" her toys in the cardboard box, "taking each one out and rolling or bouncing it on the floor." This particular morning she did not accompany these moves with her usually joyful "hi"; rather, she became listless, her sounds took on a grumpy quality, and her two fingers went into her mouth while she was sitting by the box and looking up at her mother in a disheartened fashion. Suddenly, Julie stood up and went, almost running, down the long corridor all the way to her bedroom. She pulled the blanket from her crib and dragged it, with one hand still in her mouth, back to the kitchen.
>
> Her mother, when discussing the incident, said that the look on Julie's face when she got up to go to her crib reminded her of somebody who knew that she had to have a cigarette that very moment. This incident demonstrated Julie's first complex, goal-directed behavior.

Not infrequently young children reject what is offered to them.

Adrian, 3, finding no pleasure in joining the play group, screams over and over: "I don't like anybody." This attitude indicates, other than dissatisfaction with the needs he feels, his inability to adapt himself to a given situation.

Negative attitudes toward demands of self-limiting adaptation are frequent at this age level where the child has to learn adaptation beyond his own needs. Expressions of an unwillingness to cooperate are frequent, such as the assertion of Debra, 3, who insists: "I don't want to march."

> A positive acceptance is noted in the following example. Lisa, 2 years and 9 months old, was scolded by her father for removing the lid from a glass bowl on the coffee table in the living room. She had been told often and explicitly not to touch the lid. The scolding by her father was followed by a long period of her crying. Several weeks later, Lisa's mother observed her one day as she was standing by the entrance to the living room. Lisa was looking toward the coffee table, then made a few steps into the room, stopped short, shook her head energetically and said "No, no," apparently addressing herself.

Creative expansion is exemplified by the statement of the 4-year-old Dana: "I want to be a police girl," she says. "Why?" "So I can help everybody." Adrian, 3, wants to be "a man, but mommie says I have to be 28 first," and Johnny, 3, announces: "I want to be a firetruck."

> A creative goal for the more immediate future was conceived by Madeline, 4. She lies in her bed ready for her mother to read a story. She has pulled her blanket over her shoulders and lies rather still. As her mother tries to figure out what Madeline has in mind, she realizes that the child has gone to bed with tomorrow's underwear and socks on. As usual, an argument ensues, and Madeline restates many times that this is "a best idea, 'cause then you just have to put your dress on tomorrow morning."

Most important is the creative expansion which the child of this age group expresses in his art work and his make-believe play.

> Beth, 2, sitting next to her mother who is writing a letter has, upon her recent request, been given a piece of paper and a crayon. She is scribbling in her usual way, going "around and around and around." Suddenly she pauses and looks at her mother's moving hand and her own production. Giving herself a command, as she frequently does, she says dreamily: "Beth, write!" Almost immediately she begins, with all her fingers still gripping the crayon, to move it in a different fashion, up and down in zig-zag lines. With her hand thus pursuing the goal she has set for herself, she bursts into shrieks which almost drown her joyous exclamations of "Beth, write, Beth, write!"

> Jenny, 1 year and 9 months, is playing on the back porch. She finds the wheel base to her milk truck in one of the toy boxes: "Mul bot. (milk bottles) No? Find." She picks up a pail from the floor. "Pail." She spies another pail. "Two pails." Giving herself the command to look for the third pail, she says: "Bye, bye." With these words she is off down the hall toward the kitchen. She returns. "Mamaaa." Three pails are dangling from the bike bars. She parks her bike and leaves again, saying "bot, bot." She is off to the kitchen once more and can be heard at the far end of the house banging bottles together and chanting "bot, bot, mul bot." She returns with her arms full of bottles and tries now to place them in the pails which hang from the handle bars of her bike, moaning as they tumble to the floor: "falling down." At last the buckets with the bottles hang from the handle bars and she pedals off down the hall.

Most of these creatively expansive activities involve, besides the creative productivity, also the satisfaction of needs, be they emotional, intellectual, or activity needs.

The order-upholding tendencies, as we indicated before, are very complex, since we assume that they comprise several integrating principles, of which organization and conscience are the most important. The penetrating studies of L. Murphy (1962) and her collaborators supply us with a great deal of relevant material. Both organizational behavior, called self-orientation, and self-evaluating behavior have been noted in many situations.

All of the 3- to 4-year-old children seemed capable of orienting themselves under various circumstances, although with considerable individual differences in their "comprehensive grasp." The active mastery "of surveying a situation in order to orient themselves clearly to it, . . . the attempt to understand, to make a cognitive map, to clarify as many aspects of the situation as possible, seems to be involved with practically all of the children who took a watchful, observing attitude in new situations. It was also true that some children were not able to act upon their observations as other children did" (Murphy, p. 41).

Equally general as the action based on perceptual and conceptual organization was Murphy's evidence of these children's self-appraisal. Varying in degree and attitude toward themselves, the children frequently evaluated their own achievements, abilities, and behavior. The observers noted a distinct need to maintain self-esteem. The origin and development of this self-esteem belongs to one of the most intriguing problems in child psychology. L. Murphy in her own interpretation refers, on the one hand, to G. Murphy who bases the self-image on early narcissism (1947) and, on the other, to E. Erikson who bases the beginnings of identity on recognition and being recognized (1956). Both experiences are thought to contribute to the "I can do" and the "I am" sensations.

But the 3- to 4-year-old child exhibits yet another phenomenon. He begins to stand up for certain things, i.e., he displays some feelings, often strong ones, about what is fair and what is due him.

> An interesting example of this is a scene reported by E. Köhler (1926) about "Annchen." Little Ann is a 3-year-old who, in one of those not infrequent attacks of jealousy and hate against a younger sibling, has bitten the finger of her little sister Eve. The parents happen to be in an adjoining room and, as they hear Eve screaming, rush in to see what has happened. For a moment they are speechless, and then the father gives Ann a beating. But this is not all. "Ann," he says, "go and ask Eve to forgive you." Now Ann is speechless. After a minute or so she throws herself on the floor and screams, completely beside herself: "No, no, I will beg pardon from Mammi, from Mitzi (their sitter), from Olga (the cook) but not from Eve, not from Eve."

Is this just the result of narcissism and the experience of being recognized? While Annchen's hurt pride may be interpreted this way, I suspect there is something else. Her father's demand is an insult to her sense of justice and does not seem right or fair to her. This insistence on fairness appears to be the beginning of a quest for what is just.

Such a quest, in turn, presupposes more than narcissism and recognition. It presupposes a direction which must originate at a level deeper than that of ego demands or ego reasoning. Fully developed, it represents one aspect of the self's intentionality in the direction of values.

This, however, is the point at which the theoreticians differ most.

L. Murphy as well as the junior author of this chapter, M. Marschak, have chosen to interpret the reported data in terms of Freud's id, ego, and superego. These concepts seem useful as far as they go and as far as what they represent can be incorporated into the basic tendency theory.

Thus Julie's need-satisfying and adaptive behavior may be usefully analyzed in psychoanalytic terms. According to Marschak, Julie's behavior also signifies a joint functioning of id and ego processes. Her striving for relief of tension, possibly of physiological origin, e.g., fatigue, leads to the ego activity of retrieving the spatially removed, comforting blanket as soon as she thinks of it. The blanket-retrieving behavior as involving both id and ego has been discussed by Winnicot (1953) who called the blanket the transitional object,* an object providing the transition from the feeling of oneness with the mother to the awareness of the mother as a separate being and to the beginning of object relationship.

Using psychoanalytical concepts, Marschak interprets Lisa's behavior as a first manifestation of the super-ego or conscience. The child has internalized the parental prohibitions and is able to curb her action accordingly. The verbal command she gives herself will somewhat later be replaced by an automatic avoidance of transgression.

Buhler, however, sees the id, ego, and superego triad as an incomplete conceptualization of creativity and of those aspects of conscience which are the result of self-realization.

Empirical Questionnaire Studies of Life Goals

While verbal tests are a doubtful source of information where a person's feelings and thinking are concerned, the senior author felt that something could be gained by asking people what they believed to be their life goals. In a field which lacks investigative tools and methods, except for the Allport-Vernon questionnaire on goals, this approach seemed rather promising, particularly since it also offered an opportunity to learn about individual life goals through a less scholastic and broader frame of reference than that of the Allport-Vernon test.

C. Buhler constructed, therefore, an inventory of 86 questions regarding life goals as they relate to the four basic tendencies toward fulfillment of human life. A list composed of possible goals which have primary concerns in these four directions makes up the Life Goal Inventory (1964). Andrew Comrey's factor analysis of a first sample of 150 cases resulted in a group of factors which actually could be organized in terms of the four basic principles. William E. Coleman then worked out scoring devices, permitting the establishment of a Life Goal Profile. This, with an additional five questions, was administered to a second sample of 200 cases, and followed by a second factor analysis by W. E. Coleman and W. H. McWhinney in 1966. The second analysis essentially corroborated the statistical findings of the first study. The end result was a list of eleven

* The universality of retrieving a transitional object, indicative of early goal-directed behavior, was demonstrated to M. Marschak on a recent mountain hike in Switzerland. Stopping for a glass of milk in a cowherd's cabin, she saw a 2-year-old child searching under a bedstead until he emerged with a piece of soft cloth which he greeted joyfully, holding it first to his cheek and then chewing on it. His mother called the cloth a "luempli," and admitted that she had made it up for him since "you cannot always hug him."

factors which was organized in terms of the four basic tendencies. The factors are:

- I. *Need satisfactions*
  - A. Satisfactions in life
  - B. Love and family
  - C. Sex and self-gratification
- II. *Self-limiting adaptation*
  - D. Self-limitation, caution
  - E. Adaptiveness and submissiveness
  - F. Avoidance of hardships
- III. *Creative expansion*
  - G. Self-development
  - H. Power, fame
- IV. *Upholding of internal order*
  - J. Moral values
  - K. Political and/or religious commitments
  - L. Success

C. Buhler subsequently administered her Goal Inventory to 40 patients who were about to enter psychotherapy. In ten cases, where considerable improvement had been noted, the test was repeated one to two years later. The Goal Inventory was also given to a number of subjects whom C. Buhler interviewed in conjunction with a study of their life histories as well as to an old-age group. (The old-age sample was assembled by A. Brind and A. Horner.) Findings of the two studies were published in C. Buhler, 1965, 1968.

A comparison of ten relatively well-adjusted and well-functioning nonpatients was made with 30 patients who were classified in three groups of ten, according to the severity of their neuroses. It allows the following tentative statements:

Theoretically speaking, we can distinguish between favorable and unfavorable goal patterns. Favorable patterns are patterns of factorial percentiles which, in a clinical evaluation, would indicate a personally and socially constructive attitude toward life. People who set their goals according to these patterns may be expected to have love in their life, to care for other people's welfare, and also to believe in their own self-realization. Furthermore, they seem to be aware of reality and able to accept reasonable degrees of limitations and/or hardships.

Unfavorable patterns are patterns of factorial percentiles which indicate a personally and socially unconstructive attitude toward life. These include patterns revealing lack of love, lack of concern for others, or else an overemphasis on the rights of others, disbelief in one's own self-realization or unrealistic expectations, disregard of reality, an inability to accept limitations and hardships, an unreasonably self-restrictive or submissive attitude and/or an exaggerated willingness to take burdens on to oneself.

The goal patterns of the well-functioning person on the whole were more in agreement with a factor distribution that could be called "favorable" to a fulfilling way of life. Their profiles show high factors B, G, and F, with the exception of older people's G being regressed. They also appear to have adequate degrees of A, C, D, and L, while the distributions of E, F, H, J, and K vary with each individual. In addition, these profiles tend to distribute themselves over medium and high percentiles.

"Unfavorable" profiles tend to show great variations of percentiles and excessively high and low scores. Depressed persons tend to score in the low to medium percentiles, while very demanding persons have excessively high scores.

The individual profile, when related to the data established in psychotherapy by C. Buhler, revealed relevant particulars which had not shown up in Rorschach or TAT tests. As a matter of fact, they repeatedly indicated certain factors which only later became apparent in psychotherapy.

While the Life Goal Inventory is still in the process of development, it corroborates, even at its present stage, the hypothesis that the four basic tendencies may be usefully applied in clinical work.

References

Bertalanffy, L. V. General system theory and psychiatry, *Amer. Handbook of Psychiatry, III*. New York: Basic Books, 1966.

Buhler, C. Kindheit und Jugend (*Childhood and adolesence*). Jena: G. Fischer, 1928. 4th ed. Göttingen: Verlag für Psychologie, 1967.

Buhler, C. Theoretical observations about life's basic tendencies, *J. Amer. Psychotherapy*, 1959, *13*: 3, 561-581.

Buhler, C. Psychological and psychiatric considerations of a questionnaire study of goals, *Acta Psychiatrica Scandinavica*, Copenhagen: Munksgaard, 1965.

Buhler, C. Old age as a phase of human life, *Hum. Devel*, 1968, *11*, 53-63.

Buhler, C., and Coleman, W. Life goal inventory, mimeographed ed. Los Angeles, 1964.

Buhler, K. *Die geistige Entwicklung des Kindes (The mental development of the child)*. Jena: G. Fischer, 1918.

Erikson, E. *Identity and the life cycle*. New York: International Universities Press, 1959.

Goldstein, K. *The organism*. New York: American Book Co., 1939.

Köhler, Elsa. *The personality of the three year old*. Leipzig: J. A. Barth, 1926.

Murphy, G. *Personality*. New York: Harper, 1947.

Murphy, L. *The widening world of childhood*. New York: Basic Books, 1962.

Piaget, J. *Dreams and imitation in childhood.* New York: W. W. Norton, 1951.
Ripin R., and Hetzer, H. Earliest learning of the newborn in the feeding situation, *Zeitschr. f. Psychologie,* 1930, 118.
Spitz, R. Hospitalism, *The Psychoanalytic Study of the Child, I,* New York: International Universities Press, 1945.
Wilder, J. Basimetric approach to psychiatry, *Amer. Hdbook of Psychiatry, III,* New York, 1966.
Winnicot, D. W. Transitional objects and transitional phenomena, *Int. J. Psycho.-Anal.,* 1953, *34,* 89-97.

Chapter 7

Infancy and Goal-Setting Behavior

Bernice T. Eiduson

No specific age has been identified for the onset of goal setting. Customarily the preschool years provide some insight into the beginnings of goal behaviors that become characteristic of later periods of life. In line with her extended perspectives on human motivation, however, C. Buhler has encouraged the search for precursors of goal behavior in infancy.

Some years ago she proposed that data reflecting some very early trends in goal setting were suggested by her own observations and those of other researchers in infancy (19). It was evident then, as it is today, that this area is speculative and untested. Yet, as Charlotte Buhler has pointed out, to think about the kinds of behaviors which may hold clues to adult goal-setting tendencies and to look for embryonic forms of the motivations which dominate and shape the course of human life is a challenging task.

Problems in Studying Goal Setting in Infants

One of the great difficulties in discussing goal-setting behavior in infancy is that we are dealing with behaviors that can only be known by inference. Everything we know about goal setting and goal behavior is derived from observation and study of the goals themselves. We infer the motivations and motivational processes that lead to various goal choices. When we see that the goals have changed, we assume that the motivations have changed.

Since our referents for goal-setting trends are derived from behavioral observations of goals, it is essential that these observations be reliable and appropriate. Furthermore, the observations must be relevant to goal behavior and must be sufficiently diverse to be characteristic of the repertoire of needs of the individual.

These requisites pose difficult problems for the infant researcher. Reliable, relevant, and characteristic observations are not easily obtained with infants, since the investigator usually deals with a repertoire of behaviors that is limited, and with phenomena which are often fleeting and transitional. Such conditions make the determination of behaviors that are reflective of goal choices often problematic.

The problem of determining the degree to which early behaviors or goal choices predict later trends and predilections also involves critical issues.

It is apparent that the task of identifying early goal trends rests on many of the assumptions that make longitudinally-based projections tenuous. In assuming that development or growth of behavior is continuous, we hypothesize that behavior seen at later stages is influenced in a predictable way by preceding behaviors. We anticipate, too, that lawful relationships between predecessor and successor in behavioral acts can be recognized; that is, that the later appearance of something identified earlier is sufficiently similar to the earlier form to be able to be perceived as such. Experimental work has shown that the danger of overweighting the significance of goal objects that later prove to be transitory is as great as the danger of overlooking goal behavior that later may indeed prove to be percursory for more complex goal motives.

Many developmental researchers have noted that identification of "transformations" of behaviors over time poses a knotty problem (51; 27). Behavior changes radically with development, for growth brings increasing resourcefulness, generality, and diversity. Therefore, behaviors or propensities seen at one moment are likely to look quite different at another moment. Also, behavior seen early often responds decisively to the shaping pressures of significant adults, peers, and environment, so that only those aspects which are unusually pronounced, consistent, and strong are likely to resist the effects of marked change or of inhibition, a fact which may distort the original activity beyond recognition.

Our knowledge about the transformations that take place in the case of specific variables is not reliable. We may assume with some assurance that a strong need for nurturance, manifested by crying when the mother leaves a 3-month-old infant, signifies the same phenomenon as clinging behavior upon entering nursery school, but can we be as sure of behaviors where the similarity in elements is not so close? Do a 6-month-old baby's crying responses at a delayed feeding and his temper tantrums when toys are not shared reflect the same goal-setting behaviors? Does the goal of task mastery remain the same when the goals are different, e.g., involve different sensory modes or motor elements?

Meaningful inferences about goal behavior demand more sophistication than we have today in discerning the fundamental response dispositions, and more "hard" evidence about the shape of continuities in behavior over time. Also, we need tools capable of measuring the comparability of the same phenomenon when it appears at different times and under different conditions.

The problem of ferreting out early motivational trends, therefore, is beset with difficulties. Yet, despite the soft and speculative base on which postulations in this area must rest, the recent reconceptualizations about motivation do suggest that consideration of goal-setting tendencies in the early months of life may be worthwhile.

Primary Needs and Goal Behavior

Survival needs

The primary needs of the infant have classically been associated with survival; they are needs for food, drink, warmth, and oxygen. The direct goals which would insure presence or satisfaction of these organismic conditions are obvious.

The food the infant seeks to gratify his hunger is the goal; and his goal behaviors are the responses appropriate to his drive toward that goal. His goal may not be as purposive or directive as the close stimulus-response relationship implies. However, Mussen points out that persons in the infant's environment respond to it as if there were a close association (64). The mother, for instance, hearing the child fretting or crying, asks herself, "What is it that he wants?"

Needs for stimulation and arousal

In recent years intensified observation and study of the infant has extended the needs categorized as primary. The alternating need for sleep and arousal is now considered to be a basic need, as have the needs for tactile and for genital stimulation (85). It has been shown that all these behaviors are present at birth, seemingly without having been learned; that they exist over time; and that they have at least equal primacy as far as need is concerned with the more directly nutritive behaviors (72).

In this enhanced concept of primary motivation, tactile contact and the search for arousal take on primary roles. Bell's factor analytic study of behavior observed when the infant was 48 hours old showed the state of arousal to be one of the five primary factors fundamental to a large number of observed behavioral parameters (5).

The engaging work of Harlow with infra-humans suggests the place of tactile contact in the hierarchy of primary needs (47). Young monkeys, separated from their mothers, were mothered by surrogates who were either made of terry cloth or wire mesh. The latter substitutes could supply milk from their nipples. When allowed free access to both, the monkeys noticeably preferred the terry cloth mothers, especially when frightened or in strange situations. When the terry cloth mother was near, the infant monkey would explore potentially fearful situations, something he would not do in the presence of the wire mesh mother.

Lustman's work on the pleasure infants derive from genital stimulation has also extended the notion of primary drives to include those which we later identify with sexuality (61). He has shown that newborn infants are sensitive to both manual and air-pressure stimulation in the genital region. In one group of infants observed for ten days, tumescence occurred at least every day in five of seven infants, and at the end of ten days in the other two infants. Tumescence in general was accompanied by what could be referred to as unpleasantness—restlessness, crying, fretting, and stiff legs—while detumescence was apparently pleasurable. This suggests that arousal per se is not invariably pleasurable.

Of particular interest has been the infant's interest in actively searching out, exploring, and manipulating his environment. This kind of selective, discriminating behavior was, until the 1930's or 1940's, essentially ignored because the infant was conceived of as a passive recipient of stimuli impinging on him from within himself and the outside world (33).

Tension-reduction model of motivation

When the infant was thought to be limited to responding to tissue needs or to stimuli from the outside, his functioning could be conceptualized in the framework of a simple pleasure–pain model (41). Pain comes from within or from some irritant without; pleasure comes when the needs are gratified or the irritation is removed. In this model, the infant is passive and is moved to action only by the need to reduce the tensions which arise in him from bodily tissues or outside irritants.

Hebb has pointed to the need of the infant to seek out sensory stimuli from his earliest days because learning cannot occur otherwise

(48). Trial and error behavior demands stimulation external to the infant himself.

In the psychoanalytic conceptualization, also, only the construct of a perception apparatus permits the change from passivity to activity. As the infant begins to take stock of the environment which impinges on him and to perceive it, he learns to incorporate it into his abilities, his modes of thinking and reaction, and his ways of handling the world with which he is confronted. In other words, what the infant projects as his ego or his personality becomes his through a process of introjection.

The limitations in the tension-reduction model for behavior were made apparent when infant research showed that the search for stimulation and exploration was a primary drive in the newborn. He frequently engaged in behavior which showed that he sought out tension-producing activities. These psychological findings drew support from physiological evidence which showed the brain to be far from a passive organ responding only to outside stimulation.

The brain as an active agent

Some time ago Lashley described the brain's activity and constancy, its rhythmicity, and its automatic maintenance of activity regardless of external stimuli (55). These characteristics are found in brain parts when they are isolated from the whole, and in processes that take place at the cellular level. Furthermore, research disclosed that the rhythmic or automatic character of brain activity regulates input (57). For example, differentials were demonstrated in the ease with which certain reverbatory pathways were set up (45), in the response of some neurons to chemicals (65), and in ways that synaptic functions limit what is transmitted (74). Reward or punishment centers were seen as "attractive" or "unattractive" cerebral areas, i.e., determining the character of input (66). The reticular activating system was shown to filter afferent impulses en route to the cortex, supplementing the usual afferent pathways (54). It became apparent, thus, that the brain of the organism was itself an active, orienting, and directing organ, consisting of components which themselves were active, orienting, and directive.

This new conception negated the notion that the brain is a machine which regulates and systematizes knowledge of the environment, stores this knowledge, and makes behavior appear smooth and regular. Unlike a machine into which any mechanism can be set, the brain appears to have mechanisms of its own. These mechanisms not only effect transmissions between the organism and its environment, but even more directly contribute substantially to how, when, and what will affect the organism.

This does not imply a reification of brain or mind, or a declaration of its independence, or the organism's independence from the environment. It is rather a recognition of certain patternings or autonomous qualities which by their structure and mechanisms predetermine to a large extent the stimuli appropriate to them. Woodger has recommended the use of the phrase "environmentally insensitive" as contrasted to "environmentally sensitive," to describe biologically the inborn or characteristic qualities of man (90). There seems to be a need for a similar refinement, in terms of "organism-sensitive" or "-insensitive" as regards stimulus data, to capture the feeling that the organism determines what part of the environment comes in as input.

Reconceptualization of motivational behavior

The relevant literature is now replete with data which show the persistence, vigor, and selectivity with which an infant pursues external stimuli. One needs only to look at the extensive areas of latent learning, stimulus deprivation, and consummatory behavior to realize that quiescence is no longer the dominant state of affairs (24). Tension-reduction drives and anxiety-reduction theories have been superseded by theories of infant motivation which take account of a more complex motivational framework. Drive theories have been more generalized in some schools, and special drives have supplemented primary ones, such as drives of curiosity, exploration, and manipulation. For example, White has conceptualized a "competence" drive as the common factor in the visual, exploratory, grasping, locomotor, linguistic, and other activities involving effective interaction with the environment (89). Such motivation shows itself most unambiguously in the playful and investigatory behavior of young animals and children, as K. Buhler has pointed out (21).

Also, Scott's work on the social development in canine and human infants (75), Brown's description of the social play of infants (17), and Berlyne's work on the variety and diversity of stimuli patterns that attract infants (7), all indicate that infants persistently and energetically seek stimulation.

Some efforts have been made to determine which of the various primary drives are the most important. For many years primacy was given to the needs related to life maintenance but this is being questioned in view of recent studies of the competing strengths of various needs. W. H. Bridger recently compared two primary needs, food and arousal, for drive strength (14). The results showed that infants sucked as much when they were satiated and experimentally aroused as when they were food-deprived and equally aroused. Hendry and Kessen found more mouthing and hand-to-mouth contact after, rather than before, feedings in infants under 3 days of age (50). Thus, while one might have thought that food intake would immediately reduce subsequent oral behavior as well as general activity, this was not the case. While primacy among primary needs has not yet been definitely established, Rheingold and Bayley (72) suggest that the nutritive drives are likely to rank lower in the hierarchy of drives than non-nutritive ones.

Infant capabilities

As the infant has come to be viewed as a discriminating, orienting, and selective organism from birth, many studies have been conducted to show the ranges of his potential resources at birth or shortly thereafter and the kinds of preferences and dispositions evidenced in his selective behaviors.

Of course, it had been known for a long time that an infant at birth has a full complement of abilities as far as his sensory and motor resources are concerned. Peiper's painstaking summary of infant behaviors (67), and Pratt's well-known description of neonatal reactions (70) detail the infant's general capacity for reacting to visual, auditory, gustatory, olfactory, and tactile stimuli. Recent research, however, has indicated some previously unrecognized refinements of sensitivities in each of these areas.

No effort will be made here to cite or summarize the vast experimental data which have enhanced our understanding of individual resourcefulness or of the potential for responsiveness at birth and during the first months of life. We will, however, mention briefly some characteristic data in the area of visual perception. The choice of visual data is arbitrary since the same discriminatory capacities are being demonstrated in the other sensitivities, such as auditory or tactile. The work in visual responsiveness, however, were it possible to present it more extensively here, would make it apparent that the once-held image of "the blooming, buzzing confusion" confronting the neonate is no longer tenable. It now appears that from the first he selects and attends to highly discrete, often complex and intricate, phenomena. We know that the infant at birth shows pupillary reflexes and responds to varying degrees of brightness. Contrary to the long-held notion that he is unable to see for the first few weeks, he is able, shortly post-delivery, to engage in visual pursuit (30), follow visual stimuli with movements of his head

(63), and show saccadic movements (28) as well as rudimentary binocular coordination (58).

Recent work has also provided us with detailed studies of visual attention which have shown how movement accompanies fixation: during the first and second weeks when an infant stares at an object, he is quiet; by the third week he shows rhythmic limb movements, smiles, and vocalizes after fixation (82). Other recent investigations have disclosed how visual attention directs a baby's development of reaching and grasping for objects (88).

Of particular interest is the research suggesting the neonate's capacity to discriminate visually among selected patterns. For example, experiments show an interest in complex stimuli (8), in contrasts, in unfamiliar visual objects as compared to familiar ones (40), and a preference for certain colors (78). Four-month-old infants, for instance, look longer at red and blue patterns than at grey ones (79). One of the pioneers in the area of visual novelty, R. Fantz, found that after 8 weeks infants will give up their habit of looking at a repeatedly exposed pattern in favor of a novel pattern, offering new cues (39). The preference in infants for novel and complex situations seems now to be reliably established, although the exact variables in the stimuli which attract them have not been conclusively determined. Is it the amount of variety or diversity in a stimulus pattern, the number of distinguishable elements, the relative versus the absolute novelty that are the significant factors in discrimination?

Berlyne maintains that incongruity, uncertainty, surprise, and incompatibility tend to attract rather than repel infants. These features set up competing tendencies or conflicts which demand resolution by the infant, and it is this drive for resolution or selection among stimuli that constitutes the basis of learning and discrimination.

As has been suggested, neonates also appear to be more discriminating in auditory responsiveness than was previously thought. For example, they react differentially to tones of 200 and 1,000 cycles per second (15). They are able to localize sound and turn their head in its direction as soon as 10 minutes after birth (87); their attention is differentially attracted by the duration of the tone (84).

Even taste and smell sensitivities are well developed at birth. Neonates respond to odors, even during sleep, by squirming, crying, or sucking (67). In one study newborns responded to olfactory stimuli as early as 32 to 68 hours following birth (36).

This work has also focused on the importance of having objects and persons available in the environment to stimulate the infant. The early work of Spitz and Wolf (80), and later Rheingold (71), Dennis (31), and Casler (26), had shown that exposure to stimulating objects was salient for the development of attention and perception, and intellectual growth in general. Piaget had postulated that externally aroused exploratory behavior (assimilation for the sake of assimilation) was an essential precursor for looking at objects and for subsequent perceptual development (42). In a more recent formulation Gewirtz has suggested the importance of distinguishing between privation, when the environment fails to provide stimuli necessary for learning, and deprivation, a state of frustration that arises when stimuli are not available to the infant (46). Under total privation neither learning nor emotional responses occur, and the infant, therefore, develops as a passive and asocial person, reacting only to emotionally startling behavior. By contrast, the deprived youngster discriminates poorly and critically so that his general response to stimuli is affected.

A similar set of differentiations was suggested by C. Buhler who, when discussing social reactions of infants, found some to be socially blind or nonperceptive, as compared to others who were socially dependent, or socially independent (56). Since social awareness of separation of self and world is a condition for the objectification of objects, the different categories of social reaction suggest the different kinds of general response to the environment.

Individual differences

The vastly enhanced differentiation and selectivity in the infant's responsiveness is of particular interest in the consideration of goal setting. It suggests that the development of interests, tastes, and predilections is not necessarily a slowly evolving, canalizing, or narrowing-down process that moves in the direction of increased specificity. It is quite conceivable—although it has not yet been demonstrated—that the specificity noted in the later focusing on certain goals has its genesis in the discriminations and orientations of the early months. The individual differences noted among primary needs suggests this notion, for infants show a wide range of differences in needs and responses, and in the time and conditions under which these make their appearance. For example, primary needs, like hunger, differ from other needs in their intensity or drive strength, as well as in their periodicity and the manner in which they can be satisfied. Differences have been noted in the rhythm of sucking (2), in the rates of sucking (56), and in the rates with which infants adapt to different feeding schedules (62). Neonates show individuality in the speed with which a rooting reflex is manifested upon stimulation of the cheek (10). A constitutional (and sex-linked) basis has been postulated to account for observed individual differences in the degree to which children like to be cuddled (73). Following a study of state of arousal, Brown has hypothesized that the infant's behavior in the first week reflects important constitutional differences in his ability to maintain physiological homeostasis (18). The amount of time per day that newborns show crying behavior is also indicative of individual differences (1).

When a variety of behavioral and autonomic (cardiac and respiratory) measures was used to study infants' responses within the first 4 to 5 days of life, individual differences which had been noted earlier showed a significant day-to-day constancy (9; 60). When movement was measured in the newborn, stable individual differences over the 5 days of the lying-in period were demonstrated (52). A study of rhythms in movement similarly showed stability within individual differences (53). These studies of motor behavior suggest differences in activity level which seem to persist beyond the first months (38).

Differences in visual fixation time and in response to light intensities (70) are characteristic of a host of studies which suggest individual differences in perceptual sensitivity. The search for relationships between perceptual sensitivities and psychological stability has also grown out of the increasing recognition of the range of individual variations.

Thus, primary drive states have been shown to vary in intensity, in tempo and rhythmicities, and in the patterns of response they trigger. The wide range of individual differences in primary needs pointed to differences in resources in infants from birth and possibly also to differences in preferences, interests, propensities, and perhaps in "early motivations."

Learned Needs

Innate and/or acquired

The reconceptualization of the infant as an active, stimulus-seeking, discriminating organism from birth has re-aroused the controversy about how many and which facets of personality are inborn and innate and which aspects are experientially determined. This is an issue which has plagued psychology, and developmental psychology particularly, for many years. It found its greatest momentum in the nature-nurture controversy of the 1930's. Thereafter, it assumed a lesser but still uneasy status in the background of psychological concerns. However, recent work in genetics, biology, anatomy, and ethology has shown that this question is, to a large extent, artificial.

It is no longer possible to separate nature from nurture either on the behavioral or on the cellular level. Investigation of genetic factors has led to exploration of the environment in which genetic factors operate. Here, researchers have been confronted with an active set of factors which condition not only what is genetically determined but often if, and when, a genetic characteristic will make its appearance.

The biological studies make it quite evident that environment can no longer be defined as something outside the organism that affects or becomes part of the organism by internalization. Environment must include intraorganismic factors as well, for the nature-nurture interaction is so meshed and interdependent, even on the prenatal level, that it becomes impossible to determine what is heredity and what is environment (35).

Study of prenatal development has shown that development is a long process of continuous changes, starting with a given genetic array acting in a given environment. The first interaction product, then, constitutes the background or the environment for the next interaction with the environment. In the case of a cell, this includes the interaction product of other cells, and in this manner all future reactions are codetermined by all preceding steps and hence also by genetic endowment. Thus, one can no longer point arbitrarily to certain factors as genetic and others as environmental, regardless of where one arrests the sequential reactions for study. As Weiss has pointed out, there is no sharp dichotomy any more, even prenatally, between geneticists and environmentalists (86).

The same arbitrariness in distinguishing primary from learned needs is apparent in investigating infant behavior. The more classical secondary needs, i.e., the desire for money, social status, and prestige which can be easily established from goal behavior, are not part of the infant's repertoire. The needs that are present as, for example, nurturance or dependency, and aggression, present problems as far as knowledge of their genesis. While even in infancy, many of these behaviors show indices of very early learning, some of the behaviors in each area also suggest that they are genetically determined and innately organized.

The lack of easy differentiation as far as the roles of heredity and environment are concerned seems to be a function of two things: the lacks in empirical evidence about the genesis of many psychological phenomena, and the artificiality in the question itself. In psychology, as in biology, the heredity-environment interaction is obviously evidenced so early, even prenatally, that the infant behaviors are in fact already resultant products (34). In addition, developmental changes take place in the infant's primary needs. The manner, the temporal and spatial changes in the ways in which he satisfies his needs, are significant aspects in his development.

The scheduling of feedings—for example, the changes in diets and the changes in weaning—presents variations in the original primary needs or the ways in which these needs are gratified. Therefore, although the need for food is a primary need in the infant, and although many of the early feeding behaviors, like sucking, swallowing, and rooting are associated with reflexive behaviors, they have been thought to be innate. However, as these feeding behaviors change with experience and become a purposeful and coordinated activity, they take on the characteristics of secondary learned drives. One study showed that the different modes of feeding—by cup, bottle, or breast—had different effects on the sucking behavior of newborns (29), with sucking being reinforced more by breast feeding than by the other modes. Another study convincingly demonstrated the classical conditioning of the sucking response (59).

This same gradual "socialization" takes place in regard to sleep behavior and elimination, where the learning of new patterns suggests the shaping of basic needs and motivations. Conditioning of head-turning and other motor behaviors has been demonstrated as constitutional muscular abilities develop.

Also, development of perceptual-cognitive abilities presents a striking demonstration of the gradual evolution of a biologically based function which takes on cognitive structuring as it interacts with experience and thus becomes subject to learning. The infant's need for arousal or for sensory stimulation, his search for experience and his perceptions of form and depth, implies that his primary perceptions were perhaps not without some innate organization. However, these basic sensorimotor responses are modified as the infant attempts to cope with or handle external realities (68). While objects at first have little permanency or autonomy of their own, an infant's conception of them eventually changes in response to his problem-solving approaches to the environment. The now classical example of the infant's reaction toward objects that disappear from his view as if they had ceased to exist, shows the functional orientation of early cognitive processes. Through the search for familiar people and objects early responses become refined. To use Piaget's terms, assimilation and discrimination occur, and differentiation of the learning of new responses take place. This adaptational process reflects the ways needs become shaped as they grow out of the innately organized field and function as learned behaviors.

Much of this learning may take place without apparent awareness or purpose. It may grow out of play or out of experience for experience's sake; and play behavior may be unrelated to needs or unconcerned with secondary drives. Stott, following Buhler's and Piaget's theoretical formulations, empirically showed, e.g., that there was no direct connection between play activities and social or organizing needs (83).

However, some activities seem more influential determinants of need behaviors. The nature of the relationship between child and mother is well recognized as formative in this regard, although numerous other persons in the environment—caretakers, fathers, and others—are involved in the development and growth of secondary drives. While the vast body of pertinent literature suggests some of the "goal tendencies" deriving from the mother-child relationship, the variables in this relationship to which this influence can be attributed are not clear-cut.

At first, for example, most specific maternal practices were thought to have concomitants (16). However, when modes of feeding, scheduling practices, weaning, and toilet training practices were studied, it was found that their reliability as predictors for later developmental features was not very high. Instead the studies showed that mothers' overall attitudes or generalized response sensitivities which encompassed a number of separate activities or single dimensions of attitude or affect to children's needs were more effective (22).

By and large, maternal behaviors have been viewed with regard to whether they have been mainly restrictive or stimulating in their influence, as in the studies of institutionalization, separation, isolation, overprotection or symbiotic relationships (23; 25; 91). While there is general agreement as to the outcome of these extreme conditions, the situation is different with more subtle variations in the mother-child relationship. How much maternal stimulation is "minimal but sufficient?" How effective are the multiple discontinuous caretakers? Or how effective is extra "handling?" How durable are the temporal changes in behavior? What aspects of the maternal relationship effect the restructuring of behaviors: the time period during which it takes place, the consistency, or the particular mothering style? How salient a factor is the temporal dimension as far as stimulation from outside is concerned? How critical are the times? Are there periods of unusual sensitivity, analogous to the age-specific psychosexual phases, for maximizing the effects of "socialization" pressures? How much do all these parameters in the infant-mother relationship really affect the infant's later behavioral trends?

While it seems evident that certain environmental variables can be singled out which are particularly pertinent to the development of motivational behaviors, the roles these play are not well understood.

Dependence-independence

This is evident as the course and development of some of the learned needs seen in infancy have been studied. In the case of the dependence-independence dimensions, for example, the aspects of personality which are associated with the need for nurturance and dependency, and the polar trait, independence, are considered derivative of the mother's role and her attitudes toward meeting the infant's needs, and letting him be dependent on her as the instrument for help. The mother's presence is the seat of emotional as well as instrumental dependence, and these both are connoted in "mothering." It has been shown that an infant's affectionate behavior, with smiling and a general increase in outgoing activity, is first apparent at 4 months (4). By that time the tactile, sexual, and emotional components of the maternal relationship have combined to produce affection-seeking behaviors.

It is generally agreed that dependency characterizes the behavior of the infant, while a child in his preschool years shows ample surges of independence. However, even in infancy, there are moves toward independence and away from mother. While not stable or persistent, these play a role in walking, climbing, in taking off and being able to be separated from mother. The studies of mother-child separation are extremely sensitive in reflecting the vicissitudes of the dependence-independence behaviors. They also show that the manifestations of clinging and overdependency are often influenced by situational factors, such as unfamiliar situations, or forms of stress (12; 49).

As far as can be established, responses to shows of independence, like frustration and punishment, determine the course of later dependency strivings. Evidence here rests on studies like those by Sears and his colleagues who have examined behaviors in the preschool child for evidence of the effects of infantile dependency antecedents (77). Such variables as rigidity of feeding and severity of weaning seem to vary directly with later dependent strivings (though there is some difference in the former as a function of sex); but severity of toilet training is unrelated to dependency behavior in preschool years. The time at which frustrations were imposed, and the lack of a reward element in the toilet training process seem critical variables in this research. Interestingly, the amount of nurturance received showed no relationship to dependency. While Beller's investigation of the relationship of oral and anal traits to dependency and independency supports Sears' early findings (6), a later study by Sears suggests that the relationship between frustration and dependency is equivocal (76).

Aggression is sometimes linked with dependency because of the role it is assumed to have as a drive in generating independent behavior, which may or may not have hostile components. However, in contrast to the dependency parameter, the aggressive drive has stimulated a great deal of speculation about its genetic and physiological components. Animal studies suggest that aggression may be constitutionally based. This notion seems to draw support from certain behavioral studies on human infants. For example, Escalona and Heider have wondered whether unusually high levels of activity are not highly correlated with aggressive behaviors. They find that the inability to control behavior as seen in high activity levels suggests internal aggressive tensions (35). Others feel that while a child may be aggressive, his activity may so influence his parent's reactions to him, that these reactions may be the critical factor in his learned aggressive behaviors (41).

To some extent the definition of aggression determines whether or not it is present in infancy (3). Tension, thrashing of arms and legs, crying, screaming, hitting out at discomforts and restraints, are found in all infants, and most researchers consider these behaviors as antecedents to assertiveness and to aggression. However, when aggression is defined as hurting someone to gain a goal, it has less place in infancy. Such behavior demands the separation of self from other and, thus, it can only be found in growth periods when a sense of self has been established.

The sense of self

Because of the theoretical issue which concerns the genesis of early ego functions, psychoanalysis has been especially concerned with precursory indices of self in the infant years. Anna Freud has explained that the ego of the infant as a sense of self-awareness (for the ego has other functions) becomes differentiated when his needs are not met (43). The contrasting nature of frustration and gratification leads to the beginnings of the ego; when a bottle is delayed there is a growing awareness of "I" and "not I." Awareness comes when the infant realizes that something must be done by his mother to meet his needs. His sense of omnipotence diminishes, and his dependence on others begins to become apparent.

The separation of mother and child also produces social awareness. If she is a responsive, good mother, the child's first experiences in perception of the other person are trusting; if she is unfriendly and harsh, his world is apt to be hateful (81).

In Piaget's sensorimotor cognitive stage, the self and environment are undifferentiated. The infant's initial egocentrism is shown by his inability to distinguish environment from self. By adapting to the external world he creates the self.

Empirical data on the emergence of the self concept include the infant's responsiveness to social surroundings by quieting when he is 4 weeks old, the smiling response to the human voice or face between the first and third months, and the self-recognition in the mirror at age 1 (32). The Spitz and Wolf data showed that first sight of the experimenter brought forth a smile by the beginning of the sixth month (81); discriminated smiling responses to the familiar person, and not the stranger, were also a phenomenon characteristic of the last half of the first year. The smiling response is subject to reward and extinction, as are other social behaviors (13). Social relationship with peers is first noted around the age of 6 months. Studies have suggested that some of these early relationships observed in a play setting resemble those seen in adult life. A considerable variety of learning and maturational experiences seem responsible for the appearance of self and social awareness: objectification of objects, perception of persons as strange and familiar, the closeness but separateness of mother, use of names and pronouns, recognition of need for communication, being held responsible for actions, and development of independent tendencies. However, even in these behaviors the possible contribution of genetically based factors cannot as yet be ruled out.

Consistency or Stability of Characteristics Over Time

Bloom, in his careful analysis of studies of human growth and development over time, points out that on the average at least one-third of the variance seen in adolescence in intellectual interests, dependency, and aggression is predictable at age 2 (11). By age 5 as much as one-half the variance at adolescence is predictable for these characteristics. Kagan and Moss (2), following individuals in the Fels study to adulthood, also showed that certain measures of aggression and passive dependency have unusual stability over time. Such longitudinal studies suggest that certain traits have identifiable roots in earliest childhood. Certain traits apparently stabilize and become persistent and others do not—and of those that do persist over time, some exist in recognizable and fairly stable form much earlier than others.

A number of considerations have been suggested as pertinent to the determination of which traits become fixed at early stages of growth. For example, it has been postulated that the environment in which a characteristic has its greatest growth period becomes formative for that characteristic. Bloom found that the characteristics which proved to be most predictable of later growth were height, intelligence, aggression in men, and dependency in women—all traits which showed a negatively accelerating curve of development which reached midpoint before age 5. This period then may be the time when early childhood influences are most likely to affect such characteristics.

Other hypotheses stress that the cumulative effects or sequential nature of development, i.e., of the ways later learning is built upon early learning, must be considered. How does the resolution of a developmental conflict at one age affect the resolution and expression of subsequent conflicts? How is the mode of expression of a behavior or characteristic modified by time and circumstance? As the infant's behavior becomes differentiated with time, so does the expression of a trait such as aggression. Therefore, prediction of aggressive behavior at age 7 demands appropriate definition of the parameters of aggression: is it direct or indirect; is it aim-specific; is external provocation an essential element?

As forms of expression in later years are studied, it appears that the repertoires of behaviors established early become sex-linked. In the Kagan and Moss work, for example, dependency was a more stable trait for girls, whereas aggression was more stable for boys. The authors interpreted this as a function of the different social significance these characteristics had for sex roles. This corroborates the findings of Escalona and Heider (38) who, in their longitudinal study of infants, found that predictability was better than chance from birth through the 5- to 7-year age period in areas where the social norms and sexual roles had become already established. By contrast, prediction was poor in the case of the more implicit psychological functions.

While aggression and dependency are like some of the physical characteristics, in that they show maximum development during early childhood, many characteristics develop and mature throughout the growth process, and thus are open to the shaping influences of a far more complex environment than the one available to the infant. The factors that impinge on these influences are diverse and numerous. How- [illegible]any studies of values, hopes, goals, work habits, and vocational aspirations show that these varied formative influences become crystallized around the milieu that is represented by social class, family structure, and family role. Children quickly learn attitudes and behaviors that are appropriate to their roles and encouraged by their social class. Once these values and attitudes have been incorporated, they can be recognized in a repertoire of behaviors, and thus are fairly predictable.

However, other characteristics seem to remain idiosyncratic, and reflective of the circumstance or condition in which they appear. Whether they are in fact so variable or whether our methods of observing them and assessing their development are inadequate to the task they present, remains unknown.

This particular issue is important in regard to understanding the precursors of adult goal choice. Our understanding here unfortunately rests on inferences obtained from observable later behaviors. The postulation of the formative influences of early experience on these later inferred motivations adds a very large speculative element to an already nebulous area. However, perhaps detailed data on the course of motivations seen early, and their responses to varying conditions and pressure, may contribute some pertinent empirical information.

I hope that the analyses of clinical data which are so felicitous to Charlotte Buhler's present interests can make some contributions to this problem. The vicissitudes of behaviors and of motivations are basic features of the case study. The patient in his preoccupation with certain repetitive themes and conflicts reveals the nature of his motives, their intensities, and the ways in which they get diverted, overlaid, and denied. In his effort to get them under control, the patient tries to understand the kinds of influences that brought them into their present status in his life. He relates how certain kinds of motives or goals are related to each other, and which have precedence at certain times. It seems to me that such detailed data could provide useful heuristic hypotheses for studies of the origin and evolution of goal behavior. Given such assumptions, empirical exploration could begin.

References

1 Aldrich, C., Sung, C., and Knop, C. Crying of newly born babies, *J. Pediatrics,* 1945, *27,* 89-96; 428-435.

2 Balint, M. Individual differences of behavior in early infancy, and an objective way of recording them, *J. Genet. Psychol.,* 1948, *73,* 57-79; 81-117.

3 Bandura, A., and Walters, R. *Adolescent aggression.* New York: Ronald Press, 1959.

4 Banham, K. The development of affectionate behavior in infancy, *J. Genet. Psychol.,* 1950, *76,* 283-289.

5 Bell, R. Q. Relations between behavior manifestations in the human neonate, *Child Develpm.*, 1960, *31*, 463-477.

6 Beller, E. K. Dependency and autonomous achievement striving related to orality and anality in early childhood, *Child Develpm.*, 1957, *28*, 287-315.

7 Berlyne, D. *Conflict, arousal and curiosity*. New York: McGraw-Hill, 1960.

8 Berlyne, D. Influence of the albedo and complexity of stimuli on the visual fixation in the infant, *Brit. J. Psychol.*, 1958, *49*, 315-318.

9 Birns, B. Individual differences in human neonates' responses to stimulation, *Child Develpm.*, 1965, *36*, 249-256.

10 Blauvelt, H. Capacity of a human neonate reflex to signal future response by present action, *Child Develpm.*, 1962, *33*, 21-28.

11 Bloom, B. S. *Stability and change in human characteristics*. New York: John Wiley & Sons, 1964.

12 Bowlby, J. *Maternal care and mental health*. Geneva: World Health Organization, 1951.

13 Brackbill, Y. Extinction of the smiling response in infants as a function of reinforcement schedule, *Child Develpm.*, 1958, *29*, 115-124.

14 Bridger, W. H. Ethological concepts and human development. In J. Wortis (ed.), *Recent Advances in Biological Psychiatry*. New York: Plenum Press, 1962, *4*, 95-107.

15 Bridger, W. H. Sensory habituation and discrimination in the human neonate, *Amer. J. Psychiat.*, 1961, *117*, 991-996.

16 Brody, S. *Patterns of mothering*. New York: International Universities Press, 1956.

17 Brown, J. Social play of infants, *Proc., Soc. Res. Child Develpm.*, 1963.

18 Brown, J. L. States in newborn infants, *Merrill-Palmer Quart.*, 1964, *10*, 313-327.

19 Buhler, C. Earliest trends in primary goal setting, *Revue de Psychiatrie Infantile*, 1958, *25*, 13-23.

20 Buhler, C. The social behavior of children. In C. Murchison (ed.), *Handbook of child psychology* (2nd ed.). Worcester: Clark University Press, 1931, 374-416.

21 Buhler, K. Dis geistige Entwielung des Kindes, 6th ed. (Berlin). Jena: Gustav Fischer, 1929.

22 Caldwell, B. M. Effects of infant care. In *Review of Child Develpm. Res.* New York: Russell Sage Foundation, 1964, 9-87.

23 Caldwell, B. M., Herscher, L., Lipton, E. L., Richmond, J. B., Stern, G. A., Eddy, E., Drachman, R., and Rothman, A. Mother-infant interaction in monomatric and polymatric families, *Amer. J. Orthopsychiat.*, 1963, *33*, 653-664.

24 Cantor, G. N. Responses to complex and novel stimuli. In L. Lipsitt and C. Spiker (eds.), *Advances in Child Develpm.*, 1963, *1*.

25 Casler, L. Maternal deprivation: a critical review of the literature, *Mon. Soc. Res. Child Develpm.*, 1961, *26*, 1-64.

26 Casler, L. The effects of extratactile stimulation on a group of institutionalized infants, *Genet. Psychol. Monog.*, 1965, *71*, 137-175.

27 Cattell, R. B., and Howarth, E. Hypotheses on the principal personality dimensions in children, and tests constructed for them, *J. Genet. Psychol.*, 1962, *101*, 145-163.

28 Chase, W. P. Color vision in infants, *J. Exp. Psychol*, 1937, *20*, 203-222.

29 Davis, H. V., Sears, R. R., Miller, H. C., and Brodbeck, A. J. Effects of cup, bottle and breast feeding on oral activities of newborn infants, *Pediatrics*, 1948, *3*, 549-558.

30 Dayton, G., and Jones, M. Analysis of characteristics of fixation reflex in infants by use of direct current electroculography, *Neurology*, 1964, *14*, 1152-1156.

31 Dennis, W. Causes of retardation among institutional children, *J. Genet. Psychol.*, 1960, *96*, 47-59.

32 Dixon, J. C. Development of self-recognition, *J. Genet. Psychol.*, 1959, *91*, 251-256.

33 Eiduson, B. T. Brain mechanisms and psychotherapy, *Amer. J. Psychiat.*, 1958, *115*, 203-210.
34 Eiduson, B. T., Eiduson, S., and Geller, E. Biochemistry, genetics and the nature-nurture problem, *Amer. J. Psychiat.*, 1962, *119*, 342-350.
35 Eiduson, S., Geller, E., Yuwiler, A., and Eiduson, B. T. Biochemistry and behavior. Princeton: D. Van Nostrand, 1964.
36 Engen, T., Lippsitt, L., and Kaye, H. Olfactory responses and adaptation in human neonate, *J. Comp. Physiol. Psychol.*, 1963, *56*, 73-77.
37 Erikson, G. *Childhood and society*. New York: W. W. Norton, 1950.
38 Escalona, S., and Heider, G. *Prediction and outcome*. New York: Basic Books, 1959.
39 Fantz, R. Origin of form perception, *Scientific American*, 1961, *204*, 66-72.
40 Fantz, R. Pattern vision in growing infants, *Psychol. Rec.*, 1958, *8*, 43-47.
41 Fenichel, O. *The psychoanalytic theory of neurosis*. New York: W. W. Norton, 1945.
42 Flavell, J. *Developmental psychology of Jean Piaget*. Princeton: D. Van Nostrand, 1963.
43 Freud, A. *The ego and the mechanisms of defense*. London: Hogarth Press, 1937.
44 Fries, M., and Woolf, P. Some hypotheses on the role of the congenital activity type in personality development, *Psychoanal. Stud. Child*, 1953, *8*, 46-62.
45 Gerard, R. Biological and social units: the position of man, *Proc., Amer. Psychiat. Assn.*, Los Angeles, 1957.
46 Gewirtz, J. L. A learning analysis of the effects of normal stimulation privation and deprivation on the acquisition of social motivation and attachment. In B. M. Foss (ed.), *Determinants of infant behavior*. New York: John Wiley & Sons, 1961, 213-229.
47 Harlow, H. F. Primary affectional patterns in primates, *Amer. J. Orthopsychiat.*, 1960, *30*, 676-684.
48 Hebb, D. O. *The organizations of behavior: a neuropsychological theory*. New York: John Wiley & Sons, 1948.
49 Heinicke, C. M., and Westheimer, I. *Brief separations*. New York: International Universities Press, 1965.
50 Hendry, L. S., and Kessen, W. Oral behavior of newborn infants as a function of age and time since feeding, *Child Develpm.*, 1964, *35*, 201-208.
51 Kagan, J., and Moss, H. A. *Birth to maturity*. New York: John Wiley & Sons, 1962.
52 Kessen, W., Hendry, L., and Leutzendorff, A. Measurement of movement in the human newborn, *Child Develpm.*, 1961, *32*, 95-105.
53 Kestenberg, J. S. Role of movement patterns in development, *Psychoanal. Quart.*, 1965, *34*, 1-36.
54 Killam, K., and Killam, E. Drug action on pathways involving the reticular formation. In Int. Sympos. Reticular Formation, Ford Found., Boston: Little, Brown, 1958.
55 Lashley, K. S. In L. A. Jeffress (ed.), *Cerebral Mechanisms in Behavior*, The Hixon Symposium. New York: John Wiley & Sons, 1951.
56 Levin, G. R., and Kaye, H. Nonnutritive sucking by human neonates, *Child Develpm.*, 1964, *35*, 749-758.
57 Lindsley, D. B. Psychological phenomena and the electroencephalogram, *Clin. Neurophysiol.*, 1952, *4*, 443-456.
58 Ling, B. A genetic study of sustained visual fixation and associated behavior in the human infant from birth to six months, *J. Genet. Psychol.*, 1942, *61*, 227-277.
59 Lipsitt, L. P., and Kaye, H. Conditional sucking in the human newborn, *Psychonomic Science*, 1964, *1*, 29-30.
60 Lipton, E., and Steinschneider, A. Studies in the psychophysiology of the infant, *Merrill-Palmer Quart.*, 1964, *10*, 103-117.

61 Lustman, S. L. Rudiments of the ego. In R. S. Eissler (ed.), *Psychoanalytic Study of Child, 11.* New York: International Universities Press, 1956.
62 Marquis, D. A. Study of frustration in newborn infants, *J. Exp. Psych.,* 1943, *32,* 123-128.
63 Morgan, S. S., and Morgan, J. Examination of the development of certain behavior patterns in infants, *J. Pediatrics,* 1944, *25,* 168-177.
64 Mussen, P. H., Conger, J., and Kagan, J. *Child development and personality,* 2nd ed. New York: Harper & Row, 1963.
65 Olds, J., and Eiduson, S. Selective effects of chemicals in the brain studied by techniques of self-stimulation, *Proceedings of the 6th International Neurological Sciences Congress,* Brussels, 1959.
66 Olds, J., and Milner, P. Positive reinforcement produced by electrical stimulation of septol area and other regions of rat brain, *J. Comp. Physiol. Psychol.,* 1954, *47,* 419-427.
67 Peiper, A. *Cerebral function in infancy and childhood.* New York: Consultants Bureau, 1963.
68 Piaget, J. *The origins of intelligence in children.* New York: International Universities Press, 1952.
69 Pratt, K. The Neonate. In L. Carmichael, *Manual of child psychology,* 2nd ed. New York: John Wiley & Sons, 1954.
70 Pratt, K. C., Nelson, A. K., and Sun, K. H. *Behavior of the newborn infant.* Columbus: Ohio State University Press, 1930.
71 Rheingold, H. The modification of social responsiveness in institutional babies, *Mon. Soc. Res. Child Develpm.,* 1956, *21*: 63.
72 Rheingold, H. S., and Bayley, N. The later effects of experimental modification of mothering, *Child Develpm.,* 1959, *30,* 363-372.
73 Schafer, H., and Emerson, P. E. Development of social attachment in infancy, *Mon. Soc. Res. Child Develpm.,* 1964, *29,* 1-77.
74 Scheibel, A., and Scheibel, M. Substrates for integrative action in the brain stem reticular formation. In Int. Sympos. Reticular Formation, Ford Found., Boston: Little, Brown, 1958.
75 Scott, J. P. The process of primary socialization in canine and human infants, *Mon. Soc. Res. Child Develpm.,* 1963, *28,* 47 pp.
76 Sears, R., Maccoby, E., and Levin, H. *Patterns of child rearing.* Evanston: Row Peterson, 1957.
77 Sears, R. R., Whiting, J., Nowlis, V., and Sears, P. Some child-rearing antecedents of aggression and dependency in young children, *Genet. Psychol. Monog.,* 1953, *47,* 135-236.
78 Simmons, W. Operant discrimination learning in human infants, *Child Develpm.,* 1964, *35,* 737-748.
79 Spears, W. C. Assessment of visual preference and discrimination in the four-month old infant, *J. Comp. Physiol. Psychol.,* 1964, *57,* 381-386.
80 Spitz, R. A., and Wolf, K. Anaclitic depression; an inquiry into the genesis of psychiatric conditions in childhood, *Psychoanal. Study of Child.,* 1951, *6,* 255-275.
81 Spitz, R. G., and Wolf, K. M. The smiling response: a contribution to the ontogenesis of social relations, *Genet. Psychol. Monog.,* 1964, *34,* 57-125.
82 Stechler, G. Attention and arousal in the infant, *Proc., Soc. Res. Child Develpm.,* Minneapolis, 1965.
83 Stott, D. H. An empirical approach to motivation based on the behavior of the young child, *J. Ch. Psychol. Psychiat.,* 1961, *2,* 97-117.
84 Stubbs, E. Effect of the factors of duration, intensity and pitch of sound stimuli on responses of newborn infants, *Univers. Iowa Stud. Ch. Welf.,* 1934, *9,* 75-134.
85 Watson, R. I. *Psychology of the Child,* 2nd ed. New York: John Wiley & Sons, 1965.

86 Weiss, P. In B. Mintz (ed.), *Environmental influences on prenatal development.* Chicago: University of Chicago Press, 1958.
87 Wertheimer, M. Psychomotor coordination of auditory and visual space at birth, *Science,* 1961, *134,* 162.
88 White, B., Castle, P., and Held, R. Observations on the development of visually-directed reading, *Child Develpm.,* 1964, *35,* 349-364.
89 White, R. W. Motivation reconsidered: the concept of competence, *Psychol. Rev.,* 1959, *66,* 297-333.
90 Woodger, J. H. What do we mean by inborn?, *Brit. J. Phil. Sci.,* 1953, *3,* 319-326.
91 Yarrow, L. J. Separation from parents during early childhood. In *Rev. Child Develpm. Res.,* 1964, *1,* 89-136. New York: Russell Sage Foundation.

Chapter 8

Genetic Aspects of Creativity

Althea J. Horner

Innate Factors

Any consideration of the genetic aspects of creativity must, of necessity, go back to the biological organism. The interaction between its structure and its function may well constitute the earliest example of creative interest and behavior. Individual differences reveal themselves at all levels of the biological and psychological organism, and we may assume that these differences are reflected in the quality and intensity of such early indications of creativity.

Eiduson (1962), in her comprehensive study of creative scientists, observed that they all had experienced a period of either physical or psychological isolation when they had turned to their own resources for solace and amusement. Their activities revealed that they often played for play's sake or spent hours daydreaming and toying with ideas and symbols. They found in these diversions a kind of intrinsic satisfaction unrelated to outcomes or products: that is, their goals and values were oriented toward the activity rather than toward the result of the activity. Although this is a point that has been emphasized by many researchers in the field, the motivating and goal-directing influence of the product of creative activity cannot be as completely dismissed as often happens. Eiduson also found that there was an exploratory quality to the cognitive behavior of her subjects. They tended to scan the perceptual field before responding in terms of organizing or structuring principles. If we want to find the origins of this preference for manipulative and exploratory behavior, be it physical or mental, we must go back to the newborn organism.

When we observe infants in the newborn nursery, we can see initial differences in the vigor of their activity, in their sleep patterns, in their responsiveness to environmental stimuli, and in the amount of their random, spontaneous movements. Putting these differences together with certain other patterns of innate behavior, we get a wide distribution of observable behavior patterns. By innate behavior we mean the exploratory and manipulative behavior which can be observed not only in the human infant but has also been demonstrated by Harlow (1956) in his work with the infant rhesus monkey. Preyer's observational study of his infant son, published before the turn of the century, first called attention to what he called "spontaneous" or internally stimulated behavior. Harlow's studies showed that manipulation motives appear very early in the life of the infant monkey. His data strongly suggest that such manipulative behavior is self-sustaining and primary, that is, not elicited by conditioning the animal to an identifiable internal drive, such as hunger, or to a learned incentive, such as food.

This innate drive toward exploring and manipulating the environment, when combined with differences in strength, activity, and responsiveness to stimuli, results in primary differences in the breadth, vigor, and quality of the exploratory and manipulative behavior itself. These differences, then, can be hypothesized as leading to differential degrees of success which, in turn, are more or less reinforcing in terms of establishing this as a preferred mode of behavior or goal.

The description of two brothers, David and Kenneth, will illustrate the point. David is six years older than Kenneth. The quality of maternal care was essentially the same for both boys, as were their environmental conditions. Both boys have measured IQ's in the superior range. David was an extremely easy baby to care for. He ate and slept well, cried very little, and was happy, quiet, and contented. He never ventured far from where he was placed and, when he was 6 months old, happily played in his playpen where he was placed for long periods of time with only a few toys left within his reach.

Kenneth, on the other hand, was far more active as an infant, and reacted more vigorously to stimuli, startling easily. He often had to be rocked and sung to sleep. When he was a few months old, his mother would place him on a small rug in her room. Time and again he would, with great effort, pull himself along on his stomach until he reached the place where the edge of the rug adjoined the hardwood floor. There he would stop and with great interest and concentration scratch first at the rug and then at the floor, obviously intent upon experiencing the difference in texture between the two surfaces. That his interest and curiosity were inherent there can be no doubt, and so was the innate physical vigor which he used to gratify his curiosity. He also obviously experienced pleasure in the mastery of his environment, that is, the extent to which he could control his position in space.

When Kenneth was 6 months old, he rebelled against being confined in a playpen and his mother, therefore, devised a series of gates and doors which allowed him the run of several rooms. The family, going in and out of this area, would use a particular door which closed tightly with a slight click. When this door did not fully close as evidenced by its failure to click, Kenneth knew that he could open the door. He would come scrambling on his hands and knees from the opposite end of the area and find his way to that part of the house that was ordinarily closed to him. He showed early an intense interest in and sensitivity to environmental stimuli, and used his keen sensorium to master his environment. Eiduson found this same kind of heightened perceptivity to sensory experience in her group of creative scientists.

The fact that both boys are of superior intelligence shows that these qualities cannot be attributed to intelligence alone, at least not to intelligence as it is measured by ordinary intelligence tests. Getzels and Jackson (1962) found in their comparison of high IQ subjects with highly creative subjects that, although there was a 23-IQ-point difference between the two groups, the highly creative group did as well academically as the high IQ group. The authors also noted that their subjects were not highly motivated by the desire for success and that their school performance, therefore, could not be characterized as overachievement. Rather, the results suggested that there are aspects of intelligence, as reflected in creativity, that are not being measured by existing intelligence tests.

It has been pointed out that intelligence tests call for answers that require convergent thinking. As defined by Guilford (1957), this is thinking that is directed toward the one right answer. And, indeed, the structure of most tests demands this kind of thinking. As Darwin said, "You would be surprised at the number of years it took me to see clearly what some of the problems were which had to be solved . . . . Looking back, I think it was more difficult to see what the problems were than to solve them." Perhaps this is the essence of creativity: to define new problems as well as to find new approaches toward solving old ones. Creativity requires what Guilford calls divergent thinking, thinking which is in the nature of searching and readiness to pursue different directions. This kind of thinking is actually penalized in the scoring of intelligence tests. One morning our 6-year-old Kenneth, while watching the toast being buttered, laughingly sang, "Yankee Doodle had a farm, e-i-e-i-butter." He was aware of and enjoyed the nonsensical product that resulted from the new combination of old and familiar elements. His singsong was an example of early divergent thinking, and the form in which it was expressed may help us understand why Getzels and Jackson's highly creative group valued a sense of humor so much more than did the high IQ group. For it is in the humor or nonsense statements of the small child that divergent thinking first demonstrates itself. However, the evaluative function of the intellect through which, according to Guilford, we evaluate our thought products, is most important even at this stage. Eiduson describes her subjects as being able to recombine and reorganize familiar conceptions, to display novelty in ideational activity, and to indulge in highly individualized and even autistic ways of thinking. She found that her scientists could relax their controls on thinking without fear of a personality disorganization but that they were also willing to test their conceptualizations against reality. It is in this area of perceptual and cognitive style that she noticed the greatest similarity in her subjects; there was no such common patterning in the area of personality.

We would also expect to find given individual neurological differences. According to Barron (1963b) some individuals are born with a greater brain capacity and can thus derive a richer synthesis from the stimuli impinging upon them. That is, they have a greater facility for organizing stimuli of varying degrees of complexity into meaningful relationships and patterns. At the extreme end of the continuum of individuals who have this increased synthesizing ability we find those who employ the more unique organizing principles that characterize the creative person. The organization of stimuli itself represents a kind of manipulation of the environment, an activity that seems inherently pleasurable to the creative adult. Barron speaks of the creative individual's positive preference for what we call disorder but which to the individual represents the possibility of a future order whose principle or organization is not yet apparent. Barron's study shows that those who rated high in originality had a preference for less simply ordered geometrical drawings, for figures which were generally considered to be disordered, irregular, or even chaotic. Thus, creative individuals had a positive liking for phenomenal fields which could not be assimilated according to the principles of geometric order but required the development or creation of new perceptual schemata to render the phenomena intelligible.

Hallman (1965) emphasizes the aesthetic motivation in the creative arts, advancing the theory that the creative individual responds primarily to the qualities in his environment, and prefers to engage in qualitative symbolic behavior rather than in survival or adaptive behavior. He says, "The qualitative response explains why the creative act consists in operations of composing, modeling, arranging, expressing, combining, fusing. It explains why objects tend to lose their more practical meanings to take on a plasticity of meanings and possibilities which enable the creative person to combine them in the interest of an aesthetic rather than a survival need" (p. 458). He directs his views explicitly at artistic activity but it would seem that their significance goes beyond that. This same need also applies to the theoretical scientists for whom a well-turned theory is a thing of elegance and beauty.

The thought of an aesthetically pleasing solution, whether artistic or scientific, brings us back to the pleasure inherent in the innate manipulative behavior of the infant. Eiduson points out that all the scientists in her study were amply endowed with intellectual capacities, that from their earliest days they probably were able to manipulate certain things, ideas and even people in their environment with great facility, that they could explore and cope with their world, and that they probably managed it with considerable skill and modes of response. Such success, as we mentioned before, may lead to a kind of satisfaction which in itself may be a reinforcing factor and tend to establish this conduct as a preferred type of behavior.

Schilder (1964), in his developmental neuropsychiatry, emphasizes the importance of what he describes as ego instincts: to seize, to hold, and to master. Every individual, he says, strives to master reality. He maintains, furthermore, that human beings have a deep interest in the world, in action, and in experimentation; that they derive satisfaction from venturing out into the world and do not experience reality as a threat to existence; that organisms, and especially human organisms, have a genuine feeling of safety and security in this world, and that threats come merely from specific situations and deprivations. C. Buhler (1954) describes what she calls a primary positive response to reality, while Erikson (1953) speaks of an initial positive reality acceptance that underlies the establishment of trust in the child. Buhler sees her primary positive response as a structural foundation for later anticipations that are determined by the positive aspects of reality. In other words, the individual, anticipating satisfaction, responds to reality in a positive manner derived from a specific potential within him. Or, to quote Buhler: "Reality is an opportunity before it is a hindrance." Only if the individual is not satisfied does he begin to realize that he has to cope with reality as a hindrance. This view contrasts sharply with that of the psychoanalytic theorists who conceive of reality as a hindrance to the gratification of id impulses.

These theorists have all described as a primary given what has eventually come to be considered one of the characteristics of the creative individual, that is, "openness to experience." MacKinnon (1961), in his study of creative American architects, discovered his subjects to be open to their own feelings and emotions as well as to what goes on outside themselves. Maslow (1963) speaks of "taoistic receptivity," a kind of non-interference or attitude of "let be." Rogers (1961) defines openness as follows: "This is the opposite of psychological defensiveness, when to protect the organization of self, certain experiences are prevented from coming into awareness except in disturbed fashion. . . . It means lack of rigidity and permeability of boundaries in concepts, beliefs, perceptions, and hypotheses" (p. 353). He implies that experiential variables, which intervene between the stage of Buhler's primary positive response and later attitudes toward environment and experience, can interfere with the establishment of creative openness to experience. We can thus conceptualize "openness to experience" as an innate given which, as is the case with any given characteristic, is later affected by environmental influences. This conceptualization necessarily assumes an adequate and intact organism.

However, it is likely that this primary receptiveness can be demonstrated to be qualitatively different from one newborn to another. Observations have indicated that the infant is shielded from the outside world by what is termed a "stimulus barrier." Stimuli coming from outside are perceived only when their level of intensity exceeds the threshold of the stimulus barrier. Differences in the level of this threshold may account for what seem to be considerable differences in the newborn's responsivity to stimuli in general. We know from Spitz's (1965) observations that infants who are severely deprived of stimulation because of environmental factors, fail to develop physically, mentally, or psychologically. We could take this one step farther and suggest that an infant with an extremely high stimulus barrier will also suffer some deprivation of stimulation and thus show some deficiencies in his development, as did the babies in Spitz's study. It has been suggested, on the other hand, that infants with an inadequate stimulus barrier are inundated with stimuli that they cannot assimilate or integrate, and that they become overwhelmed with anxiety, predisposing them to the formation of later psychological defenses against environmental stimuli (Bergman and Escalona, 1949). We might say, therefore, that there is an optimum range of this innate openness to experience that allows the child to develop maximally, without predisposing him toward gross and indiscriminate withdrawal from stimulation. Our creative artists and scientists-to-be might logically be hypothesized to be endowed with this optimum level of stimulus receptivity.

The studies of Escalona (1963) suggest, though, that this may be only partly true; that, because the stimulus barrier of the potentially creative individual is actually somewhat low, this particular growing child makes a kind of selective choice as to which stimuli shall be shut out and which admitted for integration.

Roe, McClelland, Barron, et al. (1963) have characterized the creative scientists as having a high degree of autonomy, self-sufficiency, and self-direction. They reported that their subjects displayed a somewhat distant or detached attitude in interpersonal relations, a marked independence of judgment, and a rejection of group pressures toward conformity in thinking. MacKinnon (1961), in his study of creative architects, found that they shared a strong wish to be left alone while also wanting to exert control over others. These men, too, had little desire to be included in a group. Eiduson found her group of creative scientists to have few intense relationships. She wondered if perhaps they had to shut out irrelevant events in order to be good scientists. They were actually highly perceptive of emotional stimuli, she discovered, although they were not especially responsive to them.

These research findings tie in with the differences Escalona found in her comparison of highly active and inactive infants, namely, that the active infants, because of a high level of receptiveness to external stimuli, found it necessary to shut out certain social stimuli so they could function at the optimal cognitive level for their stage of development.

Escalona also found that the behavior of the active babies, who were 28 weeks old, was less closely dependent upon maternal or external stimulation in spontaneous play activity. Not only were they more active, but they showed spontaneously more highly integrated behavior. Unlike the inactive babies who either mouthed or waved a toy without looking at it, or looked at an object without manipulating it, the active babies combined and integrated these different modalities of apprehending an object, enhancing their ability to master it. What was most interesting, though, was what happened when these babies were subjected to intense social stimulation. The inactive babies performed at a more highly integrated level of behavior, although they reverted to more simple levels when left on their own again. The highly active babies, however, who showed more highly integrated levels of behavior when left alone, showed a reversion to simpler levels of behavior. These facts alone demonstrate that Escalona was not dealing with actual differences in abilities but with differences in conditions under which these kinds of behavior appear. In terms of the most basic interaction effects of the environment upon biological givens, these findings show how the same maternal interventions can encourage the activation of developmentally important behavior in some infants while hindering that of others, and how a condition—in this instance, spontaneous activity —which is optimal for the emergence of significant learning experience for some infants, fails to provide these experiences for others.

It does not seem unreasonable to hypothesize that our infant creative scientists and artists—who show more highly integrated cognitive abilities when left to their own spontaneous and independent behavior, and great perceptiveness but reduced responsiveness to social stimuli—would have fitted the description of Escalona's active babies, and that early in their development they had found that in order to master their environment, to function at their optimal cognitive level, they had to shut out excessive social stimulation. This would imply a kind of active choice on their part, a rejection of intense emotional involvement in favor of the use of cognitive and manipulative skills. (One woman scientist reports how, at the age of 4, she deliberately built a wall of blocks around herself so that she would be undisturbed and able to sit and "think.") What is really needed, then, from a scientific point of view, is a longitudinal study which would follow infants to maturity to see whether the conclusions derived from combining the findings of infant studies with those of studies of creative adults can be justified.

Not only are there inherent differences that are apparent at birth, there are also differences in the rate and degree to which maturational changes take place. The child's interest in the manipulation of his environment goes hand in hand with developmental changes in his manipulative ability and skill. And as his abilities mature, his interest in exploring and manipulating his environment lead to the experience of different results or outcomes of his behavior. Buhler (1931) describes how, when he is 5 to 7 months of age, the child can handle blocks separately and hammer with them, experiencing the creation of sound as the result of his own efforts; how he can bring them into relationship with one another when, a little later, he is able to knock them together; and how, when he is

10 to 12 months old, he comes upon another relational experience when he discovers that things can be fitted together. The realization that things have a relationship to each other is for the child, according to Buhler, a creative experience. This search for meaningful relationships is, of course, part of the scientific process, and goes back to the early days of infancy. But at that stage the child has not yet experienced creating a new product from the elements at hand; he has merely discovered certain potentials inherent in the objects themselves. When he is about 1½ years old and discovers that blocks can be piled upon one another to make a tower or a house, or lined up to make a train, he combines certain inherent spatial relational aspects of the material with his creative imagination, endowing the product of his exploratory and manipulatory behavior with creative meaning. He may then go on to devise more complex structures, again endowing them with surplus meaning, which is the distinguishing feature, and giving them a creative aspect rather than having them appear as accidental results of trial and error manipulations. C. Buhler sees this as "an experimental handling of material, with the purpose of creating something new. This may at first be only vaguely foreseen, but gradually becomes more and more clearly envisioned."*

Thus the potentially creative adult shows as a young child not only the ability to manipulate successfully the materials of his environment but also his sensitivity to the creative potential inherent in these materials. When Hallman described the aesthetic motivation in artistic creativity, he emphasized the use of materials that lent themselves to composing, modeling, arranging, combining, or fusing, and the plasticity of meanings and possibilities inherent in the materials at hand. This creativity shows itself in many tasks and, as the individual gets older, is applied to an ever-widening range of environmental materials with which he comes in contact, such as the sand in a sand-box when he is 3, the paints and crayons when he goes to school, and the language in which he develops greater competence and understanding as he grows up. For language also is a material with which the creative person can work, creating, for instance, new ideas and concepts. The mathematician who works creatively with numbers and highly theoretical formulae does so at an even more abstract level.

Gagné (1965) states that although a child's curiosity, openness, freedom, and honesty may have a great deal in common with the most sophisticated practice of science that one can describe, one cannot

* Personal communication, 1966.

equate the two because of the many intervening steps the child must take in terms of cognitive sophistication. Gagné considers it the role of education to encourage and increase the child's curiosity, and to choose materials and subjects that have innate appeal as well as a high potential to arouse the need for the desired skills. I agree, although it appears that, since a common education does not have an equal impact upon all who are exposed to it, there are some whose interest and response to the efforts of educators far exceed that of others.

Barron (1963a) believes that a highly organized system of responding lies behind any given original response, and that certain patterns of relatively enduring traits facilitate the production of original acts. Thus, when we take a longitudinal view of the development of the creative individual, we can see a continuity that begins at birth and progresses through childhood, the school years, and the achievement of professional status.

Environmental Factors

Bloom (1963) insists that it is highly unlikely that creativity is a characteristic that an individual possesses under all circumstances. He believes that there are variables in both the individual and the environment that facilitate or hamper creative effort. What, we may ask, are the environmental variables that are common to those who function creatively?

Returning once more to the infancy and early childhood of our creative individuals, and using Escalona's observations, we hypothesize that intense social stimulation or pressure had a deleterious effect on them. MacKinnon (1962) pointed out how the mothers in his study did not interfere with their children but granted them the freedom to explore and function for themselves. We may postulate, then, that for the potentially creative infant to function optimally and to experience the kind of success in functioning which reinforces his interest in mastering his environment, he must have a mother who does not interfere and offers him help only when he seeks it. It may well be that this requires what MacKinnon calls "autonomous" mothers. We should add that an autonomous mother is *not* a rejecting or indifferent mother. She is a mother who values her own autonomy and respects that of her child, fully accepting his active exploration of his world. There are mothers who find such exploration intolerable, preferring a clean, quiet, passive, and inactive child. Such mothers might well punish and severely inhibit the very behavior that is the forerunner of creativity.

Emphasis was also put upon the child's interaction with the materials of his environment, presupposing an environment that offers him materials to discover and with which to demonstrate his creative skills. Culturally deprived children usually lack such materials, and the deleterious effects of that deprivation are being closely examined by psychologists, sociologists, and educators.

According to Goertzel and Goertzel (1962), it is the family value system that has the strongest impact upon the child with ability. If his parents respect ability and have themselves strong intellectual and physical drives, he is more likely to become outstanding. The love for learning acquired in these intellect-oriented homes appears to have a kind of autonomy; it is not associated with a desire for material gain. Common to the homes in the Goertzel study was the fact that parents and children enjoyed each other, and that they worked and played together. The children had considerable intellectual and physical freedom, and there was an absence of anxiety about safety and health. There was a lot of fun and humor, and great tolerance for minor misdemeanors. Mothers whom their children remembered as being especially beautiful were not found to have influenced their children in constructive ways. What was evident in this and other studies was the preponderance of dominating mothers, women who today might have their own careers but who at that time used their capable offspring as outlets for their own drives and abilities.

MacKinnon (1962) found the parents of his creative architects to have great respect for their children and confidence in their ability to do what was appropriate. From the very start, these parents granted their children unusual freedom in exploring their universe and making decisions for themselves. These attitudes appear to have contributed greatly to an enrichment of experience as well as to a sense of personal autonomy that was characteristic of this group.

MacKinnon, like Goertzel and Goertzel, found that his subjects lacked a close relationship with the father. There were no very strong emotional ties with either parent, the relationship being balanced so as to foster neither overdependency nor feelings of rejection. As MacKinnon said, "It was the kind of distance that had a liberating effect so far as the child was concerned." What was conspicuously absent was the kind of emotional exploitation of children by their parents that is so often found in clinical patients.

Goertzel and Goertzel commented that their group had the kind of mothers who in today's society might have their own careers. MacKinnon (1962) found this actually to be the case; his study showed a high incidence of autonomous mothers who led active lives, with interests and sometimes careers of their own. This would suggest that it was not the prodding and pushing of the domineering mothers that led to the success of the children but rather the high value that both they and the mothers of the architects set on the realization of a person's potential.

In the Getzels and Jackson study there was a striking difference between the value emphases of the mothers of the high IQ subjects and those of the highly creative group. The mothers of the high IQ group put far more emphasis on providing the "correct" upbringing for their children, on conforming to conventional standards, and on their children's doing well scholastically. They also tended to be more worried about the dangers of the world and were more concerned about their children's behavior and choice of friends. Friends were evaluated in terms of social characteristics, such as being from a "good family" or "having good manners," rather than in terms of values or interests, which was the basis of preference used by the parents of the highly creative subjects. All in all, the high IQ children came from homes that limited individual divergence and minimized risk. The parents of the highly creative children, on the other hand, behaved much like the parents in the other studies of creative individuals cited in this paper, encouraging individual divergence and risk.

Values and Goals

The emerging common patterns of thinking, behaving, and valuing that seem to characterize creative individuals carry with them certain goals toward which the individual moves. That these are not limited to conventional success was demonstrated by Getzels and Jackson whose study showed that the highly creative group not only valued success itself less highly but also those personality and social characteristics that had been agreed upon by both groups of subjects—high creatives and high IQ's—as being necessary to the achievement of adult success in our society.

The lack of deep involvement that Eiduson's scientists showed, and the aloneness that characterized Getzels and Jackson's high creatives, make it clear that the goals of these individuals are not centered on their relationships with other people. MacKinnon's architects, also, were not particularly interested in being part of a group.

Career aspirations of Getzels and Jackson's high creatives were in the direction of the more unconventional vocations, such as adventurer, inventor, and writer, and indicated a greater than usual willingness to take career risks. Job security, therefore, is certainly not one of the goals of the creative individual.

If, as it seems, creative individuals are not highly motivated in terms of conventional success, security, or close interpersonal relationships, what are the goals that direct their efforts and their lives?

We may say that the interest in mastery, the pleasure in bringing order to chaos and complexity, and the satisfaction experienced in establishing something new and meaningful indicate that the goals of the creative individual involve his relationship with himself and his task. There are those for whom the creative process itself is as valuable as the product that terminates the process. In the terminology of K. Buhler (1927), creative persons experience a kind of "function pleasure," which can be seen as a partial goal. Their interest in their product is conditioned by the degree to which it validates the process, thus enhancing the function pleasure and the satisfaction they derive in their drive toward a meaningful existence.

Our focus has been on the process involved in creativity rather than on the product of the creative effort. Researchers have used productivity as one of the criteria by which they define the creative individual, although they de-emphasize the significance of the product when they describe him and the ways in which he functions. This dismissal of what constitutes the essential criterion of creativity as unimportant to creativity appears to be operationally inconsistent. It may well be that the product does not have the conventional motivational implications of success and achievement as defined by our present culture, i.e., money and/or prestige. Getzels and Jackson, in fact, did find that their high creatives valued conventional success less than did their high I.Q. group. MacKinnon (1961) found that, although his creative architects were strongly motivated to achieve in situations in which independence of thought and action were called for, they were not so motivated where conforming behavior was expected or required. Thus, here too, achievement motivation was not the primary drive.

However, this does not mean that the product per se is not important for the creative individual. As Clarence Darrow (1932) said, "Doubtless . . . the emotion to live makes most of us seek to project our personality a short distance beyond the waiting grave." A woman psychotherapist expressed the same feeling in the following way: "If my life is to be meaningful the world must be a different and better place because of the fact that I existed." For her the process of psychotherapy was meaningful and gratifying but no less than the feeling of accomplishment she experienced when a case was successfully terminated. And a number of scientists from the Jet Propulsion Laboratory, for instance, have described their feelings of elation when the product of their creative process, the moon probe, met with success. Such observations clearly show that the product is motivational in nature and that it imparts goal directedness to the process of organizing fragmented activity into a meaningful whole. Furthermore, the product is the culmination of the process and as such a part of the process; it is the criterion by which the creative individual evaluates the validity of the process. To some degree, the product also must have validity when viewed from the external world. The product of creative scientific thought must be consistent with the objective facts of nature. The product of the creative architect, for instance, must serve a purpose beyond expressing his aesthetic needs; people must be able to live and work in it; it must meet their functional needs as well. Going back to Guilford's evaluative function of the intellect, it is at the stage of the product that this function must operate. MacKinnon (1962) differentiates artistic from scientific creativity in terms of the product. He maintains that the products of artistic creativity are expressions of the creator's inner states, needs, perceptions, or motivations. In other words, the artist externalizes something of himself and puts it into the public field. The products of scientific creativity, however, are unrelated to the creator as a person, because the scientist in his creative work acts largely as a mediator between externally defined needs and goals. MacKinnon sees the architect as a combination of artist and scientist.

The creative individual, then, meets not only his own needs but those of the external world as well. He must to some extent meet the stylistic demands of his time and culture, at least if his product is to be accepted. Many may argue this point, insisting that the product stand on its own merit and reasoning that styles change, and that what is unacceptable at one time may be heralded as a masterpiece at another. Beethoven's music, for instance, was ridiculed during his life because he used a totally new form. Moreover, a creative product that does not yield to the stylistic demands of its time may actually be instrumental in changing them. Frank Lloyd Wright's architecture, for example, has done just that. And so the product has creative significance not only for the individual himself but for the society in which he lives, which creatively changes and evolves as it incorporates within its structure the new and unique expressions of its members.

MacKinnon's architects rated higher on the Allport-Vernon scale in aesthetic and theoretical values than other professionals. Bloom found among a group of graduate students a preoccupation with problems rather than with the subject matter of courses, and a lack of competing activities and interests such as concern for family and personal life, social relations, status, prestige, and money. Maslow (1962) describes how creativity can be seen in all kinds of individuals—including housewives and athletes—for whom competence in the tasks that confront them is combined with a kind of pleasure in the aesthetic elegance that can be brought to the task. Competence and elegance, mastery and aesthetics seem, along with the interest in creating something new and meaningful, to be at the center of the creative individuals' value system.

This value orientation is apparent in the very young child who shuts out intense emotional involvement with people around him in order to deal more effectively with the materials of his environment; it is evident in the older child who takes pleasure in wading deeply in literary fantasies, experimenting with a chemistry set or collecting butterflies, and who prefers this to being on a baseball team or going to parties or dances; it is also evident in the youth who prefers a course of study in college that challenges his thinking and imagination to subjects that will qualify him for a position in as secure and respected a field as law or accounting. Rather than to retreat from the problems that confront him and take refuge in the goals of comfort and security, rather than turning his back on the complexity of life by disregarding those possibilities that are anxiety-provoking in their uncertainty or the manner in which they conflict with one another, the creative individual considers the many possibilities open to him and tries to bring them into harmony and balance. The creative person may combine the talents of a poet, writer, painter, and statesman as exemplified by Winston Churchill. He need not limit himself or feel that he must adjust to things as they are. He can expand his own existence and, if he wishes, overcome existing circumstances. This concept is reflected in one of Buhler's life-goal factors, aptly called "creative expansion." (C. Buhler and W. Coleman, 1964.) Goertzel and Goertzel tell us that "normality," as evidenced by a lack of intrapsychic tension, by adequate social, economic, and familial adaptation, and by satisfactory integration with other persons, implies a lack of creativity, imagination, and spontaneity. "The comfortable and contented do not ordinarily become creative." They found in their study of 400 eminent men and women that three-fourths were troubled as children in terms of social, economic, physical, or interpersonal matters. The fathers of about half of the subjects were failure-prone in the routine of everyday life. In the words of the authors, "In the homes which cradle eminence, creativity and contentment are not congenial. Both parents and children are often irritable, explosive, changeable, experimental. They are prone to depression and exaltation. They make terrible mistakes and win wonderful victories" (p. 130). Only 58 of the 400 subjects were found to have experienced the stereotyped supportive, warm, and relatively untroubled home, and even here the authors suspect omission of data.

So we might say that the value a person places on creative goals and activities, and all that this implies, determines the choices he makes at each turning point in his life cycle. C. Buhler* has found that for some creative old-age subjects the aspect of function pleasure assumes a particular importance in that it helps them to accept the decline in external involvements and opportunities.

In summary, then, studies of creative people lead us to view creativity as a quality that initially resides within the biological givens of the newborn child, is enhanced by certain parental values, especially those of the mother, and ultimately develops into an important determinant in the choice of goals at various stages of the individual's life cycle.

References

Barron, F. The disposition toward originality. In C. W. Taylor and F. Barron (eds.), *Scientific creativity: its recognition and development.* New York: John Wiley & Sons, 1963. (a)

Barron, F. The needs for order and disorder as motives in creativity. In C. W. Taylor and F. Barron (eds.), *Scientific creativity: its recognition and development.* New York: John Wiley & Sons, 1963. (b)

Bergman, P., and Escalona, S. Unusual sensitivities in the very young children. In R. Eissler, A. Freud, H. Hartmann, and M. Kris (eds.), *Psychoanalytic study of the child.* New York: International Universities Press, 1949.

Bloom, B. S. Report on creativity research by the examiner's office of the University of Chicago. In C. W. Taylor and F. Barron (eds.), *Scientific creativity: its recognition and development.* New York: John Wiley & Sons, 1963.

Buhler, C. *Kindheit and Jugend.* Leipzig: S. Hirzel, 1931.

Buhler, C. The reality principle: discussion of theories and observational data. *Amer. J. Psychother.,* 1954, *8,* 626-647.

Buhler, C., and Coleman, W. Life goals inventory, 1964.

Buhler, K. *Die Krise der Psychologie.* Jena: Gustav Fischer, 1927.

Darrow, C. *The story of my life.* New York: Scribner, 1932.

Darwin, F. (ed.), The autobiography of Charles Darwin and selected letters. New York: Dover Books, 1958, 216.

Eiduson, B. *Scientists—their psychological world.* New York: Basic Books, 1962.

Erikson, E. H. Growth and crises of the "healthy personality." In C. Kluckhohn and H. A. Murray (eds.), *Personality in nature, society, and culture.* New York: Knopf, 1953.

Escalona, S. Patterns of infantile experience. In R. Eissler, A. Freud, H. Hartmann, and M. Kris (eds.), *Psychoanalytic study of the child.* New York: International Universities Press, 1963.

Gagné, R. M. Psychological issues in science—a process approach. In *The psychological bases of science—a process approach.* AAAS Commission on Science Education, 1965.

* Personal communication.

Getzels, J. W., and Jackson, P. W. *Creativity and intelligence: explorations with gifted students.* New York: John Wiley & Sons, 1962.

Goertzel V., and Goertzel, M. G. *Cradles of eminence.* Boston: Little, Brown, 1962.

Guilford, J. P. Creative abilities in the arts, *Psychol. Rev.*, 1957, *64*:2, 110-118.

Hallman, R. J. Aesthetic motivation in the creative arts, *J. Aesthetics and Art Criticism,* 1965, *23*:4.

Harlow, H. F., Blazek, N. C., and McClearn, G. E. Manipulatory motivation in the infant rhesus monkey, *J. Comp. Physiol. Psychol.*, 1956, *49*, 444-448.

MacKinnon, D. W. The personality correlates of creativity: a study of American architects. *Proceedings of the 14th International Congress of Applied Psychology,* Copenhagen: Munksgaard, 1961.

MacKinnon, D. W. The nature and nurture of creative talent. Walter Van Dyke Bingham lecture given at Yale University, New Haven, Conn., April 11, 1962.

Maslow, A. H. *Toward a psychology of being.* Princeton: Van Nostrand, 1962.

Maslow, A. H. The creative attitude, *The Structurist,* 1963, No. 3, 4-10.

Roe, A., McClelland, D., Barron, F., *et al.* A look ahead. In C. W. Taylor and F. Barron (eds.), *Scientific creativity: its recognition and development.* New York: John Wiley & Sons, 1963.

Rogers, C. R. *On becoming a person.* Boston: Houghton Mifflin, 1961.

Schilder, P. *Contributions to developmental neuropsychiatry.* New York: International Universities Press, 1964.

Spitz, R. *The first year of life.* New York: International Universities Press, 1965.

III Early Emotional Dynamics as Codeterminants of Goal Setting

The third part of this book opens with a theoretical discussion by Arthur L. Kovacs. This author predominantly adheres to the psychoanalytic egopsychology. What makes his contribution particularly valuable in the context of this book's basic orientation is that he himself critically evaluates a position he holds at the outset.

After a few pages he already refers to psychoanalysis' focusing primarily on psychopathological processes as one of the weak points which present-day theorists try to remedy in the interest of understanding more "normal" behavior and development. In the main section of his chapter, Kovacs gives a systematic presentation of the significant aspects of egopsychology.

In this "critique," Kovacs points to the validity of the self-theorists' viewing man as a person instead of a machine, seeing human interaction instead of tension-reducing processes, understanding motivation in terms of growth and fulfillment instead of homeostatic processes, and conceiving of man as an unfolding actualizer instead of a synthesizer. His sharp and objective survey does justice to the complexity of the present theoretical situation in the field of emotional dynamics as related to goal setting.

In Chapter 10, C. Buhler tries to categorize the early environmental influences on goal setting; here she finds a correspondence between the individual's basic tendencies with influences exercised by the environment. The categories love and care, demands and discipline, information and opportunity, and, finally, models and ideals are useful to show the environment's relation to the child's own tendencies toward need satisfaction, self-limiting adaptation, creative expansion, and upholding of the internal order.

M. Meyer, in Chapter 11, relates the healthy and unhealthy goal development in children to the compatibility of the child's goals with his native endowment and the developmental stage. He distinguishes goals for external and internal achievement, and describes the healthy pattern of goal setting as a harmonious integration of the child's innate physical and psychological characteristics with the demands and opportunities provided by the environment.

R. Ekstein demonstrates in Chapter 12 incidences of pathological goal setting in psychotic adolescents. He shows four varieties of deviations from the normal struggles of this age phase. There are adolescents luxuriating in long-term unrealistic phantasy goals, while actually they are "stuck" in extremely short-term goals. They are unable to project a unified integrated self from the present to the future, and are involved in existential conflicts of life-threatening proportions.

Earlier chapters of Part III consider how parents may influence an individual's initial goal setting in a detrimental manner. In Chapter 13 T. Tomlinson discusses the part the psychotherapist plays in helping a patient to a healthier and more mature goal-setting attitude. He presents psychotherapy essentially from the humanistic point of view, intended not only as a "cure" in the sense of making functional what previously was dysfunctional, but also being instrumental in aiding the patient to direct himself toward more self-realizing goals.

Chapter 9

Ego Psychology and Self-Theory

Arthur L. Kovacs

Any comprehensive theory of personality faces at least three tasks: 1) to describe the inner organization of personality—how such things as needs, attitudes, character traits, and similar concepts are organized and interrelated within the psychological "skin"; 2) to describe how this organization has developed and how it carries within it dynamics which will unfold in the future; and 3) to describe how the individual personality organizes its interactions with other personalities and objects in the world. Various viewpoints about personality structure and about psychogenetics, inherent in the first and second of these tasks, are expounded elsewhere in this volume. The present chapter is an attempt to set forth some considerations about how the person contacts his reality and how these contacts are given coherent structure.

At the present time there seem to be several highly visible and contrasting points of view about the nature of man's interaction with his world. One of the most popular of these, of course, is psychoanalytic ego psychology. This chapter will attempt to summarize and to clarify this way of conceptualizing man's commerce with life outside himself and to explicate the assumptions inherent in it. It is the product, of course, of a theoretical orientation which uses concepts of force and energy and attempts to be systematic, although sometimes in a self-contradictory fashion. As such, it is open to critical evaluation from persons whose orientation is more humanistic, who use concepts of unfolding and of growth, and who are concerned with the self and not the ego as a core organizing concept.

After describing ego psychology within the limits of these very few pages, then, some critical observations about the problems which it poses will be made from the useful and contrasting vantage point of self-theory.

The term "ego psychology" is one which any reader of the psychological literature encounters with increasing frequency. It appears in a myriad of publications flowing from psychoanalytic theory. That we have fads in our technical language is one of the facts of our professional lives. Conceptualizing a test protocol, a therapeutic event, or an aspect of theory construction from the standpoint of so-called ego psychology currently marks that activity as fashionable, and it conveys to the parties involved a sense of sophistication and omniscience which traditionally has adhered to the use of such concepts as "dynamic" or "unconscious." But any good clinician knows that he must not confuse the secondary gain of a symptom with its primary function. So it is with the term "ego psychology." We, as psychologists, must be critically concerned with whether its utility extends beyond that of simply enhancing the self-esteem of its users.

CONTEMPORARY EGO PSYCHOLOGY

An adequate understanding of current theorizing in the domain of ego psychology depends upon some working familiarity with the vicissitudes of Freud's writings about the ego—a topic about which he changed his mind repeatedly and drastically during the course of his life. Those readers who are not already conversant with the relevant literature would find it helpful in understanding what follows to review some of the books and papers Freud produced (Freud, 1914; 1920; 1923; 1936; 1937; 1954; 1955) which have provided the germinal seeds for contemporary psychoanalytic ego psychology. It should be noted here, however, that psychoanalysis at the time of Freud's death was essentially a theory of psychopathology focussed primarily on conflicts and disturbances which were conceptualized as located somehow "within" the person. From this point of view, it may indeed be said that the overriding goal of contemporary ego psychology is nothing less than that of broadening current psychoanalytic theory to account for "normal" as well as "abnormal" behavior, including considerations of how the personality maintains synthesis, integrity, and future-oriented strivings in both an interpersonal and cultural milieu. Its adherents attempt to explain in a more parsimonious manner the mechanisms involved in adaptive behavior, rational action, values, ethics, "mental health," and the integrated fashion in which man ordinarily functions without having to commit the reductionistic fallacy of translating these phenomena into libidinally driven, usually pregenital, motives. Psychoanalysis has now evolved to the point where, for instance, every artistic creation no longer has to be conceptualized as simply a higher order derivative of fecal play, as if reference to the latter could indeed ever "explain" the former. Psychoanalysis now aims to become a general psychology and not merely a theory of psychopathology.

Ego psychology also promises to bring psychoanalytic theory into greater harmony with the data of the biological and social sciences. These data make it clear that the phenomena of human behavior are continuously distributed and are relative to the time and place in which they are studied as well as to the frame of reference of him who does the studying. Freud had a tendency to think in terms of separate units and a small number of determinants of behavior: cathexis and countercathexis; conscious, preconscious, and unconscious; id, ego, and superego; drive and defense; the pleasure, reality, and nirvana principles; narcissism and object love; eros and thanatos, etc. The concepts of ego psychology, as will be seen below, are more flexible and do not force the data of human behavior into such conceptual straitjackets.

Finally, the current theorists who have left their imprint upon ego psychology have aimed to purge psychoanalysis of much of its previous mystical and pseudo-biological underpinnings. The gathering of data from life histories, from biographies, and from the direct observations of infants and children are now employed more systematically to generate hypotheses about the functioning of man without recourse to phylogenetic notions of the kind involved in, say, assumptions about a racial unconscious and universal symbolism; to prehistoric constructs such as those found in speculations about the primal horde; or to biological instincts like eros and the death instinct, to give a few examples. These kinds of premises have obfuscated psychoanalysis, are unproven, and probably are unprovable by any accepted empirical rules. Ego psychology uses other conceptual tools.

In order to achieve these goals—the formulation of a "normal" psychology, the integration of psychoanalysis with the other sciences, as well as purging it of mysticism and pseudobiologizing—contemporary theorists have had to rework extensively the legacy left by Freud. Certain traditional postulates have been seriously questioned. I will elaborate on this shortly in much greater detail. For the present, let me note that the postulate that all psychic energy was ultimately libidinous has been thoroughly attacked. Aggression and the difficulties of its management within the personality has now been accorded a more central role than previously. The structural point of view which stresses the importance of those functions labeled collectively the "ego" has been much further elaborated, and the untenable position that the maturation of apparatuses characteristic of the human organism (such things as intellectual, perceptual, and muscular capacities) were somehow derived from the "instincts" has been set aside.

With these comments by way of introduction, then, let me begin a more detailed survey of the contemporary status of ego psychology.

The Structural Point of View

Freud described the psyche as being divided into three often competing, most often conflicting, systems: id, ego, and superego. While he did not conceive of these as being completely independent of each other or as being invariably opposed to each other, the Freudian emphasis was mainly on strife between systems. The ego psychologists, particularly Hartmann, Kris, and Lowenstein (1946), have left this position. First, Hartmann (1950) objects to the reification implied by the very concepts id, ego, and superego—as if three incompatible homunculi were quarreling inside one's head. Hartmann maintains that systemic concepts like ego are really no more than convenient shorthand notations for describing a set of functions. The important personality functions which the term "ego" subsumes include, but are not exhausted by, such things as defense, perception, intelligence, thinking, reality testing, memory, access to motility, and synthesis. Hartmann and his collaborators then go on to change Freud's emphasis, that is, to stress the interdependence and interrelatedness of each psychic system with the others as well as that of the various functions within each given system.

Thus, a function of one system can be used by another system. For example, while masturbation is ordinarily conceived of as being an outlet for libidinous strivings and therefore as a discharge channel closely allied to the id, masturbation may come to be used defensively by the ego to divert drives which might lead to a dreaded actual sexual encounter. A function of one area may be taken over by another area in the same system. Rational thought is ordinarily considered an ego function which participates in problem solving and adaptation. It can, however, as the clinician is well aware, become invested with defensive meanings as found in obsessional disorders. Next, a function of one system may be captured by another system. One of the most readily apparent instances of this phenomenon is, of course, to be seen in the symptoms of the classical conversion hysterias. Here some previously conflict-free ego function—motility, perception, etc.—under pressure of a moral imperative of the kind "Thou shalt not look, touch, or hit . . ." becomes completely submerged and functionally ceases to be a part of the individual's behavior repertoire. A set of adaptations to one set of forces may lead to impairment of adaptation to another. The dynamics of early marriage seem to typify this principle. Consider the difficulties encountered by a hypothetical adolescent girl who flees the troubled existence she experiences in living with authoritarian, punitive, rejecting parents by entering an early marriage. Her initial reaction to the marriage is often one of fairy-tale bliss as she successfully separates from her family. But all too frequently the equilibrium is completely unstable. She soon becomes painfully aware of developmental lacunae which impair her ability to adapt to the demands of adult responsibility, of sexual intimacy, and of child birth and child rearing. Finally, a preponderance of one adaptive ego function may mean a weakness in another, equally adaptive in and of itself. Here might be noted, for instance, the successful counterphobic character who appears superficially to be outgoing, aggressive, capable, fearless, and free from anxiety. A slight alteration of the stresses which impinge on his life, however, would reveal a personality organized around a deficiency in the vital capacity to tolerate anxiety and a flight into frequently premature and maladaptive solutions to conflict-laden life situations.

Contemporary ego psychology, then, is marked by increasing sophistication about how various personality functions are structurally organized and about how these functions complement, interfere with, and abrogate other functions, regardless of the traditional system—id, ego, or superego—to which these have been assigned.

The Development of the Ego

Current theorists hold that the ego develops out of the interaction of several sets of forces: the maturation of inherited characteristics and apparatuses in interaction with the vicissitudes of sexual and aggressive drive development; and the influence of external reality, including the social milieu, the specific impact of those responsible for the child's socialization, and other, more idiosyncratic, learning experiences. Each of these will be discussed in turn.

Maturation

Freud's original formulations held that the ego developed out of the id (1923). Hartmann and his collaborators have pointed out the logical fallacy involved in such a formulation. To hew to such a position would be to insist that the innate apparatuses of the neonate, the germinal seeds of such later ego functions as perception, memory, control of action, etc., are all part of the id. These latter-day theorists prefer, rather, to speak of ego and id functions as both belonging at birth to an "undifferentiated phase." Given what Hartmann describes as an "average expectable environment" (1958), then independent, active development of ego functions proceeds from this undifferentiated matrix. Some adherents of the so-called English school (Fairburn, 1952; Guntrip, 1961) would even insist that the structuring of id functions as well as the development of the ego is created out of the impact of early human relationships upon the at first relatively unformed neonate.

Contemporary ego psychology, in addition to granting relatively greater autonomy to the maturation of ego functions, also deemphasizes to some degree the instinctual roots of man's behavior. It is now quite commonplace for psychoanalysts to assert, for example, that intellectual-perceptual apparatuses have usurped in man the adaptive functions of specific inherited behavior, characteristic of lower organisms. Man's childhood is long and protracted and characterized by only gradually waning helplessness and dependency precisely because of the complex interplay between maturational factors on the one hand (the unfolding of mastery over libidinal and aggressive drives and of increasing facility with perception, memory, intellect, and control of motility), and environment on the other (experience, learning, and the context of human relations in which these are embedded). The relationships between these variables, of course, are extremely intertwined and often synergistic. Mastery of speech, for example, partially determines shifts in the mode of expression of anger, if certain rewards and opportunities for identification are provided by the child's agents of socialization. Growing sexual curiosity during the phallic and oedipal periods can serve as an important motive in galvanizing a quest for knowledge whose acquisition can thereby enrich the ego's repertoire. And as a further instance, the slow accretion of the notions of space, time, and causality (Piaget, 1955) gradually prepares the ego to deal with frustration in terms of secondary process thinking and provide possibilities for more sophisticated, less crippling defenses than do developmentally primitive ones, such as withdrawal, denial, and projection (Kovacs, 1958). The maturation of a variety of apparatuses, then, some related to the drives and some to what will become ego functions, all influence the development of the ego.

It follows from this principle that the importance of a particular experience in molding further development depends upon the specific developmental phase of the child's ego, id, and superego. The loss of a father through death may have little direct impact on a child during the first few weeks of its existence, for the psychoanalytic theorists would hold its ego is not yet capable of forming object relations. What a different impact such an event would have during the fourth or fifth years of his life! Similarly, the lancing of an abcess in the groin would be a much more trivial procedure for a little boy during his second year of life—in spite of the pain and stress involved—than it would be some time later when the growth of phallic interests and concommitant castration fears have reached their peak. These examples make it clear that life experiences become crucial if, and only if, the demands or responses of the environment conflict with developments brought about by maturation, whether that maturation be of altered instinctual demands (id development) or of altered intellectual-physical apparatuses (ego development).

Implicit in the comments I have made thus far about the development of the ego has been a return to the middle period of the development of Freud's theorizing. Once again current conceptions of ego development and functioning stress the fact that the ego unfolds independently of the drives and that it has its own reservoir of psychic energy available for the accomplishment of its functions. From the beginning, many of the functions of the ego are autonomous in their relationships to drives and conflicts, although they may be later captured by conflicts (see below). Not only does the development of the instincts have an impact upon ego development, but these autonomous ego functions can and do serve as models for later instinctual sequences. To illustrate this, it has been suggested that the child's early experiences in learning to walk, the pleasure of initial experiences of the exultation of mastery alternating in cycles with the physical knocks and blows of falling and being hurt, give form to later castration fears as the child discovers its genitals. An expectancy is established that the joy of new experience, in this latter case libidinous, must be tempered with anxiety that such joy can quickly lead to direct physical pain (Hartmann, 1952).

It must also be obvious from what I am describing that current ego psychologists strongly stress the fact that the exercise of the ego's functions as they mature is in and of itself pleasurable; that there are sources of gratification in thinking, perceiving, remembering, exploring, moving, etc., which have little or nothing to do with libidinous gratifications. With such an assertion, psychoanalysts begin to find some common ground with such academic psychologists as Tolman (1932), Seward (1963), and Allport (1961), and with such humanistic psychologists as Buhler (1959) and Maslow (1962). The maturation of the ego, like a nuclear chain reaction, is circular and self-perpetuating. Maturational advances in one function facilitate advances in others. Increased perceptual sophistication aids memory, as does the development of language. Learning the difference between self and nonself brings about a shift in defense mechanisms now available to the growing child. The development of the capacity to locomote aids reality testing, for the growing child can now locate and contact things previously perceived only at a distance. These examples could be multiplied endlessly. It is sufficient to note, however, that as the ego's functions begin to coalesce because of maturation, the various apparatuses which mediate these functions become increasingly defined and viable and organized into a system "ego."

I will close this section on the maturation of the ego by ending where I began. That is, I wish to make a few observations on the differentiation of the systems, the growing separateness of the ego from the id as each develops from the undifferentiated phase. Man's protracted helplessness and his dependence upon the ministrations of those who care for him are both his curse and his blessing. While the relationship between object relations and ego development will be discussed in greater detail in the following section, it should be noted here that the ability to distinguish self from nonself is a fundamental step leading to the increasing differentiation between ego and id. The blind, unselfconscious need to survive gives way in this fashion to the need to be loved. The child comes to set portions of himself against the expression of other portions of himself, those expressions which bring displeasure and loss of love from parents and others significant in his immediate life. And as differentiation takes place between psychic systems, man becomes equipped with his very special, very precious organ of adaptation, the ego. This, ultimately, is what sets man apart from lower organisms. In animals, instincts mediate relationships with the environment. In man, adaptation is entrusted to another institution, the ego.

Object relations

Just as certain ego functions unfold "naturally," according to preordained developmental sequences, these very same ego functions are subject to, and thereby either facilitated or distorted by, the nature of the growing child's object relations. It is not an exaggeration to state that every phase in the differentiation of the psychic systems and in the development of ego functions corresponds to a step in the formation of stages in the development of the child's interactions with significant others. Both processes, differentiation of the psychic systems and relation of self to external objects, are interdependent.

Indeed, in order for the differentiation of id, ego, and superego to take place, it is necessary that the growing child be subjected to a degree of deprivation and/or restraint. This, of course, is inevitable because parents or their substitutes could never be completely and immediately gratifying to children. What current theorists now stress, however, are the positive consequences of an optimum level of interference with, frustration of, and socialization of childhood behavior. As long as the demand for immediate gratification prevails in the parent-child relationship, the absence of the care person is experienced as a threat. With repeated frustrations, however, signal anxiety begins to appear in the child's response repertoire. Through this signal the child learns to maintain the love and support of the environment, even in the face of the parent's absence, while at the same time more effectively achieving gratification by controlling immediate impulses. It also should be noted that other people are extremely important in the child's attempts to learn about reality. From the beginning the very ways a child acquires knowledge are subject to distortions, distortions inflicted upon him by the misrepresentations and idiosyncrasies of those who teach him. While pleasure and approval await the child who conforms to the demands of reality in his society, it should not be overlooked that such approval may be forthcoming for adapting to erroneous as well as correct views of reality. And these distortions can involve either outer or inner realities. Here language plays a paramount role in the learning process, since language itself is full of imprecisions and thereby the author of its own distortions. Thus every child learns a view of reality which is in part cultural convention and in part familial myth.

The Functions of the Mature Ego

In this section I will attempt to survey and synthesize the comments of various psychoanalytic theorists on those functions which characterize the operations of the mature ego.

Primary autonomous functions

Among the most basic, primitive, and primarily autonomous ego functions must be listed the motor functions of the organism. In the typically psychoanalytic manner of reifying concepts, Hartmann (1964) accords to portions of the ego the task of carrying out the imperatives of other segments of the ego and, indeed, of other functions belonging to the systems id and superego. The musculature is conceived of as being the vehicle for the final translation of inner urgings into actions in the world. As was noted, the development of motor functions is viewed as being primarily autonomous. Under ordinary circumstances increasing mastery and control by the organism of the motor apparatus is not a libidinal, conflict-laden process (although it may become involved in conflict, as in hysteria) but depends solely on the interaction of maturational forces with what Hartmann (1958) calls an "average expectable environment" for its flowering.

In addition to mastery of motor performance and coordination, certain cognitive processes are conceptualized by the ego psychologists as being primarily autonomous. Such things as the mechanisms of perception and the aptitudes ordinarily brought together under the rubric of intelligence are listed among the skills of the ego. Related domains of ego-functioning of particular familiarity to academic psychologists would, of course, include such things as memory, learning, comprehension, thinking, concept formation, verbal fluency, planning and anticipation, etc. All these conceptual tools for the organization, storage, retrieval, and internal reworking of the data of the senses allow man to profit from experience, to evaluate his current situation, and to plan purposefully for his future. They are viewed by the ego psychologists as unfolding under the impact of ordinary maturational developments in interaction with ordinary experiences from nuclei which are innately given by the nature of the organism. Again, only in psychopathological conditions do such attributes become distorted, abrogated, or involved in conflict.

Defenses

A further set of phenomena subsumed among those which collectively make up the ego consists of those functions that comprise the mechanisms of defense. These mechanisms have been and are one of the enduring concerns of psychoanalytic theory. It is assumed that the reader is reasonably familiar with Anna Freud's classic work on defense mechanisms (A. Freud, 1946), a publication which marked a significant post-Freudian attempt to bring order and coherence to a topic which cried out for systematic treatment. The comments which follow are offered as a description and amplification of still more recent attempts to explicate the operations involved in the functions of defense.

Defenses develop genetically from several different sources. Many of the sources of defense may be traced back to primarily autonomous preliminary stages of ego functions belonging to the earliest portions of the undifferentiated phase of development. One of Freud's initial descriptions of how the psyche functions (1920) contains the notion of a "stimulus barrier" which acts to dampen sensory input and to spare the tender organism from a traumatic influx of sensory energy. Whatever the neural processes involved in the operation of the stimulus barrier, it is now postulated that these processes come to be elaborated into such mechanisms of defense as denial and repression as the infant develops and increasing structural differentiation takes place. Hartmann (1958), taking an even more radical position, goes so far as to suggest that nuclei of defensive processes may exist in the undifferentiated phase even at birth and that already in the neonate there is a kind of beginning structural canalization which serves to oppose instinctual gratification.

Defenses coalesce not only out of processes in the newborn which later on in his life will be located under the label of ego but also out of processes later to be designated by the psychoanalytic id as well. Let me cite as an example those operations which are often referred to as introjection. Introjection originally appears during the earliest oral period as a libidinous device for psychically taking in and holding on to a love object from which some loss is threatened. Yet the mechanism of introjection forms the substrate out of which the defenses of incorporation and identification later arise with increasing differentiation of the maturing child.

Many maneuvers of the psyche labeled as defense by psychoanalytic theorists involve the cognitive rearrangement of perceptual events (Kovacs, 1958). Hartmann (1958) considers these kinds of defenses (displacement and projection, to note two examples) to be the unfolding of mechanisms whose beginnings may be found in the earliest modes of thought, so-called primary process thinking. The lack of organization of experience into categories of space, time, causality which characterizes primary process thought, as well as the ready and rapid displacement of cathexis from one idea to another, serve as the raw materials with which subsequent, more sophisticated cognitive defenses will be constructed. Thus the mechanisms of defense represent adaptive mechanisms which evolve out of raw materials already present during the undifferentiated phase of development, raw materials which, when they appear in adult life, may even be greeted as manifestations of systems other than the ego. Note that I have here stressed the importance of the mechanisms of defense as adaptive tools of the organism. Contemporary ego psychologists repeatedly point out that defense is not necessarily or even ordinarily to be equated with pathology. Many, many defenses are appropriate, reality-syntonic, adaptive, and necessary to man's very survival as a human being.

To close this section on current ego-psychological notions dealing with the nature and functions of the mechanisms of defense, some observations on the relationship between defenses, on the one hand, and character and personality, on the other, seem to be in order. Certain defense mechanisms permanently modify the structure of the personality and contribute importantly to individual uniqueness. Among the most potent of these are, for example, repression, identification, and reaction formation, all of which tend to give rise to enduring, highly stable character traits. The development of such defense mechanisms through maturation of the perceptual and motor raw materials out of which they are composed tends to hasten the growing differentiation and distancing between the id and the ego as the primary undifferentiated phase retreats into the past of earliest infancy. But more importantly, defenses of this type are among the foundation blocks of the personality. Indeed, it is often extremely difficult to draw a line between a personality trait and a defense; often it might be more accurate to consider, rather, how a given personality trait serves purposes of defense, synthesis, and adaptation, all at the same time.

The conflict-free areas of the system ego: its secondarily autonomous functions

It was previously noted that such functions of the organism as perception, memory, locomotion, etc., as they make their appearance in infancy, are not at first embroiled in conflict. But they may become so under the impact of the experiences involved in socialization and their ordinary directions may then be blocked, extirpated, or rechanneled. Conversely, as development proceeds, activities and functions emerge from the undifferentiated phase and from conflicted domains of the personality which can only be described in terms of their having achieved "secondary autonomy." That is, with developing maturity, certain skills, interests, aptitudes, and values emerge in the growing person and come to be exercised and pursued in their own right and not necessarily because they provide channels of discharge for id derivatives. These are conceived of as being endowed with neutralized energy and as being important nuclei around which the ego comes to be organized. Such functions are not necessarily coterminous with what had in the beginning been primarily autonomous functions, but they may share some elements in common with the latter.

Freud (1923) at one time felt that what appeared to be the ego's aims and interests grew out of the "self-preservative drive" and were therefore part of the id. The ego psychologists (Hartmann, 1964) point out that goals, values, interests, skills, aptitudes, etc., follow the "laws" of the ego—particularly reality testing—and not of the id. Their energy may indeed even be used against id satisfaction as, for example, when a writer sits down to write a long chapter on a technical subject for many hours at a time and in the process has to renounce companionship, rest, sometimes food, and many other necessary and desirable things. The degree of autonomy achieved by ego interests is a function of the degree to which these interests are invested with neutralized energy and are no longer in the service of the libidinous striving from which they might have developed but are now pursued in and of themselves. To state this another way, secondarily autonomous functions are pleasures offered to the individual through the exercise of the skills and interests of his ego as contrasted to the pleasures offered to him through id discharge or obedience to the imperatives of the superego. Secondary autonomy may be measured in terms of pleasure resulting from the activity itself as contrasted to pleasure derived from the effect of the activity. Here Hartmann comes close to the concept of "function pleasure" and possibly demonstrates the impact of an early apprenticeship served with the Buhlers.

Many of the ego's secondarily autonomous functions are experienced by the individual phenomenologically as "goals." These are hardly ever unconscious, that is, unavailable to introspection; but the degree to which they can be brought from the preconscious into clear conscious articulation serves as an additional measure of the degree to which goals have reached secondary autonomy. Again, an important point bears repeating. While goals may originate in the superego (as incorporated representations of the goals of those who socialized the growing child) or in id strivings, both kinds are potentially capable of being taken over by the ego and pursued autonomously. The ego's goals also may collaborate with or work against other ego functions. Thus the pursuit of the delights of intellectual interests may foster the achievement of a valued career. On the other hand, for example, devotion to the composition of a fugue may interfere with the immediate aim of earning a living. Note that secondarily autonomous functions are exercised in constant interaction with all other functions of the system ego. Lastly, the principles whereby the competing aims of the ego—indeed, of the entire personality—become harmonized are referred to by Hartmann (1958) as the organizing functions and by Nunberg (1948) as the synthetic functions of the ego, and serve as the next important domain of ego psychology to be discussed in this presentation.

Organizing functions

The organizing functions of the ego must be approached from three different points of concern: 1) self-preservation, 2) action, and 3) the reality principle. An understanding of these points is integral to an understanding of the process of bringing harmony to the disparate, often contradictory and competing, demands of various portions of the personality.

1. *Self-preservation.* Contemporary ego psychologists view the organism's attempts to maintain its integrity as a function of one portion of the organizing domain of the ego, not as an instinct or drive, as Freud

(1914) postulated during a period of his theoretical development. While the reality principle, libidinous strivings, and certain moral imperatives more clearly to be ascribed to the superego all participate in preserving the organism's existence, the role of these id, ego, and superego functions now is accorded a position in human survival secondary to a more central ego function, "self-preservation." In animals, instincts and innate drives tend to protect the organism from situations of danger which would threaten their existence. In man this burden has been more clearly laid upon the ego. The ego is the mediator between drives and the external world; drive representation cannot be actualized without the ego's intervention. This is not true in lower organisms. Stated another way, the self-preservation of animals is more closely tied to the pleasure principle. In man, however, self-preservation is more closely allied to perception, judgment, choice, and reality-testing ability.

In the earlier eras of psychoanalytic ego psychology, Freud (1920) postulated that aggression served self-preservation drives, thus involving himself in a cumbersome paradox: destruction somehow leads to self-preservation as it is turned outward and away from the individual. Contemporary ego psychologists have strong reservations about Freud's formulation of Thanatos as a guiding principle in mental life (Hartmann, 1955). It might be more fruitful and parsimonious to postulate that man is endowed with a certain quantum of free aggression, serving as the energizer of destructive acts which may then be directed either inward against the self or outward against things or others. But man also has the capacity to neutralize this energy and to sublimate the derivatives of his drives so that neutralized aggression thus can become available to the self-preservative areas of the ego. The ego psychologists would maintain, for example, that ultimately it was neutralized aggression which galvanized the Indian of the Pacific Northwest as he sat for hours patiently fashioning a wood and bone harpoon to use against the migrating salmon. But what transformation from crude "destructiveness" has to take place before such purposeful, integrated activity is possible! It also should be noted that the capacity to neutralize has a great deal of survival value. The Indian who simply attempted to crash boulders into the stream soon would starve to death.

2. *Action.* The second concept necessary to an understanding of current psychoanalytic notions about the organizing functions of the ego is the concept of action. Normal action is defined by an involvement with some intention directed toward some goal. In the beginning the neonate is primarily—but perhaps not totally—reactive. As development proceeds, reactive motor outlets are replaced by increasingly intentional, inte-

grated behaviors coincident with the internal mastery of the reality principle and the increasing differentiation occurring in the ego from which emerge goals and values. It must be noted, however, that while the control of action is an ego function, any concrete action most probably bears the stamp of all three psychic systems: id, ego, and superego, in varying proportions. Thus all systems influence action, and action serves any and all systems.

The ego's participation in the directing of action seems to be compounded out of at least three lesser functions of the system ego: anticipation, internalization, and objectification. The ability to anticipate is, of course, a prerequisite for any form of intentional act. The psychoanalytic theorists traditionally have stressed the importance of anxiety in helping the organism in the task of anticipation. And, indeed, they have usually been unable to conceptualize the possibility of anticipation as a characteristic of the infant before the use of anxiety as a signal had been partially mastered. But there is now developing agreement among ego psychologists and those active in the study of child development that a positive, directive, selective anticipation of a world in which to become active may not be nearly so dependent upon the development of signal anxiety as had been postulated and that it may exist at birth as a kind of innate predisposition of the human organism. Bernice Eiduson, in her contribution to this volume, notes that ". . . there has been a shift of thinking in recent years about the infant: previously thought to be a passive recipient of experiences, now regarded as an active seeker-out of experiences. The kinds of experiences that he seeks out are generally thought to be subsumed under a) those things which stimulate or interest him; b) those experiences which are likely to be pleasure giving; c) those experiences which may arouse tensions and in which there is some pleasure in the tension aroused itself; and d) those experiences which meet needs for exploratory drives. It is generally assumed that the infant seeks out persons and things and even in a certain repetitious manner seeks out and reseeks out those things which challenge him. Therefore, it is not so far-fetched to say that infants 'seek goals' or that their activity is purposeful. It is only far-fetched when we assume that the goals of infants are like adult goals—symbolic, indirect, sublimatory." [A fuller discussion of the theoretical issues involved may be found in an article by Charlotte Buhler (1954), cited with approval by Hartman (1964).] These changing notions about how the neonate orients toward the world of experience represent a vital, growing bridge between psychoanalysis and child study and represent a significant step forward in formulating a science of man.

It is now generally agreed, however, that as the ego matures and its skills are mastered, particularly perceptual, reality-testing, and judgment skills, and as certain kinds of inhibitions begin to be placed in the path of reflex action in response to the developing dependability of the anxiety signal, the growing person increasingly is able to find a variety of outlets for his wishes. In this way anticipation serves a facilitating as well as an inhibiting role.

The notion of internalization is a convenient shorthand label for the observable phenomenon that with increasing maturation there is a growing independence from the immediate impact of presenting stimuli. The psychoanalysts have typically viewed the neonate's response system to be one patterned on the nature of the reflex arc, stimulation leads easily and mechanically to response. While this view of the newborn's response repertoire is now at last being modified (see immediately above), there is agreement that with development there occurs a rapidly proliferating ability to work and rework "inside" the organism the information contained in stimuli and a consequent vastly increased range of response potentialities.

Finally, objectification refers to the differentiation of the self from the objects and people of the environment, both physically and mentally. This process, too, seems to be crucial in aiding the shift from reflex to intentional action.

An interesting sidelight to the topic of action concerns the relationship between action and insight. Hartmann (1947) stresses the necessary interdependence of these two complementary modes of relating to the external world. Insight into reality—that is, the internal registering, assimilating, reworking, "understanding," and planning which make use of the perceptual and cognitive apparatus—serves to guide a great deal of the action of the mature person. Yet the data gained in the pursuit of action also function as a most crucial means of acquiring further knowledge about the world and of promoting additional insight. Both sets of functions interpenetrate and are synergistic to each other in normal adaptation. In such psychopathological syndromes as the obsessive-compulsive disorders or in phobias, we can see how the ordinary synergy can be disrupted.

Let us now turn to a consideration of the roles of both rational and irrational actions in human affairs. It must first be noted that action most often is in the pursuit of some aim, or end, as opposed to instinctual behavior which simply presses for discharge. Normally the "ends" of given actions are usually only turning points. Life is a flux with the achievement of the aim of any particular action serving as a platform upon which to mount a progression toward the aim of some subsequent action. Thus the child is toilet-trained to prepare him for attendance at nursery school so, in turn, he can be better prepared for kindergarten, which will help him adjust to elementary school in preparation for mastery of the skills to be imparted in junior high school so that he might get the grades necessary in high school for attendance at the college of his choice, which will prepare him for a career in which he might be able to pursue economic affluence and become a consumer of . . . ad infinitum. Some ends, however, seem to become relatively fixed and resistant to change. For most people there is a rather large set of aims which are pursued repetitively for long periods of the life span, and these seem to be rather impervious to modification or resistant to renunciation under the impact of experience. The ego psychologists maintain that such "fixed ends" usually are in the service of the superego and have been incorporated en masse from the agents of the child's socialization. Man's acceptance of, indeed, his enshrining of, certain "unchangeable goals" seems to be a very human characteristic, although the nature of what constitutes the good to be striven for varies immensely from culture to culture. Kaiser (1965) maintains that man is in perpetual flight from a sense of his own separateness, his own aloneness. Eternal verities provide man with a "delusion of fusion," which gives rise to the subjective experience of certainty and serves as a buffer against the anxiety of his existential plight. Hartmann (1947) agrees that the pursuit of fixed goals can indeed have usefully adaptive consequences and cautions, as in the case of the concept of defense, against labelling behavior which is in the pursuit of rigid goals as being in and of itself pathological.

The terms "rational" and "irrational" tend to be bandied about by personality theorists without much concern for semantic precision. For the psychoanalytic ego psychologist, the concept of the rational is defined in terms of logically "correct" thinking; it implies a consideration of empirical facts and their connections according to commonly accepted rules of logic. "Irrational" is reserved for processes which are predominately affective or instinctual. The irrational follows the laws of the primary process; the mental representations of the instincts are irrational as are the representations of other kinds of unconscious material (i.e., derivatives of the repressed). Conceptions of rational and irrational do not imply value judgments about the "goodness" or "healthiness" of the thought processes to which these labels are applied. Rather, they are employed in a strictly descriptive fashion and are not meant to imply anything further.

Hartmann (1947) particularly is concerned with the excess meaning which many of his colleagues and other personality theorists attach to the notion of the rational. It is not uncommon for "rational" to be equated with "reasonable" or "appropriate" at various points in the literature on human behavior. This equation only has some validity if what is considered reasonable or appropriate is in itself based upon the exercise of intelligence, insight, and logical thought. Far too often, however, the reasonable or the appropriate in human affairs is so labelled on the basis of value judgments rather than of empirical knowledge. It was both reasonable and appropriate, for example, for the British to behave in an imperialistic fashion during the last century, given certain assumptions about the moral and intellectual inferiority of distant national groups and a paternalistic desire to "bear the white man's burden" by bringing the fruits (?) of British civilization to such poor, benighted people. The assumptions of racial inferiority by which such actions were buttressed have proven to have had a shaky empirical base. What had smugly appeared to be rational behavior now appears merely to have been "reasonable" behavior based on exploitative and self-aggrandizing values.

The concept of the rational also tends to merge indiscriminately with a glorification of rationalism in the writing of some theorists (cf., Ellis and Harper, 1961). For such thinkers, effective human action must ultimately stem from a certain omnipotence of the intellect. Man is most effective when he most apes the computer; fantasies, wishes, and affects are useless noise in man's information circuits. On the other side of the debate, certain Eastern philosophies and Western psychotherapists (cf., Perls, Hefferline, and Goodman, 1958) tend to focus on the irrational as the ultimate wellspring from which effective human action must flow and tend to minimize the importance of cognition and the role of empirical knowledge in providing a crucial portion of its foundation. The ego psychologists feel that overemphasis on either rationalism or irrationalism is not helpful in seeking an understanding of man. Insight into the nature of man's rational actions must contain a synthesis of both poles.

We come at last to the essence of rational action. Rational action is behavior which is directed according to means, ends, and consequences. It involves a balancing of ends against means, means against consequences, and ends against each other. These calculations are carried out on both conscious and preconscious levels, and the calculations involve both inner and outer reality. To some extent, the skills involved in rational action are independent from one another. That is, one person may have an excellent facility for balancing means against ends but be very poor at appraising certain portions of his reality situation. Conversely, another may be excellent at apprehending his own inner states and the nature of the world about him yet lack the tools for weighing the implications of various courses of action. And, as a final note, it must be observed that the goals toward which action is directed are in and of themselves neither rational nor irrational. Such terms can be applied to goals only when the goals in question are part of a complex of a larger ends-means configuration as turning points on the way to yet more distant ends.

Hartmann (1947) also notes that rational action need not be either "useful" nor serve the self-preservative portions of the ego. What any particular society defines as being "useful" usually is invested with both id gratifications and superego values. Typical of many different cultures, however, is a philosophy which holds that those actions are useful which lead a person toward greater social status, influence, success, wealth, or comfort, as these actions are defined in the particular instance. While such goals may be traced genetically to instinctual roots, as differentiation takes place they often become secondarily autonomous and desired in their own right. The pursuit of usefulness can be carried too far. Every clinician is familiar with the middle-class man on the make for success who seems to caricature all the "right" middle-class virtues, yet he exists alienated from contentment, isolated from those whom he professes to love, and prey to depression and psychosomatic problems. Sometimes what is truly rational consists in the renunciation of what is useful.

As was noted, the concept of rational action does not imply the pursuit of self-preservation either. Self-preservation is organized by a portion of the ego but involves participation of functions belonging to all systems of the personality. If "rational" is reserved for that behavior which protects or enhances self-preservation, then the special meaning of the term is lost. Indeed, if we remember that rational is to be reserved only for those behaviors logically directed in terms of means, ends, and consequences, then the self-immolation of the Buddhist monks in protest of the Saigon regime may fully merit the label "rational," if we assume that the monks are deeply cognizant of their inner states, of the pain to be endured, of the fact of their death and its meaning, and the possible utility of death in galvanizing public opinion and social action. To sum up, the concept of rational behavior is not a magic one. It does not inevitably refer to actions which are either useful or in the service of self-preservation.

There is, then, an undeserved tendency in our society to equate the rational with the healthy, the good and/or the right. The reality is that rational action well may be put to destructive and even self-destructive uses. Yet this tendency to lump rational action with other positive attributes is a useful illustration of another principle of ego psychology: man tends toward an agglutination of values. That is, elements of human behavior which are positively valued in human affairs tend, in man's mind, to be identified together or even to be connected causally. The ego psychologists point out that man often makes spurious connections between phenomena which are based on a common value judgment rather than on facts. And, to borrow a leaf from learning theory, there is also a tendency toward an irradiation of values in man's perceptual apparatus. If a segment of behavior is valued positively in a culture, then the phenomena which surround it also will tend to be valued positively, and vice versa. Here we may observe a mixing of superego schema with ego schema and can clearly note that the superego is organized in layers which are governed by the rules of primary process thought and not by the rules of reality testing.

3. *The reality principle.* The third set of phenomena which seems to underlie the organizing functions of the ego is that which is traditionally subsumed under the notion of the reality principle. The concept is employed in at least two different senses in psychoanalytic literature: it can refer to the use of the ego to appraise "real" features of both the inner and outer worlds or to the ego's restraint of the immediate tensions inherent in id strivings. In the second sense, the reality principle at first glance seems to be opposed to the more hedonistic pleasure principle which Freud claimed inherent in all human activity. The latter-day ego psychologists, however, prefer to resolve the issue by asserting that the reality principle itself is merely the ego's attempt to secure "assured" pleasures in the future, pleasures which can be reached only through planning and appropriate appraisals of reality. In this sense, hedonism is retained. Indeed, man even engages in the exercise of autonomous ego functions, so the current argument goes, because such exercise gives him pleasure in and of itself. Turning to reality in the search of gratification, therefore, is seen as being ultimately in the service of the pleasure principle and involves ego functions in the areas of cognition, purposeful action, postponement, and anticipation. In this fashion, man exchanges the uncertainties of immediate gratification for the more lasting delights of future, assured ones.

Thus the ego ultimately uses the pleasure principle in order to gain mastery over inner and outer reality. The maturing child does not renounce instinctual gratification only to avoid punishment and to secure the love and approval of his parents. Quanta of pleasure also may be obtained by participation in the adults' world. While it seems paradoxical, the implication of these observations is that there is pleasure in giving up pleasure, and this in itself provides a strong motivating force for the child in accepting the demands of the reality principle.

Throughout this section the term "reality" has been employed rather uncritically. Hartmann (1956), however, attempts to explicate the meaning of the term from a psychological point of view. He holds that two kinds of knowledge contribute to man's apprehension of reality: objective knowledge marked by verifiability and empirical validation, and socialized knowledge of a more conventional kind marked by a rather uncritical, intersubjective acceptance. The former is inevitably contaminated by the latter; only at distant times and places does man often become aware of how large a part value judgments play in what poses as objective thinking. It is, of course, easy for the contamination to take place. The world of experience—and it is, after all, only the world of immediate experience that man can ever directly apprehend—is not easy to define. It is clear that the world of experience and the scientific world are not coterminous; science often deals with variables not available to direct experience. It also is clear that coherence and organization markedly affect the assimilation of "reality" perception; dissonance with an already existing apperceptive mass is likely to result in some disturbance in the use of objective knowledge. What we call reality, then, is formed by the nature of our own histories which unfold in a particular time and place and by the nature of the mental apparatus itself. Adults, through the organizing function of the ego, establish a working, but constantly changing, equilibrium between objective knowledge and inner and outer subjective worlds. In this fashion the economic and dynamic status of knowledge is given to change through its continuous interplay within the psychic structure which characterizes man.

Adaptation

The ego psychologists are much more concerned about how man "fits in" to his physical and social environment than were the early psychoanalytic pioneers. Freud (1920) tied adaptation closely to the workings of the reality principle. Faced with a conflict between inner urgings and outer reality, man had only two choices: to modify himself (autoplastic) or to act against the environment (alloplastic). Hartmann (1947), in particular, has greatly enlarged these early notions. He not only has contributed a description of a third possible solution to the dilemma of human existence—a change in the relationship between inner and outer, e.g., searching for and finding a more appropriate environment for oneself—but has vastly expanded psychoanalytic notions about the nature of those variables which are involved in bringing about effective adaptation.

Current thinking emphasizes that adaptation is not simply a consequence of the learning of the reality principle. Indeed, it is not even entirely the province of the ego, although the ego is most powerfully involved in the constant struggle for adaptation. The id and the superego both have their important roles to play in adaptation, too. In this regard it is erroneous, for example, to take for granted that rational behavior necessarily leads to effective adjustment to the demands of the environment. There are a myriad of activities necessary to man's effective performance which only can unfold in an adequate fashion if reason is held in abeyance. For example, many behaviors involved in man's very survival are carried out in an automatic fashion organized at a preconscious level (reactions in the moments before an automobile accident, to name one instance), behaviors which, if deautomatized, might result in disaster. And it should be noted, conversely, that some forms of neurotic symptoms are manifested as a hyperrational reviewing of reactions which ought otherwise to go on without reflection.

While it is true that the inability to withhold action directed toward momentary pleasure in order to secure greater gain through the medium of rational action often interferes with adequate adaptation, the other side of the coin may be equally valid. That is, if goals are only the means to greater ends all organized by some logical plan, nothing can be enjoyed in and of itself. Man's behavior under such conditions is incomplete, provisional, and dehumanized. Means-ends calculations may run wild and not be adaptive at all. Or, from a slightly different point of view, highly differentiated functions, such as rational action, do not guarantee optimum adjustment. These functions need to be coordinated and supplemented by other systems, some even on a much more primitive level. The totally rational human being is a hollow caricature of himself!

It may be said, then, that there is an important place for regressive, archaic processes in effective adaptation. Even in scientific inquiry, a detour into irrational elements of thinking often is a way station on the path to discovery. The use of symbolic elements and visual imagery has played a powerful role in man's increasing mastery over his physical environment. And in the field of the arts, regression in the service of the ego (Kris, 1952) is an essential ingredient in the process of creative or artistic production. "Mental health," therefore, cannot be evaluated simply on the basis of the admixture of the rational and the primitive in the life of a given individual. On the contrary, any evaluation of adaptation must rest ultimately on the nature of the equilibrium between substructures of the personality and the total personality's relationship to the environment. A related issue involves adaptation and conformity. The ego psychologists caution against equating these two concepts. Although "conforming to conventions" or acting out of "common sense" may be practical and efficient and lead to approbation from the environment, such actions may not serve the whole personality optimally. True adaptation involves attention to inner and outer, self and society, rational and irrational, and gratification and delay. Emphasis on any one of these poles violates the real meaning of adaptation.

Neutralization

The final ego function which captures a great deal of attention from current psychoanalytic theorists concerns the ego's role in the control and distribution of so-called psychic energy. Freud wrestled all his life with the question of whether or not all the energy available to man was ultimately sexual in nature. Current thinking, however, accords to aggression a status equal to sexuality. Aggression is viewed as an independent drive which seeks discharge on its own and not merely as a response to deprivation or restraint. The economic function of such discharge is not solely the release of energy which otherwise would be self-destructive, but seems to provide quanta of pleasure as well. Yet man's aggression leads to conflict with important others; as development proceeds, this outer conflict soon is partially transformed into an inner conflict between libidinal and aggressive wishes directed toward the same object. For enduring human relationships, both libidinal and aggressive drives must, in the end, be tamed—subjected to some degree of neutralization—and it is this process, carried out by the ego, which has attracted a great deal of theoretical interest (Colby, 1960; Hartmann, Kris, and Lowenstein, 1949; Hartmann, 1964).

It seems to be the current consensus that the energy which ultimately galvanizes the ego is partially desexualized and deaggressivized energy and partially derived from a preexistent pool of drive energy belonging to the primary ego functions. The concept of neutralized energy is one which carries with it the notion of degree, of gradations. All neutralized energy is not neutralized to the same degree and may, to a greater or lesser extent, retain some of its original drive properties. For example, the postulated relationship between sadism and the profession of surgery may be much more intense in some individuals than in others. Both the amount and extent of energy that is neutralized provide significant clues to an individual's ego strength and resistance to psychological stress. The less the energies are neutralized—remaining closer to their original drives—the greater are the possibilities for psychopathological reactions.

Neutralization is effected by the ego by two mechanisms: a shift in mode of discharge and a shift in aims or directions. The first of these processes refers to a binding, a slowing down, of the discharge of energy, the gradual renunciation of primary process organization in favor of secondary process organization. The second mechanism involves either a kind of "taming" of the intensity of discharge or a displacement of its target, or both. The extent to which the original aim has been changed is indicative of the degree of neutralization.

To sum up, then, the ego neutralizes libidinal and aggressive energy and is, in turn, further enhanced in its functioning by the pool of neutralized energy so created. Such energy at the disposal of the ego exists in all shades and gradations of neutralization. In this sense, current theorists no longer see man as at the mercy of his biology but are struggling to understand the means by which he is able to escape being the victim of his drives. Through the concept of neutralization they have provided a set of notions about the means by which man may master and transcend the raw givens of his being.

CRITIQUE

Psychoanalytic ego psychology perhaps may best be evaluated as a coherent theoretical system concerned with the development of man-in-the-world by contrasting it to another point of view which, for want of a better term, might simply be called self-theory. While self-theory lacks the sense of systematization characteristic of ego psychology, many of its organizing concepts are such as to throw the philosophical roots of ego psychology into the boldest, most stark relief. I shall organize this discussion, then, around four nuclear issues: man as a machine versus man as a person; biological reductionism versus human interaction; energy versus growth; and synthesis versus self-actualization. In each of these polarities, as will be obvious below, the first term represents a primitive, often unexplicated, assumption of ego psychology, while the second constitutes an opposing stance taken by the proponents of self-theory.

Man as a Machine Versus Man as a Person

Psychoanalytic ego psychology remains anchored to the rationalism and empirical optimism of the nineteenth century and to the medical training not only of Freud but of most of its latter-day advocates. As such, it adopts the principle that the most efficient way to go about understanding the nature of man is to assume that he is analogous to a machine, that the processes which define him can be understood best through the empirical method, and that the kind of empiricism which characterizes the physical and biological sciences—while hard to achieve at the present stage of psychoanalytic knowledge—would represent the ultimate means of assessing man. It is for these reasons that psychoanalytic concepts are cast in the mold of "functions," of "mechanisms," of "structures," and of "energies." In this fashion the model of man is that of a cunning computer hooked both to sensing devices and tools for carrying out actions, the whole being funded with energy produced not by storage batteries but by chemical processes in biological tissue. If sufficient human computers are investigated and analyzed by the psychoanalytic method, general laws for their operation can be devised, based on the regularities in all human computers.

Many theorists of different persuasions are extremely unhappy with such philosophical orientations. For psychologists of a more humanistic bent the model of man as a machine not only does not aid but does violence to the study of man and may even have destructive heuristic implications. Polanyi (1958), for example, insists that man must be studied *as a person.* To consider man as a unique person rather than as a variant of a common mechanical contrivance, Polanyi maintains, leads not only to a different kind of science than that predicated on classical physics and the rationalism of the nineteenth century, but to a science which may, in the long run, give man the tools with which he might better deal with his fate. The data of the kind of science advocated by Polanyi would be better gathered on the basis of personal participation and shared experiencing with the human being or beings to be studied. Participant-observation, rather than the subject-object dichotomy, as in the physical sciences, may be the key to fuller mastery of the secrets of man's nature. And from such an orientation have come new developments in psychotherapeutic technique. Interested readers may wish to look at Kovacs (1965, 1966) and at Bugental (1965) for more detailed expositions of this point of view.

Allport (1961) also is critical of what he considers to be inappropriate scientism in the field of personality theorizing. He makes use of the distinction between nomothetic laws (the kind sought by the physical sciences) which apply to objects of a given class, and ideographic laws which seek to make predictions about the unique case. Through extensive use of personal documents, Allport is able to make a convincing case for the utility of the ideographic approach in exploring, understanding, and predicting the course of the life of a single individual. Whatever the appeal of an approach to man based upon the model of the machine in an age devoted to the machine, to engineering, to the physical sciences, and to medicine, the work of the kinds of personality theorists described here makes it clear that such an orientation may indeed not be the most useful or the richest nor provide us with the ultimate principles which will allow man not only to survive but to flourish as man.

Biological Reductionism Versus Human Interaction

This polarity is related to, but not coterminous with, the one above. It is concerned with the question of the ultimate determinants of man's nature. Psychoanalytic ego psychology remains closely tied to man's biological endowment. The core task for man as posed by the ego psychologists is one of finding suitable outlets for the discharge of biological energy within the confines of a society which has taboos and mores about such matters. In the painful course of learning this kind of control, man develops an ego, a piece of regulating machinery, which gives him his particular flavor: the ultimate meaning of life for man lies in the efficient reduction of biological tension while, at the same time, keeping to a minimum the friction which such reduction might cause with the environment.

Several disparate groups of personality theorists, some of quite distant theoretical persuasions, question the dependence of man's nature on man's biology. Both C. Buhler (1933) and Balint (1952) seriously question whether man is indeed only a biological organism even at the very beginning of his existence. Buhler and her students have carried out an interesting set of experiments based upon observations of children in earliest infancy. They seem to suggest that the neonate is, in fact, oriented toward and responsive to other human beings from the dawn of his life. These data are consistent with the thinking of Balint, who is a psychoanalyst. He questions the basic assumption of primary narcissism upon which much of psychoanalytic theory is built. For Balint, libidinal drives—the seeking of pleasure—are *from the very beginning* intimately tied to the search for an object, an "other," with whom to interact. Libidinal development itself, according to Balint, depends on "good" human commerce.

Fairburn (1952) and Guntrip (1961) also are convinced that from birth man is searching for satisfactory interaction with others. These two members of the so-called English school of psychoanalysis go even further, however. They insist that man's nature can be understood only as the precipitate of his experiences with the other persons with whom he has interacted and with whom he continues to interact. Indeed, even the expression of his "biological nature" is not truly biological in origin but is created out of interpersonal commerce. In this fashion man creates his id as well as his ego. These two theorists forcefully warn against what they consider to be the fallacy of reductionism in an attempt to understand man. Man is not the same thing as the human body. The ultimate explanation of man's essence must be a psychological one and not a physiological one.

Finally, the contributions of Erikson (1950) to this controversy richly deserve to be mentioned. He, as much as anyone, has done a great deal to elucidate how man comes to bear his unique stamp. He parts from his psychoanalytic colleagues in refusing to view human development as a process merely involving the unfolding of the "instincts." Development is a much more complex task, according to Erikson, consisting of the search for solutions to phase-specific demands which emerge from the interaction between biological maturation and social expectations. The search extends throughout the span of the life cycle and may be divided into eight nuclear conflicts: trust versus mistrust; autonomy versus shame and/or doubt; initiative versus guilt; industry versus inferiority; identity versus identity diffusion; intimacy versus isolation; generativity versus self-absorption; and integrity versus disgust and/or despair. Erikson sees man not as searching for surcease from biological tension but as concerned with the forging of a viable identity which will give meaning, purpose, and coherence to his life within the confines of his particular culture.

Energy Versus Growth

It should be clear from the above comments that the ego-psychological image of man has him tied to what Maslow (1955) calls "deficiency motivation." Man appears to be a closed energy system when viewed from the psychoanalytic framework. External stimulation or internal changes in homeostasis result in the accumulation of energies which then must be discharged to reduce the organism once again to some optimal level of tension. While some of the organism's energy is primarily autonomous and some is neutralized, giving rise to aims and activities which are relatively distant from the instincts, man is yet conceived of as an annihilator of tension, as a being whose highest purpose is to discharge energy of one kind or another. Maslow disagrees quite intensely with such a philosophy and argues instead that man's orientation is at least as often toward growth, toward fulfillment, rather than toward the overcoming of some state of arousal or deprivation.

Erikson (1950) and C. Buhler (1964) seem to agree with Maslow and, from slightly differing points of view, stress the importance to man of the development of a coherent self: a self marked by self-awareness; by an understanding of the roots of his existence in a past personal, social, and cultural world, and by the possession of a schema for projecting his fate into his own personal future. For Erikson, the creation of this identity is a true work of art. The self works and reworks the raw materials of existence to produce that coherent organization of meaning and self-knowledge which gives life as it is being lived a sense of purpose and direction. Man hungers for purpose in his life as much or more than he hungers for biological satiation. To these notions, C. Buhler (in press) adds that man's striving for wholeness and for synthesis is characteristic not only of the cross-section of his inner and outer life at a particular moment in time. Indeed, it is possible to view one person's entire life and see that his whole life course bears evidence of a strain toward longitudinal synthesis as well. Without coherence, growth, intentionality, and meaning, man's biological being can survive; but somehow man himself, in all his personhood, cannot.

Ego as Synthesizer Versus the Self as an Unfolding Actualizer

We have come at last to the heart of the quarrel between the psychoanalytic ego psychologists and those I have chosen to label the self-theorists. For the psychoanalysts, man's uniqueness is to be found in the particular flavor of his ego, with its manifold mechanisms which mediate defense and adaptation. The ego is a juggler which takes pleasure in its own performance, tossing and catching inner urgings, energy accumulations, outer demands, and its perception of outer possibilities. Yet the ego has little life apart from its role as a juggler. Hartmann (1958) is unequivocally clear that "fitting together," or synthesis, is the highest aim of the ego.

The self-theorists feel that such a view of the uniqueness of man is quite limited. Man, so they insist, is really a teleological creature. Maslow (1962) stresses man's purposefulness; that is, that man's self is endowed with certain potentials, the unfolding and actualizing of which constitute man's life work. May (1958) describes what he calls man's "movement toward something." By this, May means that man can find his humanity only through the transcendence of the achievement of simple survival. Man, May argues, must find meaning in existence, if he is to be man.

These contemporary anatomists of the self are part of a growing cultural stream in psychology, a stream which owes a debt to such pioneers as Goldstein (1939), Fromm (1941), and Horney (1945). Many persons, although in somewhat different ways, see man as being endowed with tendencies toward growth, toward the realization and actualization of potentials which inhere in and define the self. From this point of view man is not a mechanism, not a set of integrated operations, and not a collection of functions. On the contrary, man first and foremost is a person, who lives, grows, and creates with purposes and intents which often transcend the boundaries of his own self.

Our understanding of the nature of man is in its infancy. I have tried within the limits of these few pages to describe one set of notions about his essence which is currently enjoying a great deal of popularity and to criticize these notions using the conceptual tools of another orientation. It is only through the free exchange of intellectual wares in the market place of ideas that knowledge can be advanced. Which of these two competing orientations will ultimately stand the test of accumulated experience is impossible to predict—probably neither of them. It is likely that some new theoretical scaffold will be erected which borrows planks from both. But whatever scaffolds subsequent generations erect, it may be that man will never quite be hung on any of them. My personal hunch is that our intellectual endowment can only let us approximate him; in some ways man is destined to remain an eternal mystery.

References

Allport, G. W. *Pattern and growth in personality.* New York: Holt, Rinehart and Winston, 1961.

Balint, M. *Primary love and psychoanalytic technique.* London: Hogarth Press, 1952.

Breuer, J., and Freud, S. *Studies on hysteria.* New York: Basic Books, 1957.

Bugental, J. F. T. *The search for authenticity.* New York: Holt, Rinehart and Winston, 1965.

Buhler, C. *Der menschliche Lebenslauf als psychologisches Problem.* Leipzig: S. Hirzel, 1933.

Buhler, C. The reality principle: discussion of theories and observational data, *Amer. J. Psychother.,* 1954, *8,* 626-647.

Buhler, C. Theoretical observations about life's basic tendencies, *Amer. J. Psychother.,* 1959, *13,* 561-581.

Buhler, C. The human course of life in its goal aspects, *Journal of Humanistic Psychology,* 1964, *4,* 1-17.

Buhler, C. Human life as a whole as a central subject of humanistic psychology. In J. F. T. Bugental, *Perspectives in Humanistic Psychology.* In press.

Colby, K. M. *Energy and structure in psychoanalysis.* New York: International Universities Press, 1960.

Ellis, A., and Harper, R. A. A *guide to rational living.* Englewood Cliffs, N.J.: Prentice-Hall, 1961.

Erikson, E. *Childhood and society.* New York: W. W. Norton, 1950.

Fairburn, W. R. D. *Psychoanalytical studies of the personality*. New York: Basic Books, 1952.

Freud, A. *The ego and the mechanisms of defense*. New York: International Universities Press, 1946.

Freud, S. On narcissism (1914). *Collected papers, 4*. London: Hogarth Press, 1953.

Freud, S. Beyond the pleasure principle (1920). *Standard edition, 18*. London: Hogarth Press, 1953.

Freud, S. The ego and the id (1923). *Standard edition, 19*. London: Hogarth Press, 1953.

Freud, S. *The problem of anxiety*. New York: W. W. Norton, 1936.

Freud, S. Analysis terminable and interminable (1937). *Collected papers, 5*. London: Hogarth Press, 1953.

Freud, S. *The origins of psychoanalysis: letters to Wilhelm Fliess*. New York: Basic Books, 1954.

Freud, S. The psychology of the dream processes. Ch. 7, *The interpretation of dreams*. New York: Basic Books, 1955.

Fromm, E. *Escape from freedom*. New York: Rinehart, 1941.

Goldstein, K. *The organism*. New York: American Book, 1939.

Guntrip, H. *Personality structure and human interaction*. New York: International Universities Press, 1961.

Hartmann, H. On rational and irrational action. *Psychoanalysis and the social sciences, 1*. New York: International Universities Press, 1947.

Hartmann, H. Comments on the psychoanalytic theory of the ego. *Psychoanalytic study of the child, 5*. New York: International Universities Press, 1950.

Hartmann, H. The mutual influences in the development of the ego and id. *Psychoanalytic study of the child, 8*. New York: International Universities Press, 1952.

Hartmann, H. Notes on the theory of sublimation. *Psychoanalytic study of the child, 10*. New York: International Universities Press, 1955.

Hartmann, H. Notes on the reality principle. *Psychoanalytic study of the child, 11*. New York: International Universities Press, 1956.

Hartmann, H. *Ego psychology and the problem of adaptation*. New York: International Universities Press, 1958.

Hartmann, H. *Essays on ego psychology*. New York: International Universities Press, 1964.

Hartmann, H., Kris, E., and Lowenstein, R. M. Comments on the formation of psychic structure. *Psychoanalytic study of the child, 2*. New York: International Universities Press, 1946.

Hartmann, H., Kris, E., and Lowenstein, R. Notes on the theory of aggression. *Psychoanalytic study of the child, 3-4*. New York: International Universities Press, 1949.

Horney, K. *Our inner conflicts*. New York: W. W. Norton, 1945.

Kaiser, H. *Effective psychotherapy*. New York: Free Press, 1965.

Kovacs, A. L. Some antecedents of denial in fantasy as a defense against anger. Unpublished doctoral dissertation. Ann Arbor: University of Michigan, 1958.

Kovacs, A. L. The intimate relationship: a therapeutic paradox, *Psychotherapy: Theory, Research and Practice*, 1965, *2*, 97-103.

Kovacs, A. L. Further remarks on psychotherapy as an intimate relationship, *Psychotherapy: Theory, Research and Practice*, 1966, *3*, 53-60.

Kris, E. *Psychoanalytic explorations in art*. New York: International Universities Press, 1952.

Maslow, A. H. Deficiency motivation and growth motivation. In R. M. Jones (ed.), *Nebraska symposium on motivation*. Lincoln: University of Nebraska, 1955.

Maslow, A. H. *Toward a psychology of being*. Princeton: Van Nostrand, 1962.

May, R., Angel, E., and Ellenberger, H. F. (eds.). *Existence, a new dimension in psychiatry and psychology*. New York: Basic Books, 1958.

Nunberg, H. The syntetic function of the ego. *Practice and theory of psychoanalysis.* New York: Nervous and Mental Disease, 1948.
Perls, F., Hefferline, R. F., and Goodman, P. *Gestalt therapy.* New York: Julian Press, 1958.
Piaget, J. *The origins of intelligence in children.* New York: International Universities Press, 1955.
Polanyi, M. *Personal knowledge.* Chicago: The University of Chicago Press, 1958.
Rapaport, D. *Organization and pathology of thought.* New York: Columbia University Press, 1951.
Seward, J. P. The structure of functional autonomy. *Am. Psychologist,* 1963, *11,* 703-710.
Tolman, E. C. *Purposive behavior in animals and men.* New York: Appleton-Century, 1932.
Waelder, R. The problem of freedom in psychoanalysis and the problem of reality-testing, *Int. J. Psa.,* 1936, *17,* 89-108.

Chapter 10

Early Environmental Influences on Goal Setting

Charlotte Bühler

From the beginning of the child's life, he is influenced by his environment, both in terms of emotional impact as well as in terms of a formative power. The emotional impact seems strongest in the early stages, when the infant is most vulnerable and sensitive to the treatment he receives from his parents. The formative process takes place more gradually and largely through his training and teaching.

It is well known that a child's perception and understanding of what he is expected to absorb and learn are greatly colored by the emotional relationships he establishes within his environment. We have made an attempt, therefore, to distinguish between the direct emotional impact of the early environment (Part III) and the ideational orientation that it consciously or unconsciously conveys (Part IV).

The major emotional impacts of an infant's early environment are love and care, and demands and discipline. The nature of these relationships influences a young child's motivation and goal setting and, indirectly, his reactions to the information and opportunities the environment offers, as well as his identification with the models and ideals his parents represent and recommend to him.

Love and care

There is no doubt that good care by a loving mother or mother-figure is a basic requirement for an infant's healthy emotional growth. Two recent reviews by Bettye M. Caldwell (1964) and Leon J. Yarrow (1964) of the literature in this field provide us with an excellent summary of available information. Caldwell concludes from her survey that while the effects of different practices in infant care still are debatable, parental attitudes seem to be of greater consequence than parental behavior. Yarrow's survey of studies of "separation from parents in early childhood" confirms the generally held conviction that maternal care is practically irreplaceable. The quality of this maternal care and of the mother-child relationship, however, does play a role, as do the individually varying needs of the infant.

How does the emotional impact of adequate or inadequate maternal love and care affect a child's goal setting? Love and care satisfy the infant's needs, thus fulfilling one of his basic tendencies. This need satisfaction, in turn, provides the security which enables him to venture out into the world, engage in activities, and make contacts with others. The large number of studies on institutionalized children indicates that such children are unable to develop adequate relationships with people. R. Spitz and K. Wolf (1964) demonstrated that withdrawal from the environment is one of their most general reactions; Bowlby (1944) and Bender (1947) concluded from their clinical studies that "maternal separation is a specific etiological agent in the development of psychopathic personalities" (Yarrow, p. 104), or of "affectionless characters," as Bowlby calls them—persons, that is, who are incapable of experiencing genuine feelings.

A high quality of maternal love and care, on the other hand, seems to prepare the child for emotional contacts with other people and to supply enough confidence to encourage the exploration of new situations. Unfortunately we lack reliable data about the positive effects of favorable backgrounds.

The following case history may serve as a brief illustration.

> Bonnie is a little girl, aged 3. She is the older of two girls of a young couple whose marriage appears to be a happy one. Mrs. Rees, an attractive 25-year-old woman, is interested in developmental tests and likes to avail herself of the benefit of regular checkups and advice regarding her children. She is devoted to her family and her home and enjoys both. She is intelligent, gentle, gay, and efficient, and takes seriously her relationship with her husband and children. Mr. Rees, an

engineer, has not shown much interest in his children so far. He adores his wife and is somewhat jealous of the attention she gives the girls. Bonnie reveals no signs of frustration over this situation as yet, but she does not pay much attention to her father when he is around, which is not very often.

Interestingly enough, her equilibrium is not shaken by her father's obvious lack of attention. How much she craved for it, though, became apparent some time later when her father suddenly began to take an interest in his bright little daughter.

Bonnie showed unusual poise when she arrived with her mother to take the test. She smiled at the examiner, though a little uncertainly. She sat willingly on the chair meant for her and did all assignments as instructed. She seemed not only cooperative but actually interested in the various objects and activities and handled some of the materials rather creatively.

Only twice did she give small signs of impatience. Once she said, a little irritated, that she could not do this, and at another time she said she was "very tired." With some encouragement, however, she continued her task.

At no time did she seem afraid. She accepted the, to her, strange situation, did not appeal to her mother for support, enjoyed functioning successfully, and accepted the one failure she was aware of without getting too upset. She felt free enough to announce her dislike of a tedious task but did it politely by calling herself "tired" rather than unwilling. She obviously had an adequate sense of her self and her role and was able to function as a person in her own right.

From the moment she arrived Bonnie gave the impression of being prepared to handle the situation. In identification with her mother's pleasant, polite, and dignified manner, she smiled and was polite and dignified. She approached her assignments with a certain determination to master them and, as she succeeded, relaxed and even enjoyed them.

Several intents can be distinguished in the goal pattern of this secure and well-loved child. She wants to be pleasant and well accepted and wants to achieve what is expected of her. She also displayed creative interest in some of the material given her, and throughout the test she wanted to sustain her self-possession and integrity.

The case of Linda, which I presented elsewhere (1962), resembles in certain features the parent-child relationship of Bonnie and her parents. Linda as a little girl behaved very much as Bonnie did. Her goal pattern could be described as being almost the same as Bonnie's and did not change through the years. She was eminently able to develop creative goal patterns within a generally adaptive behavior. When grown up, she increasingly turned toward a creatively expansive orientation as was to be expected in a normal development.

The child who starts out with an unaffectionate mother may not be quite as badly off as the institutionalized child because the former at least has a mother to call his own. Comprehensive research, as well as clinical evidence, has shown a variety of emotional disturbances and psychosomatic illnesses to be associated with a deficiency of "motherliness." The different behavior syndromes that develop as the result of a child's relationship with a "cold" mother always seem to contain the elements of depression and hostility.

> A case in point is that of Louise, a woman in her early thirties who in hypnosis recaptured three short episodes of experiences she had had with her mother at what, as was established later, must have been her tenth month of life.
>
> In the first episode she saw herself sitting on the floor of the kitchen and looking at her mother, who seemed to be standing far away at the stove. She longed for her mother to turn toward her, but this did not happen.
>
> Then she saw herself jumping up and down in her cradle looking for her mother and hoping she would come through the door. Nobody came.
>
> In the third scene she saw herself in the arms of her mother, whose head was turned to talk to a neighbor. Louise again yearned for her mother to turn to her but in vain.
>
> Waking up crying, Louise admitted that this was the way she had always felt, "being nothing at all" to her mother, just existing.
>
> This feeling of worth or worthlessness, based on the feeling of being loved or unloved, probably contributes most to a person's or even already a child's, sense of self.
>
> Louise has suffered from a lack of confidence and from depression ever since she can remember. She became submissive in order to be accepted, she withdrew and resigned herself to being unable to obtain or achieve what she wanted.

Not all children, however, are alike in their reactions to given conditions. Bettye M. Caldwell's (1964) comprehensive survey demonstrates conclusively that it is the individuality of a child which determines, to a considerable extent, how he interprets and uses the influences of his environment.

Thus the effects of proper love and care or of their absence represent only predominant trends and not absolute rules.

Demands and discipline

Among the greatest benefits of psychoanalysis is the fact that it has disclosed the damaging consequences of extreme parental demands and discipline.

W. C. Becker (1964) in his recent review of relevant literature discusses the presently available information on "consequences of different kinds of parental discipline" (p. 169 ff.). Using factor analysis studies, he finds three general dimensions of parental behavior: 1) restrictiveness versus permissiveness; 2) anxious emotional involvement versus calm detachment, and 3) warmth versus hostility. Since the emotional involvement factor has not yet been sufficiently researched, he presents the available data primarily under the aspect of warmth and hostility in interaction with restrictiveness and permissiveness. Considerations regarding consistency of discipline are dealt with separately.

The highly informative table of research findings that follows appears in Becker's article (p. 198).

Table 1. Interaction in the Consequence of Warmth versus Hostility and Restrictiveness versus Permissiveness*

	Restrictiveness	Permissiveness
Warmth	Submissive, dependent, polite, neat, obedient (Levy) Minimal aggression (Sears) Maximum rule enforcement, boys (Maccoby) Dependent, not friendly, not creative (Watson) Maximal compliance (Meyers)	Active, socially outgoing, creative, successfully aggressive (Baldwin) Minimal rule enforcement, boys (Maccoby) Facilitates adult role-taking (Levin) Minimal self-aggression, boys (Sears) Independent, friendly, creative, low projective hostility (Watson)
Hostility	"Neurotic" problems (clinical studies) More quarreling and shyness with peers (Watson) Socially withdrawn (Baldwin) Low in adult role-taking (Levin) Maximal self-aggression, boys (Sears)	Delinquency (Gluecks, Bandura and Walters) Noncompliance (Meyers) Maximal aggression (Sears)

* Reprinted with permission. W. C. Becker, Consequences of different kinds of parental discipline. In Martin L. and Lois Wladis Hoffman (eds.), *Child Development Research I*, New York; Russell Sage Foundation, 1964, 198.

Inconsistent discipline seems to contribute to "maladjustment," conflict, and aggression in the child.

On the whole, it may be assumed that warmth and permissiveness facilitate the growth of sociable, yet independent children, and that parental hostility has debilitating effects. Becker, however, cautions against sweeping conclusions because the degree of restrictiveness and permissiveness may make a difference.

Our question again is, how goal setting is influenced by the various degrees of demands and discipline, the procedures used to socialize children. Normally, children are eager to relate to the people around them. One of their basic tendencies is that of self-limiting adaptation which expresses itself as a willingness to go along with others and fit in. They want to belong and be accepted, and appropriate demands and discipline might help develop the kind of social personality they wish to have. There are, however, unfavorable demands and discipline patterns which, as Becker's survey shows, almost invariably result in maladjustments of various kinds.

In the behavior syndromes which develop in reaction to Becker's four discipline patterns, the most apparent deviations pertain to degrees of dependency, compliance, aggression, outgoingness, and creativity.

More specifically, a favorable pattern would show a child's intents as being somewhat independent without being noncompliant, to be "successfully aggressive" and outgoing, and, obviously as a result of these constructive relationships, to be free enough to be creative.

There are three unfavorable patterns of intents. One is the child who is dependent, compliant, and not aggressive, but neither friendly nor creative. The second is the child who quarrels or is shy, self-aggressive, and withdrawn, and the third is the child who is noncompliant, maximally aggressive and possibly delinquent, i.e., destructive.

There is no mention of the creativity aspect in the last two types. The main reason for this omission seems to be that the relevant studies have largely focused on characteristics of the social personality. There is also the possibility that the socio-emotional problems of these children are so great as to hamper their productivity.

The intents of these four groups, if seen in their major social orientations, may be classified as conforming dependency, constructive independence, noncooperative withdrawal, and noncooperative aggressiveness or destructiveness.

Assuming that these four groups represent the basic social orientations of children, their conditioning and the patterns in which they occur become more complex when we introduce the variables of demands and of gifts.

In Becker's review, warmth and permissiveness develop constructive independence and creativeness in a child. Warmth and restrictiveness, on the other hand, result in conforming dependency and noncreativity.

D. C. McClelland's (1953) careful studies on the "achievement motive," however, show not only high achievement, but also greater independence in children whose parents make high demands and who are emotionally distant, if not unloving.

There is a difference, then, between parental severity which is nonpermissively demanding behavioral obedience per se and that which is nonpermissively asking achievement and mastery. The latter furthers independence of achievement in conjunction with behavioral conformity.

We also need more differentation between the "warm" and the "hostile" parent, since the "distant" parent is not necessarily hostile.

Even more complex is the relationship between the environment and the development of a child's creativity. The term "creativity" here means the potential that, as stated by Getzels and Jackson (1962), may be "found to some extent in all persons" (p. 16).

While there is still much speculation about the nature of the creative process, lately certain ideas have been increasingly substantiated by empirical studies. (See Chapters 6 and 8 for a detailed discussion.) In the present context, however, the main relevant finding is the fact that "repression operates against creativity" (MacKinnon, 1962).

In other words, a restrictive environment would have to be offset by other very favorable conditions for a child to develop his creativity. For example, a child's personality could be so strong, or his thinking so "field-independent" (Witkin et al, 1962), that he is able to assert himself regardless of the restrictive environment. Or his creative gifts could be so pronounced and his parents so ambitious that, while otherwise restrictive, they allow his apparent talents to unfold.

Many of the scientists in B. Eiduson's study (1961) had restrictive backgrounds which, however, did not prevent them—if, indeed, it did not actually encourage them—to develop new and different conceptual and perceptual styles. Getzels and Jackson's investigations (1962), on the other hand, show the families of the creative children to be more permissive than those of the highly intelligent but noncreative children. The latter, mostly learners and conformers, do not seem to feel in discord with their restrictive environment.

The picture is further complicated by the influence of the family's value system. It is not only the parents' domination as such which influences the development of the child's potentials, but also the values they hold. An example of this can be found in Strodtbeck's (1958) studies of the different educational goals of different subcultural groups. (See Chapter 14.)

The relationship, therefore, between parental demands and the development of a child's gifts is quite complex. The variables of the emotional atmosphere, the severity of discipline, the parental demands and expectations, as well as the child's own gifts and inclinations, interact so multilaterally that the prediction of the goal-setting behavior of a growing individual can only be very tentative.

Information and Opportunities

We know that the level of a person's aspirations is codetermined by the kind of information, education, and opportunities available to him. The role that these factors play in the development of a person's goal setting has been studied mostly by social psychologists who see it primarily in terms of social class impacts. A great deal of information exists about the different aspiration levels of various social classes and the fact that, generally speaking, higher-class families seem to influence their youngsters in the direction of higher occupational status aspirations. H. Hyman (1953), for instance, observed that the desire for upward mobility varies with social class level and occupational category. These differences, however, are relative only within the general trend toward upward mobility so characteristic of American culture. There is, as R. W. Mack, R. J. Murphy, and S. Yellin (1962) call it, "a culturally defined success drive shared by persons at all levels of our social structure" (p. 484). This means that to some degree everybody participates in the "American dream" of the availability of opportunities, which is at the root of the mobility ethos. It is not surprising, therefore, that American youths strive to improve on the position of their parents.

Educational psychologists have conducted a different type of group studies in which they examined the effects of specific opportunities. Surveys on the effect of group experiences in nursery schools (J. W. Swift, 1964) and peer relations in childhood (J. D. Campbell, 1964) on goal setting, have shown only inconclusive results.

J. W. Swift points out that nursery school and group situations provide enriching experiences only to the degree that the child is ready to utilize them and the teacher is able to support the child's interests and goals. The influence of peer groups on motivation is generally acknowledged, as is the fact that it seems to increase during the school years and becomes a decisive factor at high-school age (J. S. Coleman, 1961).

What are the goals for which a child may utilize the stimulation and aspirations impressed upon him by his environment? The basic tendency toward creative expansion shows itself from the beginning in the impulse to try things and to experiment with the handling and use of materials and tools. (See Chapter 6 for additional examples.) But only recently have we been able to learn more about the qualities of different gifts in children.

An unusually instructive example is the previously mentioned study of Getzels and Jackson (1961) in which the highly creative and the highly intelligent children are compared regarding their own and their families' goals. We see two groups of children with an equal opportunity of exceptional schooling, but who have different gifts on the one hand and different environmental ambitions on the other. It appears that the child's own gifts and his family's orientation are more decisive for the choice of his aspirations than are the opportunities offered by the school.

Whatever knowledge we have of the effects of early stimulation, we know that information and opportunities or denial of learning practices on children's goal setting is of a causistic nature.

Anne Roe (1953) finds that a high percentage of professionals comes from homes with intellectual interests, a finding recently confirmed by J. A. Chambers (1964). B. Eiduson (1961) reports childhood memories of scientists who had an early exposure to educational experiences and an opportunity to practice educational activities. One chemist remembers vividly how his mother would drive him to New York for plays, museums, and concerts. He says that it was expected he would participate in what was offered to him "in some implicit way. . . . Both of my parents actually were interested in self-discipline, and the self-discipline with which I grew up was something that just came from the atmosphere of the home, I'm sure, more than anything else. This made me want to do well in school and get something out of it, and I never had to be rewarded for doing well" (p. 41).

In a study on the "Development of Individuals' Potentials under Different Environmental Impacts" (in preparation), I compared 80 psychotherapy cases regarding the aftereffects of the presence or absence of early cultural privileges and intellectual stimulation.

The cases have from low to high middle-class backgrounds, the ratio of male to female is 3 to 5, and their ages range from 18 to 65, with the majority being in their middle years. All of them have emotional problems of various kinds. In many of these cases the cultural background factor plays a minor or major role in their personality problems, a role which is either positive or negative, depending on opportunities, pressures, and deprivations. A little more than a third of the individuals had culturally underprivileged childhoods, yet about half of them have made adequate to superior lives for themselves. In spite of this success, practically all of them are plagued by inferiority feelings, shame, or resentment regarding their backgrounds. They feel that in some way or other the lack of cultural stimulation and education in their childhood has been damaging to them.

> Typical of the pattern in which several men, who have otherwise successful careers, experience this damage is the case of Ellery, 39. Ellery got himself through engineering school under great deprivation, in nearly complete social isolation, and founded and developed a tool manufacturing company out of nothing. Neither his successful career and subsequent outstanding social position, nor his marriage, home, or family, freed him from his deep feelings of worthlessness and inadequacy. While these feelings undoubtedly originated in the lack of mother love as a child, they were strongly enhanced by feelings of social inadequacy. These feelings impaired his development as a person and prevented him from building up fulfilling human relationships.

> The other pattern of detrimental aftereffects of a deprived cultural background became apparent in the case of Gertrud, a 28-year-old nurse. Gertrud, an unusually bright girl, had repeatedly been encouraged by her superiors to acquire additional training and to work toward advancement in her professıon. Gertrud, however, was reluctant to do this. She did not feel that she had the qualities necessary for a leadership position nor the drive to develop herself any further. She knew she ought to, but always felt herself drifting back into that childhood atmosphere of mental laziness and emptiness.

> Some of the patients who have remained unsuccessful blame it on the deprivations they suffered in their early years. Louise, a woman in her middle thirties, feels extremely unfulfilled because there was no money in her poverty-stricken childhood to develop her considerable musical talent. In fact, her father discouraged her from the pursuit of any interests beyond working toward the increase of the family income. Louise did not have the strength to stand up for the goals and values she believed in.

Fewer than a third of the sample come from families with a high cultural background. These were families in which one or both parents had had an academic education, professional training, and cultural interests.

The majority of these individuals made successful use of their educational and cultural opportunities. There are, however, a few where excessive parental pressure led to strong antagonism against higher education and corresponding careers. There are also two cases in which extreme spoiling prevented the development of appropriate self-discipline.

Summarizing the findings of this study, it may be said that the opportunities offered by a rich cultural background help to motivate the growing youth to work toward culturally valuable goals. Excessive pressure and excessive spoiling are apt to cancel out the benefits of the available opportunities.

Correspondingly, the cultural deprivation experienced in a deprived background may deaden and paralyze a person. Even if he is strong enough to overcome the disheartening condition, he may continue to carry with him the feelings of resentment and inadequacy which it created in him.

Models and ideals

From the beginning of his life the child is subject to the direction of parents who do things in certain ways, set up certain rules of behavior and principles of action, and who also demonstrate certain behavior patterns of their own. This includes a great many different things. There are the simple practices and habits of everyday behavior, moral principles and other rules. There are interests, ambitions, and plans, and there are attitudes toward people and life in general. The child either accepts these attitudes and influences or obstructs and rebels against them.

The child himself begins very early in life to look for a model and for directives which he can follow. From the imitating of perceived sounds and movements to the imitating of adult actions in make-believe play, the infant and nursery-school-age child are continually relating themselves to the examples they observe.

Furthermore, beyond the mere copying, the 2- to 5-year-old begins to develop an interest in rules and other organizing principles. His own order upholding tendencies normally lead him in the same direction as the adult wishes to guide him. Whether, however, they lead him to accept or to reject the leadership his parents provide depends on a number of conditions.

A child's positive or negative identification with his parents may be subconscious and remain so, or it may eventually become conscious. The identification has both an emotional and a cognitive aspect. The usual assumption is that the emotional aspect is the decisive one, and that in an emotionally satisfying relationship with his parents the child will be willing to accept whatever habits and principles his parents teach and demonstrate to him. It is also assumed that a "well adjusted" personality development is furthered by this kind of positive identification.

However, these widespread assumptions can be challenged on several counts, some of them relevant to the present discussion of the parents' impact on children's goal setting.

The most favorable situation is the one in which both parents are in harmony and agreement regarding their own values as well as their principles and upbringing techniques, where the child feels loved and appreciated and where, luckily, his own identification and preferences naturally line up with those of his parents.

This happy situation rarely exists. Little Bonnie, who was previously introduced, experienced it, particularly when her father also began to take an increasing interest in her, almost matching that of her mother. Bonnie, even at the difficult age of three, seems to agree with her parents' goals for her.

Not all cases, though, in which there is harmony, love, and affection offer a child the model and ideals that are good for him.

Myrna's case is one where, despite favorable emotional dynamics, there was little in terms of goals and values with which she could identify.

Myrna loved her parents. They were simple and gentle people who raised their two children with kindness and tolerance. But they were also colorless and without any outside interests. Myrna's father, a county employee in a lower income bracket, often was ill, and Myrna learned early to feel concern for her father's health problems. Her mother was rather plain and drab; she did her housework and was friendly and easygoing, but had not much to say about anything.

Myrna was impatient with this environment. She had many ideas of things she wanted to do and many questions she wanted to have answered. But there was no stimulation or instruction forthcoming.

At the age of four Myrna met the person who became her model and her ideal. It was a neighbor, a woman whom she had come to admire greatly in the course of a friendly relationship that had developed between them. One day Myrna told the woman that she wanted to give her mother a birthday present she had made herself. The neighbor offered to show the little girl how to embroider a doily for her mother, and for a few weeks Myrna found herself sitting in her neighbor's handsome living room, being entertained with cookies and fruit juice while embroidering her doily.

From then on, Myrna kept the ideal that she would become the same type of "nice lady" that the neighbor was. Simultaneously with her admiration for this woman, Myrna loved both her parents. She was quite close to her gentle and kind father and felt a kind of protective affection for her mother.

In cases where no interests or ideals are offered at home it seems that a child has to depend almost entirely on his own initiative to find values and goals to focus on. This is easier for a child with talents such as Myrna's. In a less favorably endowed individual the development of goals and values may be entirely arrested or continued only up to a certain point.

> Gertrud, who also was mentioned before, is a case in point. At the time she entered psychotherapy she felt she led a dreary, depressing existence. She was 24 and a registered nurse in a hospital. This career was the only objective she had ever envisioned and pursued, much to the pride of her family who were small-town people with jobs in the lower middle-class income bracket. They led quiet, uneventful lives with no interests or ambitions. "There was no book in our house," says Gertrud, "and there was never any talk about anything but daily events, neighbors, church or the like."
>
> At age 6 she made the acquaintance of a distant cousin who happened to visit relatives in Gertrud's town. This cousin was a nurse and the first person ever to speak of activities and places that sounded interesting. Gertrud was a fairly intelligent girl and longed for some mental stimulation. She decided that she was going to become a nurse and in that capacity see and visit other places.
>
> This she did, incidentally being the only one of a family of five who ever accomplished anything. But after she had reached her goal, she was stuck and did not know where else to go. Her problem was the more pronounced, as she was shy and socially somewhat retiring. She also had not been able to enter a satisfying sex and/or love relationship.

If the mentally empty home, where the child is not helped to develop ideas and ideals, is also encouraging a defective development, the situation becomes even more damaging. I could describe a variety of conditions where parents either set up bad models, have warped or prejudiced ideas for their children's futures, or have ideals and goals which prove to be totally inappropriate for the particular child.

In view of limited space one example will have to suffice. It has been selected to show how erroneous it is to assume that positive identification in an emotionally satisfactory relationship must have favorable results.

> Lorna is one of two children in a closely knit family with mutual affection between parents and children. Lorna, while she loved her mother, was particularly attached to her father, an intelligent man of strong convictions who fascinated and dominated her completely.
>
> Her own inclinations were artistic, and from an early time on she was enthralled by dance and music. She also liked to draw and paint. Her father did not think much of these endeavors, but he believed in

helping people and tried to lead Lorna, first through stories and later through books and discussions, into the field of social work. Lorna followed obediently, repressing her own interests and considerable talents.

She played this role all through college and into a marriage with a sociology major who, in many ways, resembled her father and with whom she thought herself in love. In her marriage she conceived of her role as that of wife and mother in terms similar to those she had admired in her mother, a woman who also had started out on a career before she got married, and had given it up to dedicate herself completely to her family.

After identifying with her father's interests and intellectual as well as moral values, and identifying with her mother's concept of a woman's role in marriage, Lorna, now the wife of a successful young professor and mother of two children, felt herself sinking into an unexplained depression. In the middle of what seemed to be an extremely happy stage of life, with a loving husband and two healthy children, she felt empty and unfulfilled. Her frantic efforts to interest herself in her husband's work and her own genuine interest in her children's development did not seem enough to satisfy her inner self.

She longed to do something completely different, to draw and to paint, to study art and to meet artists, all wishes she felt guilty about because they would take time from what seemed to her to be the important and responsible things to do. After revealing her seemingly irrational depression to her husband, Lorna entered psychotherapy. But it took considerable time until she realized what had happened to her. In her admiration of and identification with both her parents, she had repressed her own personality so completely that she had developed an entirely artificial identity. When she gradually got rid of her false identity and allowed her real self to emerge, the development, and eventual successful practice, of her considerable artistic talents brought her a sense of fulfillment that she had missed throughout her previous life.

The problem of the growing youth to find appropriate goals for himself is complicated by the fact that, on one hand, his potentials are still unknown and, on the other, the influence exercised by his parents' ideas and ideals may not be suitable for him. A situation in which parents demonstrate a valuable life of their own and at the same time help their children to find themselves does not seem to prevail very frequently, desirable though it is.

The models and ideals that parents present to their children should ideally serve two purposes: the child's socialization and his eventual self-realization.

As L. Kohlberg (1964) emphasizes in a comprehensive survey of writings on the "Development of Moral Character and Moral Ideology," theoreticians like Piaget (1932), G. H. Mead (1934), and J. M. Baldwin (1906), view the parental training "as influential only as a part of a world or social order perceived by the child" (p. 395). They focus mostly on the family (Baldwin), the peer group (Piaget), and the larger social institutions (Mead). The imperative to develop the self to its fulfillment through appropriate need satisfaction and accomplishments within the context of one's own culture, is not conceived of as a moral goal in the studies of moral development.

Parents also are more concerned with their task of socialization than of helping their child to integrate aspects of self-realization. They begin with their "good" and "bad" in the very earliest stages and often hold a small child to their own moral philosophies, regardless of how they may affect the child.

"Is he a good boy or a bad boy?" says Steven aloud, philosophizing to himself. At 2 years, he walks around, deeply in thought about this problem. "No, he is a bad boy," he decides emphatically and for the moment with great satisfaction. He took his value choice at this point in his own hands.

Roger's mother had a conviction that peace in the world could be brought about if children stopped fighting. Thus she forbade her son not only to fight but also to fight back. This moral principle had the most disastrous consequences for Roger, until he finally took it upon himself to fight back, regardless of his mother's dictates.

Linda, on the other hand, had a mother who furthered her daughter's personality development from the earliest stages. She helped her to pursue her intellectual interests against her husband's prohibiting influence, and made Linda aware that everybody, even young children, have certain rights if they respect those of others.

When and on what basis does a young child try to integrate his actions with some value aspect? The usual assumption is that avoidance of punishment is the first operative orientation and that this begins in the preschool age, say 2 to 4 years, as soon as prohibitions and punishments are understood.

The question is, however, whether a child does not attempt simultaneously or even before at 1½ to 3 years to find a value orientation when he begins, tentatively, to set his very first considered goals. When the 1½- to 2-year old begins a sentence with "I want to . . .," and then, sometimes in a most arbitrary and capricious manner, decides on something or other he wants or does not want, that seems to be the first exercise in choosing and experiment in willful goal setting.

The spontaneous value orientation which the child is seeking at this point is rarely understood nor is it helped by the environment.

References

Baldwin, J. M. *Social and ethical interpretations in mental development.* New York: Macmillan, 1906.

Becker, W. C. Consequences of different kinds of parental discipline. In M. L. Hoffman and L. W. Hoffman (eds.), *Child development research, 1,* New York: Russell Sage Foundation, 1964.

Bender, L. Psychopathic behavior disorders in children. In R. M. Lindner (ed.), *Handbook of correctional psychology.* New York: Philos. Lib., 1947, 360-377.

Bowlby, J. Forty-four juvenile thieves, *Internat. J. Psychoanal.,* 1944, *25,* 1-57.

Buhler, C. *Values in psychotherapy.* New York: Free Press, 1962.

Buhler, C. Development of individuals' potentials under different environmental impacts. In press.

Caldwell, B. M. The effects of infant care. In M. L. Hoffman and L. W. Hoffman (eds.), *Child development research, 1.* New York: Russell Sage Foundation, 1964.

Campbell, J. D. Peer relations in childhood. In *Child development research, 1.* New York: Russell Sage Foundation, 1964.

Chambers, J. A. Relating personality factors to scientific creativity, *Psychol. Mon.* 1964, *78,*7.

Coleman, J. S. *The adolescent society.* New York: Free Press, 1961.

Eiduson, B. *Scientists—their psychological world.* New York: Basic Books, 1962.

Getzels, J. W., and Jackson, P. W. *Creativity and intelligence.* New York: John Wiley & Sons, 1962.

Hyman, H. The value systems of different classes. In R. Bendix and S. Lipset (eds.), *Class, status and power.* New York: Free Press, 1953.

Kohlberg, L. Development of moral character and ideology. In M. L. Hoffman and L. W. Hoffman (eds.), *Child development research, 1.* New York: Russell Sage Foundation, 1964.

Mack, R. W., Murphy, R. J., and Yellin, S. The protestant ethic, level of aspiration, and social mobility: an empirical test. In B. H. Stoodley (ed.), *Society and self.* New York: Free Press, 1962.

MacKinnon, D. W. What makes a person creative? *Saturday Review,* 1962, *69,* 15-17, 69.

McClelland, D. C., et al. *The achievement motive.* New York: Appleton-Century-Crofts, 1953.

Mead, G. H. *Mind, self and society.* Chicago: Chicago University Press, 1934.

Piaget, J. *The moral judgment of the child.* New York: Free Press, 1948 (1932).

Roe, A. *The making of a scientist.* New York: Dodd, Mead, 1953.

Spitz, R. A. Hospitalism: an inquiry into the genesis of psychiatric conditions in early childhood, *Psychoanal. Stud. of Child,* 1945, *1,* 53-74.

Spitz, R. A. Hospitalism: An inquiry into the genesis of psychiatric conditions in early childhood, a follow-up report, *Psychoanal. Stud. of the Child,* 1946, *2,* 113-117.

Spitz, R. A., and Wolf, K. Analytic depression, *Psychoanal. Stud. of the Child,* 1946, *2,* 313-342.

Swift, J. W. Effects of early group experience: the nursery school and day nursery. In *Child development research, 1.* New York: Russell Sage Foundation, 1964.

Witkin, H. A., Dyk., R. B., Patterson, H. F., Goodenough, D. R., and Karp, S. A. *Psychological differentiation.* New York: John Wiley & Sons, 1962.

Yarrow, L. J. Separation from parents during early childhood. In M. L. Hoffman and L. W. Hoffman (eds.), *Child development research, 1.* New York: Russell Sage Foundation, 1964.

Chapter 11

The Development of Healthy and Unhealthy Goal Setting

Mortimer M. Meyer

Implied in the title of this chapter is the assumption that goal setting is a combination of developed and inherent faculties. There are, however, such relatively stable and unchanging factors as native endowments of the individual. These are indicated by Buhler in an earlier chapter of this volume as "inherent activity trends," and "individual aptitudes and talents." There also are the stable, important influences that social and cultural mores have on the developmental process. For this presentation, consideration essentially will be given to those influences which impinge more directly upon the child and affect his individual development more specifically. In the earliest years the parents normally are the crucial influences, not only in terms of their direct relationship with the child, but in terms of the total environmental *Gestalt*, as reflected in such things as the physical characteristics of the home, the parents' relationship with each other, and the goal-setting directives for themselves and other children in the family.

The role that goals play in the development of the child through his relationship with his parents is manifold. Consideration of these goals in their individual aims and outlook would result in a myriad of fragments which would not highlight the basic pattern. Consequently, in this chapter goals will be considered in terms of two major trends which are not the only possible basis for consideration of a pattern, but were chosen because they are useful in considering the problem in the framework of a psychology which takes into account the conscious and unconscious aspects of motivation. It should be noted carefully that consideration of the development of goals in a brief chapter and without integration into other aspects of development is bound to result in some oversimplification with the concomitant possible apparent distortion of other aspects of development.

These two trends are goals related to direct external achievement and goals related to inner values. Clearly these are not separate and, in fact, it is anticipated that there will be a harmonious integration of them. However, they are sufficiently distinct for the considerations at hand. Although parents are crucial in the earliest years of the developing goal-setting patterns, the attitudes concerning goal setting for the child do not wait for his birth. Attitudes about goal setting for children are established in the parents during their own development, but usually are not likely to become a conscious or motivating force until marriage. For some adults, directly upon marriage children become an important part of their outlook. For others, however, this consideration does not occur until pregnancy. For still others the question of goals for children is delayed even further and sometimes never becomes a part of conscious thinking by the parents. Nevertheless, as indicated above, right from the time of the child's birth parental attitudes toward the child make evident their outlook on goals for him, and thus influence him. In the case of the parent for whom goal setting is part of the wish to help the child achieve a full life of his own, his influence on the child is markedly different from that of the parent for whom the child becomes a second opportunity to achieve those goals which the parent never did. It is still different from the influence of that parent who expresses no concern or interest in the child's goal setting.

In large measure it is to retain the love of his parents and to allay the primary anxiety of infancy and childhood that the child wishes to incorporate goal patterns set by the parents. When parents use the child's handling of anxiety in this way as a continuing means of having him conform to their wishes, regardless of his readiness and ability to develop his own goals, this mechanism of reducing anxiety remains the essential one and carries with it severe psychological dangers. The danger involved is pointed out by Klein (1949):

> It is necessary for the child's future stability that this mechanism of mastering anxiety should not predominate to excess. If the child's interests and achievements and other gratifications are too completely devoted to its endeavours to win love and recognition from its objects, if, that is, its object-relations are the pre-eminent means of mastering its anxiety and allaying its sense of guilt, its mental health in future years is not planted in firm soil. If it is less dependent on its objects and if the interests and achievements by means of which it masters its anxiety and allays its sense of guilt are done for their own sake and afford it interest and pleasure in themselves, its anxiety will undergo a better modification and a wider distribution—be levelled down, as it

> were. As soon as its anxiety has thus been reduced, its capacity for libidinal gratification will grow, and this is a pre-condition for the successful mastering of anxiety (pp. 259-260).

In addition, there is the obvious danger that the child will never have direct access to his own capacities for their development in his own way. The importance of love as a motivating factor should not be permitted to obliterate such other motivating factors as the expectation of gratification in an action, described by Buhler (1954) as the positive reaction to reality.

The process of incorporating, developing, and establishing goals is an extremely complicated one, because the manner in which it is accomplished or rejected is dependent upon basic factors, such as the inherent biological and psychological characteristics of the child, the relationship of the goal to the developmental level of the child, the character of the love relationship between parent and child, and the cultural environment. For example, the loving attitude on the part of the parent is not necessarily consistent throughout the child's growth. A parent may feel comfortable, relaxed, and truly accepting of the infant, so that the child perceives love as gratifying and the parental goal demands as comfortable and feasible. The same parent, however, may develop marked discomfort and anxiety as the helpless infant develops into a child who asserts his wish for some independence and expresses some direct aggression. The previously truly accepting parent may now become directly unaccepting or develop special modes of behavior to defend against the discomfort and anxiety and the direct emergence of the unaccepting attitude. The result is a strained attitude toward the child and impairment of the comfortable love relationship. Consequently, the child's readiness and wish to incorporate parental goals will be affected accordingly, and the child, who formerly incorporated parental goals readily, may now become resistent and/or try to regress behaviorally to the style which was accompanied by true acceptance with resultant blocking and distortion in further development.

The basic factor in the consideration of healthy versus unhealthy goal development is the compatability of the goals set for the child both in terms of native endowment and the developmental stage. Consequently, the influence of the environment on the child's goal setting is an important one with opportunities for favorable and unfavorable outlooks. In the earliest years the parents are the most direct environment. Thus where the parents have an understanding of the child and recognition of his specific assets and liabilities, the child has an environment favorable for the development of goals based on his own characteristics and thus compatible to his own personality. With their interest in the child's self-development based essentially on the child as an individual, the parents are attuned to the emerging characteristics as well as their responsibility for the child's social adaptation. The goals for the child then emerge from a relationship with his parents in which a harmony between their needs and socializing function and his individual needs is achieved. Such harmony is essential if the child is to develop in a manner consistent with his own endowment and interest. Unless he can have this consistency, eventual self-fulfillment becomes impossible, since the native qualities or the developed interests are being made subservient to the wishes of others. Buhler, in previous chapters of this volume and in *Values in Psychotherapy* (1962) has numerous illustrations of such interference with self-fulfillment.

Goals For External Achievement

For example, such parents are sensitive to the infant's tenuous attempts to reach out for independence in the feeding process, and they have tolerance for the fumbling ineptitude of the infant's first attempts. The infant then experiences a move toward independence as a goal within its capability, as being without undue stress, and bringing the rewards of mastery as well as parental approval. Thus, the goal of control for the infant can be set in terms of recognition of the readiness of the infant in terms of physiological and psychological development so that goal achievement is incorporated by the child as a feasible and pleasurable concept. A satisfactory experience at this level sets a foundation for reasonable and flexible goal setting in the child's future standards of his expectation of receiving from others. Such an expectation is crucial not only to the receiving from parents but in any joint effort, whether it be the teacher's giving in the learning situation or the colleague at work. This phase of development is followed by the period of bowel and bladder training, wherein the goal set for the child is that of direct control of bodily activity. This new and additional achievement, when accomplished in a harmonious atmosphere, carries with it for the child the conviction that he is able to attain the self-regulation demanded by external sources. This conviction is important for its later service as a basis for coping effectively with those situations, such as the school room, where an appropriate goal of self-control is necessary for maximum learning. With development proceeding on this carefully and appropriately regulated level, an important additional accomplishment is achieved.

The parent, by regulating the development of goals appropriately, helps the child to incorporate as one of his goals a sense of order. The child, flooded by many stimuli around him, recognizes that by establishing a hierarchy of importance of the stimuli and an ordered manner of responding, he is likely to achieve greater effectiveness and greater satisfaction. Such recognition is accomplished in simple ways. The child is encouraged to complete one task before beginning another, thereby helping him see the advantage and pleasure of one completed task over two incomplete ones. Another simple method is the frequent occurrence of delaying the award of a piece of candy from before dinner to after dinner, with accompanying explanation for the delay. The child develops a pattern based on a sense of orderliness in dealing with the world so that integrated and executive functions of ego process become highly coordinated as a basis for the later development of goals and goal achievement. This goal is clearly related to Buhler's (1959, 1964) upholding the internal order.

Such a development in ego process is crucial for effective accomplishment in later life when the child must take on the responsibility of ordering his achievement, because it is through the ego process that effectiveness is accomplished. When the ego does not develop the capacity for maintaining orderliness the basis is laid for serious disturbance, because the individual is helpless in the face of a variety of pulls which he cannot master. It is not infrequent to observe adults who start one activity after the other and complete none. Although in the child's development thus far he has not been required to achieve in the larger sense with which adult living is concerned, nevertheless, the mold has been set by the parents, through the process of achievement, in terms of the acquisition of skills in motor coordination, muscle development, and socialization. Buhler (1928) finds that it is at this time, approximately from 5 to 8 years, that the child shows evidence of a capacity to commit himself to a task. She found that at age 5 the psychologically healthy child could set and accept tasks to be accomplished. Erikson's (1963) later concept of a capacity for industry appears to be similar to that presented by Buhler. This basic outlook that energy becomes available for task setting and acceptance is critical for the child's next step, that is, his entrance into and success at school. From this point on the influence of many individuals outside the family begins to play a part in attitudes and patterns of goal setting. These influences, however, are more likely to be related to the specific goals than to the pattern of goal seeking which had been laid down in the preschool years. Although no elaboration is offered, mention should be made that the presence or absence of a sibling is another variation in the environment which can be of marked positive or negative significance in a number of ways. An older sibling can be a source of stimulation by the example he sets in his own growth or development, or he can be a deterrent. Where the older sibling, for reasons of his own, needs to prove his superiority, he may stimulate excessive competition or deride every effort of the younger child to such a degree as to destroy initiative in the younger child. Such a relationship may replace the development of personal goals with submission to externally oriented ones. Similarly, parents may provide opportunities for siblings to complement each other by their individual differences, or they may make destructive, derogating remarks.

Thus far the discussion has dealt with the development of a healthy basic pattern for goal achieving and has assumed that the parents have been able to relate and adapt their own goals to the child's needs. That the first accomplishment is not a simple one is readily evident, not only from the vast amount of clinical material which points out the failure of communication between parents and child, but from experimental work, such as that of Escalona (1954). Her investigation demonstrates that normal and abnormal psychological development well may be related to the compatability of the child's indigenous qualities and the indigenous and psychological characteristics of his parents. The reinforcement of a goal-seeking pattern is dependent upon the individual's experiencing some form of gratification from it. When the parents are able to help the child to walk at the time he is physiologically and psychologically ready, they reinforce in him the pleasure of achievement. When the parents, because of needs of their own, set goals for which the child is not ready, gratification not only may be diminished to the point of absence, but frustration may reach excessive proportions. Such a situation induces distortions in the developing goal-setting patterns. For example, where the parents make demands too early for goal achievement but provide considerable gratification for it, the child is likely to make every attempt to fulfill the goal and may well do so. But the developing pattern carries with it the experience that goal achievement takes extreme effort and brings great reward. Where the demand is excessive, so that with or without the anticipation of gratification the child cannot achieve it, goal setting becomes fused with frustration. A practical illustration is often seen clinically, where the parents have a child whose mental endowment is low. The parents are frequently unable to accommodate their expectation level to the level of the child, with the result that the child begins early to develop the attitude of inability to achieve and the belief that people will always be excessively demanding of him. Thus he becomes fearful of setting goals for himself, including those which may actually be within his reach. The reverse situation sometimes occurs where the child is far brighter than the parents, and the parent is unable to understand the intellectual superiority of the child. This is often seen by the parents as a threatening challenge and an interruption in their routine pattern, and is interpreted as the child's being "smart alecky." The result again can be that of making the child fearful of goal setting.

The above general discussion of the setting of outer goals can be considered in more specific developmental psychoanalytic terms as described by Erikson (1963), that is, in terms of the level or levels at which the incompatible demands are made. In approximately the first year of life the infant's relationship to his parents is one in which he is concerned about being the recipient, initially more passively and then more aggressively. Thus goal setting by the parents at this time influences the goals for external achievement of those infants who are dependent upon receiving from others. Where parental giving tends to be grudging, unadapted to the child and only at the convenience of the parent, the child is likely to interpret that taking and getting are so unpleasant that no goal should be set which involves dependence on others. Consequently cooperative attitudes are not developed and, for example, school activities which require goal setting, based on getting something from the teacher, may suffer badly. On the other hand, with parents who give readily and overabundantly, again without adaptation to the child, the infant experiences no need to set a goal, and goal setting also develops poorly. The expectation is fostered that getting involves no effort, and dependency on others is substituted for the setting of goals for self-achievement. Late in the second year the child is normally faced with the need to learn bowel control. Such control implies the capacity to retain or delay, and to let go or to give appropriately. Variation from an appropriately adapted training for this mastery again results in the appearance of maladaptive approaches of goal setting. The parent with rigid, excessive demands for the goal of bowel control is likely to meet with stubbornness, which then becomes ingrained in the child's character and is reflected in his goal setting, i.e., he stubbornly refuses to give up a goal he has set for himself or to alter his goals when they are in conflict with the goals of others. When the parents are excessively lenient and set no goals for bowel control, the child's character development is likely to reflect the excessive leniency in a subsequent lack of perseverance, that is, the appropriate amount of stubbornness to carry a project through to completion. School again may be used as an illustration. Such a child is likely to be one who sets goals but shows little perseverance toward achieving them, and little distress about failure to reach them.

The next phase, described by Erikson (1963) as the period of "locomotion and the genitals," is that period in which the child deals with the development of abilities to be intrusive and inclusive. Intrusive refers here to the ability to enter into the activities of others and to move away from total self-centeredness. When parents in this phase overstimulate the child's goal setting by setting excessively high goals, the child is likely to respond by being excessively competitive and being concerned only with his goal of successful competition and intruding into the activities of others in order to surpass them, thus losing sight of the particular goal for achievement. When goals of the parents at this time tend to discourage intrusiveness, for instance, by excessive requirements for compliance or the inhibition of aggressiveness, there is impairment in the child's ability to develop adequate readiness for appropriate competitive effort to strive for a goal which he has set. Such a child is timid in a competitive situation and is likely to develop a pattern in which his goal setting is dependent on the wishes of the authority figure. This development has particular significance for the learning process in terms of how it affects the child's attitudes toward the learning goals. As Erikson has pointed out, "If we take intellectual functioning as an example of a part function, we find that it is either integrated with or will be distorted by organ modes." Thus if at this time the child has accepted the desirability of moving away from self-centeredness to enter into the activities of others without excessive intrusion, he can make the most of the intellectual situation. However, where intrusion into group activity as a goal has been hampered, the child becomes fearful of the intrusion in the classroom situation, hangs back, and is unable to undertake the necessary active participation. Where the drive for achievement as a means of competition has become the end in itself, the child is likely to lose sight of the values in the achievement and to be busy with his competitiveness as a means of surpassing instead of learning. Previous disturbed development can show itself clearly here as, for example, with the child who during the early period learned to expect to be fed without any effort on his part, and who translates this experience to the classroom and expects the teacher to teach him without making any effort to learn.

The discussions thus far have dealt with the setting of compatible and incompatible goals. A third possibility is a situation where the parent expresses little concern or interest in establishing goals for the child. Frequently in such cases a parental substitute such as a maid, governess, or housekeeper is at hand to pick up the neglected area and to serve in the parents' stead. Nevertheless, it is not quite the same because there is likely to be engendered in the child many questions about the parents' attitude toward himself and the goals he absorbs from the parental substitute. Such goals always have a taint of being "secondhand." Akin to this type of situation is one in which no parental substitute is supplied. The child, through observing the family relationship in the home of a peer or of a supportive relative, sees how different the parent-child relationship can be and may vow that for his children it will be different. With this goal in mind, he then sets up goals for himself which rise aggressively, almost as a matter of rebellion, instead of growing out of a constructive base. Then, too, there are the many situations in which there are no substitutes, and the child must gain goals by default. The very failure of the parent to set goals carries implications for the child. In the extreme situations, where no one displays any interest in the child, experimental evidence has shown that severe depression and apathy occur with drastic characterological results, sometimes ending with death in infancy (Ribble, 1965). Where interest in the child is sufficient to prevent him from such severe effects but insufficient for goal establishment, an apathy toward achievement is likely to result as part of an over-all aimless life pattern.

It should be pointed out that in general it is assumed that the parents play an important, though not total, part in transmitting to the child the social heritage as a source of enrichment compatible with his own development. Occasionally, however, there are parents who, because of their own psychological needs, cannot carry out this responsibility. Instead, they will ridicule, overtly or covertly, the social milieu in a manner that establishes in the child a goal of negativism and rebelliousness. Sometimes such influence is exerted in the guise of encouraging individuality or avoiding the effects of excessive conformity. When such children, in turn, become rebellious toward their parents, the parents are likely to be taken by surprise, to feel affronted, and to blame the children and everyone else.

Although the goals for outer achievement discussed previously are related to inner goals through both the developmental process of the child and the process of activating goals, they are sufficiently distinct so that the outer behavior may not always reflect directly the inner goals. To explore this differentiation further it is necessary to describe the concept of inner goals as it relates to the concept of outer goals. Inner goals deal with the efforts of the individual to achieve inner satisfactions as separated from outer achievement, and in this sense serve as motivating forces. Thus two individuals may be motivated to achieve the goal of vocational success, but in one case it involves, to a marked degree, the goal of inner satisfaction gained from achievement which corresponds to the concept of self-realization as described in the field of humanistic psychology; such achievement may be reinforced by outer approval but is not dependent upon it. In the other case the individual is motivated to obtain that same external goal by the need to satisfy parents or parental images rather than by the need for self-realization. The development of such inner goals is of major importance in the foundation of the personality because they provide an internal self-stimulating basis for action, a self-reliant attitude toward accomplishment, and a sound foundation for desirable self-esteem.

Ordinarily the development of inner goals is concomitant with the development of outer goals. Parents start the young child on developing outer goals with the attitude that it is for his parents that he is achieving, but gradually the child begins to enjoy the achievement for the sense of mastery it gives him. This enjoyment provides a basis for the development of skills which have little direct bearing on useful achievement but rather further the goal of inner satisfaction. As the child begins to mature the parents begin to encourage achievement by telling him that something is worth doing because of the satisfaction the achievement will bring and in this way encourage identification with their own inner goals. As with outer goals, the parents' attitudes and actions are important in the course of development of inner goals. In addition, as with the outer goals, the handling of different levels of development contributes to the final attitudes toward inner goals. Where the parent is attuned to the child's developing needs, he will encourage him to enjoy the mastery of any given step at the earliest level, but in a manner that stimulates the child to try to reach mastery of a next higher level as soon as appropriate. For example, the alert parent is ready to take advantage of the child's signs that he is ready to give up drinking milk from the bottle and replace it with drinking from a cup. The parent will do the same when the child shows readiness to move from crawling to walking. With this freedom to develop the child establishes the inner goal of self-growth as an inherent goal but always with pleasurable memories of having reached earlier levels of achievement rather than with anxiety-laden memories. This goal seems to be equivalent to Buhler's (1959, 1964) basic tendency called creative expansion. Such an inherent goal serves as a stimulus from within for continuing self-growth and thus resolves the immature dependency upon external sources for motivation. Parental interaction at the individual growth steps influ-

ences the specific formation of the inner goals as well as the formation of the specific patterns of goal achievement. Thus when parents can schedule satisfaction of the child's feeding needs appropriately, the child learns to accept gratification through taking-in as a justifiable inherent part of living and as a desirable inner goal to be satisfied. This acceptance serves as an important part in the foundation of the concept of "taking in for the pleasure of taking in," such as a love of learning as a source of personal gratification rather than as a matter of pleasing someone or just "getting good grades." The pleasure it can bring fosters the wish to learn and reinforces the basic trust in others as a source of learning. In similar fashion when parents help the child gain self-control, as dramatically experienced in the period of bowel and urinary control, the child develops a sense of mastery of retention and giving. Such mastery serves as an important foundation for self-control as a generalized function in which the child views it as a basic goal of living. This goal is constantly reinforced by society's demand for self-control which, in turn, is then seen as congruent with his own goal. Buhler's (1959, 1964) basic tendency, called self-limiting adaptation, seems to correspond to this goal.

While the child is young the importance of the development of inner goals and their outer manifestation generally is not evident. Their importance, however, is manifest in simple ways at first and gradually in more crucial ways. Thus parents take it for granted that when the child is able to play by himself he finds his own amusements. This is an ability dependent, in part, on the developed inner ability to know what one's goal is, in play as well as in other kinds of activities that result in inner gratification. Only when the child persists with the phrases, "What shall I do now? I don't know what to do, play with me," does the parent begin to feel uneasy and wonder whether something is wrong. This situation is more serious for the older child who is in high school or college and flounders with complete inability to decide what future activity will bring him gratification. While in military service, this writer saw many such young men with excellent capabilities who could never make a decision and waited to be told what they should do with their futures. In the child's early years such behavior is often viewed as representative of the "good child." He "never thinks for himself at all." An example is that of a parent who wondered why her 7 year old would not feed himself, tie his own shoelaces, and the like. He seemed to have no motivation toward maturity. This same parent was the one who proudly explained how quickly her baby had learned not to touch the spoon as she fed him, thereby not making the mess that the self-feeding baby is likely to create. There was no realization that robbing the child of the early experience of the gratification of maturation and replacing it with such externally controlled goals could affect later development. Often it is the adolescent's struggle against excessive dependence on parental goals and guidance, while accepting his goals as his own, that makes for the turbulence which tends to characterize parent and child relationships during adolescence. Parents should be able to accept the adolescent's need to establish the individuality of his inner goals and the sense of inner directedness which these goals provide. They can be crucial both to his ability to make an effective future and the character of his future relationship to his parents. Although this period may bring much disturbance in the relationship, the final resolution, including a feeling of acceptance of his own inner goals by his parents and himself, ends the adolescent's need to struggle to separate himself. It is where the parents fight the adolescent's need for the establishment of his own goals that the adolescent's struggle is prolonged, and wholesome development is threatened. Often the result is the exact opposite of the parents' intent, and the adolescent remains a permanently rebellious individual, ever pursuing his inner goals to the upset of his outer goals. Where parents have been severely controlling from the child's earliest years, an obedient child may develop who will grow and be a comfort to his parents' aspirations, but with the resulting complete dependence upon direction from others will also come the permanent loss of inner gratification. It is not a matter of removing all influence, as some parents infer, but rather to examine the kind of influence and direction given.

It is quite evident that the development of goals, like all personality characteristics, cannot be attributed to any single factor. Goals are the result of the interaction of a number of factors of which the two most crucial are the inherent characteristics of the child and the attitudes and the actions of the parents. However, the importance of cultural attitudes and an occasional key figure outside the family is not far behind in the influence upon child and parents in this interaction. It should be noted that the presence of a particular talent can be critical in the interaction for a child with a special talent. For such a child the denial by parents of an opportunity to exercise such talent may be experienced as severely frustrating or, if jointly denied by parents and child, may result in a sense of emptiness; it may also breed perpetual conflict between parents and child as the latter struggles to develop the innate talent. Where the parents, because of their own needs, try to impose a goal for which the child has no talent, not only failure is likely to ensue but also a sense of frustration, struggle, or emptiness, as well as a lack of self-realization. On the other hand, where the parents can foster such talent, it can become a wholesome, mutually gratifying experience for all concerned. In general, the parent can participate in the development of the child's inner goals by offering him additional stimulation to develop the process of inner goal establishment by posing questions that require the child to think about those things that bring inner gratification. Such recognition on the part of the child becomes an important stepping stone toward establishing the inner goals for adult living. Thus in addition to helping the child to recognize the things that he needs to do, he can be encouraged to think about and talk about those things that give him personal gratification. In this way he achieves personal gratification in a creative and socially constructive style based on his own needs, and this process becomes an inherent part of his personality.

It is clear that the development of goal setting is the result of a long-term process, beginning early and involving the interaction of a variety of people and factors. The healthy pattern of goal setting results from a harmonious integration of the child's innate physical and psychological characteristics with the demands and opportunities provided by the environment, so that internal and external goals develop in coordinated fashion. Such a harmonious integration involves not only permitting the child to develop "the primary 'positive' response" to the reality around him, as described by Buhler (1954), but providing him with guidance, where necessary, to assist him in recognizing his abilities, and offering him appropriate stimulation. Encouragement must be given at a pace and with goals appropriate for the levels of development through which the child goes. In contrast, where such harmonious integration does not occur, unhealthy patterns develop. The particular unhealthy pattern will be influenced by the area or areas of ineffective integration, as indicated in detail in this discussion. The evidence of the unhealthy pattern will be noted in such characteristics as exaggeration of striving, manifested in excessive competitiveness for a goal where the gratification arises from successful competition instead of from a growth experience. Other manifestations are seen in the individual who can achieve well, but only where the goal is provided by an outside source or where he undertakes many different goals and achieves none. Instead of harmonious integration, an unbalanced and inappropriate development has taken place.

References

Buhler, C. *Childhood and adolescence*. Leipzig: S. Hirzel, 1928.

Buhler, C. The reality principle, *Amer. J. Psychother.*, 1954, 8:4, 626-647.

Buhler, C. Theoretical observations about life's basic tendencies, *Amer. J. Psychother.*, 1959, *13*:3, 561-581.
Buhler, C. *Values in psychotherapy.* New York: Free Press, 1962.
Buhler, C. The human course of life in its goal aspects, *J. Humanistic Psychology*, 1964, *4*:1, 1-18.
Buhler, C. Aiding the patient to find his identity and the values consonant with it, *Psychotherapy*, 1965, 2:2, 89-91.
Erikson, E. *Childhood and society*, 2nd ed. New York: W. W. Norton, 1963.
Escalona, S. Emotional development in the first year of life. In M. J. E. Senn, *Problems of infancy and childhood.* New York: Josiah Macy, Jr., Foundation, 1954.
Escalona, S. Patterns of infantile experience and the developmental process. *Psychoanalytic study of the child, XVIII.* New York: International Universities Press, 1963.
Klein, M. *The psychoanalysis of children*, 3rd ed. London: Hogarth Press, 1949.
Ribble, M. *The rights of infants*, 2nd ed. New York: Columbia University Press, 1965.

Chapter 12

Psychotic Adolescents and Their Quest for Goals

Rudolf Ekstein

I suggested elsewhere that the frequent turmoil during puberty and adolescence hides a crisis about which it is frequently difficult to decide whether it expresses a sign of growth or is a symptom of pathology, particularly the pathology of schizophrenic and similar psychotic states (Ekstein, 1966c).

Anna Freud, in a well-known paragraph from her classical text, *The Ego and the Mechanisms of Defense*, published as early as 1936, has summed up the dilemma with a few master strokes. She describes adolescents as:

> . . . excessively egoistic, regarding themselves as the center of the universe and the sole object of interest, and yet at no time in later life are they capable of so much self-sacrifice and devotion. They form the most passionate love relations, only to break them off as abruptly as they began them. On the one hand they

> throw themselves enthusiastically into the life of the community and, on the other, they have an overpowering longing for *solitude.* They oscillate between blind submission to some self-chosen leader and defiant rebellion against any and every authority. They are selfish and materially-minded and at the same time full of lofty idealism. They are aesthetic but will suddenly plunge into instinctual indulgence of the most primitive character. At times their behavior to other people is rough and inconsiderate, yet they themselves are extremely touchy. Their moods veer between light-hearted optimism and the blackest pessimism. Sometimes they will work with indefatigable enthusiasm and, at other times, they are sluggish and apathetic (Freud, 1948).

About fifteen years later, Erikson (1950) characterized the problem which the adolescent has to solve during this phase of development as the search for a permanent adult role, for occupational, social, religious, and personal commitments which lead him through an identity crisis which is insoluble unless society grants him a psychological and social moratorium. This moratorium releases inner organizing forces, enabling the adolescent to move toward young adulthood.

Pumpian-Mindlin (1965) has described this phase of the search for commitment, the temporary role diffusion, the playing with and the acting out of future choices, in terms of omnipotentiality, the megalomaniclike belief of the adolescent that he can reach any goal while, at the same time, committing himself to nonpermanency. Potentially then, he can reach any goal or none, and during this phase the adaptive or maladaptive struggles of the adolescent will determine the outcome, while he is being watched with anxiety and envy by the parent generation.

Frequently these young people give us distorted pictures of pseudoidentification with the adult world. These distortions have been puzzling to the clinician and have encouraged the equally distorted pseudojudgment that adolescence itself is a kind of illness. But it is true that often in this period one can hardly differentiate between psychopathology and normal growth crisis. However, some clear clinical syndromes can be delineated.

In what follows I wish to make remarks about the schizophrenic adolescent whose development parallels in many features that of the average adolescent. His psychopathological state, however, expresses itself in symptoms which, while remindful of the average adolescent crisis, carry in themselves the germs of destructive illness leading to the inability to solve such age-specific problems as the establishment of goals and purposes and the acquisition of skills by which to achieve these goals.

Charlotte Buhler's (1959) lifelong studies of the human life cycle and the patterns of establishment of goals, which then, in themselves, become a motivating, organizing, and character-building force, have given us many guidelines. So, too, have Erikson's (1962) discussions of the different life stages of man and his studies of ego virtues. These will be helpful as we attempt to throw some light on the schizophrenic adolescent's abortive struggle to develop life goals or *Lebensziele.*

In Charlotte Buhler's terms, the adolescent's attempts at setting life goals are first more experimental and programmatic than realistic. He sees and sometimes tries himself in various roles, but his commitments are temporary. While programming these adult roles, he projects himself in his phantasies into the future. All his moves in relating himself to the future realities of life, however, are provisional and preparatory rather than final. This probing by adolescents is bound up in existential-type conflicts. The question "Who am I?" plagues the thinking youth. He feels thrown into conflicts which he cannot resolve and in which he feels utterly alone. Not infrequently, his despair leads him to doubt his ability, his wish to cope with life, and makes him feel hopeless about himself and sometimes even suicidal.

All these problems occur in an exaggerated form in the case of the pathological development. The neurotic youth may tend either to make premature decisions and enter finite relationships, such as a very early marriage, or else he may luxuriate in fantasies of future glory and happiness. Thus a borderline schizophrenic and later homosexual girl, Edda, spent her free time at age 12 lying on her bed and dreaming about going to Hollywood with a suitcase full of brilliant plays, visiting and charming various famous actors and actresses, and becoming famous herself overnight. She prepared maps, studied roads to Los Angeles, put money aside, and packed a suitcase with clothes and some of her poems. However, it never got beyond that. (Case reported by C. Buhler in preparation.)

The psychotic youths described in the following paragraphs demonstrate four different forms in which their goal setting deviates from the normal, First, they have long-range fantasies, which, as such, are phase-characteristic but in their cases are completely unrealistic. Second, in reality they remain "stuck" in short-term goals, which may occur from childhood on or at any age, but which, in the psychotic case, appear as projects of major proportions. Third, they are unable to integrate themselves and to project a unified self from present to future. And fourth, they experience existential-type conflicts, which again, although they may be found in normal adolescents, in their case become serious struggles involving the question of life or death.

I invite the reader to follow me as I describe some clinical material illustrating these struggles in the psychotherapeutic work with a female schizophrenic adolescent, the vicissitudes of whose treatment I have previously described (Ekstein, 1966a, Chapters 3, 12, 14, 22; 1966b).

At first Theresa was hardly reachable and often out of contact. As she slowly ventured out of her autistic world and tried to join the world of her peers as well as that of the adults who were part of her social situation, she tried desperately to cope with a catatonic-like paralysis which kept her from putting into action whatever plans she was capable of developing. These plans seemed to remain forever part of her infantile, her primitive fantasy world. They reminded one of promises that small children offer their parents in an attempt to secure love but really are not meant to be kept. The difference, however, between the small child who offers the promise as a love-restoring device, and Theresa, our patient, is that the small child, as time passes, learns to deal with the promise in the fullest sense of the word and attempts to live up to it, while Theresa's promises could never be kept. They were but static symptoms of her regressed position. They were forgotten as soon as the psychotherapist was out of sight, and they could be compared to a repressed dream which one wishes to remember in order to report it to the therapist. When she finally remembered the promise, the mere recollection of it was experienced as if it were the fulfillment of the promise itself. However, as she continued on the slow road to recovery, frequently hardly noticeable, she learned to live up to small promises, which she could now fulfill on the installment plan, as it were.

Her practical life goals that she discussed during this phase of her psychotherapy concerned such issues as being able to leave the shower room, not after hours and hours of preoccupation with delusional fantasy activity while under the shower but after a specified time which would permit her to be on time for the volunteer worker who brought her to the clinic for the appointment. Somewhat later she experienced as a major achievement the newly gained capacity to take a bus by herself and to remember the number of the bus. This task occupied her mind for weeks and months until she could triumphantly report that she had reached this goal, which she saw as a magnificent achievement, although her performance was completely out of proportion to what would ordinarily be expected of a young person her age.

If one were to see these goals as the life goals she had set for herself, one would have to see them as no more and no less than very small, very tiny short-term goals. For instance, she described during an interview how her social and psychological paralysis finally abated after many weeks and how she was now "moving around a bit, helping the Sisters a bit" in the Catholic home where she then resided. Obviously, this very small investment in the world of reality, the world of social action and of actuality, indicated that much of her psychic energy was invested in other areas of her life. Her life goals, therefore, were of a different nature than the ones that make up the ambitions, the purposes, the activities of adolescents who belong in the ordinary range of psychopathology or normal behavior.

We will come back to Theresa later. First I want to offer similar material from other patients in order to stress certain interesting aspects of these small, short-term goals.

Another research patient was Donald, also a schizophrenic adolescent (Caruth and Ekstein, 1964; Ekstein, 1965; Ekstein, 1966a, Chapter 22). He was occupied in establishing his goal behavior with plans for the next few months, such as to be able to eat lunch together with the other children in the private school he attends. It took him months of mastering his anxiety and fear until he was capable of accomplishing this. Other actions concerned his fear of using the public bathroom, of joining children in a baseball game, or of eating and talking together with his parents. He was impelled to discuss these problems for hours and weeks with obsessive rigidity, and one gained the impression that a powerful struggle developed around a seemingly tiny issue.

A third patient, Danny, again an adolescent suffering from an adolescent schizophrenic character disorder, wanted to live up to the promises he thought he owed society and himself and to his ambition to become a musician, a song writer. These promises to be fulfilled found practical expression in the attempt to finish a poem. He had written the opening lines and was able to complete it only after weeks and months of endless obsessions about it, accompanied by escapes into psychoticlike acting-out phases. His own enthusiastic response to the finished poem was temporary proof to him that he had a great future, but in the face of a minor frustration the enthusiasm vanished without a trace.

What and where are the true investments of such patients? The first patient, Theresa, is sometimes capable of establishing a feeble bridge between her inner world, her delusional preoccupation, and her attempts to communicate with the psychotherapist. She does this by means of what I have called *borrowed fantasies.* She can talk about herself only by metaphoric allegories borrowed from television shows or movies to which she is addicted. As she watches these shows, she sometimes remembers enough of one so that she can communicate the plot, frequently in a changed and bizarre form, and uses the show like a coat hanger on which she hangs her inner life during the transference struggle. The show becomes the brittle and unreliable bridge between her chaotic inner world and the vague desire to talk about that inner world.

During the hour (Ekstein, 1966b) in which she attempted to report to her therapist that she was now successful in "moving around a bit," she used the screen play *Black Orpheus* in order to describe the vicissitudes of the current transference struggle. She saw herself as Eurydice who was involved with Orpheus, but who was, at the same time, also persecuted by the hateful, jealous, and revengeful Aristaeus. She dies a bitter death and Orpheus is to resurrect her. But as he turns around, spurning Pluto's injunction, and listens to her desperate pleas, he loses her again. She described, through her powerful identification with the heroine, her underlying basic philosophy, which then established the psychotic goal behavior of this patient. She considered herself as dead and, at the same time, miraculously alive. She lived through and died a thousand deaths and tried to become alive over and over again. She shared with the therapist the powerful and almost convincing fantasy that she was going to kill herself by the end of the year and, at the same time, told him that she has improved so much that she will never touch herself again, blurring the difference between masturbation and suicide. She has gained self-control and she wants to live. But then she projects the very suicidal and/or sexual fantasy into a homicidal or raping expectation, claiming that someone, some man, perhaps some woman, will kill her, attack her, by the end of the year. Her search for love and for acceptance, her struggle against death, are matched at the same time by the search for death. Her fear of death is matched by the fear of life, and, like Eurydice, she moves backward and forward between the positions of life and death; and the helper, the beloved one, the rescuer, the therapist, at times is seen as the saviour and at other times as the crucifier, the dangerous murderer, the raper.

One can see then that underneath the conscious, the reality-oriented attempt to master small tasks and to be committed to short-term goals, is a powerful psychic system which is characterized by the inner struggle, the alternating commitment to life and to death. One well might say her goal is to stay alive. She does not search for goals which are going to make her life meaningful, but rather she struggles for existence itself. The meaning of her life is a life and death struggle.

She finds herself exposed to these powerful anxieties, these inner terrors, to such an extent that one well can say of her, if it is permitted to coin a new word, that she does not struggle with omnipotentiality but, rather, that she is beset by omni-impotentiality. She defends herself against the awareness of this omni-impotentiality, this utter helplessness, this terror of dying, by means of a defensive fantasy which changes the omni-impotentiality into megalomania. It is for this reason that, in spite of the fact that she does not do more than "move around a little bit," learn to take the bus, learn to count money, and so on, she also speaks of goals such as of becoming a famous movie star, an outstanding singer, a great dancer, etc., goals that are indeed megalomanic because she can and does do nothing in order to move toward them. They are not goals but fantasies which are to cover up the helplessness, the fear of destruction, the terror of destructive impulses. They are promises to herself by which she tries to restore her self-love and to cope with self-destructive tendencies. These megalomanic fantasy goals are self-promises which are not meant to be kept; they are comparable to the promises of the small child to the parent, and just as the latter promises are made to restore the parent's love, these are to restore self-love, megalomanic narcissism. They are the psychotic version of what Schlesinger (1964) called primary promises.

The same is true of our second patient, Don. He, too, even though his accomplishments sometimes move at a snail's pace and are characterized by obsessive repetitiveness which paralyzes him as well as the therapist who attempts to listen (Caruth and Ekstein, 1964), establishes himself in fantasy as a powerful genius, a potential world leader, a great pianist, one who will impress the world with enormous success. But behind these megalomanic expectations looms large his omni-impotentiality, his utter helplessness, and his weakness, his fear of loss of self and loss of object, such as when he tells us that he needs proof that he exists. He sometimes looks at his therapist and wonders whether this experience he has refers to a real person or to a movie-screen picture of the therapist. He must then touch the therapist in order to establish for himself that there is reality. Sometimes he does not believe that he himself exists, since he cannot see himself. He would believe that he exists only if he could see his own image, and then he needs this evidence to prevent himself from being devoured by anxiety and terror. Descartes' *cogito ergo sum* is replaced by a "you touch me or let me touch you therefore I know that I am and that you are."

The third adolescent, Danny, when threatened by loss of object or self-experience, or with a kind of psychic death, tries to restore object and self-world by destructive acting out through wild aggressive attacks, through suicidal gestures, of which it is never quite clear, if one follows the meaning of the delusional material, whether they are to be understood as homicidal or suicidal.

We find then in these patients a variety of common denominators which all relate to the issue at hand: the quasi-search for goals in the psychotic adolescent. As we watch their rudimentary mastery of reality, we find that they have endless problems with social adjustment, school learning, work situations, and that they cannot master actuality, that is, apply reality testing to appropriate need gratifying action. Even in those rare moments when islands of reality testing are comparatively intact, we realize that little energy is available for social mastery, for putting the reality testing into a context of actuality and organized achievement.

We notice that small, short-term goals dominate their lives as far as realistic problem solutions are concerned. We find also that these patients, within their fantasy activities, see their power, their talents and their gifts, and their possibilities for success way out of proportion to the ordinary daydreams of adolescents. Unlike the successful artists, the writers, of whom Freud once said that they achieve through their fantasies what they have dreamed about in their fantasy, namely, honor, power and the love of women, these schizophrenic adolescents have not found the way to translate fantasies or daydreams into truly goal-directed behavior. But still, they see themselves, in spite of evidence to the contrary, as great persons, as world rulers, as creative artists, singers, millionaires, who must wait for the fantastic fulfillment of their wishes or live with the delusionary conviction that they have reached their goals, without ever having to relate these wishes or delusions to any kind of realistic behavior. The primary process does not lead to the secondary process but ends up in a dead-end street. They cannot see any relationship between these fantastic elaborations of their inner dreams and the very small investment they are able to make in their everyday dealing with social issues.

Their megalomanic fantasies, however, are not stable, are not constant, and give way frequently not only to underachievement and nonachievement but yield also to terror, to deep-seated anxieties, to the fear of death and annihilation. They fear that they and the world will perish, so that most of their inner investment does not constitute a struggle to find meaning in life, to initiate purposeful goal behavior, but rather results in a stay-alive struggle, the warding off of *Weltuntergangsphantasien* (fantasies of the world's end).

It must, of course, be emphasized that as these patients struggle for survival and struggle against self-destruction, their use of such existential notions must be understood within the context of schizophrenic thought disorder and disturbed schizophrenic object relations. When we refer to object relations, we do not have in mind the context of interpersonal relations, rather, we refer to the capacity or incapacity of patients to maintain object and self representations within themselves. Theresa, in her use of the theme of Eurydice, gave us a powerful picture of what keeps her from coming to the "upper world," the world of Orpheus and reality, of light and insight, and what keeps her from maintaining this world so that she can establish more than token purposes, more than short-term goals, and can really give meaning to life rather than having to remain committed compulsively to the only meaning she sees in life, the desperate struggle to stay alive, to not die. She struggles backward and forward, between the attempt to gain the object and to reestablish the self representation, and the regression in which she loses both and is paralyzed once more in a catatonic-like disaster.

From studies such as Spitz's (1965) we know that the separation and individuation process in the small infant establishes the capacity to maintain self and object representations, an achievement which is then the basis upon which to build realistic goals in life. Adolescents who do not suffer from such weak object and self representation, who are in no danger of really losing them and have resolved this struggle, can move toward purposes in life, can change or maintain these purposes, can develop toward individuation and identity very much along the lines which have been described in the studies of Buhler and Erikson. They sometimes do give the impression that they are about to lose these achievements and, since the adolescent must give up the early objects' ties in the family and replace them with new ties, he lives through phases where these objects and self representations are on shaky ground. But, as we observe such patients during treatment, we see that they go through the ordinary vicissitudes of neurotic transference manifestations and that they utilize the object representation of the analyst in order to bring about reality-oriented life purposes and goals. This the schizophrenic adolescent is unable to do. He therefore develops transferences which are at times only of a neurotic order, but more frequently are actually psychotic transferences in which separation of self and nonself gives way to fusion-states where there is no clear-cut separation between self and object, between therapist and patient. Sometimes these transferences give way to quasi-separations in which either the self or object representation is maintained at the expense of the other. These are then the more autisticlike states in which patients seemingly cannot be reached during short phases of the therapeutic process.

We suggest, then, that the inability to maintain goals and goal-directed behavior, the incapacity to establish life purposes which are realistic, stem from the fact that schizophrenic adolescents are unable to maintain object constancy. Unlike their neurotic counterparts who suffer from omnipotentiality, these schizophrenic youngsters suffer from omni-impotentiality, a feeling of impotence which permeates all spheres of life, including the inability to maintain self and object representation. Their defense against this omni-impotentiality, this dread and this hopeless struggle for survival, this constant terror of death, is megalomania, which very frequently looks like the omnipotentiality of the ordinary adolescent but actually is but a forged, a nongenuine replica of it. Since most of their energy, then, must be used in order to reestablish some form of psychic equilibrium, their actual moves seem to be poverty-stricken, slow, token gestures, empty promises, tiny, short-term achievements.

Our stress on the issue of object constancy is to indicate the direction in which research in psychotherapy with such patients must proceed. Many case studies (Ekstein, 1966a) in our research help us to establish new techniques utilizable in this struggle toward object constancy. The neurotic adolescent must learn to resolve the unconscious conflict with objects of the past and the present. But still, his is a conflict between separate individuals, between different representations of self, of past and present, and of objects of past and present. The psychotic adolescent offers us a pre-object world and a pre-self world, fused with the partial achievement of object and self representations. As long as there are unstable introjects, the purpose and the goal of life will be a desperate and hopeless struggle for existence, a compulsion to endlessly repeat past misery. But when object constancy is achieved, when capacity for object relations is developed, such existence will be the basis for new meanings and for permanent and realistic life goals, for the release and development of adaptive capacity toward self actualization and the positive use of reality as a source of challenge and nurture (Ekstein, 1966a, Chapter 13).

References

Buhler, C. *Der menschliche Lebenslauf als psychologisches Problem,* 2nd rev. ed., Göttingen: Verlag für Psychologie, 1959.

Buhler, C. *Intentionality and self-realization,* San Francisco: Jossey-Bass, in preparation.

Caruth, E., and Ekstein, R. Certain phenomenological aspects of the countertransference in the treatment of schizophrenic children, *The Reiss-Davis Clinic Bulletin,* 1964, *1*:2, 80-88.

Cooper, B. Casework in the separation of the psychotic child from the parent. Unpublished, 1966.

Ekstein, R. To sleep but not to dream: on the use of electrical tape recording in clinical research, *The Reiss-Davis Clinic Bulletin,* 1965, *2*:2, 87-92.

Ekstein, R. *Children of time and space, of action and impulse: clinical studies on the psychoanalytic treatment of severely disturbed children.* New York: Appleton-Century-Crofts, 1966. (a)

Ekstein, R. The Orpheus and Eurydice theme in psychotherapy, *Bulletin of the Menninger Clinic,* 1966, *30*:4, 207-224. (b)

Ekstein, R. Turmoil during puberty and adolescence: crisis or pathology? *Reiss-Davis Reporter,* 1966, *5*:2, 2. (c)

Erikson, E. H. *Childhood and society.* New York: W. W. Norton, 1950.

Erikson, E. H. Reality and actuality, *J. American Psychoanalytic Association,* 1962, *10,* 451.

Freud, A. *The ego and the mechanisms of defence.* London: Hogarth Press, 1948.

Pumpian-Mindlin, E. Omnipotentiality, youth, and commitment, *J. American Academy of Child Psychiatry*, 1965, *4*:1, 1-18.
Schlesinger, H. J. A contribution to a theory of promising: I: primary and secondary promising. Unpublished, 1964.
Spitz, R. A. *The first year of life*. New York: International Universities Press, 1965.

Chapter 13

The Psychotherapist as a Codeterminant in Client Goal Setting

Tommy M. Tomlinson

The basic aim of this chapter is to explicate the rationale and method of a therapeutic approach which is generically known as "humanistic." The goals of humanistic psychotherapy will be spelled out and their unique characteristics described. Certain issues will be discussed which bear on the justification of the humanistic approach, e.g., client selection, the legitimacy of personal experience as therapeutic data, the place and function of values in the humanistic approach, problems of evaluation of effects, and the effects of various types of therapeutic interventions. The chapter will conclude with a discussion of the relationship format and theory of therapeutic change of a single, but representative, humanistic method—client-centered therapy.

Broadly speaking the entire mental health institution, especially that portion with therapeutic intentions, e.g., mental hospitals, clinics, etc., is supposed to have a humanistic philosophy. Beginning with Pinel's philosophy it has been customary to say that mentally disturbed people should be treated with respect, dignity and compassion, in short, humanistically. In a sense, every person who views and treats mental patients as humans and accords them a person status is a humanist.

In addition to (or perhaps in response to) the pan-humanism which is supposed to, but often does not, characterize psychiatric and psychological practice, there is a subgroup whose entire therapeutic philosophy and method is based on the concept of humanism. Its fundamental premise is the same as that of the total profession: each man is of worth and entitled to respect. From this basic position, however, they move in the direction of framing a rather elaborate set of therapeutic principles and goals. The aim of this chapter will be to explicate these principles and goals. To do this one first must define what is generally meant by the "humanistic" approach to treatment and then identify those who are amenable to the methods that characterize this view.

Humanistic approaches generally are concerned with the development of self-sufficiency, self-realization, self-worth, self-actualization, and like kinds of more or less ideal concepts. They are oriented toward the development of full human potential, and the aim of the therapy goes beyond simple symptom removal, or "adjustment," and into the somewhat transcendental realm of creativity and self-fulfillment. Because these goals do go beyond simply removing the source of pain and because they do invite the client to personal fulfillment by transcending his pre-therapy state of being, one must use care in identifying the clients who can profit from this approach. Verbal therapies of any persuasion place rather severe limitations on the type of client who will be admitted into therapy. Bergin (1966), for example, asserts that before a client is accepted into therapy he must as a rule meet and fulfill certain qualifications, e.g., he must be insightful, self-oriented, intelligent, relatively well educated, not severely disturbed, etc. Thus even in the standard therapeutic world the client must possess certain personal characteristics which make him a promising candidate.

The client who can successfully utilize an "actualizing," i.e., humanistic, therapy must to an even greater degree fulfill the requirements outlined by Bergin (1966). To take a prominent example, consider the restrictions placed on the prospective client's qualifications by client-centered therapy. The goals of this type of therapy include the development of independence by freeing the individual from unrealistic internal as well as crippling external demands, i.e., personal autonomy which is rooted in the person's own valuing process (Rogers, 1964). Implicit in the goal of personal autonomy is the idea of personal responsibility. The measure of success is the degree to which the client can responsibly extract from life the supplies which contribute to his own actualization.

These are reasonable goals to hold for certain groups of people. Yet these goals are not likely to be reasonable or feasible for many clients who do not fulfill the criteria cited by Bergin (1966). To find a single one of these criteria in a given person is to move against expectation. To require them in any substantial combination means a reduction of qualified candidates to a relatively small number. In this light the first point with regard to humanistic therapies is one of perspective. When we talk of this therapeutic form we are not speaking of one which relates to all or even a substantial proportion of the potential client population. Rather, it relates to a limited percent of those who conceivably need "help," and these limitations are imposed by the nature of the goals and procedures of the humanist approach. This is not to say that humanism in therapy is not of benefit to any client regardless of his incapacity to profit from or move toward the higher-order outcome. Ekstein (see Chapter 12), for example, describes how schizophrenic children are enabled to set and achieve very low-level goals, and Buhler (1966) has noted that a more honest personal life can be achieved by poorly educated clients. Yet as the following excerpt will illustrate, humanistic-existential concerns are not the concerns of the severely disturbed, among others.

The scene is a local hospital where groups of student therapists and chronic schizophrenics have been observing each other interact (Barthol, Groot, and Tomlinson, 1966). The aim of the intergroup observation was to expose the patients to "normal" interaction and thereby provide a model of social interaction, as well as to expose the patients to the style of problem expression and coping which characterizes presumably effective people. Diaries of the experience were kept, and reported excerpts were taken from one of the male students.

Following the first meeting the student writes, "There's a big difference in the level of communication between the students and the patients. The students had an intellectual discussion of difficulties of communication. The patients don't attend much to what is going on." At a later meeting he reports, "The students are very intellectual and bright. If I talk to patient X, patient Y interrupts; if I talk to patient Y, patient X dozes." He concludes his diary with this statement, "The students were supposed to supply a model of normal persons to the patients and also to demonstrate that normals have problems too. Yet these students are sophisticated, intelligent and young and tend to discuss problems like the 'existential dilemma' and the 'meaning of life.' These ideas have little to do with my patients. I wonder whether the patients saw us as quite real or not . . . maybe more normal nonpatients should be used."

Certainly a trained therapist would have kept the content of the interaction within the limits tolerable to this type of patient. But the point is clear: existential concerns and problems of meaning are not the stuff of which therapy with severely disturbed people is made.

Humanistic therapies are geared to handle those personal considerations which have been identified as cosmological (Hobbs, 1962) or existential (Buhler, 1962). By cosmological is meant the business of deriving a code of conduct when one is confronted with two or more such codes, at least one of which is in conflict with another. This is the malaise of the late adolescent, more especially the college student. It is their rather intense concern to work through a suitable code of personal ethics and morals in a world where the "old ways" seem to be either failing or merely the mouthings of hypocritical adults. The aim of therapy is to come to grips with these problems of cosmology and proceed to a systematic understanding of a personal place in the world and the ideals by which the person will conduct his life.

At a presumably deeper level lie the existential concerns of those who are attempting to supply meaning to a life which has lost its meaning or perhaps to survey the past and try to draw meaning out of an existence where none is immediately obvious.* This appears to be the problem of the middle-aged person.

In summary, the humanist therapies seem most appropriate for bright, verbal, introspective, 20- to 50-year-old people, whose main source of anxiety derives from a need to have purpose and meaning in their lives. It is to the needs of these people that the humanists dedicate the treatment style described in the remaining pages.

Values and Humanistic Therapy

There are a number of spokesmen for the humanistic idea, e.g., Maslow (1959), Buhler (1962), Fromm-Reichmann (1956), and Rogers (1961), and while their individual approaches to therapy may differ, the

* The word "meaning" as used in this chapter has two different definitions. Which of the two applies depends on the context within which it is used. "Meaning," as in the phrase "meaning of life," is defined as the data of one's existence and by itself contains no evaluative inference. The evaluative dimension of "meaning" is typically couched in terms of "meaningfulness," i.e., the degree of meaningfulness the individual attaches to the substance (meaning) of his life. Thus a view of one's life as meaningful assumes an existence which has both substance and is valued positively. A meaningless life also has substance, but the substance fails to fulfill the individual's criteria of usefulness or purpose. The nature of the substance itself is in large part irrelevant to its evaluation; what is useful and has purpose for one person may be useless and purposeless to another. In like manner, what is called purposeful or useful will differ from person to person, although, as with substance, there will be some general agreement as to what kinds of life cycles fulfill these criteria.

The second definition of meaning is used in the connection with therapy rather than with philosophy. Meaning in this instance refers to the nature of the symbolization process by which an individual describes his personal experience. In Gendlin's (1964) discussion, meaning refers to one's sense of having experience which exists on a continuum from preconceptual to complete symbolization. The symbolization process permits the individual to attach meaning to his inner experience. The development of meaning in this sense is the central aim of the "humanist" therapies.

basic goal remains the same. Therapy is not viewed only as a "cure" in the sense of making functional what previously was dysfunctional, but also to provide a situation wherein the client can surpass his previous developmental level and move in the direction of greater exploitation of his human potential with its attendant increase in satisfaction with life.

This basic consideration cuts through all other considerations of theory or technique. For example, Buhler (1962), although accepting the general merits of the Freudian position, disagrees with Freud's position that the conscience has its sole roots in the rules of society. Her disagreement centers on the humanist position that the conscience may have its roots in essential aspects of the self and is not, therefore, simply a repository of the rules delivered by the agents of society. The basic point is the belief that people can work out their own solutions to living which will include a personal set of rules of conduct which may or may not be deviant from those sanctioned by the norms of society. Implicit in this position is the belief that man is not a victim of his past, i.e., his behavior is not unalterably determined. Rather, he can make his own future, given the opportunity to free himself from his past and given the atmosphere within which to work out the plan of action.

Accompanying the assumption of self-determination is the correlated and necessary assumption of man's responsibility for his own behavior. One of the aims of the therapy is the generation of personal responsibility which goes beyond simple self-control. Viewed from the humanist perspective, man must come to recognize his own contributions to his fate, i.e., his responsibility for his current state and his capability for changing it. Thus if the emerging client is ever to engage in a more creative life than is typified by his past, he must be able to assume a degree of responsibility that is freeing rather than constraining. This point is important, since the usual notion of being responsible carries with it the connotation that the responsible person never engages in behavior which moves against the "accepted" mode of conduct, e.g., he never breaks a rule knowingly. Green (1946) seemed to be saying this when he suggested that therapy could never induce creativity, since man is always constrained by his fellows and the rules of society.

There are two assumptions in Green's (1946) statement which are needful of clarification. The first is that creativity must necessarily incur negative sanctions from society, i.e., that creative or innovative behavior will bring the individual into conflict with the rules and norms of society. In the first place most of the "creativity" which grows out of the therapeutic experience involves the client's approach to his problems of living. He may elect a new, heretofore untried approach to coping with the exigencies of his existence. Behavior of this type is quite unlikely to be constrained from expression by a repressive society. Should the client actually engage in the common definition of creativity, i.e., invent or discover something new, it again seems unlikely that he would be greeted by disapproval. In fact, society tends to uniformly reward people for creating something new.

There are times, however, when society will bring its force to bear on the person who attempts a new approach to living. Typically, such resistance to expression is encountered by the person who elects to move against the "established" way of life. Under these circumstances the "offender" usually is cited as irresponsible because he appears to be deliberately disregarding the rules of society, the assumption being that no responsible person would intentionally violate a behavioral norm. Yet the client who moves through a therapy experience in which he critically examines the premises underlying his behavior will very often conclude that many of the constraints which are imposed externally serve to cripple the development of his own and society's full potential. An outgrowth of this realization may be a decision to abide no longer by those rules which retard development, but such a decision and the action which follows must be made responsibly. The crucial consideration is whether the decision to move also includes a willingness to accept the sanctions against the move which might be delivered. Thus, for example, a person might deliberately choose to break a harsh and illogical law and remain a responsible person, providing he does not intend to evade his responsibility for having done so. Or more typically, a person may choose a path of personal conduct of which he knows a certain proportion of his world will disapprove, yet with full awareness and responsibility he may decide that the outcome is worth it and so proceed.

Some may worry about "psychopaths" exploiting their fellow man as a result of being able to act in the way described. The likelihood of such an event is slim. As Hobbs (1962) points out, we are all the product of roughly the same socialization processes, and the people who tend to engage in the kind of therapy being described are most often oversocialized rather than undersocialized. One of the aims is to free them from the unnecessary crippling constraints and externally imposed rules. Should the development of personal knowledge be misused, it still is difficult to fault the humanist approach; knowledge can always be perverted by a few, but that fact has not lessened our search for it.

Thus the product of the humanist ideology is a man who knows where he has been and where he is going, who enjoys the freedom of action resulting from felt autonomy and personal responsibility and, by being so, embarks on the road to self-fulfillment.

The reader will note the word "ideology" in the preceding paragraph; it means that the humanist therapist has a position to present to the world. There is built into the value system and the philosophical scheme a systematic view of the "good life." To deny this would be to deny that there are distinctly humanist goals in therapy. There are clear goals, and they deal with a conception of personal conduct and the fulfillment of man's potential which separate this point of view from any other.

The philosophical and scientific problems which are encountered with the announcement of the intention of advancing a given conception of life are manifold. The psychotherapeutic professions have argued at great length about the need to maintain a scientific, i.e., uninvolved, stance vis-à-vis evaluations of personal conduct, good vs. bad life styles, approved outcomes in therapy, etc. The argument has hinged on the idea that therapists should maintain a nondirective or noninfluencing attitude, i.e., should not inculcate into their patients their own attitudes and beliefs. Increasingly, however, the trend has been in the direction of openly stating that certain therapists have distinct ideas of what is desirable in their patients' behavior. The humanist position, however, while obviously advocating a defined position, nevertheless can maintain this stance of nondirection. The aim of the humanist is not to supply meaning to the experience of the client (in fact he may actively avoid doing so), but rather to supply the client with a situation in which he himself can come to supply his own meaning. To be sure, this situation is one in which the therapist actively advocates personal autonomy, but it is exactly the achievement of this goal that permits the client to interpret the meaning of his own life in his own terms. The advocacy of the goals of personal freedom by their very attainment lead to a reduced susceptibility to therapist influence and permit the therapist to remain in a nondirective role.

As a final example of humanist thinking it will be useful to examine the role of personal knowledge in this system. The concept of personal knowledge derives from Polanyi's (1958) systematic and general treatment of the part played by human experience in the "scientific" enterprise. The concept as applied to psychotherapy seems more suitable and useful than the concept of insight. Thus rather than discussing "insight" therapies, it would be more appropriate to discuss "personal knowledge" therapies. The aim of the latter is to generate in the client an awareness of the meaning of his experience. Instead of coming to see previously unrelated aspects of one's experience as related together with its relevance for current behavior, that is, to achieve insight, the overall goal is the generation of information about oneself which leads to a better or more congruent articulation of the meaning of one's total behavior, whether the behavior stems from an internal feeling process or from overt, cognitively mediated action.

The discussion of the role of personal knowledge in psychotherapy will take place in the context of the current issue which exists between the humanists and those representing a more behavioristic or, more precisely, a behavior control position. The issue which has been drawn, e.g., London (1964), concerns the relative merits of "insight," i.e., personal knowledge, vs. "action," i.e., behavior change, as therapeutic change agents.

The actionist therapists take the position that since the insight therapies have failed to produce credible evidence of their ability to change behavior, they should be removed from the therapeutic marketplace. They adduce evidence (Wolpe, Salter, and Reyna, 1964) taken from studies of behavior control methods of treatment to support their contention that the action approach is the only justifiable treatment technique in terms of the production of observable behavior change. The certitude with which they advance their position is not matched by the evidence (Breger and McGaugh, 1965), but the central point of this paper is not to challenge their data, rather it is to make a case for "insight," i.e., verbal, and more especially, humanistic, therapies.

The case turns on the validity of personal knowledge, that is, personal awareness, as a desirable and legitimate therapeutic goal. In the first place there is something of a paradox in the position of the actionists who rely so heavily on the scientific foundations of their practice and yet, at the same time, disparage that most scientific of enterprises, the gathering of information. The peculiarity seems to stem from the fact that the behaviorists apply what the laboratory produces to the client, whereas the humanist allows the relevant information to come from the immediate source, the client, and the client then applies the information to himself and to his interpretation of the world. The issue thus resolves itself into one of information credibility. The humanist accepts the client's accounts of his experience as legitimate data; apparently the behaviorist does not, beyond what is necessary to identify the client's problem. The discovery of personal experience, the development of personal knowledge, are the goals of the humanist. The shaping and control of unwanted behavior are the goals of the behaviorist.

From the standpoint of the humanist the acquisition of personal knowledge is desirable, even necessary, if the person is to survive in the modern world. Speaking directly to the problems attending the deliberate control of behavior, Roe (1959) points out that awareness is essential for counter-control against unwanted manipulation. She suggests that "awareness of our own needs and attitudes is our most effective instrument for maintaining our own integrity and control over our own reactions." This sort of personal control is among the goals seen as desirable by the humanists. It is a goal which by definition cannot be shaped in the behavior control sense. Thus the two camps are at odds as much over the issue of goals as they are over methods and outcome. At stake is whether the accumulation of personal knowledge as an end in itself is sufficient to justify the continued application of the humanist method. The problem is particularly touchy, since the goal of personal knowledge has no obvious or logical relationship to behavior change. Thus to measure the result of a humanist therapy in terms of observable behavior change may be like measuring length in terms of weight; it simply isn't relevant or appropriate. The generation of "meaning" and the removal of "symptoms" may be quite unrelated, but both are legitimate goals; and they need not occur in concert for the therapy to be evaluated positively.

In support of personal knowledge it is difficult at this stage to either conceptually or practically extend typical behavior change techniques into the task of providing meaning about one's experience. For example, one is hard pressed to understand just how the removal of a phobic response, as an end in itself, is related to the generation of a value system or the discovery of meaning in life. Yet it also is clear that not everyone wants, needs or is able to achieve the goals described by the humanists as being desirable. But for those who can and want to go the route of personal knowledge, the question of efficacy in terms of symptom removal becomes meaningless and irrelevant. Clients in search of meaning come to therapy not to lose a symptom but to gain understanding. The question is begged if one suggests that merely reducing the anxiety about having to understand is a "cure." The quest for personal knowledge, the need to know about oneself as well as the world, is a motivation which as a personal (therapeutic) goal is both pressing and legitimate. To deny the point is to deny the purpose of science itself.

Thus the quest for meaning through personal understanding and knowledge, while no panacea, is a defensible therapeutic goal. To be sure, the quest is necessary and the therapy useful to only a limited number of people, but it *is* necessary and it *is* useful to them. The fact that the therapeutic experience speaks to a relatively small proportion of the population is irrelevant; the only real consideration is that those who can use it get it, and those who can't use it receive something else. That is a problem of diagnosis and treatment decision. The issue of efficacy and ethics arises only when clients who are not suitable to the therapy or not in search of the humanist goal are invited to engage in the pursuit of those goals.

The Outcome

What can the client expect to gain from personal knowledge? Buhler (1962) summarizes a number of idealized therapeutic goals which are suggested by various therapists, e.g., Lorand who judges therapeutic success in terms of the client's ability to "get along" better after treatment, Thompson who sees success in the light of reduced feelings of inferiority, lessened anxiety, relief from repressions, etc., Fromm-Reichmann who speaks of the client as being free to create and move in the direction of self-realization, and Rogers who sees his therapy as a method to release a "constructive tendency" in the client. There is little in these brief statements which makes clear what exactly the client can expect to take away from psychotherapy. The level of abstraction contained in the concept "constructive tendency" makes it virtually impossible to describe behaviorally the actual gains which result.

Hobbs (1962), in an article critical of the use of the concept "insight" as an explanation for behavior change, suggests five sources of gain which may accrue to clients who emerge from therapies with a humanist focus. Each of these sources of gain involves learning by the client, that is, the accumulation of personal knowledge. They are not dependent upon "insight" for their efficacy in producing personal knowledge or behavior change, though the client may gain insight and therefore a better understanding of himself during the therapeutic period. From Hobbs's (1962) view, however, the insight is more a product of the learning than it is responsible for it.

Psychotherapy, Hobbs says (1962), provides the client with the opportunity to learn the following things:

1. Through the sustained experience of intimacy with a therapist who makes no personal demands, who does not insist that the client be someone other than who he is at the present moment, the client can risk uncovering his "authentic," or real, self. The client is in a position to take a chance on being close, honest, and open with another human being without the threat of punishment. As he learns to risk himself with the therapist, he also learns that interpersonal intimacy is possible and that

the development of "personal authenticity" (Bugental, 1965) removes the need for interpersonal facade and deception.

2. The client in this relationship has a chance to reduce the anxiety which attaches to various symbols of unpleasant experience. He can, for example, gain a new and more appropriate view of those early authority figures which cause him so much pain in his present life situation. By so doing he can develop a more effective repertoire of responses to the symbols. At the least, he can learn that he doesn't have to be afraid of symbols of authority.

3. The therapist, by being always genuine and nonjudgmental, can provide the client with an opportunity to see how his own interpersonal and experiential distortions interfere with the conduct of a rewarding relationship. The therapist refuses to respond to the "neurotic stupidity" which the client acts out, and by so doing he confronts the client with a relationship which does not reinforce his customary ways of interacting. The client can learn from the therapist that simple, direct and honest relationships do not require deceit and need not be feared.

4. By consistently refusing to supply meaning to the client's own experience the therapist provides the client with training in independence. The locus of control and the locus of evaluation reside entirely in the client. The choices the client makes evolve from his own thinking, and by making such choices he learns that he can trust his own wisdom to guide himself through life.

5. Finally, and from the humanistic point of view perhaps most importantly, the client has the opportunity to develop or perfect a cognitive system, or cosmology, by which to provide meaning to his experience. It is in the generation of meaning that humanism probably makes its most vital contribution. Since the meaning that an individual gives to his existence must be uniquely suited to his own life situation, the absence of overt influence by the therapist is absolutely essential.

Attempts to "adjust" the client on the basis of systematically shaping him to conform to the current societal norm is an error on several counts. The most obvious is that the norms are continually changing. Green (1946) made the point twenty years ago that inculcating the prevailing value system into a client is, at best, a stop-gap, since the moral and ethical system is in a state of rapid change, and the client sooner or later would be out of step and in conflict again.

A second error resides in the nature of the therapy structure. Unless the therapist lives with his client, he can never know exactly the conditions under which the client must live. Overt suggestions for behavior change or direct applications of "action" methods are invariably based on inexact and, at times, wholly distorted perceptions of both the therapist and the client. Furthermore, if suggestions for change are given and followed, the likely outcomes assume two forms: if the change is effective, the therapist is reinforcing dependency in the client (the client learns that following the therapist's suggestion leads to improvement and, as a result, he fails to learn to follow his own lead); if the change attempt fails to work, the client comes to mistrust and doubt the therapist's understanding of him with consequent damage to the relationship. From the standpoint of learning personal autonomy it seems clear that direct attempts to influence client behavior will have an adverse effect. The object of this type of therapy is to get people to assume responsibility for their own lives and their own behavior. Therapeutic behavior which works against that goal is at the end destructive, however well intentioned the therapist may be in "helping" the client.

Thus the goal is to help the client generate his own meaning system, but one which is sufficiently open-ended to permit future self-propelled change. The structure and process of the learning experience which provides for such "cosmological flexibility" has been described by Rogers (1957) and more recently elaborated by Gendlin (1964). Rogers (1957) has advanced a conception of the type of relationship within which personal knowledge and individual growth are maximized. The nature of this relationship, though conceived within a client-centered context, nevertheless is appropriate to the broad humanistic interest and provides a working definition of the type of relationship which should lead to the development of personal autonomy, self-responsibility and increased awareness of one's own experiencing process as a valid guide for living.

As the "necessary and sufficient" conditions for the production of personal growth, Rogers (1957) suggests that the following characteristics should be present in the therapist's behavior:

1. *Positive regard.* The therapist must value or "prize" the client. He must have a fundamental respect for the person as a person. This concept assumes a basic commitment to the worth of the individual and the principle that each man has the right to self-worth and self-determination. Positive regard may or may not include personal liking for the individual, although it seems likely that if one values a person, he is likely to "like" him also.

2. *Congruence.* In the relationship to his client the therapist presents himself exactly as he is; there is no facade or pretense at being something other than a human being. He is open to his own feelings and willing to

acknowledge them to himself and, if necessary, to the client. He can allow himself to be aware of his own fears or his own perplexities without having to erect defenses to deny these feelings.

3. *Empathy.* This condition involves the therapist's ability to understand the meaning of his client's words. As the client describes his experiences (both internal and external), the therapist is empathic to the degree that he perceives and understands the client's descriptions "as if" they were his own. The condition of empathic understanding is fulfilled when the therapist moves in the same world of meaning as the client. At that point he truly understands the client.

4. *Unconditionality.* This condition is closely related to positive regard, in that it calls for the therapist to avoid placing "conditions of worth" on the client. By this is meant that regardless of how the client presents himself, whether he says good or bad things about himself, the therapist will not make evaluations of "good" and "bad." He accepts whatever the client says without passing judgment.

5. *The final condition for growth.* Given the presence in optimum degree of the four therapist conditions, the client must perceive their presence at least to a minimal degree. He must be able to experience being understood, positively regarded, etc., before growth can take place. Though many therapists of a humanistic persuasion would disagree with the assertion that these are the "sufficient" conditions, few would hold that they are not "necessary." Thus they describe the ingredients of a relationship which should promote personal growth in the client, regardless of the particular theoretical position of the therapist. Some therapists, for example, would say that interpretations also are necessary for successful and effective growth experiences, but that does not take away from the desirability of this form of relationship as a context within which the therapist works with his client.

The evidence which bears on the interplay of the therapeutic conditions and therapy outcome stems from two principle sources. Barrett-Lennard (1962) operationalized the "conditions" in the form of a "relationship inventory." Observers (or the client and therapist) respond to 64 Likert-scored statements which tap the dimensions of the conditions, e.g., positive regard: "He respects him"; empathy: "He nearly always understands what the client means." The results indicate that there is a positive significant association between the rated degree to which the conditions are present and independently measured therapeutic outcomes. A study by Truax and Carkhuff (1965) suggests further that when the conditions are present, i.e., the therapist is being empathic, congruent, etc., patients maintain a level of self-exploration which drops significantly when the conditions are withdrawn. From these data it may be concluded that these conditions of the relationship not only set a growth-inducing context for the therapeutic interview, but, in fact, their absence retards the self-exploration which is necessary for the growth process to take place. Thus it seems clear that the conditions are indeed "necessary" for therapeutic growth. Without them the self-exploration which leads to personal knowledge fails to occur.

Two questions remain: 1) how in this relationship does self-exploration produce personal knowledge, and 2) what kind of knowledge does it produce? At the core of the humanist-existentialist position is the concept of experience. Central therapeutic questions concern the manner in which the client construes his experience, how the therapist can come to know and understand the client's experience of the world, and how the client can come to know and more realistically evaluate the meaning of his own experience and experiencing process. Gendlin (1964) recently developed a theory of personality change which employs the client's experiencing process, that is, his sense of having experience as the primary mode of personal growth. By differentiating between "experience" (concrete psychological events) and "experienc*ing*" (a felt process), Gendlin describes how the "experiencing process" (concrete, bodily feelings) may be used to discover the "basic matter of psychological and personality phenomena."

Gendlin (1964) points out that anyone at any time can refer directly to his inward sense of experiencing, and, by so doing, one's sense of having experience provides a "direct referent" to internal feelings. The feeling or direct referent to which the person refers contains meaning. Frequently the meaning is not well symbolized and thus not susceptible to detailed articulation. The feeling is, however, in awareness and may, therefore, be referred to, however unclearly. The unverbalized–implicit–meanings can be better or more completely symbolized if they are directly referred to and talked about. The process of focusing on a preconceptual meaning provides the client with the chance to complete or carry forward the preconceptual, implicit meaning of a bodily feeling.

Gendlin (1964) also notes that this process of self-exploration is best completed in a relationship of the kind previously described. When a person can feel safe enough to focus on an anxiety-producing bodily feeling, he is in a position to thoroughly explore the heretofore vague, implicit meanings that accompany the anxiety experience.

As the client begins to refer directly to his bodily feelings, the anxiety which ordinarily accompanies the experience and which typically prevents focused self-examination begins to dissipate. The dissipation of the anxiety is the client's cue that he is correctly symbolizing the felt meaning.

The paradox of anxiety reduction accompanying focused attention on a feared experience or experiencing process is rather easily resolved. The client is made anxious by his ignorance of the meaning of his feelings. He can't understand why he feels the way he does, and it is frightening to him. His inability to gain mastery over his feelings, to understand their full meaning, leads him to feel helpless with himself. Coming to know the complete meaning of one's feelings is fear-reducing because the person is fulfilling his "need" to know about himself. He is now in control of his feelings; he knows exactly what they mean. He can continually refer to his experiencing for confirmation that the current symbolization of the bodily feelings is correct. It "feels right" to have described his experiencing process in a certain way. An erroneous description of the internal process "feels wrong," the client knows he is incorrect, and anxiety rises.

Thus step by step the client *unfolds* his felt meaning. He may grapple with a felt referent by attempting to symbolize it in a number of ways. He may dramatically hit upon the "right" description as, for example, when he announces, "Yes, that's it. That's the way I've always felt, but I didn't know what it meant."

During these periods of unfolding, as the client more and more accurately symbolizes the direct referent, there will be times when he sees a more general application of the discovered meaning. He may say something to the effect that he now sees that he treats everyone in terms of the uncovered construct, or that he has repeated the same behavior over and over again but without previously recognizing the fact.

As the more general nature of the direct referent, i.e., the experiencing process to which the client is referring, becomes known, it begins to feel different. The heretofore implicit meanings are now changed. The direct referent is seen in a new context and now, as a product of *referent movement,* the client shifts his focus to the new meaning of the referent.

The process of directly referring to an imprecise, preconceptual felt meaning and of unfolding and symbolizing aspects of the referent leads to referent movement. As the referent moves, the client starts again on the "new" referent and repeats the process. The continuous exploration of changing but more completely symbolized referents exerts continuous pull on the client's attention. It is something he must attend to, something he must finish. He may be sidetracked, but he is compelled to return to the felt referent. The compelling nature of referent exploration is called the *self-propelled feeling process,* and it is this self-propelled quality that permits the client to proceed on his own. As one becomes able and accustomed to focus on and symbolize vague internal feelings, he also is enabled to continue the process alone. A therapist who can facilitate the unfolding, who can help the client to verbalize the implicit meanings, is critically important. But for purposes of initiating what has been called the "actualizing process," the client must develop the capability to refer to and understand his feeling process without the help of a therapist. In this light, therapy is an experience which initiates the growth process. But for continued growth to occur, the client must learn to use his inner, organismic experience as a guide. It is only then that he can know what he wants and needs and can fully engage in the behavior which leads to his own fulfillment.

To sum up, the therapy which grows out of humanistic considerations moves beyond conventional treatment interests in the direction of not only helping the disturbed person but also of providing him with an experience which will contribute to his long-range growth and self-realization. The goal is not merely to return the person to some previous level of psychological functioning, but to contribute to an enhanced richness of living which surpasses that which was known before.

The process by which this goal is attained focuses sharply on the relationship between the client and his therapist, and on the development of a heightened awareness of inner experience to provide meaning to one's personal experience. As the person comes to know how he feels and is able to symbolize that experiencing process accurately, he effectively comes to rely upon himself to provide meaning to his experience and set himself meaningful goals of life. His susceptibility to external influence drops proportionally as he learns to trust himself to provide meaning to what he sees. He is freed to give himself direction and to develop his own style of life, one which is uniquely suitable to him. He is enabled to move to, if necessary, unconventional, hopefully creative goals, since he is not constrained by growth-retarding self and societally imposed rules. But he is responsible to his fellow man and gives cause for their disapproval only when his own sense of personal integrity permits him no recourse. Having done so, he willingly acknowledges his action and his responsibility for the direction he takes, having learned that it is he and only he who chose to act.

References

Barrett-Lennard, G. T. Dimensions of therapist response as causal factors in therapeutic change, *Psychol. Mono.*, 1962, *76* (Whole No. 562).

Barthol, R. P., Groot, H., and Tomlinson, T. M. The use of student volunteers as role models for psychiatric patients in a quasisensitivity training laboratory. Paper given at the American Psychological Association Conference, New York, 1966.

Bergin, A. E. Some implications of psychotherapy research for therapeutic practice, *J. Abnormal Psychology,* 1966, *71,* 235-246.

Breger, L., and McGaugh, J. L. Critique and reformulation of "learning-theory" approaches to psychotherapy and neurosis, *Psychological Bulletin,* 1965, *63,* 338-358.

Bugental, J. F. T. *The search for authenticity*. New York: Holt, Rinehart and Winston, 1965.

Buhler, C. *Values in psychotherapy*. New York: Free Press, 1962.

Buhler, C. Humanistic psychology: its concepts, its cultural significance, its meaning for people in their personal lives. Unpub. manuscript, Los Angeles, 1966.

Fromm-Reichmann, F. Notes on the history and philosophy of psychotherapy. In F. Fromm-Reichmann and J. L. Moreno (eds.), *Progress in psychotherapy*. New York: Grune & Stratton, 1956.

Gendlin, E. T. A theory of personality change. In P. Worchel and D. Byrne (eds.), *Personality change*. New York: John Wiley & Sons, 1964.

Green, A. W. Social values and psychotherapy, *J. Personality,* 1946, *14,* 199-228.

Hobbs, N. Sources of gain in psychotherapy, *American Psychologist,* 1962, *17,* 741-747.

London, P. *The modes and morals of psychotherapy*. New York: Holt, Rinehart and Winston, 1964.

Maslow, A. H. *New knowledge in human values*. New York: Harper, 1959.

Polanyi, M. *Personal knowledge*. Chicago: University of Chicago Press, 1958.

Roe, A. Man's forgotten weapon, *American Psychologist,* 1959, *14,* 261-266.

Rogers, C. R. The necessary and sufficient conditions of therapeutic personality change, *J. Consulting Psychology,* 1957, *21,* 95-103.

Rogers, C. R. *On becoming a person*. Boston: Houghton Mifflin, 1961.

Rogers, C. R. Toward a modern approach to values, *J. Abnormal and Social Psychology,* 1964, *68,* 160-167.

Truax, C. B. Experimental manipulation of therapeutic conditions, *J. Consulting Psychology,* 1965, *29,* 119-124.

Wolpe, J., Salter, A., and Reyna, L. J. *The conditioning therapies*. New York: Holt, Rinehart and Winston, 1964.

IV Socio-Cultural Factors as Codeterminants of Goal Setting

In Part IV, an attempt is made to determine the impact of socio-cultural factors on goal setting, particularly with respect to their influences on the ideational content of goals. Socio-cultural experiences indeed involve emotional forces together with those of an ideational nature. Some people say that they prefer the Catholic Church because its service appeals intensively and directly to their emotions. Others adhere to the traditions of the Jewish religion because it makes them feel that they belong, even if they do not attach specific meaning to the rites. Some young people of our time feel that they are bringing about a new era by wearing long hair, living in unconventional ways and producing ecstatic drug-induced states sometimes with and sometimes without basing their behaviors on specific ideology. Modern social psychology has investigated the effects of ideology, rooted in socio-cultural forces, on the lives of individuals. Particular significance attaches to these effects in the areas of occupational and personal goal setting, as shown, for example, in studies of achievement motivation and aspiration.

In Chapter 14, C. Buhler and A. J. Horner interpret the roles of education in the process of goal setting, focusing on the function of ideational persuasion in the educational process. The authors choose the previously established frame of reference of love and care, demands and discipline, information and opportunity, model and ideals in probing the areas in which education's ideational content reveals its impact. They discuss the roles of various cultural traditions in handling the young child, the effects of authoritarian versus democratic upbringing, and the ideals of conformity versus free self-expression. Finally, Buhler and Horner consider the practical and theoretical goals of formal education and the widely observed transition to peer group influence on modern youth, replacing the traditional influence exerted by parents and elders.

In Chapter 15, R. Friedman and M. Wallace deal with the relationship between vocational choice and the formation of life goals. They review and evaluate theories of occupational choice, and weigh the effects of family and broader external socio-cultural-economic environment on this choice. They pay special attention to the significance of early job experience in shaping later goal setting and occupational patterns.

In Chapter 16, W. H. McWhinney investigates the part played by small groups in goal development. He holds that distinctly human goals have their origin, development and confirmation in the context of small group experience. He describes group influence on goal development as becoming effective through information, identification, inclusion and reification.

In Chapter 17, F. Massarik discusses goal setting as influenced by institutional factors. He begins with the thesis that the institutional environment into which the individual is born and through which he moves in the course of his life serves as a major codeterminant of the goals that he sees as relevant and potentially attainable. Massarik notes that the individual learns to think and speak in terms of particular goals, whereas other goals remain for him a foreign language beyond his ken. In this sense, affected by his institutional environment, the person internalizes a "goal vocabulary," focusing on certain goals while excluding others. The author illustrates the influence of class and other institutional factors on goal setting by reference to several brief cases, including one of an itinerant laborer and another of a girl at the fringe of hippie society.

In Chapter 18, J. Livermore Sanville examines some ways in which cultural tradition acts as codeterminant of human choice. Her examples include an adolescent Negro boy from the Caribbean, who, in spite of obstacles, commits himself to a career aim based on modern education; an American Indian who had chosen to return to the life and culture of his forebears; and a man of Turkish origin who chose to identify with the American culture. In each case, the choice of cultural values arises from an inner struggle complicated by emotional dynamics. Sanville examines the interrelations among these factors and the occasional emergence of the choice from what appears to be an individual's independent action of evaluation.

Chapter 14

The Role of Education in the Goal-Setting Process

Charlotte Bühler and Althea J. Horner

When we hear the word "education," we are likely to think of it in terms of the narrowly defined process of formal schooling. Goldschmidt (1960) gives us the broader definition which we would like to use here: "What we include under the term education is the total process by which the infant acquires knowledge, understanding, attitudes and orientation that are characteristic of his culture" (p. 172).

This definition includes both formal education and the subtle, informal processes by which we acquire cultural values and attitudes. As for the latter, we turn to the anthropologist who, with his comparative studies of culture, is in a better position than the psychologist to clarify how some of these processes take place. We will temporarily disregard the psychological viewpoint and its focus on the individual's personality and behavior in order to examine the interaction between the individual and the cultural forces influencing him. How do these forces affect him, his feelings about himself, his understanding of human relationships, and his ideology?

Cultural traditions are the result of a group's reactions to varying interpretations of life and the world. They are reflected in the rearing and training process and have an emotional and intellectual impact on the growing individual. This impact, in turn, generates certain patterns of feelings and thoughts and is so pronounced in a person's formative years that it would be difficult to determine what he would be like without these traditions. Marvin Opler (1965), for example, feels that: ". . . the regulatory controls, the styles of expressions, the ordained goals and social role behavior are defined within the definition of the situation (its meanings and communicated symbols) long before anyone of us is privileged to select and construct a life pattern, or indeed, add personal understanding and interpretation to it" (p. 193). F. L. Strodtbeck (1958) shows how culturally determined principles influence the modes of the growing individual's self-direction and goalsetting even in subgroups of the American culture.

Rejections of cultural patterns and the substitution of individual choices of goals and ideals occur generally only in those individuals who are genetically strongly endowed or are exposed to conflicting culture patterns, as demonstrated by Jean Livermore Sanville in Chapter 18.

In spite of the valuable material which anthropologists have contributed in the last half century, the psychological interpretations of the psychological effects of various educational systems and principles of upbringing on the individual still are very hypothetical.

The following discussion and examples will serve to illustrate the impact of cultural patterns on various areas of a person's life.

Love and Care

It is only recently that we have begun to question how different principles of infant care affect the individual. As far as the emotional dynamics of the mother-child relationship are concerned, it has been demonstrated clearly, specifically by R. Spitz (1945) and in a survey by J. Bowlby (1952), that the mother's absence from the young infant is bound to damage his development.

The various traditions reflected in how a mother handles her infant have caused a variety of reactions. M. Mead (1951) has speculated about the difference of feelings in infants who are constantly being carried around on their mothers' backs or in their arms, and in babies who, most of the time, are left alone in a cradle or play pen. She has also dealt with the different effects of the method of up-bringing in which a child is being made to feel at home with any parent in the community and the one in which he knows only his mother or her specific substitute. By comparing Israeli children, who were raised in the Kibbutz with its pattern of multiple mothering, with Israeli children who were raised on the family-centered farm, A. Rabin (1965) found that the Kibbutz children were far less affectively involved with members of the family than were the others, and therefore they also had fewer opportunities for conflicts with the family.

Some recent American experiences point up the difference in another set of principles. In the twenties many mothers, under the influence of J. Watson (1924), handled their babies in a matter-of-fact and impersonal way. This method soon proved highly unsatisfactory because many of these children became difficult, rebellious, and complaining. Under the cultural influence of psychoanalytic teachings, some of the mothers later changed their views and began to pay much attention to and cuddle their babies.

Demands and Discipline

The different principles which we have been describing represent not only specific ways of giving the infant care and affection, but also different expectations regarding the child's cooperation. In this area it is particularly crucial to clarify the distinction between individually conditioned emotional impacts and the effects of cultural ideology. In Chapter 10 we reported on a study by Becker who distinguishes between the emotional effects of permissive and restrictive parents, of parents who show anxious emotional involvement and those who display calm detachment, and of parents who are warm and those who are hostile. He finds that a child's dependency, his compliance, aggression, outgoingness, and creativity are conditioned by the impact of these emotions. Hostility has the worst effect and does even more damage if it is paired with permissiveness rather than with restrictiveness. Restrictiveness paired with warmth is not necessarily damaging, although it fosters dependency and may result in a lack of creativity.

These findings contradict to a degree the conclusions reached by Adorno et al. (1950) in their well-known study, the *Authoritarian Personality*. Their concept of the authoritarian personality is that of a syndrome which develops as the result of rigid discipline on the part of the parents, with affection that is conditional in the sense that it is dependent upon approved behavior. This kind of personality, they claim, grows up within a framework of dominance and submission and eventually is overly concerned with status values and an admiration of power.

The traditional fixation on authoritarian principles is explained by these authors as the result of insecurity and uncertainties which the authoritarian personality cannot tolerate and against which he defends himself with standards and rules. The authoritarian personality, furthermore, is thought to harbor hostility against anybody who attacks his convictions which he uses for his self-defense.

On close inspection, however, this eloquent theory does not hold water or at least cannot be stated in such general terms. As R. Christie, M. Jahoda et al. (1954) showed, there are different kinds of authoritarian relationships. It is not true that all people brought up in cultures in which authoritarian principles prevail, are as neurotically defensive as Adorno et al. describe it. To be sure, there are cultures in which authoritarian principles prevail but as long as they are accepted, they constitute a closed system in which a young person can grow up without hostility and defensiveness. It is only when the cultural development of a whole civilization casts doubts on the justification of certain procedures and convictions that defensiveness arises.

This brings us to the problem of insecurity. While human beings at all times must have felt more or less insecure, there is no doubt that our present existential insecurity is being experienced by more people than ever before. The result of our modern thinking is an uncertainty that some people can tolerate and others find unbearable. The latter may choose to hold on or retreat to religious and ethical convictions that are contained within certain traditionally accepted dogmas. This, however, does not make them neurotics. If they are neurotic, i.e., defensive and hostile in their efforts to cope with reality, it is as a result of personal difficulties and their lives' unfortunate emotional bases. In other words, their insecurity is rooted in their personal history and not in the uncertainties of their convictions. The emotionally stable person usually finds ways and means to cope with existential uncertainties, a point which we will discuss further in Part V of this book.

Thus seemingly democratically tolerant parents, if they are insecure persons who do not dare to take a stand and do not trust their own judgment, may have insecure children because their tolerance is merely an escape from the responsibility of having to offer their children some kind of a hold. On the other hand, authoritarian parents may take a stand but do it without true conviction. This makes them defensive within the framework of our present culture and makes their children insecure and/or hostile.

We have tried in the foregoing considerations to disentangle the personal and emotional reasons for choosing or automatically favoring a certain type of discipline as against acting under the influence of culturally established standards. The latter are presently undergoing great changes in many places and most certainly in our Western civilization.

The benefits of conformity versus free individual development, of strict discipline versus extreme tolerance, of authoritarian versus democratic principles have led to many debates and experiments. Most notable among the experiments are those of Lippitt and White (1939, 1943), which grew out of the work of Kurt Lewin. In these well-known studies, youth club members were put alternatively under the guidance of authoritarian, democratic, and "laissez-faire" leaders and a comparison was made between the effects these three types of leadership had on the members.

There is obviously a great difference between demands and discipline, as well as models and ideals, that are based on abstract ideologies and those that are dictated by the more practical principles of life.

Erikson (1943), in his studies of the social character of the Yurok Indians, concludes that: "systems of child training . . . represent unconscious attempts at creating out of human raw material that configuration of attitudes which is (or once was) the optimum under the tribe's particular natural conditions and economic-historic necessities" (iv). Goldschmidt (1953) states that, generally speaking, comparative studies of primitive cultures have shown that these societies value those personal attributes that make for economic usefulness. Examples of how primitive societies orient their children toward practically and economically useful habits are numerous, and only a few are mentioned here.

M. Mead (1930), for example, reports how, in the Manu society, respect for property is taught from the earliest years. A good baby is one who never touches anything and also never asks for anything that is not his. This is reminiscent of the French attitude toward their children's handling of personal property. M. Wolfenstein (1955), after having observed French children playing in a park, points out how parents emphasize the preservation of a personal possession, and how different this is from American parents who tell their children that they must learn to share. Thompson and Joseph (1947), in a study of the Hopi Indians, note how their early teachings are related to the way they view the world and to the economic necessities of their kind of life. From the very start sex roles and expected associated behaviors are impressed on the child through interpersonal relationships. A little girl is told she will grow up to be a good cook, a boy, that he will be a swift runner. Margaret Mead (1930) also relates that the Manus, whose homes are built over water, teach their children early in life to feel at ease with water. Motor skill is highly valued in this culture and to achieve it is one of the primary goals of child training.

All these practices of guidance must originally have been conceived of in the interest of certain goals and values, some of which were forgotten while the traditions lived on.

Information and Opportunities

Information is conveyed by words and actions. Long before an infant can be taught by words, he learns through experience. His own curiosity and his desire to master things and to communicate with his environment impel him to imitate people. Piaget (1963) has noted this kind of imitation in infants just 2 weeks old. Margaret Mead considers the forces of imitation as much more potent than the adults' techniques for exploiting them. She believes that a child's receptivity to his surroundings is more important than any stimulation, and that as long as every adult with whom he comes in contact is saturated with tradition the child cannot escape a similar saturation. She admits that this applies primarily to a homogeneous culture, such as that of the Manus, but maintains that this theory has played a significant role in modifying America's faith in education as a universal panacea. Culture, in her opinion, is far more influential as regards a child's future than are the formal learning experiences of school. "The child can only be as rich intellectually as the culture from which he comes," she says. The implications for the culturally disadvantaged child in our own society are obvious.

True as it may be that learning through imitation and identification prepares the basic matrix for education's successful development, the formal educational process that takes place in the school is of central importance because it is systematic and representative of a culture.

The school's immediate goals are to convey information and to offer opportunities. In our Western civilization, however, the role of the schools always has been viewed within the broader aspects of a more comprehensive goal, a goal of personality or character formation in the framework of society, human development, or mankind's ideals. From the beginning there has always been a question of how to combine the pursuit of the practical goals of useful learning with the theoretical goals of serving certain ideas. About 1600, Comenius, a great educator who firmly believed in man's love of liberty and was committed to support it, discussed the possibility of teaching children in a way that would enhance their human development.

The problems that arises from the school's having to serve short-term as well as long-term goals has long been a central issue in educational discussions. John Dewey (1956), the father of modern American educational philosophy, devoted much thought to this problem and suggested the philosophy of combining teaching with the child's development of experience, thus integrating him into the social process. Bertrand Russell (1926) greatly favored the English notion of acquiring knowledge along with character education. And in one of his more recent publications, the educator R. Ulich (1964) defines the dual task of education as follows: "The school fails unless it sets the perennial against the contingent. It teaches science and literature, and through them about the world of nature and of humanity" (p. 31). In *Education and the Idea of Mankind,* he outlines the history of the ideology on which Western education was founded and indicates some of the problems which education faces today, a time which is given over to a complete re-evaluation of our educational systems and procedures. The anthropologist G. D. Spindler (1963) goes right to the center of the problem by pointing out, in his *Education in American Culture,* how "little is known on an empirical basis about American value systems." Rhoda Métraux (1955) agrees with him and, trying to clarify some of the "implicit and explicit values" in the American educational system, relates them mostly to the process of growth and development.

Among the new values that our educational system strives to enhance are the individual's creativity, his free inner development, and the fulfillment of his potential. There also is an increasing recognition of such values as self-understanding, communication, and the understanding of others.

Several modern schools try to focus on one or the other of these aspects. Well known is the experiment of A. J. Neill (1960) in his school "Summerhill," in which he hopes to develop a child's potential through removal of pressure. As he sees it: "The molded, conditioned, disciplined, repressed child—the unfree child, whose name is legion, lives in every corner of the world. He lives in our town just across the street. He sits at a dull desk in a dull school; later, he sits at a duller desk in an office or on a factory bench. He is docile, prone to obey authority, fearful of criticism, and almost fanatical in his desire to be normal, conventional, and correct . . ." (p. 95). Neill's educational goals are the development of self-regulation, which he believes can be strengthened through an atmosphere of love, trust, understanding, and responsible freedom. He sees the culture of England as basically "anti-pleasure," trying to mold the child into a disciplined creature who will put duty before pleasure. He believes that the child's inherent potential can be fully developed only through a policy of noninterference with his growth and removal of pressure. This is not to say that he confuses freedom with license; what he is trying to achieve is "responsible freedom." Neill considers creative expansion the dominant value which in turn can only be attained through noninterference and nonpressure. He bemoans the many attempts to foist an academic education on youngsters whose tendencies lie in other directions. It is interesting to note, however, that only a small number of his students choose further academic training. Does this prove a fallacy in Neill's methods? Academic achievement in the Summerhill setting is not set forth as an admirable goal to be pursued. No incentives are offered and there is no stimulation of creative mental efforts at the critical period where a person's creative expansion begins (C. Buhler, 1959). The concept of a critical period for learning, which was derived from Lorenz's (1935) work on imprinting in ducks, is relevant here. It was found to be relevant also in McClelland's (1961) studies of the development of achievement motivation during childhood to which we have already referred in Chapter 10.

Studies about creative persons, as reported earlier in this book (see Chapter 8; B. Eiduson, 1962; and Goertzel and Goertzel, 1962), also show very definitely that early stimulation and example play an important role in the development of creative talent. An atmosphere of learning, as it seems to prevail in the Chicago school from which Getzels and Jackson (1962) obtained their material, appears to be far more inspiring than a laissez-faire attitude. It is hoped that this atmosphere of learning and interest in the individual will develop his potentialities as they relate to himself and to his fellow men (G. Murphy, 1958; H. Otto, 1966), a development which is particularly emphasized by the new movement of humanistic psychology.

Models and Ideals

As we have seen, the environment provides the growing individual with ideas and ideals. They are implied in the modes of love and care, of demands and discipline, and in the techniques of giving information and offering opportunities. Besides these indirect techniques, however, there are direct procedures by which models and ideals are held up to children.

Some of the values implied in the training of young children were mentioned before. The early direct teaching of values and beliefs seems to be handled more systematically in cultures other than our own. Spindler (1963) described certain socially required qualities of the Menomini, qualities which the individual in that culture comes to see as ideal: equanimity under duress, control of overt emotionality and aggression, and autonomy. Mead (1930) emphasizes how cultural pressures may inhibit striving and keep it within traditionally defined boundaries.

Our own culture has relatively few unitary goals and values. In a forthcoming study of 50 middle-class persons' memories of the values that were impressed on them as young children, only very few appeared to be of a general nature (C. Buhler, 1962). Essentially they had to do with cleanliness, good manners, honesty, and cooperative behavior. Sears, Maccoby and Levin (1957), in *Patterns of Child Rearing,* list as objectives of the observed restrictions and demands good manners; good behavior at home; neatness; orderliness; successful toilet training; success in school; rejection of dependency; low permissiveness of aggression, sex play, and masturbation; and immodesty. There is a difference of emphasis when it comes to the more complex values, depending mostly on social and cultural group participation and on individual temperaments and philosophies of life. But before we discuss some of these areas, we must again distinguish between the dynamic impact the environment has on the child's acceptance of models and values and the role ideology plays in an individual's life.

As far as pressures are concerned, there is a notable trend toward an increased influence of peer groups. This holds true even for the previously very authority-oriented German youth (Schelsky, 1958). Two interrelated reasons for this are the older generation's own uncertainty regarding values, as well as the Western civilization's failures in wars and the resulting political chaos, which have robbed the present youth of much of their confidence in authority.

In Freudian terms this means that superego values, i.e., the incorporated values of parents and leaders, are being replaced by ego ideals, i.e., objectives chosen by the younger generation on its own. This would be a truly progressive development if the ideals were really set up as a matter of choice. But only in part is there a truly considered choice at play. Most of the time the present youth's goal setting is strongly determined by a rebellious attitude on one hand, and a pleasure-seeking trend on the other. It should not be overlooked that this rebellion usually results from the fact that the youth of each generation works toward new patterns of life. These new goals and values, however, often remain vague and confused, and only the negative and rebellious orientation comes to the fore. Also, many of the seemingly new directions turn out to be not freely chosen ego ideals but goals adopted under pressure; adult pressure has been replaced by peer pressure. As Coleman (1960) found in high school social systems which do not reward scholastic achievement, students considered as "intellectuals" were not the ones with the most ability. Rather, the ablest students sought status in more profitable areas such as athletics. In other words, approval of and conformity with others remains a decisive determinant of the average person's goal setting, except that the peer group assumes the role previously played by the adults.

Sherif and Cantril (1947, p. 252) hypothesize that "the degree of influence of age-mate reference groups and membership groups varies directly with the degree of psychological weaning from grown-ups and the intensity of adult-youth conflict." When the young adolescent finds himself caught between the values of his parents and the conflicting values of his peers, he is put into the position of having to make a choice. Whether he chooses for or against the values of his parents will often be highly influenced by the quality of his relationship with them. The less the parents meet and have met the emotional needs of the child, the more likely he is to turn to his peer groups for support and to accept their values as well. In clinical work with adolescents we so often meet parents who blame everything that has gone wrong on the child's bad companions. What is striking in these situations is the frequency and degree to which the parent-child relationship has obviously been a troubled and unsatisfying one since early in the life of the child.

Not all individuals are equally subject to group ideals and group pressures. Cartwright and Zander (1955) investigated why some individuals yield to these pressures and others resist them. Reviewing several studies done in this area, they conclude that pressures are exerted differently. More pressure is put on the person who is disliked and less on the person with high prestige. As Goodenough (1945) noted, if the individual has a strong enough personality (which probably results in prestige), he can bring others around to his way of doing things. Cartwright and Zander also concluded that individuals perceive group pressure differently and cite Gordon's findings that the degree of conformity is related to the degree of the person's group identification, his conception of the group's attitude toward nonconformity and of his own role in relation to the group, as well as to his own special personality traits. A third factor affecting conformity is the degree of attractiveness the group has for the individual, and this determines the extent to which he will go to be included in the group. When a person wants to remain in a group because he finds it attractive, the threat of rejection is powerful potential punishment.

The enormous strength of peer-group pressure seems to make it just as hard for an individual to become himself today as parental pressure did previously. The struggle to find oneself, which we observe so frequently in our psychotherapy patients, seems to be no easier for the peer-dominated than the parent-dominated individual. In view of the strong appeal that group interaction has in our time, and of the very encouraging results which group psychotherapy and sensitivity training have had, it is possible that the introduction of this kind of procedure as a regular course in the last year of high school may bring about a favorable solution to the problems of adolescents' group activities. If adolescents could be shown that their respective group can help them in developing positive feelings about themselves, their bent toward destructive activities might be curbed.

We mentioned before the widespread interest in the reform of educational methods, which goes hand in hand with a reevaluation of educational goals and ideals. Educators frequently ask, what exactly do we want to accomplish; what are our values? As G. D. Spindler reminds us, the latter are not really clear. There is no doubt, though, that ours is an "achieving society," a concept which was introduced and defined by McClelland (1961). The pursuit of excellence which J. Bruner (1961) defines as the goal of American education today is obviously related to our society's high acclaim of achievement, as McClelland also indicates. The latter finds, with Calvin, that need for achievement (*n* Ach) in a continual striving for perfection (p. 49) scores high in American education today. But what does this achievement goal imply? In starting out with Max Weber's famous theory on the tie-up of the development of modern protestantism with the development of modern capitalism through enhancement of independence and achievement, McClelland comes to the conclusion that the achievement motive is actually an economic profit motive. Economic profit, he holds, is what ultimately motivates the achiever. He further recommends the cultivation of other-directedness in our educational system, because the other-directedness that he sees cultivated by peer groups in his opinion increases achievement. This, however, seems to stand in direct opposition to his finding that: "subjects with high *n* achievement tend to do better than subjects with low *n* achievement only at non-routine tasks that require some degree of personal initiative, or even inventiveness, for solution" (p. 216). It also contradicts his theory that man is more "a creator of his own environment" than he has previously been given credit for. What truly creative person has ever been an other-directed person? All through history truly creative persons have been the most inner-directed of all, and to assume that the creation of great works of music, art, and science was motivated by the idea of economic profit is obviously absurd. Of course, McClelland does not claim that; but he does, for example, relate the rise and fall of literature and science in England to that country's economic growth and decline. In other words, he sees creative productivity as a by-product of the "expansive mood" of certain times. This still does not mean that the creative person is motivated solely by considerations of profit or that he is outer-directed. On the contrary, it means that a group's collective high status and standard of living permits its creative members to be inner-directed, economically unconcerned, and interested in excellence for excellence's sake.

This idea is not too different from the previously mentioned concept of Bruner that excellence is the goal of achievement, a goal which may be considered inherent in achieving. Any other functions that excellence may have in the achiever's life must be judged to be secondary, even if they are predominant in his mind.

Parents and teachers usually emphasize excellence as such. But case studies seem to suggest that parents' early overemphasis of economic or social motives in teaching their children studying or working habits is emotionally quite detrimental. As McClelland and his collaborators showed, later achievement levels depend greatly on early stimulation as well as on the example that parents set. Identification with parents or teachers as models is an important factor, as the many recent studies on creative personalities have brought out. Eiduson (1962), for example, found in her study of the creative scientist that the main, and sometimes only positive, tie between him and his family was related to his achievement. The emphasis on achievement as related to other personality characteristics varies greatly in different social as well as subcultural groups, and also in different families. A few examples follow.

The effect of the social-cultural environment upon achievement goals was examined by Ausubel and Ausubel (1963) who concluded that:

> During pre-adolescence and adolescence, segregated Negro children characteristically develop low aspiration for academic and vocational achievement. These low aspirations reflect existing social class and ethnic values, the absence of suitable emulatory modes, marked educational retardation, restricted vocational opportunities, lack of parental and peer support, and the cultural impoverishment of the Negro home. Because of loyalty to parents and rejection by the dominant white group, Negro adolescents develop ambivalent feelings toward middle-class achievement values and the personality traits necessary for their implementation (p. 34).

McClelland reported that the high *n* Ach level among Jews was related to the fact that the Jewish religion itself stresses perfection in conduct and insists on a measure of self-reliance as a means of understanding God's relationship to man. That is, the individual is supposed to know the law himself, and to consult the rabbi only when he needs help in understanding a difficult point.

Strodtbeck (1958) found that the Jews were the only group which did not show a drop of *n* Ach level in the lowest socio-economic category. There is no doubt, he says, that the average *n* Ach among Jews is higher than that for the general population of the United States, and he explains this in terms of McClelland's ideal condition for the production of a high *n* Ach level. Jewish families set high levels of aspiration for their children. According to McClelland, there is an interaction between religion and social class in the genesis of *n* Ach, with social class being a more important determinant than ethnicity or religion. However, Strodtbeck's findings about the Jews' *n* Ach level in the lowest socio-economic group contradict this view.

As far as Catholics are concerned, McClelland found that their achievement values were closely related to their degree of Americanization and that the values of the modern middle-class American Catholic reflected the general culture rather than his religion. He concluded, therefore, that the effect religion has on a person's *n* Ach level depends on the degree to which the religion is "individualistic" and emphasizes personal responsibility rather than reliance upon ritual and the religious expert (the priest).

Strodtbeck also found completely different value systems in culturally different groups. His comparative study of Italian and Jewish families shows how differently each group values the family and the individual, and how one regards man's destiny to be beyond his control while the other believes in the perfectability of man and his ability to control his fate.

The individual's ideational development is thus a complex process in which emotional pressures as well as cultural ideals and prejudices play a role. It is not a once-and-for-all proposition, because his own mental growth as well as his experiences in life often modify his original ideals and ideas. Eventually he develops a unique value structure which for some persons consists of a rigid system of opinions and principles and for others remains flexible and open-ended.

Cantril (1940), in opposition to the initially quoted opinion of Opler, summarizes the individual's evolutionary development as follows:

> Although we do conform in large measure to the common values of society and do desire a certain amount of social recognition, in addition to this—and often much more important in terms of felt significance—we cherish certain values which may be shared by our family circle, a few professional colleagues, a local community group, or a political party. And sometimes we cherish, as most important of all, those values which we have worked out for ourselves and think of as our own . . . In such instances, we care about recognition only from a very few people, or the status we may want is status only in our own eyes (p. 45).

This statement reminds us that in the realm of models and ideals the individual's own self-determination can play a more decisive role than what he learns from his environment. Given a strong personality and the relative freedom which our present Western civilization provides, an individual may well set his own goals and ideals starting early in life (C. Buhler, 1962).

References

1 Adorno, T., Frenkel-Brunswik, E., Levinson, D., and Sanford, R. N. *The authoritarian personality.* New York: Harper, 1950.

2 Ausubel, D. P., and Ausubel, P. Ego development among segregated Negro children. In A. H. Passow (ed.), *Education in depressed areas.* New York: Teachers College, Columbia University, 1963.

3 Bowlby, J. *Maternal care and mental health.* Geneva: World Health Organization, 1952.

4 Bruner, J. *The process of education.* Cambridge: Harvard University Press, 1961.

5 Buhler, C. *Der menschliche Lebenslauf als psychologisches Problem.* Leipzig: S. Hirzel, 1933(2nd ed. Göttingen: Verlag für Psychologie, 1959.

6 Buhler, C. Theoretical observations about life's basic tendencies, *Amer. J. Psychother.,* 1959, *13*:3, 501-581.

7 Buhler, C. *Values in psychotherapy.* New York: Free Press, 1962.

8 Buhler, C. Human life goals in the humanistic perspective, *J. Humanistic Psychology, VII*:I, 1967.

9 Campbell, J. D. Peer relations in childhood. In M. L. Hoffman and L. W. Hoffman (eds.), *Child development research.* New York: Russell Sage Foundation, 1964.

10 Cantril, H. *The invasion from Mars.* Princeton: University Press, 1940.

11 Carroll, J. B. (ed.), *Language, thought, and reality; selected writings of Benjamin Lee Whorf.* Cambridge: John Wiley & Sons, 1956.

12 Cartwright, D., and Zander, A. (eds.). *Group dynamics: research and theory.* Evanston: Row, Peterson, 1953.

13 Christie, R., and M. Jahoda (eds.). *The authoritarian personality.* Glencoe, Ill.: The Free Press, 1954.

14 Coleman, J. S. The adolescent subculture and academic achievement, *Amer. J. Sociol.,* 1960, *65,* 337-347.

15 Davis, A. *Social class influence upon learning.* Cambridge: Harvard University Press, 1949.

16 Dewey, J. *The child and the curriculum: the school and society.* Chicago: University of Chicago Press, 1956.

17 Eiduson, B. *Scientists—their psychological world.* New York: Basic Books, 1962.

18 Erikson, E. H. Observations on the Yurok: childhood and the world image. University of California Pub. In *Amer. Archeology and Ethnology,* 1943, 35 iv.

19 Erikson, E. H. *Childhood and society.* New York: W. W. Norton, 1950.

20 Flavell, J. H. *The developmental psychology of Jean Piaget.* Princeton: Van Nostrand, 1963.

21 Getzels, J. W., and Jackson, P. W. *Creativity and intelligence.* New York: John Wiley & Sons, 1962.

22 Goertzel, V., and Goertzel, M. G. *Cradles of eminence.* Boston: Little, Brown, 1962.

23 Goldschmidt, W. Values and the field of comparative sociology, *Amer. Sociol. Rev.* 1953, *18.*

24 Goldschmidt, W. (ed.). *Exploring the ways of mankind.* New York: Holt, Rinehart and Winston, 1960.

25 Goldschmidt, W. Record album: *Ways of mankind.* National Assoc. of Educational Broadcasters.

26 Goodenough, F. L. *Developmental psychology: an introduction to the study of human behavior*. New York: Appleton-Century, 1945.
27 Hartmann, H. On rational and irrational action. In H. Hartmann, *Essays on ego psychology*. New York: International Universities Press, 1964.
28 Kluckhohn, C. *Mirror for man*. New York: McGraw-Hill, 1949.
29 Lewin, K. *Resolving social conflicts*. New York: Harper, 1948.
30 Lewin, K., Lippitt, R., and White, R. K. Patterns of aggressive behavior in experimentally created "social climates," *J. Soc. Psychol.*, 1939, *X*, 271-299.
31 Lippitt, R., and White, R. K. The social climate of children's groups. In R. Barker, J. Kounin, and H. Wright, *Child Development and Behavior*. New York: McGraw-Hill, 1943.
32 Lorenz, K. Der Kumpan in der Umwelt des Vogels, *J. Ornith.*, 1935, *83*, 137-213; 289-413.
33 McClelland, D. *The achieving society*. New York: Van Nostrand, 1961.
34 Mead, M. *Growing up in New Guinea*. New York: Morrow, 1930.
35 Mead, M., and Macgregor, F. O. *Growth and culture*. New York: G. P. Putnam's Sons, 1951.
36 Mead, M., and Wolfenstein, M. *Childhood in contemporary culture*. Chicago: University of Chicago Press, 1955.
37 Métraux, R. Implicit and explicit values in education and teaching as related to growth and development, *Merrill-Palmer Quarterly*, 1955, *2*, 27-34.
38 Murphy, G. *Human potentialities*. New York: Basic Books, 1958.
39 Neill, A. J. *Summerhill*. New York: Hart, 1960.
40 Opler, M. K. *Culture, psychiatry and human values*. Springfield: Thomas, 1956.
41 Otto, H. *Exploration in human potentialities*. Springfield: Thomas, 1966.
42 Piaget, J. *The moral judgment of the child*. London: Kegan Paul, Trench, Trubner and Co., Ltd., 1932.
43 Piaget, J. *Play, dreams and imitation in childhood*. New York: W. W. Norton, 1951.
44 Rabin, A. *Growing up in the kibbutz*. New York: Springer, 1965.
45 Russel, B. *Education and the good life*. New York: Avon Books, 1926.
46 Schelsky, H. *Die skeptische Generation (The Sceptical Generation)*. Düsseldorf: E. Diederichs, 3rd ed., 1958.
47 Sears, R. S., Maccoby, E. E., and Levin, H. *Patterns of child rearing*. Evanston, Ill.: Row, Peterson & Co., 1957.
48 Seward, G. H. Cultural conflict and the feminine role: an experimental study, *J. Soc. Psychol.*, 1945, 22, 177-194.
49 Sherif, M., and Cantril, H. *The psychology of ego-involvements*. New York: John Wiley & Sons, 1947.
50 Sherif, M., and Sherif, C. W. *Reference groups*. New York: Harper & Row, 1964.
51 Spindler, G. D. (ed.). *Education and culture*. New York: Holt, Rinehart and Winston, 1963.
52 Spitz, R. A. Hospitalism: an inquiry into the genesis of psychiatric conditions in early childhood, *The Psychoanalytic Study of the Child,* 1945, 5 S.
53 Strodtbeck, F. L. Family interaction, values and achievement. In McClelland *et. al., Talent and society*. Princeton: Van Nostrand, 1958.
54 Thompson, L., and Joseph, A. *The Hopi way*. Chicago: University of Chicago Press, 1947.
55 Ulich, R. (ed.). *Education and the idea of mankind*. New York: Harcourt, Brace, and World, 1964.
56 Watson, J. B. *Behaviorism*. New York: People's Institute, 1924.
57 Wolfenstein, M. French parents take their children to the park. In Mead and Wolfenstein (eds.), *Childhood in contemporary cultures*. Chicago: University of Chicago Press, 1955.
58 Young, W., and Hixon, J. *LSD on campus*. New York: Dell Books, 1966.

Chapter 15

Vocational Choice and Life Goals

Robert Friedman and Melvin Wallace

In our society, no discussion of the growth and the evolution of the individual and his life goals would be complete without consideration of the world of work and its role in human experience and individual development. One of the major milestones in the life of a person is reached when he begins to contemplate job interests and opportunities and to make plans to obtain the education and skills required for the work of his choice. For most individuals in Western culture, this process is begun in late adolescence and completed soon thereafter.

This chapter is concerned with the relationship between vocational choice and life goals. It reviews theories of occupational selection and provides a critique of these formulations. It proposes that the individual selects a vocation on the basis of his involvement in two types of experience: 1) his interaction with the family social unit, his closer environment, and 2) the interplay between himself and the objective factors that comprise his larger external environment. It also reviews the influence of the first vocational experience on life goals, the ways in which feelings, attitudes, and behavior are shaped and molded by the impact of the first job.

Although most of the background information referenced below comes from material generated from and most applicable to the population of the United States, the factors influencing vocational choice will be considered across culture, class, and ethnic lines.

Theories of Occupational Selection*

Efforts to provide explanations of the causes underlying occupational choice may be categorized as: 1) single-factor, and 2) multi-factor

* There is considerable literature devoted to the theories of occupational choice, and the reader who wishes to pursue this question in depth is referred to the bibliography.

theories. Among single-factor explanations of vocational choice, the best known is the "accident" theory. Primarily based on autobiographical material, this point of view contends that chance facts, events in the external environment over which the individual has no control, exert a powerful influence on occupational decision making. Ginzberg (6) cites the examples of the artist Whistler, who stated he would have remained an Army officer if he had not happened to fail the science examination at West Point, and David Ricardo, the economist, who developed a passion for economics through stumbling across a copy of Adam Smith's *Wealth of Nations* while on vacation. Another single-factor theory stresses the effect of unconscious impulse. Psychoanalytic literature contains many case examples of this viewpoint, the most typically cited being the selection of surgery as an outlet for sadistic tendencies.

Critics of single-factor theories have pointed out correctly that the individual has options in the response to an "accident," and the nature of the response is conditioned by a complexity of internal and external factors. The reaction of the individual to accident or impulse is not an automatic, stereotyped response. Gross (8) states the case forcefully: "Everyone is exposed to accidental occurrences and contacts, and therefore we must ask why some are apparently in a state of readiness to respond and others not. The problem is one of selectivity" (p. 146).

The second category of vocational choice theory is the multifactor, developmental sequence approach. This group of theories emphasizes the conception of occupational selection as an evolutionary process that starts in childhood and continues to develop through life. These formulations emphasize the factors of (self-concept), ability, social-cultural values and goals, and opportunities as influenced by race, sex, ethnic group, religion, class, geography, and economic conditions. Ginzberg's (6) hypothesis proposes a series of choices divided by three time periods, fantasy (ages 6-11), tentative (11-17) and realistic (young adult). He states that the occupational choice process is "largely irreversible" and that compromise between what an individual wants and what he can get is involved in every choice. The writings of Hughes (12) and Gross (8) assert the significance of social-cultural factors; Gross labels his view "occupational social selection." Hoppock's (11) premise is that need satisfaction is the dominant concern. Super (22) postulates life stages: the exploratory state (in which the individual moves through fantasy, tentative, and realistic phases to a vocational commitment), and the establishment stage (in which the individual "tries out" the occupation and either continues in it as a stable choice or decides to take entry jobs into other vocations until a stable choice is made).

It is our view that a common weakness in multifactor theories is their failure to specify which factors are decisive for whom and under what circumstances. Multifactor theories do not allow for extrapolations to explain individual cases. If vocational choice theories are to make a contribution to vocational counseling, their application to individual problems must be both feasible and illuminating.

Whether vocational choice is essentially a rational, ordered sequence of development steps in an individual's life cycle or, as Forer (4) suggests, "a somewhat blind, impulsive, emotional, and automatic process," or a blend of the two, does not seem to be settled by available studies and theoretical presentations. It seems clear, however, that the selection of an occupation is a crucial stage in the development of an individual. Vocational decision is the culmination of both conscious and unconscious efforts at self-actualization. It is the product of the individual's experience in his family (his closer environment) and his interaction with the realities in the world of work. Each of these considerations will be discussed in turn.

The Individual in Interaction with Closer Environment

What are the personal, subjective factors that impel the individual to aspire to, prefer, or choose an occupation? The answer to this question is to be found in the individual's personality, his values, and his goals.

The influence of personality or the self-concept on vocational choice is complex. Forer (4) points out one aspect of this relationship when he states "persons of different kinds of personality . . . seek to enter occupations which are peculiarly important to them by dovetailing with the ways in which they characteristically handle their problems. The personality or self develops within and is partly shaped by the family unit. The process of establishing an identity begins at an early age and continues for a long period of time. Interests change, abilities develop, potentials unfold, limitations become apparent, and values and goals are absorbed through family interactions. The maturation of identification brings with it changes from the early fantasy imaginings of being a policeman or a fireman to the more deeply considered adolescent preference for the vocation of a teacher or parent. Wish fulfillment, distortions in self-concept, a neurotic need to fail, escape from feelings of inadequacy, or conflicts in parent-child relationships can play a significant part in the decision-making process."

Merton's (16) study of medical students provided illustrative data regarding the issue of identification. He found that although sons of physicians are among the first to consider medicine as a career, those doctor's sons who postponed interest in medicine until adolescence took longer to make a final decision than those others who considered medicine earlier in life. Identification with father and family tradition would seem, therefore, to be both a facilitating and an inhibiting factor in vocational selection. Problems in father-son relationships may result in the avoidance of the simplest, most direct form of identification (imitation), and resistance to making the decision for medicine as a career may take the form of tentative or exploratory choices for veterinary medicine, dentistry, a physical science, or a less clearly related field such as social science. One doctor's son may choose to avoid competing with his father by selecting art or business as a career, another may pick medicine as an opportunity to obtain psychological independence by defeating his father (outdoing father's medical achievements). Merton speculated that decision delay may reflect the struggle between the opposing forces of family influence or father identification, on the one hand, and the felt need to establish a separate identity, on the other.

Another researcher who has alluded to the pattern of power and authority within the family and its impact on children's later behavior is McClelland (15). He suggests that vocational achievement and success are related to the arrangement of power among the three roles of father, mother, and son. He states that the way power is handled in the family will influence the son's attitudes toward achievement within the family and outside of it.

Other parental attitudes influence the occupational choice determination of their children. Some parents are uncertain about what action to take in this area and thus may arouse anxiety in their children by assuming a noncommittal approach. Parents project their own ambitions onto the career choices of their children and reflect the attitude of "I want my child to have what I never had." Such an orientation may result in children revolting against parental wishes in the choice of a career. In addition, these attitudes also may give rise to the limiting of the occupational information made available to the child from the father or to a biased picture of the father's own world of work based upon the father's zeal to have his child avoid what he considers to be an unsatisfactory employment experience. Therefore, the child discovers prohibitions against specific vocations or, at best, has limited exposure to those with which his family has little sympathy or interest. Gross (8) described the problem in this way:

> It is not simply a matter of an outside group's forbidding the individual entrance; rather he is effectively prevented from entering by the fact that the group in which he grows up simply does not know about the occupation, does not understand it or is unsympathetic towards it. This situation places an additional burden on him who would enter such an occupation; he must fight his own group (p. 149).

In his examination of parental response to children's career concerns, Ginzberg (5) pointed out that parents may exert pressure toward a particular career choice, avoid involvement with the child's problem, or so emphasize the unsatisfying, burdensome aspects of the job that a negative orientation to work itself is engendered in the child.

Thus we see that many of the vocational goals and values acquired by a person can stem directly from family experience. Pursuing this point further, we observe that the importance of making "a good living" is often a key family value, irrespective of income level or socio-economic status. Such a value can become transformed into a vocational goal by children who accept it. The preference for, and status value attached to, business in one family may be rejected as inferior in worth to the professional pursuits valued in another family. Social position, family attitudes toward the sex-identification of certain jobs (e.g., nursing is for females), community power, the poor immigrant rising above the New World ghetto, the Horatio Alger upward mobility climb syndrome—all of these may exert considerable influence on the eventual choice of vocation. In a culture where the "good life" is equated more with material possessions than intrinsic rewards and work satisfactions (e.g., self-fulfillment, creativity, and social contribution), the boy or girl whose family values stress work satisfaction, pride in craftmanship, or social needs is fortunate indeed.

One might conclude that the logical resolution of the dilemma presented by opposing sets of values would be for the individual to choose an occupation that not only provides money, security, and status, but that also proves to be fulfilling. Rosenberg (21), however, found that values of work satisfaction and self-realization were psychologically most distant from the instrumental values of money and security and, indeed, tended to be mutually exclusive. Further, a recent survey by Grafton (7) showed that 40 percent of students queried would change, or consider changing, their present career selections on the sole basis of opportunity to make more money. Vocational counselors consistently report that a large percentage of students are pursuing careers because of family pressures, having abandoned aspirations more congruent with self-concept and self-actualization potentials.

A different kind of influence, and one with a potential for causing emotional conflict, involves the particular moral and ethical principles learned in the family. For example, the boy who has been taught that integrity, truth, and justice are "good" may ponder the desirability of becoming an attorney, if his concept of an attorney is that of one who undertakes to defend someone he knows is guilty and tries to get an acquittal (perceived as a perversion of justice) in order to collect a fee (fees are the route to the other learned value of living standard, security, the "good life"). A frequently discussed conflict regarding values learned in the family is the situation where the expressed family value (integrity) is seen as negated by the parent's behavior (unfair business practice, cheating on income tax).

It seems clear that the individual's dynamic interaction in his family environment includes confrontations between his own self-concept and familiar occupational values and goals as influenced by class, and religious, ethical, and sex factors. Vocational decisions stem in part from long experience in the closer environment and are responses to both conscious and unconscious personal needs. In supporting this point, Forer (4) states that occupational choice "is an expression of basic personality organization and can and should satisfy basic needs." Demos (3) also points out that vocational choice is as satisfying as its activeness in serving as an outlet for the individual's emotional needs.

Whether vocational choice will be satisfying or frustrating will depend not only on the closer environment but also on the larger external environment. The next section of this chapter is devoted to this question.

Realities in the External Environment

The decision-making process leading to occupational choice, as pointed out above, is influenced considerably by the individual's personality, values and life goals. For each person such considerations also play a role in efforts to attend to those objective realities which characterize the world of work. Several of these "objective realities" are identified and described in the following paragraphs.

Social-Cultural Occupational Values

There have been many studies of the cultural folkways, mores and traditions that influence or prescribe the individual's work experience. Even in primitive cultures, work reflects more than individual efforts toward need satisfaction. Work also is an expression of social relationships. Gross (8) uses the term "occupational social selection" to describe a process in which society, rather than the individual, makes the choice of vocation through the impact of authority relationships, status system, predetermined division of labor, moral conceptions of right and wrong, and the structure of the economy. Further, Gross points out that although the range of occupational choices is wider in our culture than in less complex ones, the wide discrepancy between vocational preferences and actual occupations found in many studies points up the crucial role of factors outside the individual in delimiting true choice potential.

Social class as a factor influencing vocational choice also has been studied in connection with mobility, vocational interest patterns and achievement motivation. Hardy perennials in American folklore are the concepts of "rags to riches," Horatio Alger, "all you need is one good break." Such notions imply that perserverance and ability will permit the individual, despite obstacles, to move up the occupational ladder, to rise in class and status. However, in their review of social mobility in the United States, Bendix and Lipset (1) point out that the majority of the work force does not make a significant change in its occupational status, and further that most upward job mobility is of a temporary rather than a permanent nature. While it is true that opportunities for upward mobility do exist, the durability of the poor boy success story through the years attests to the reality that overcoming class limitations in occupational opportunities is more often the exception than the rule.

Hollingshead, in *Elmtown's Youth,* (10) found that jobs held by adolescents as well as their occupational value judgments were influenced significantly by their family's position in the class structure:

> The pattern of vocational choices corresponds roughly with the job patterns associated with each class in the adult work world. Therefore, we believe that the adolescent's ideas of desirable jobs are a reflection of their experience in the class and family culture complexes. These adolescents also know the position of themselves and their families in the prestige system, and they understand the connection which exists between the father's occupation and the family's economic and prestige positions (p. 285).

The person asked to free-associate to the stimulus of an occupational label such as doctor, lawyer, or bus driver, would be likely to produce material dealing not only with prestige value, but also social class standing, monetary compensation, authority-power, and educational or training prerequisites. In determining whether the occupation in question is appropriate for his own choice, the individual would consider the extent to which the "image" of the job matches his self-concept in terms of ability, class appropriateness, upward mobility potential, and family influenced value judgments. The stereotype of an occupation, reinforced audio-visually in today's society through television, advertising, and films, conveys much information about the life style, folkways, and mores of the occupations. Ben Casey, Perry Mason, and Ralph Cramden may be more potent in their representations of doctor, lawyer, and bus driver than authoritative, analytical descriptions in vocational handbooks. For a girl considering nursing as a career, the name Florence Nightingale has significance in shaping the image of this vocation and casting it in a heroic mold. Honor, glory, and a starched bright uniform are more appealing aspects of nursing than the bedpan—the stereotype can serve a constructive purpose, if it recruits personnel to a vital field of endeavor.

Other social-cultural factors also may be considerations in vocational choice. The religion, caste, race, or nationality of the group to which an individual belongs predisposes him toward one or another occupational decision. The objective reality of vocation-bound caste membership or discriminatory exclusion from a trade or profession by virtue of religion, race, or national origin could be a decisive factor in shaping occupational choice. McClelland (15) contrasts attitudes of Jews and Southern Italians in regard to educational and intellectual pursuits as examples of culture-differentiated group values. The long tradition of veneration for learning in Jewish history and religion has maintained itself for centuries. An hereditary caste system, such as that found in India, narrows choice possibilities to a point where decision-making may be virtually unnecessary. Discrimination in job opportunities drastically reduces the range of choice for the Negro in America. Ginzberg (5) illustrates this point dramatically by alluding to the bleak outlook of Negroes in the South who, until relatively recently, were restricted primarily to jobs involving menial labor. Vocational opportunities for immigrant national groups also were limited. The Irish policeman in large Eastern cities in the late nineteenth and early twentieth century is perhaps the best known example of this phenomenon.

The classic illustration of the influence of religious values on occupational determination was in evidence during the Middle Ages. Many Christian churches prohibited their members from becoming money-lenders. As a result, in many countries, money-lending became a forced monopoly of the Jews. As church opposition to money-lending as an acceptable career modified in the course of the Industrial Revolution, the money-lending monopoly reversed its composition and Jews, with a few exceptions, were rapidly displaced at the top echelons of banking and finance.

Perhaps the most decisive element in the hierarchy of social-culture occupational values stems from sex differences. Very early in life the boy or girl learns something about sex-determined or sex-influenced work opportunities. For the girl, notions of restriction in vocational opportunity, first experienced in the family setting, become more clearly defined as she progresses through school and then into the work world. For the girl with a budding scientific interest, the "fantasy choice" preference for a career as chemist or physician may soon become more realistic as information about her own competitive academic ability, medical school quotas for women, industry preference for male chemists, operates to lower her sights toward becoming a nurse or medical technician. Conditioned by the dominant social convention that women's place is in the home, the girl who wishes to capitalize on this reality by becoming an expert cook may be chagrined, but nevertheless influenced, by discovering that the best paid jobs in the culinary arts (chef) are monopolized by men! By contrast, there are few sex-typed jobs monopolized by women that attract the interest or aspirations of men.

Despite the acceleration of the entry of women into the labor market during and after the Second World War, research by Caplow (2) and Gross (8) has indicated that vocational sex limitations are relatively unaltered in the overall picture. In support of this view Ginzberg (5) clearly sets forth the conflicts and difficulties women in our society face in attempting to combine the roles of wife and mother with those of a career.

Economic Factors

Although "subject to change without notice," the condition, structure, and idiosyncratic features of the economy are probably the most visible and easily understood of the objective reality factors influencing vocational choice. Information is readily available concerning boom or depression, business cycle effects upon job availability, degree of competition in the labor market, and earning potential. At any given time the status and economic trends found in one section of the country may vary considerably from those discovered in another area. The recent shift in the textile industry from concentration in the New England States to dispersal in the South left a number of towns in New England with limited local employment opportunities for those already in the labor market as well as for the young people coming into it. Gross points out that in a small town with only one industry the likelihood is greater that a young person will enter that industry than where the economy is more diverse. Gross (8) also notes, however, that the small town may widen the job horizon of its youth by the very fact that it offers very little to them in terms of choice.

One of the less predictable (by the individual) but increasingly crucial aspects of the economy is automation. Hardest hit by automation at present are semi-skilled and unskilled workers, particularly Negro workers who had gained a foothold in the mass production industries of the North during and after the Second World War. An interesting sidelight on technological change as it influences occupational choice is the recently increased status of a liberal arts college background. This is considered to be good general preparation (and job insurance) in a labor market which increasingly stresses specialization in jobs, but where the demand for various specialties may shift rapidly in a short period of time.

The character of a job itself may vary with the setting, with corresponding changes in the qualities that employers look for in job applicants. The owner of a small grocery store may want to hire a clerk with an outgoing, gregarious personality—a person who can chat with customers while filling their orders. In the streamlined supermarket, however, a store manager would consider most small talk with customers as inefficient use of the clerk's time. Thus, a person who can be content to work without much verbal communication with others would be more desirable for the supermarket than the hail-fellow-well-met.

Another economic factor in occupational choice is the cost of acquiring the training needed for certain vocations. The increasing expense of a college education can be a major barrier and thus a limiting factor for those in lower income groups. Specialized training for professions such as medicine, dentistry, or law is even further out of reach for many individuals who otherwise might have chosen these vocations. Some skilled trades require particularized vocational training beyond high school graduation, and this also can be costly. Although scholarships and publicly supported vocational schools offer hope to a select few, many individuals abandon preferred occupational selections because of the reality factor of training expense.

A related factor which can exercise considerable control over vocational selection is the financial status of the family. For example, the child who drops out of school because his earning power is needed by the family for economic survival or the maintenance of an acceptable standard of living discovers that his area of choice is reduced to relatively unskilled occupations. The couple who marries early may find that its financial position requires one or both partners to delay or give up the preferred occupational choice in favor of another selection which will allow for sufficient income immediately. The goal of becoming an engineer can be temporarily or permanently sidetracked because it requires long training, whereas the choice of automobile mechanic for the same individual may represent a condition of sufficient present competency for purposes of earning a living.

Family inheritance is cogently analyzed by Gross (8) who points out the difference between "transmission" of an occupation and "forced inheritance:"

> The former refers to the situation in which a father actually teaches his son certain skills or helps him in some way to enter his own occupation; for example, the teaching of farm practices to a farmer's son by his father. But the son of a factory laborer may wish to stay *out* of his father's occupation and may *try* to do so but because of economic or educational limitations or because of a narrow cultural perspective, may end up, like his dad as a factory laborer (p. 153).

Family business proprietorship and preference given by medical schools or trade unions to sons of graduates or members are other potentials for occupational inheritance. Rural Ireland provides an example of more complex occupational inheritance effects. When the father chooses from among his sons the one to inherit the farm, he often precipitates migration by the other sons for whom a vocational choice now becomes mandatory if the farm can support only one family.

Institutional Factors

The school

The organizational structure of the educational system at the secondary level affects vocational choice. It presents choice factors over which the young adolescent has little control. Selection of type of schooling (academic or vocational high school), courses (academic, commercial, vocational), choice of a major if the decision is for college, termination at college graduation or continuation to graduate or professional school—these alternatives often are forced on the adolescent. The young student frequently is pushed into conflict with himself, family, or peer group by having to make a choice, with no experience as a basis for decision. Problems inherent in such forced choices have led to the addition of the "general course" category in some high schools. Once the educational training decision is made, many occupations are eliminated from consideration because of the long training period required.

It also should be recognized that the educational establishment excludes from training for high-status occupations those individuals that it feels lack academic ability, aptitude, and ambition. In many circumstances socio-economic characteristics (ethnic group, religion, financial status, class, sex) also may be seen as drawbacks to aspiring youngsters. In an attempt to be "realistic," many high school counselors advise minority group students to avoid job areas that traditionally have been discriminatory, thus further perpetuating the kind of status quo in the labor market that is a leading cause of social unrest.

A similar bias operates with the counseling of girls, who are often discouraged from considering the professions (law, medicine, engineering, architecture, dentistry) because of quota systems (open or sub-rosa) in leading professional graduate schools. The counselor may be unaware that a bright and enterprising young woman does have a chance to enter almost any profession, and that predicting the degree of chance may call for expertise the counselor does not possess. For example, many attorneys, including women, enter the field through small specialized law schools rather than the traditional university route, because these smaller schools are less likely to have quota systems.

The school reflects the values and mores of the society at large. Quota systems for professional schools, the heavy concentration of minority groups (Negro, Mexican-American, Puerto Rican) in vocational courses in high schools, the reinforcement of occupational stereotypes along with the expressed or implied judgmental bias against manual occupations as contrasted to nonmanual (working with the hands or working with the head), these are some of the unfortunate realities found in education today.

Another issue in the school's effect on vocational choice is the lack of opportunity of most students to experience work firsthand. Although one can vicariously fantasize a job as described in the occupational handbook, a real experience may be necessary for the "information" to be complete. Despite some vocational education programs funded under the Smith-Hughes and Barden Acts, most students graduate from high school with very little understanding of the work world, the disciplines required, competition, repetitive work, supervisory relationships, the possible boredom, or satisfaction that may obtain.

Ginzberg's (6) model of childhood "fantasy" choice, adolescent "tentative" choice, and young adult "realistic" choice is useful in considering the question of work experience. The young child with the lemonade-stand can perceive work as play, and even the disappointment of not selling much lemonade can be tempered by the satisfaction of consuming the unsold merchandise. The preadolescent with a paper route may experience the dullness of repetitive work, but also experience the pleasure of extra spending money, and even the monotony does not last more than a few hours. The high school student beginning to face the necessity of selecting an occupation usually is in the position of assessing himself (his interests, abilities, values and goals) in a vacuum, that is, without opportunity to test the reality of the assumed identity in interaction with a work environment. The need for experiences by which to validate, modify, or correct distortions of fact or fantasy is great, but unfortunately the opportunities are few. It is true, however, that some students are able to gain work experience through part-time, after-school jobs, vacation jobs, and vocational education school-work plans. It is likely that the rural area subculture provides more incidental work experience for the farm youth than for their city counterpart. The rapid mechanization of much of the nation's agriculture will tend to equalize this difference to a large degree. An exception is the case of children of migratory farm workers, who often leave school for months at harvest time to work alongside their parents in the fields or orchards.

The sterility of American education in regard to work experience should be a major concern of educational planners. Incidental work experience, combined with effective vocational guidance services, could provide the individual with a meaningful exposure to the larger environment and thus afford a comprehensive and objective basis for the person's occupational choice.

In recent years vocational guidance in secondary schools has become increasingly widespread. The mid-century White House Conference on Children and Youth (24) reported that over 40 states were planning increased vocational guidance services. Advances in theory and technique have accompanied the growth of services provided; although there are many unresolved theoretical, practical and methodological problems in the field, these services do present a positive stimulus which encourages the student to consider vocational choice factors. Providing information to the student about himself (interests, abilities, limitations), about occupations, job opportunities, and changing trends in the labor market is a valuable contribution. Enhancement of counselor skills through federally financed training programs to provide additional competence in individual and group guidance techniques is a positive development.

Government

Services related to vocational choice are offered by a wide network of federal and state employment offices. In addition to serving as an employment bureau, these offices provide information and vocational testing and counseling, particularly to high school graduates and others entering the labor market. Supported by federal funds, most state employment offices are able to maintain a professional level of service. Because of continual contact with training and job opportunities, these offices also are able to make available current occupational information and practical assistance.

Federal agencies have been involved with vocational matters for many years through training grants, depression-spawned CCC (Civilian Conservation Corps) and National Youth Act activities, and as major employers. Currently, the Peace Corps, Job Corps, Vista, and Youth Corps are providing a variety of employment opportunities and experiences. These programs offer intrinsic work satisfaction by upgrading the skills of illiterate and semiliterate youth and adults by providing vocational training at semiskilled or skilled levels for unskilled unemployed persons. Antipoverty programs spurred by the Negro social revolution are now attempting to widen areas of realistic vocational choice through education, training, and the breaking down of barriers to employment faced by minority group workers in industry, trade unions, and governmental service. These government-sponsored efforts are widening areas of effective choice for many individuals who have been consigned by discriminatory hiring policies to low paid menial jobs or to "last hired, first fired" occupational status. Although these programs have not yet had mass impact, it is likely that progress will continue. The changing nature of factors influencing vocational choice is well illustrated by the current challenge to the stereotype of the Negro worker as being unskilled and untrainable. Not only is industry being pressed to reassess hiring policies, but job protection through union membership is under scrutiny. Although some unions have helped expand job opportunity for Negro workers, others, particularly the building trade unions, have effectively prevented Negro entry into occupations. The harmful social effects of unemployment on the person, family group, and larger society, the frustration and despair, no longer are mainly the concern of sociologists but are now a matter of major public concern.

Another increasingly important factor which affects vocational choice is military service. Ginzberg (5) pointed out that 25 million men have served in the armed forces since 1940. He described the effects of military service on occupational choice as the widening of occupational horizons through travel, social contact with fellow soldiers from different parts of the country and of diverse occupations, training in skills that are transferable to civilian vocations, and the extension of education and training through veterans' benefits to many who otherwise would be obliged to rule out occupations for which they were well suited but could not afford.

It is to be noted that the possibility of being drafted impels some young couples to make decisions in favor of early marriage with resultant narrowing of occupational choice stemming from financial pressures. Also, some young men are enrolling in college or beginning graduate work in order to avoid the draft. This additional educational experience could have a direct bearing on job choice in addition to delaying entry into the job market. Another factor to be noted is that some employers may be reluctant to hire draft-eligible young men, thus somewhat restricting their range of job choice.

On the other hand, military service makes possible early marriage with steady income and family financial allowances with the added incentive of vocational education at government expense.

A graphic connection between military service and vocational choice is observed in recruitment posters which emphasize the possibility of selecting a specific vocational training program as part of the enlistment procedure. For the young serviceman in noncombatant job classifications the military provides the first and therefore a most valuable exposure to the world of work, including experience with authority relationships, work task hierarchies, ratings, rewards, promotions, and status seeking. The service also allows less risky vocational exploration, seldom found in civilian life, where possibility of job failure may entail considerable financial loss or threat to self-esteem. At the same time, opportunities for changing assignments, specialties, or work environments rarely are individual options in a military organization. Therefore, the effects of military service on the vocational decision-making process present possibilities for both positive and negative consequences.

Interrelationships among Factors in External Environment

Social-cultural, economic, and institutional factors of course do not alone affect vocational choice. As aspects of reality, they are intertwined and interrelated. Their combination provides information about vocations which individuals may perceive as opportunity or lack of it. An example is the girl who considers that being a housewife is the proper vocational role for a woman. She decides to accept a temporary vocational role of ministering to the sick. Her family values stress security of employment. She therefore finds that nursing is an ideal choice, since it satisfies all these requirements and is a vocational skill consistently in demand.

Another example is the young Negro whose values and goals lean toward developing a skill that will permit him upward mobility out of the urban ghetto. He finds a vocational school which would "accept" him for training, but the school points out that apprenticeship possibilities in the industry or through the union are nil and therefore the training will be useless.

In the first case, the girl's interpretation of the information available defines opportunity. In the second case, lack of opportunity is the conclusion drawn from the available information, and a goal-satisfying objective has been shunted aside. The boy discovers that a more "practical" vocational choice needs to be made.

It should be noted that the factors set forth as aspects of the real world of work are not fixed, static, and unchanging. The post-Sputnik era has seen many changes in status of occupations. Sputnik brought about enhanced prestige and opportunities for the engineer, mathematician, physical scientist, and a whole host of quasi-professional technical job classifications. The mass entry of women into the labor market during and after World War II opened up to women many vocations previously monopolized by men. In some cases, such as assembly line tasks requiring high manual dexterity, it was discovered that women outperformed men, and women are now preferred as workers in a number of industrial vocations.

The interrelationships among social-cultural, economic, and institutional factors, and their impact upon vocational choice, also is affected by the social climate which obtains. In a relatively stable period, values, stereotypes, economic factors, and institutional pressures may seem to be more predictable than in a time of social upheaval. If the Negro youngster of today senses an expanding job horizon as a result of a general expansion of educational and vocational opportunities, then abilities, interests, values, and goals may become more decisive as factors in his vocational decision. On the other hand, if a depression occurs and a student must drop out of school to help support his family, this economic reality may cancel out individual interests, abilities, values and goals, and immediate employment opportunity in any job may decide the issue.

The period of late adolescence and transition to young adulthood carries with it as a developmental task the crystallization of identity and the structuring of life goals. Choice of vocation is a key step in the move from the psychological life space of the family into society at large. If the adolescent's ego development has enabled him to begin to function autonomously, the vocational choice is more apt to be a self-actualizing one. If, however, the individual cannot break family ties and must remain psychologically dependent, the decision is less likely to be consonant with the individual's own values and goals. The independent person can, during this time in the life cycle, crystallize a reality-based choice or resist pressures for premature commitment. Dependency may result in vacillation and inability to make a vocational decision or in the acceptance of a designated vocational role that is contrary to the true self.

Thus it is difficult to predict which external factor or set of such factors will take highest priority in the vocational choice and decision-making process of a given person at a given time. The individual's aspirations are continually affecting his exposure to and his understanding of the information provided or restricted by objective environmental factors. Distortions either based upon individual internal conflicts or inaccurate perception of the environment affect the vocational decision-making process. For each individual the time at which a life's work is selected is in itself a crucial milestone. As suggested in the preceding illustrations, the individual's readiness, his interpretation of what is available, and pressures from within or without, determine when and on what basis an occupational determination is made.

It is to be pointed out, however, that vocational decisions are not always the products of logical and systematic analysis of pertinent facts and data. Forer (4), for example, believes that the "choice of a vocation is not primarily rational or logical, but is a sometime blind, impulsive, emotional and automatic process and is not always subject to practical and reasonable considerations."

Caplow (2) contends that the bases for decision are often trival:

> A student decides to study law because he has gotten his highest grades in history courses, dislikes the idea of teaching, and knows that courses in history are required for entrance to law school. A grade school pupil elects the vocational high school because someone has told him that automobile mechanics get high wages. A high school sophomore transfers from the academic sequence to the clerical course to be with her best friend. The crucial decision to leave school and go to work may reflect the most casual dissatisfaction or the lure of a passing opportunity (p. 218).

It seems to us, however, that Caplow's position would be more accurate as a description of a tentative choice rather than of a full commitment to a vocation, and that Gross (8) is correct in stating that the illustrations used in the quote above describe precipitating events rather than basic causes.

A tenable position is the assumption that vocational choice follows a sequential, longitudinal path: the individual sizes himself up, assesses the available information from the environment regarding job opportunities, relates the appraisal of self and opportunity to values and goals, and goes through a decision-making process that culminates in the selection of and entry into a vocation.

Effect of First Vocational Experience

It would be hard to overestimate the role that work plays in human experience. Work can be creative, actualizing, and ego building, or it can be boring, repugnant, and ego deflating. Vocational activity is on a par with marriage and family as a crucial setting in which realization, modification or frustration of previously set goals takes place.

The work experience itself can modify goals and shape individual behavior. It is the purpose of the discussion below to delineate the specific ways that the first vocational experience affects not only vocational choice but life goals as well.

First, we turn our attention to factors inherent in the job itself. In describing "occupational ideologies" Caplow (2) points to two major occupational influences arising out of the nature of the job: 1) customs, folkways, and traditions, and 2) standards of conduct which are enforced because of the real or supposed effects which their violation would have on job performance. The man in the grey flannel suit usually will identify with and consciously or unconsciously imitate standards of material consumption, prevailing mores, patterns of social behavior, recreation, as well as the prevalent attitudes of an organization or profession.

Caplow (2) also discusses two occupational groups which he distinguishes on the basis of the effect of group membership on individual values and goals. He describes one type as being tightly organized, with a "range of political, religious, recreational, and economic values, which cannot be easily summarized by the outside observer, precisely because it is a full appreciation of their nuances which constitutes membership." The other type of group is more loosely contained.

Similar views regarding group conformity, adherence to occupational or social class behavior and value stereotypes, and the decline of individualism have been the subject of a number of recent books. These works include analyses of socio-economic status factors [C. Wright Mills' *The Power Elite* (18) and *White Collar* (19)]; studies by Riessman (20) and others on life styles of working class people; and treatises by Oscar Lewis on the "culture of poverty" [*Five Families* (13) and *Children of Sanchez* (14)].

Jobs in isolation are becoming rare as the impact of communications technology is more widely felt. The railroad worker of today is much more aware of the world about him through modern communications techniques than was his counterpart of a century ago.

Shorter work-day and work-week factors are also new cultural patterns which bring modified life styles and changed personal activities. The individual who works fewer hours and can take longer paid vacations discovers that his goals of leisure and recreation must be reformulated. Basic changes in his thinking about himself, his values and his goals may result.

In pursuing a career, one learns the rules of the game (the group's mores, values, and goals) and then makes the accommodation as preparation for the move upward. Merton and Kitt (17) have interpreted "brown-nosing" in the army as an example of this kind of behavior. One result of the first job experience may be that the goal of immediate material well-being is subordinated to the objective of upward mobility and later financial rewards. A chemist whose B.A. is sufficient for job entry into the field of chemistry but inadequate for the status and rewards open to the Ph.D. goes on to further education, thus deferring the satisfaction of some of his life goals to a future time.

Studies of medical school students have shown that the altruistic, humanitarian, humanistic values of medical students often are changed to values and goals of success, status, power, and financial reward as the student finishes internship, a special form of first vocational experience. In other words, not only do values influence vocational choice, but the reverse process, vocational choice modifying values, also operates.

Whether the worker is a success or a failure, satisfied or disgruntled on his first job significantly affects his view of himself and what he wishes to do in life. If pride, personal satisfaction, enhancement of self-image, and opportunity for creative expression result from a first vocational experience, then the primacy of life goals based on intrinsic work satisfaction can be maintained. Failure or dissatisfaction, of course, may lead to seeking another job or a different field of work, but if job change is not possible, extrinsic goals or extra-vocational goals (hobby, recreation, avocation) may take precedence in the goal hierarchy of the individual.

Another important consideration is the time in the individual's life cycle at which he has his first work experience. The adolescent dropout's first vocational experience is considerably different from the lawyer's first position in a law firm after long training. Typically, the dropout will tend to find that his inexperience and lack of training will qualify him only for low-paid, less stable, unsatisfying, and often temporary jobs. The law school graduate may find himself on the bottom rung of the ladder in terms of money and status, but his long-term outlook is much different from that of the dropout.

Hollingshead's survey in *Elmtown's Youth* (10) revealed that the main goal of lower-income-level youth after their first job experience was to change to a skilled trade. He found that dissatisfaction after the experience of a job may change a goal that was predicated on getting *any* job. Here, too, the general lack of work experience in adolescence often has the effect of encouraging the setting of a career life goal that is so unrealistic that major shifts in goals are required after a first job. In some cases an after-school, summer, or incidental job may have important positive effects on life goals. One example is the aspiring teacher who finds that working with children in a summer camp is not for him and that working with objects is more satisfying than working with people. Government-sponsored programs such as the Peace Corps, Vista, the Job Corps, and varied anti-poverty programs are giving many young people a first vocational experience, an experience containing opportunities for constructive personal growth.

Military service, when it represents the first vocational experience, has complex effects upon an individual's life goals. As mentioned previously, military service can result in broadening occupational horizons and an expansion in occupational opportunities. It can precipitate or expedite earlier marriage, with consequent effects on goals. Emphasis on security, fringe benefits, and extrinsic factors may become dominant over intrinsic attraction of more creative and satisfying, but more gratification-delaying, occupational goals.

A sometimes overlooked factor in military service is the conflict of values and goals that can be encountered when the soldier whose moral or religious convictions say "thou shalt not kill," and whose social outlook is characterized by a strong belief in the preservation and enhancement of the inherent worth of each individual, finds that killing, the destruction of individuals, is an occupational goal. More research is needed on the effects of combat training and experience on the value systems and goals of participants.

Summary

A crucial phase of an individual's life cycle is reached at the time his vocational choice is to be made. Coming at the late adolescent and early maturity period, the selection of a vocation is a particularly complex process. It involves a person's efforts to find a sense of identity, a sense of self as he seeks maturity and adulthood. It is the culmination of experiences of self-hood occurring within the family context together with exposure to the realities of the world of work.

The choice of one's life work emerges from the interplay of personal values and self-image with social-cultural, institutional, economic, sexual, and religious factors. It represents a personal commitment and is influenced by the person's values, capabilities, and personality organization. It then becomes, consciously or unconsciously a means of satisfying personal needs and aspirations as reflected in life goals. One's vocational choice is tested forcibly during the initial job experience as the person moves toward psychological homeostasis and personal fulfillment.

References

1 Bendix, R., and Lipset, S. B. *Class, status, and power.* Glencoe, Ill.: Free Press of Glencoe, 1953.

2 Caplow, T. *The sociology of work.* Minneapolis: University of Minnesota Press, 1954.

3 Demos, G. D., and Grant, B. (eds.). *Vocational guidance readings.* Springfield: Charles C. Thomas, 1965.

4 Forer, B. Personality factors in occupational choice, *Educational and Psychological Measurement,* 1953, *13,* 361-366.

5 Ginzberg, E. *The optimistic tradition and American youth.* New York: Columbia University Press, 1962.

6 Ginzberg, E., Ginzberg, S. W., Axelrod, S., and Herma, J. L. *Occupational choice: an approach to a general theory.* New York: Columbia University Press, 1951.

7 Grafton, S. Pressures that push children into the wrong careers, *McCall's,* June, 1966.

8 Gross, E. *Work and society.* New York: Thomas Y. Crowell Co., 1958.

9 Henry, N. B. (ed.). Sixty-first yearbook of the national society for the study of education, part II, *Education for the Professions,* University of Chicago Press, 1962.

10 Hollingshead, A. B. *Elmtown's youth,* New York: John Wiley & Sons, 1949.

11 Hoppock, R. *Occupational information,* New York: McGraw-Hill, 1957.

12 Hughes, E. C. *Men and their work.* Glencoe, Ill.: Free Press of Glencoe, 1958.

13 Lewis, O. *Five families.* New York: Basic Books, 1959.

14 Lewis, O. *Children of Sanchez.* New York: Random House, 1961.

15 McClelland, D. S., Baldwin, A. C., Bronfenbrenner, U., and Strodtbeck, F. L. *Talent and society.* Princeton, N. J.: Van Nostrand, 1958.

16 Merton, R. K., Reader, G. G., and Kendall, P. L. *The student physician: introductory studies in the sociology of medical education.* Cambridge, Mass.: Harvard University Press, 1957.

17 Merton, R. K., and Kitt, A. S. Contributions to the theory of reference group behavior. In R. K. Merton, and P. K. Lazarsfeld, *Continuities in social research.* Glencoe, Ill.: Free Press of Glencoe, 1950.

18 Mills, C. W. *The power elite.* New York: Oxford University Press, 1956.

19 Mills, C. W. *White collar: the American middle class.* New York: Oxford University Press, 1951.
20 Riessman, F., Cohen, J., and Pearl, A. (eds.). *Mental health of the poor.* New York: Free Press, 1964.
21 Rosenberg, M. *Occupations and values,* Glencoe, Ill.: Free Press of Glencoe, 1957.
22 Super, D. E. *The dynamics of vocational adjustment,* New York: Harper and Bros., 1942.
23 Super, D. E. *The psychology of careers.* New York: Harper and Bros., 1957.
24 Witmer, H. E., and Kotinsky, R. (eds.). Personality in the making, *The mid-century white house conference on children and youth,* New York: Harper and Bros. 1952.

Chapter 16

Role of the Small Group in Goal Development

William H. McWhinney

Within the small group certain distinctly human goals have their origin, develop and are confirmed. It is this hypothesis that is elaborated here and for which some argument is provided in the following pages. The claim is made that once the individual matures enough to be able to participate in a peer group, the face-to-face contact with peers and near peers serves as a basic instrumentality for goal development. Implicit in this view is the additional proposition that the individual does not achieve a conscious realization of himself by himself, nor does he become aware of himself simply by being aware of the society in which he exists. Self-awareness is a result of an interactive process. The society and its agents—parents, teachers, commanding officers, and other less official masters—do provide the sense of social acceptance, its standards and the constraints. But it is more likely that the individual's membership group will provide the environment in which he may establish and test the directions which are appropriate to him.

In previous chapters, the roles of antecedent conditions (the genetic heritage), and of the specific microcosm of the social system (the family and childhood schooling) have been developed. These provide the conditions which mold and confine the infant's possibility space as he matures; these are the conditions which set basic performance standards. The peer group has the additional potency to provide the individual with goals, aspirations, and direction. Thus in this section we concentrate on groups made up of near peers, those persons who are nearly of the same age and whose roles in society are similar. Significant are the adolescent ("play") groups, the young adult's school and work group, and to a lesser extent the adult social group. Such groups affect behavior in ways different from family groupings in which the roles are stable and sharply different. While a task group may include persons associated in a hierarchical relationship of power, differences are less stable and psychologically less potent than those in the family. Yet even more than in the case of the family, the individual among his peers affects and is affected by behaviors, attitudes and goals of persons who have immediately relevant abilities, positions, knowledge, and potentials. Further, operating among near peers, the individual can exercise leadership toward change and development of his environment in a way denied the younger member of a family group, or a private individual in the vast and amorphous socio-political structure.

There is surprisingly little evidence that bears on the central hypothesis proposed here. The experimental and theoretically oriented psychologists have shown little concern for the development of goals seen as future-oriented complexes of desired states, possibilities and behavioral strategies aimed at attaining these desires. There are exceptions; Lewin's paper (Rapaport, 1951) "Intention, Will and Need" deals with goals as embodied in future psychic fields; Spranger (1924) developed a schema of central life values on which the Allport-Vernon scale was based; Charlotte Buhler studied, primarily through biographies, the development and growth of life goals over the course of human life (1933), and Maslow (1954) notes that only Dewey and Thorndike did not display the general neglect psychologists have shown for expectations; Eli Ginzberg (1951) is one of the few who have collected other than clinical data on the development of goals per se. (See his study of the process by which boys come to select an occupation.)* However, there is an extensive armory of studies attempting to establish the behavioral correlates of attitude and value change and, while the relationship of attitudes to goals has not been well established, there is sufficient proof of the meaningfulness of attitudes to consider the evidence on the sources of attitudes and values relevant in a quest to understand the importance of the peer group in the individual's goal formation.

* It is interesting to note the nearly complete absence of the mention of *goals* or related notions suggesting orientation to the future in the American psychological literature before the mid 1950's. Possibly the current interest indicates a concern for the future that scientists lacked prior to the "atomic age."

Sources of Attitudes and Their Modifications

Attitudes and changes in attitude have been the subject of innumerable studies by sociologists, political scientists and market analysts and a central concern for social psychologists. But the vast majority of these studies is concerned only with the question of who holds what opinions and attitudes. We can get some clues as to the source of attitudes from the studies which associate the attitudes of adolescents and youths with their parents and teachers, workers and school mates, co-members of clubs, unions, etc. Of particular interest here are those investigations which deal with the source of attitudes for adolescents and young adults; most of them stress the role of the parent or teacher as both the source of an attitude and the principal agent of its acceptance. The emphasis on the parental role follows the Freudian view of the primacy of the parents in the formulation of the personality while the emphasis on the teacher may follow simply from the fact that most researchers are themselves teachers and have studied students at all levels of schooling. Though there is pervasive evidence that in some cultures the child adopts his parents', and to a lesser degree, his teachers' attitudes, the causal linkage has not been established. The similarity of environment, culture and information sources of the child and of the adult could equally well account for the observed correlations.

Coleman (1961) in his recent study of the American adolescent concluded that " . . . our adolescents today are cut off, probably more than ever before, from adult society. They are still oriented towards fulfilling their parents' desires, but they look very much to their peers for approval as well. Consequently teen-age societies may develop standards that lead away from those goals established by the larger society" (p. 9), and "Adolescence is a period of transition from childhood to adulthood. As part of that transition comes a shift of orientation, away from the preceding generation, toward one's own generation. This transition has been taking place since early childhood; even a young child often responds more to the pressures of his fellows than to the desires of his parents" (p. 138).

Newcomb (1943) in his study of students at Bennington College enables us to identify the source and agents of attitude change. He classified the students according to their orientations toward their families and toward their student peers. Those who had the latter orientation were the ones who most readily adopted new values and attitudes which, not surprisingly, were the values and attitudes of the (relatively liberal) faculty. This study and many others attest to the influence of the teacher as a model for the life style of the student. It is even suggested in Sanford's *The American College* (1962) that without such models the adolescent would not mature into adulthood. But it is more safely argued that the teacher's attitudes happen to be the ones available to the face-to-face groups which form in every student body. It is hypothesized here that the agent of adoption is the membership group though the source is the expressed attitudes of the faculty. Newcomb, in an article in Sanford's collection, quotes a study by E. K. Wilson which indicates that with greatly varying opportunity for direct personal contact with college students, he did not detect any comparable variations in the adoption of the faculty attitudes by the students. Similarly, Hymans (1959) in a review article of the correlation of political views held by the youths and their parents, found few reports which would support the hypothesis that the parent was the dominant source of the youth's attitudes.

The Sources of Goals

The small group is involved in all the processes of individual goal formation, except the genetic one and early infanthood. But in some processes the group is but a mediator, the bearer of an ideal or of social reality. The peer group merges at its boundaries with the encompassing society and in particular with the ethnic group and/or class of which it is an element. To a large extent, the group vocabulary is determined by the class in which it operates, and the range of achievement goals it supports is determined by the class and ethnic constraints. For those processes by which the group merely transmits the society's demands, we can accept the framework Massarik discusses (see Chapter 17) for a unidirectional causal development of the individual as a product of society. Societal structure, however, has little bearing on how one establishes goals for his interpersonal life with his colleagues, in his family life, and in his involvement with himself in his physical being. Societal structure does place limits on the degree of one's involvement with his family and colleagues, and it denigrates an extreme level of narcissistic self-involvement. But within wide limits, society does not determine how the individual will or should value his human relationships. Similarly, except in the most restrictive and traditional societies, social forces have little influence on the particular level of self-limitation one adopts as appropriate, on the goals for self-development or the maintenance of moral and social commitment. Society may, however, be quite important in establishing meaningful constraints and directions on one's goals regarding public and leadership roles, and, therefore, on the directions in which one may strive for success.

In almost all dimensions of the individual's activity, society provides constraints and norms, but if we are to understand the process by which he develops goals we need to develop an insight into the ways in which he and his immediate associates interact while formulating and establishing the direction in which his life energies will be expended. The remainder of this section presents a scheme for displaying the various modes by which goal adoptions are produced via the group. It is developmental in the sense that within any given portion of one's social space the modes occur sequentially and, at least in the beginning, at about the same ages for all persons in a particular culture.

The Basic Modes of Goal Adoption

The group as a mediator of social forces represents simply a communication link between the individual and society, the intrument through which pressures and constraints are applied to the individual. The group as the locus of social interaction represents a field of supports and forces operating to transform the group and to provide the persons in the group with direction, confrontation, and the confidence to be individuals. Between these extreme roles which the group can play in a person's goal formation are two other discernible modes of implementation: 1) the adoption of a goal by the individual may be incidentally accomplished as he comes to identify with a significant group member or an ideal type for the group; and 2) an individual's choice of goals may be affected significantly by the dynamics of being included in a small group where he derives value from cooperative participation. Let us look at these four modes of goal development in more detail.

Information

A small group is foremost a source of information essential to goal formation and adoption. The family, as a small group, is almost the sole source of significant information from infancy to three or four years of age, not only because of the child's physical limitations but because the family selects almost all the elements of the child's environment. In spite of the vastly wider world available to the adult, the information that most affects his behavior continues to come in large measure from the several small groups to which he belongs. For the adult or, more generally, for all noninfants, information bears on goal formation as possibility and likelihood, both of which are mediated strongly by the small group in which he operates.

Possibilities

Information influences goals by providing the individual with knowledge of the possibilities to which he may aspire and the taboos and the practical constraints which may restrict possibilities. In societies rich in mass communication media, it might seem that the small group plays a minor role in the acquisition of information by the individual. But because of the massiveness of information available to the individual, he must rely to a great extent on an immediate companion to help him evaluate what portion of the information he personally receives should be used. Katz and Lazarsfeld (1949) believe this indirect acquisition of usable knowledge to be a two-step process. Lazarsfeld initially proposed that information, particularly of an attitudinal nature, is received or legitimized through an "opinion leader" who either plays the role of innovator in getting acceptance for new attitudes, or of a censor who supports those items which concur with the present views and values. While their evidence comes from adult studies, Coleman (1961) finds the same process among the adolescents he studied.

Reachable goals

It is not only information about goals and norms that the small group mediates, but also information about the likelihood that one might reach such a goal or succeed in adopting a norm of a broader and different society. David C. McClelland (1953), in his work on achievement needs, has provided evidence of the important role information concerning risks plays in goal adoption. He indicates that a rational, achievement-oriented person will not strive for objects he cannot reasonably expect to attain. Festinger (1950) theorizes about the same phenomenon in his study of social comparison processes; he notes that a person concerns himself with goals which others hold and with their performance only when their goals and performances are reasonably close to the attainments he considers possible for himself. The middle-class man seldom aims to enter the highest strata of society, though he may well strive to reach the status of the person who is most successful financially and socially among his colleagues and regular associates. He does not experience a feeling of failure in not having achieved the upper-class status. The "C" student doesn't have a goal of straight "A's"; in fact, he scorns the "A" student, calling him a "grind" or "bookworm" to reduce the need to accept the "A" goal (Becker and Siegal, 1958). While the peer group provides useful boundaries by which to delimit one's goals, it also provides a vehicle for increasing the level of target achievements; this has been observed in group therapy situations as well as under experimental conditions (Wallach et al., 1962). The presence of the group supports the included individual in setting higher, more difficult goals for himself. The mean goal level for group members increases following discussions, discussions which reduce fear through information but which also provide support by establishing a norm of higher achievement.

A currently topical example of the use of both of these goal effects of information is the "seed" project in which top Negro high-school students are tutored in their own schools or boys' clubs toward university admission. The expected effect is to have the other students become aware of the real possibility of college attendance, as attested to by the tutored group member. Working with the students while they are still within their own community increases the likelihood of the two-step adoption process, i.e., the initially chosen student influences his immediate circle of friends and they in turn carry the message to their colleagues, thus spreading the goal through the community.

Identification

There is another aspect to the change process described in the above example. Not only does a person in the community of the boy who is going to college provide information on a sense of feasibility, but the training process also provides an idol, a *reference individual* to whom the younger boy may look and with whom he may identify. For the individual, the process of identification is an important source of goals; the group facilitates the process. A group member may take a single real or idealized figure as a model for his behavior and, in so doing, adopt his goals as well. As Homans (1950) shows in describing the Norton street gangs, such a figure may be a leader in the group; or it may be a hero figure, such as John F. Kennedy, Hitler, or Jackie Robinson, who is external to the group and known only in an idealized form. In the more traditionally oriented society where value systems are relatively stable, the impact of the parent, other adult family members, teachers, and public figures often provides unmediated sources of values and aspirations. In a less stable environment the younger person may be less confident of the relevance of such sources to his world and test the transmitted values with his colleague's views. In such turbulent societies the community often calls on the peers to attempt to direct the youth away from activities and directions which the adult society disparages.

Adoption of goals as well as behaviors is fostered by the group information processes and by group norms. The powerful influence of the face-to-face peer group on the values of the young adult is attested to in

The American Soldier (Stouffer *et al.,* 1949). Merton in his theoretical comment on this massive study found confirmation of the hypothesis that

> insofar as subordinate or prospective group members are motivated to affiliate themselves with a group, they will tend to assimilate the sentiments and conform with the values of the authoritative and prestigeful stratum of that group. The function of conformity is acceptance by the group, just as progressive acceptance by the group reinforces the tendency toward conformity. *And the values of these "significant others" constitute the mirrors in which individuals see their self-image and reach self-appraisals* (Merton 1957, p. 254, italics added).

Identification can take place with a "way of life" of a reference *group* just as it can be with that of an individual. The earliest studies of the reference group, carried out by Hyman (1942), to uncover the psychology of status, indicate that subjectively the informants identify with the attributes of a class that, more often than not, is a higher class than one to which an objective evaluator would have assigned them. For some this identification was a fanciful protection from reality; more commonly the subjective uplifting seemed to reflect more realistic values and goals. But the fact that the objectively attained standards and the observed behavior differed from the person's subjective class assignment indicated that the identification with a reference group of which he is not a member does not have the impact of the reciprocal "mirror imaging" in the peer group that produces behavior appropriate to membership in that group.

Adoption of the behavior patterns and implied values and goals of another is a one-way process. It requires neither an exchange between the individual and the model nor a confrontation with the question of how appropriate the whole adopted identity is to the individual's capability and position in society. Bandura, in a series of studies with young children, found that they more commonly adopted the behavior of a model who demonstrated power than of one who was the recipient of desired possessions (Bandura, Ross and Ross, 1963). This finding supports the opinion of others that the goals most easily adopted are the egocentric ones which aid in the development of the self-image. Specifically it appears easy to adopt an idol's image for one's physical-sexual (narcissistic) self, and, with greater maturity, the leadership goals in the relevant societies. Adoption of goals so central to one's immediate person as those from an idol increases the risk of serious loss of direction, either if the idol is "broken" or if the goals and resultant behaviors are simply added as alien elements to the ego (Adelson, in Sanford 1962). However, if the significant group of which the individual is a member supports, as a group, the lost idol or the assumed goals, confrontation will be delayed; the group may live in a fantasy world in which the common goal orientation prevents confrontation with the reality of the larger society. Such in-group existence provides the goals which were adopted through identification with sufficient time and support to become deeply ingrained. (See Festinger: *When Prophesy Fails,* 1956.) The deviant's subculture, the adolescent's gang, the political radical's cell or club—they all protect the individual's goals, achieved through identification, from confrontation with social reality. In Piaget's model of the development of moral judgment in children, the identification follows as "secret and untouchable (rules) emanating from adults and lasting forever" (p. 18, Piaget, 1932). The imitative adoption of another's goals is not a social act because "each (seeks) to imitate the play of older boys and of the initiated, but more for the satisfaction, still purely personal, of feeling himself to be a member of a mystical community where sacred institutions are handed down by the leader out of the remote past, (rather) than from any real desire to cooperate with his playmates" (p. 36, *op. cit.*).

Most adults operate or have operated within a wide variety of small groups which have overlapping influences on the goals they maintain. In perfectly rational consideration of those idols appropriate to oneself, one would certainly find conflict and again suffer uncertainty. However, in the complex fabric of events, aspirations, and goals, the confrontation of one's identification with another may be avoided by compartmentalizing one's relations with different groups, allowing one to maintain idols appropriate to each group. Piaget describes an analogous situation in the behavior of boys using various rules of the game. When the child confronts a statement of rules other than those he has been given by the power figures of his world, e.g., the slightly older boys, he initially accepts the different rules as defining different games. The variances are not noticed as producing an anomaly as long as the group involved in each game plays the appropriate rule. Maturation into consciousness and acceptance of the incongruity in rules makes the individual aware of the need for cooperation in accepting a set of rules by which the group will operate. If he wishes to play, to be included in the group activity, he must come to accept the group's rules or norms. The extreme form of goal setting by identification with group norms is represented by brainwashing. In this technique, and in other related identification mechanisms, such as those found in the public confession of the Quaker sect, the personality becomes dependent on the social environment to the point of aloofness from itself. The individuality is absorbed into that of the group or its leaders. The goals, therefore, particularly those of a more explicitly rational nature including those regarding leadership and public roles and continued self-development, similarly become functions of the group with which the individual identifies (Baudin 1954).

Inclusion

The individual's need for continued social acceptance, for being a party to human intercourse, for inclusion in a closely knit, small group provides one of the strongest pressures in the selection, if not the formation, of goals. The individual who wishes to maintain relations with other humans in formal or casual groups must behave as though he has accepted the values, standards, behaviors, and goals which are appropriate for the groups' existence. The strength and form of group pressures on attitudes and behaviors have been a major subject of study experimentation and survey research for social psychologists, at least since Kurt Lewin's experiments in the 1930's concerning the response of children to different forms of leadership. Among other early classic studies which exhibit the (adult) group's power to modify perception and establish norms are Lewin's study (1943) of the value of commitment to one's peer group in attaining changes in one's attitude toward certain *declassé* foods which were underutilized during wartime, and the studies by Sherif (1936) and Asch (1958) on the effect of group pressures on the individual's perception and willingness to be seen as compliant. Coleman's study of adolescents quoted above further documents the importance of inclusion as a determinant of the school child's behavior.

These studies and hundreds of similar ones demonstrate the essentially political fact that one will modify his attitudes to obtain the privileges and goods given to a group member, and that these modifications, once accepted, often become habitual or learned responses. Roethlisberger and Dickson's (1939) famed Hawthorne studies and Homans' (1950) insightful combination of these, with other studies of small groups, attest to the depth of acceptance by the individual of group norms and to the wide range of matter on which the individual is constrained by the groups to which he belongs. However, these studies refer only to the attitudes and norms. They neither prove nor consider the question of how such pressures can modify the goals of the individual. In fact, in the majority of cases of simple economic pressure, one would not expect a change in the individual's goal even if such pressure were successful in obtaining his compliance while within a specific group.

The adoption by the individual of goals manifested in a group's behavior seems to come about by two methods: through identification, as discussed above, and through a rational, nonegocentric development, described by Piaget (1932, etc.) in his discussion of the rules of the game.*

In describing a child's maturation, Piaget noted that as the child comes to participate in social contacts with a nonfamily peer group, he finds a diversity in the ideas of correctness, values, and appropriateness. Piaget's study of diversity dealt specifically with the use of rules of a game of marbles. The young child, prior to his becoming socialized into the peer group, held as inviolable the rules handed down by authority figures. In the peer group, Piaget's subject child confronts a variety of rules differing in detail and in major elements from those he had been taught. To be able to play the game under such circumstance requires the child's recognition that the other players are necessary to the play; therefore, the rules chosen must be satisfactory to all in order to induce their continued playing. "The thing is not only to fight the other boys, but also, and primarily, to regulate the game as a whole set of systematic rules which will insure the most complete reciprocity in methods used" (Piaget, *op. cit.*). The awareness of the need to have reciprocal rules through which to coordinate action leads to social awareness and eventually to "interest in the rules for their own sake." The adoption of a coordinative view requires redefinition of one's goal which cannot be simply and egocentrically economic; coordinating involves others. Through confrontation with the diverse behavior of the other group members, the individual comes to take a more relativistic view beyond his egocentric locus. The relativistic view which incorporates others develops standards of self-limitation, acceptance of other authority, and a sense of social commitment.

Reification

The informational mode of goal development is essentially impersonal. The identification mode may be impersonal or intrapersonal, but it is *from* one real individual or from the priesthood of the idol to a recipient; the inclusive mode involves an exchange—the recognition of each by the other. Reification creates goals when the individual recognizes himself and his potential through the agentry of persons in his immediate world, through their confirming his reality as an existent self, a potential being, as opposed to simply accepting him for what he is. Piaget's model of a child maturing provides further clues to the reification process. In the fourth stage Piaget observes the child maturing be-

* While Piaget's empirical source was limited to children under 15 in rural Switzerland, the general developmental scheme has been validated by the observations of others. For example, Kohlberg (1963) reports a similar scheme, broken into six stages, based on boys under 17 living in urban USA.

yond the relativism of inclusion and the sustaining need for cooperative interaction in order to deal at a level at which he can handle invariants over interpersonal relationships—"the rules for their own sake." Piaget points out that at this stage the individual is handling social relations in a manner parallel to the way in which he handled the sensory-motor relations as a young child, i.e., by learning the invariant of a topology in spite of the varying appearance, arrived at from different viewpoints. The parallel process in the reification is the learning of the invariants of one's self in spite of the unvarying appearance one has in different social relationships. Reification cannot occur in privacy (see also Kohlberg, 1963). It is a dyadic (I-thou) or small group occurrence.

> For the inmost growth of the self is not accomplished, as people like to suppose today, in man's relation to himself, but in the relation between the one and the other, between them, that is, pre-eminently in the mutuality of the making present—in the making present of another self and in the knowledge that one is made present in his own self by the other—together with the mutuality of acceptance of acclimation and consummation (Buber, 1957, p. 104).

In becoming one's self, the goals of self-development, of leadership, of maintaining particular moral and social philosophies, and of personal success become independent of imitation and of comparative references. Such independence frees one from the false modesty induced by comparison and from the need to depreciate one's self, enabling one to strive for continuing personal development and growth. The totality of the *goal aspects* of one's life is opened in reification: "I not only accept the other as he is, but I confirm him, in myself, and then in him, in the relation to this potentiality that is him, and can now be developed, it can evolve, it can answer the reality of life" (Buber, 1957).

References

Asch, S. E. Effects of group pressure upon the modification and distortion of judgments. In E. E. Maccoby (ed.), *Readings in social psychology,* 3rd ed., New York: Holt, Rinehart and Winston, 1958.

Becker, W. W., and Siegal, S. Utility of grades: levels of aspiration in a decision theory context, *J. Exp. Psychol.,* 1958, *44,* 81-85.

Buber, M. Distance and relation, *Psychiatry,* 1957, *20,* 97-104.

Bandura, A., Ross, D., and Ross, S. Vicarious reinforcement and imitative learning, *J. Abnormal Soc. Psychol,* 1963, *67,* 601-607.

Coleman, J. S. *The adolescent society.* Glencoe, Ill.: Free Press of Glencoe, 1961.

Festinger, L., Schachter, S., and Back, K. *Social pressures in informal groups.* New York: Harper & Row, 1950.

Festinger, L., Riecken, H. W., Jr., and Schachter, S. *When prophecy fails.* Minneapolis, Minn.: University of Minnesota Press, 1956.

Ginzberg, E., Ginsberg, S. W., Axelrod, S., and Herma, J. L. *Occupational choice.* New York: Columbia University Press, 1951.
Homans, G. C. *The human group.* New York: Harcourt, Brace and World, 1950.
Hyman, H. H. *Political socialization.* Glencoe, Ill.: Free Press of Glencoe, 1959.
Kohlberg, L. The development of children's orientations toward a moral order, *Vita Humana,* 1963.
Lazarsfeld, P. F., and Katz, E. *Personal influence.* Glencoe, Ill.: Free Press of Glencoe, 1955.
Lewin, K. Group decision and social change (1943). Reprinted in E. E. Maccoby (ed.), *Readings in social psychology.* New York: Holt, Rinehart and Winston, 1958.
McClelland, D. C. *et. al. The achievement motive.* New York: Appleton-Century-Crofts, 1953.
Maslow, A. H. *Motivation and personality.* New York: Harper & Row, 1954.
Newcomb, T. M. *Personality and social change.* New York: Dryden, 1943.
Piaget, J. *The moral judgment of the children,* New York: Harcourt, Brace and World, 1932.
Rapaport, D. (ed.). *Organization and pathology of thought,* New York: Columbia University Press, 1951.
Roethlisberger, F. J., and Dickson, W. J. *Management and the worker,* Cambridge, Mass.: Harvard University Press, 1939.
Sanford, N. (ed.). *The American college.* New York: John Wiley & Sons, 1962.
Sherif, M. *The psychology of social norms.* New York: Harper & Row, 1936.
Spranger, E. *Psychologie des Jugendalters (Psychology of adolescence).* Leipzig, 1924.
Stouffer, S. A. *et al. The American soldier,* Princeton, N. J.: Princeton University Press, 1949.
Wallach, M. A., Kogan, N., and Bem, D. J. Group influence on individual risk taking, *J. Abnorm. Soc. Psychol.,* 1962, *62,* 75-86.

Chapter 17

Goal Setting as Codetermined by Institutional and Class Factors

Fred Massarik

"What do I really want out of life?"

To most, this question and its elusive answer appears highly individual, unique, even idiosyncratic. Still, the very personal process of setting major and minor life goals unfolds within a fabric of pervasive and apparently impersonal social forces. These forces, emanating primarily from institutions and social class structure, envelop the person in such measure that often he takes their effects for granted, paying little heed to their origin and function. They affect the process of goal setting in the crucial contexts of family, education and occupation, and they leave their mark on nearly every area of human concern. Institution and social class both shape and reflect in large measure what we shall call the individual's "goal probability frame," the likelihood that certain goals will be chosen by him, and his "goal vocabulary," the language of goals that he learns to speak and that serves him in articulating his aims and objectives.

In Search of the Institution Concept

Although the concept "institution" has a long history of use in the sociological literature, its definition remains imprecise. Schneider, in *A Dictionary of the Social Sciences* (Gould and Kolb, eds., 1964), summarizes an uneven collection of attempts at definitions by emphasizing the focus on "distinctive value-orientations and interests, centering on large and important social concerns . . . accompanied by distinctive modes of social interaction." Writers of elementary textbooks, often reflecting the broad intellectual currents of academic doctrine, include under "institution" a manifestly heterogeneous array of entities and functions: education and crime, art and bureaucracy, schools and prisons, offices and museums—to note a few. What is it, then, that provides a unifying principle for these assorted ideas? Two meta-concepts characterize the conceptual melange subsumed under the institution label.

First, institutions set broad boundaries, making normative demands on their constituents. In some sense, all institutions require tokens of association, whether proffered willingly or reluctantly. Role expectations, representing norms of how to act "appropriately," are created by the institutional milieu. Even dyadic and small group interactions often embody institutional processes. A student and a teacher, their respective roles in part tied to institutional prescription, interact in the classroom, the latter itself a physical manifestation of institutional concerns. In turn, this interaction is an overt symptom of how education as an institution operates at this point in time. Similarly, if crime is considered an institution, although one that is at odds with other social systems, a Mafia leader and his triggerman aide no less than the law's judge and jury give empiric substance to the institution concept. In each case, behavioral norms, traceable to institutional constraint and ideology, set boundaries within which individual behavior is to proceed.

Second, temporal continuity provides institutional patterns with leverage in impact, reaching many people over extended time spans. While particular forms of institutional expression, for instance, a graduate seminar in education or a particular antisocial criminal act, are of relatively brief duration, the institution as a whole displays long-term persistence. Any incident of human interaction may be regarded as an ephemeral "splash" but the institution's existence is analogous to a slowly altering stream. There may, at a microlevel, be considerable observable movement within that stream but for the institutional current the gross effect is one of substantial persistence from one proximate distinguishable time stage to the next.

The effects of normative demand and temporal continuity make institutions particularly significant in the establishment of life goals. Normative boundaries within which important aspects of human existence and social interaction develop, constrain the range of goals to which an individual is likely to aspire. Explicit and implicit pressures operate on him to strive in one or another direction. While the operation of these pressures does not necessarily invalidate the notion of individual choice and the possibility of transcending external circumstance, it does serve to highlight the prevalence of pushes toward certain goals under institutionaly specific circumstances. A case in point is the grading system in schools:

> In formally organized school systems, grades are mechanisms of motivation and reward. Some students may care less about grades than others. Still, institutional emphases on performance, as measured by the grades yardstick, set goals for the majority. Extreme deviations from the norm, utter disregard of the grade criterion and/or poor performance, impel the individual to a position outside the institution: he is expelled or withdraws; he "flunks" or he quits.

The significance of temporal continuity is demonstrated by the slow rate at which institutional values change:

> Though there has been considerable discussion concerning the abandonment of grades as a normative and goal-setting mechanism, the large majority of universities and practically all public schools at lower levels continue to employ this evaluation method. Many young people over extended time periods thus find their goals determined in part by the institutional force of the grading criterion.

The twin processes of normative demand and temporal continuity equally apply to social class, a concept that we shall use to illustrate the impact of pervasive social forces on human goal setting.

The Significance of Social Class

The meaning of the term "social class" is relatively clearer than that of "institution," and normally denotes a relative position in some hierarchy of socio-economic well-being, prestige or power; it is often specified by some quantitative index, such as the well-known measures of Warner (1960), Centers (1949), and others. As G. D. H. Cole (1955) has noted, class may be defined in at least three ways: 1) in terms of one or a combination of objective characteristics, such as the person's occupation, income, or relation to the process of production; 2) in terms of the person's own testimony as to the class to which he assigns himself, whatever the basis of his choice; or 3) in terms of the testimony of the person's friends and neighbors.

The notion of social class in America still plays a somewhat anomalous role. The popular ethos of American life has been nourished by the folklore of infinite social mobility and by an illusion of utopian classlessness. No serious observer of the contemporary scene takes such lore at face value. As Berelson and Steiner (1964) have shown in their compilation of social science knowledge, sociological literature abounds with data describing objective and subjective social class placements and their associations with voting, with family structure, with religious behavior, and with any number of other facets of human life. In turn these placements often relate to human life goals.

Research on Class and Goals

It is now some years since Lundberg (1955) observed that "Actually what is needed is a more direct and comprehensive study of the value systems of the population as the basic determinant of their 'class' affiliation." We still know comparatively little of the impact of social class placement on the individual's personal world view and on his values and goals but some revelant research is available.

At the overall level of goal attainment, for instance, Bradburn and Caplovitz (1965) have found an expected, though moderate, relationship between happiness and socio-economic status. Ninety percent of respondents of high socio-economic status described themselves as "very happy" or "pretty happy," while the corresponding figure for those of low socio-economic status were 78 percent. Similar relationships between components of class measures, such as education, income, and happiness, further illustrate the consistent tendency for the subjectively experienced sense of goal realization to be associated with a relatively higher socio-economic level.

When particular age groups are selected for special attention, the relationship persists. Rose (1960) found that among the elderly, "middle-class respondents think themselves to be in better health, happier, have fewer disrupted relationships and personal problems . . .," than lower-class respondents.

Not only do class differences influence the patterns of general satisfaction with life, but the process of striving for achievement also is closely linked to class factors. Douvan (1956) concludes that "The extent and nature of achievement responses . . . depend on social class membership. More autonomous and general success strivings characterize members of the middle class, while achievement motivation of working class individuals is more highly dependent on the reward loading of the task situation."

As Strodtbeck (1958) notes, family and religious variables are linked complexly within the framework of class structure and with the latter's impact on achievement strivings. The role and significance of power, as exercised, for instance, by the father in the home, is particularly tied to class factors and in turn affects achievement strivings. But, although the link between class and search for achievement appears repeatedly, one must heed Leonard Reissman's caveat (1953) as suggested by his study of age factors in achievement motivation, namely, that "the relationship between class and aspirations is not a simple one." Complicating elements, particularly those related to personality and reference-group circumstances must be considered. The unique personality structure and the particular 'people who matter' in the person's life, be they family, friends, associates, – physically remote or present – exert further impact, co-mingling in goal determination with the class factors here under discussion.

The class structure level from which the individual begins his strivings is crucially important in the establishment of goals which in themselves become possible stepping stones to personal happiness and/or to higher class placement. While the accident of birth does not unalterably fix the individual's placement in the matrix of class relationships, its impact in defining the general constraints within which eventual mobility occurs is undeniable. Much research on "social mobility," as for example parts of Lipset and Bendix's work (1960), may be interpreted in support of this assertion. The humble still may become great, the mighty yet fall from their pedestals. Democracy even tends to institutionalize a certain amount of downward mobility: the ex-President may be called "Mr. President" by his associates, but many of his prerogatives again approximate those of the ordinary citizen, however special a citizen he may be upon the termination of his elected term. But whatever the nature of mobility, and however permeable the boundaries between classes may have become, the individual's point of entry into the social system remains crucial in specifying not simply the probabilities of his objective and subjective class position later in life, but also the pattern of goals that he is likely to see before him.

Gans (1962) notes that class subcultures, by their very nature, are human responses to opportunities and deprivations. He concludes that the very lack of skills, related to lack of opportunity in an area such as education, brings about "fatalism of the working and lower classes . . . and (lack) of interest in personal development and object goals." In this sense, as has been documented particularly in the study of the American Negro, significant relationships appear between opportunity and behavioral and motivational patterns (Broom and Glenn 1965; Pettigrew 1964; Lees 1964; Myrdal 1944). In many circumstances, deprivation breeds further deprivation by reducing the motivation to seek that which appears unattainable. At the other end of the scale, as indicated by observations of upper-class and upper-middle-class suburbia, the very surfeit of material luxuries may suggest to the children that they cannot rival the accomplishments of their fathers, once more potentially reducing motivation toward greater achievement in adulthood.

Goal Probability Frames

Research evidence, for example that of Strodtbeck (1958), has indicated that it is difficult to isolate those effects on goal setting which are specifically attributable to any one of the coacting factors, or to general social milieu, education, occupation, family, primary groups, influential individuals, and the like. For instance, the family itself reflects the major values of the class to which it belongs. Class in turn is an outgrowth of the action of socio-economic forces, and its characteristics are evolved in part, as Schumpeter has observed (1955), by changing adaptations and aspirations of constituent family units which continually form and dissolve. By the same token, the influences of other goal sources interrelate in a complex manner to define the individual's goal pattern. While it is difficult to pinpoint the source of a given goal, the social class and institutional environments into which a person is born and through which he moves in the course of his life, serve as major goal codeterminants, establishing probabilities that a goal will or will not be chosen. They achieve this effect by circumscribing what the person comes to see as relevant and as potentially attainable.

Class placement (and the individual's position in any institutional setting) defines particular goal probability frames. Each frame serves as a limit-setting band within which particular goals are found more or less frequently, while the frequency with which these same goals appear outside this band declines. We may visualize this in terms of the schema shown here:

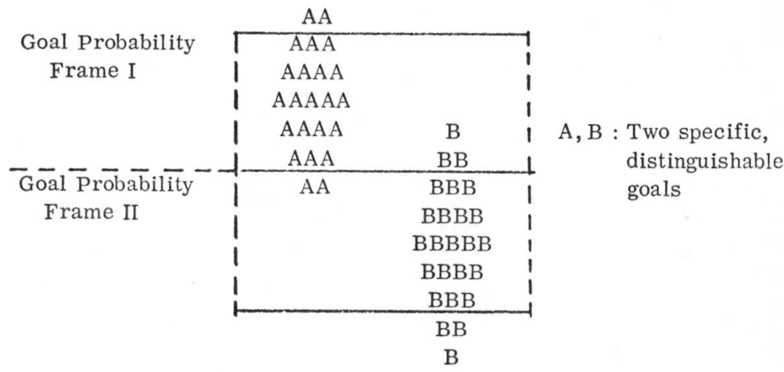

Figure 1: Hypothetical Goal Probability Frames.

Goal A predominates in frame I, while goal B appears typically in frame II. For instance, a desire for a life of material opulence and fun may be a prevailing goal of the "jet set." In a middle-class setting, however, such goals of abounding luxury would either not be seriously considered or else would be actively rejected in preference of the more practical, standard suburban aspirations ("three-bedroom ranch style home," "a Chevy in the garage," etc.). Presumably, the more central a person is to the class, the more will he espouse the dominant goals; this is shown in the the schema by the higher frequency of goals A and B at the center of the respective frames.

There is, of course, no ironclad exclusiveness of goals, neatly separating classes. Especially in societies permitting considerable interclass mobility, goals will overlap, sometimes significantly, among identifiable class structures. Thus, goal A, though pervasive in frame I (viz. the jet set), may be found among a discernible minority of persons in frame II (viz. middle-class suburbia); and the converse would be true for goal B. Empirical data specify the extent of overlap.

Concepts of class consciousness are predicated on assumptions of high homogeneity of goals within separable probability frames, and on firm divisions between the latter. Whatever the constraints of initial class placement, there are those who, by force of circumstance and internal drive, set goals for themselves which facilitate movement across the original boundaries. These moves constitute the dynamics of social mobility.

Goal Vocabularies

At the cognitive and linguistic level, the person learns a vocabulary of goals in the context of his class setting. Through a network of communication sources, ranging from mass media to the intimate interaction in a small group and family, a specific semantic and syntactical structure is created. This structure becomes the modus operandi for expression of human goals.

C. Wright Mills (1956) and other chroniclers of the American Zeitgeist have observed that there is no such creature as a truly "self-made" man. The forces that shape upward mobility do not rise, full-blown, from a self-contained psyche. The very goal of becoming a "self-made" man, for instance, and more particularly the subgoals of "success," etc., that are in its ingredients, involve sets of concepts and cognitive orientations, which crystallize in a transactional process, partly rooted in the class environment.

The concept of goal vocabulary suggests that in the course of these transactions the individual learns to think and speak in terms of particular goal formulations, while other formulations are part of a language still beyond his ken. He becomes selectively aware of goal configurations which are to be relevant to his life: certain goals will be articulated and experienced while others are outside his universe of discourse.

Let us illustrate the foregoing with an excerpt from an interview with a 58-year old unmarried Negro, here called Charles Matson. Charles has a fourth-grade education, is a resident of a low-income area of Los Angeles, and has recently arrived from Mississippi:

> Interviewer: What are you doing now?
> Matson: Huh? . . . nuthin' much . . . nuthin'.
> Int: Are you working?
> Mat: Yeah . . .
> Int.: What kind of work?
> Mat: Cleanin' bricks.
> Int.: Who pays you?

Mat: Uh . . . that man there . . .he gives me a penny for each brick.
Int.: What do you make a day?
Mat: Three dollar . . . maybe three or four.
Int.: What are you going to do when you finish this job?
Mat: I don' know . . . relief . . . maybe go south down to Diego.
Int.: How about a year from now . . . what do you think you might be doing then?
Mat: Don' know . . . uh . . . maybe work in Diego.
Int.: If things are going real well for you . . . what would you be doing . . . if you turned lucky all of a sudden?
Mat: Uh . . . I'd have a tee-vee . . . I'd drink beer and watch tee-vee. (Laughter).

Would we have expected the respondent to formulate a reply to the last question in terms of goal concepts such as: placing an order for 100 shares of IBM, joining the research staff of the System Development Corporation, buying a Chagall painting, or even, working toward a high school diploma?

It is intuitively clear that the probability of responses such as these is negligible. It is not merely the impossibility of attaining such goals as buying NYSE stocks, joining SDC, buying a Chagall, or going to high school; it is rather that these formulations are likely to be outside the respondent's experience. His life to date, notably in his placement in the class and institutional structure, involves some relationships meaningful to certain goals while others are void of personal meaning. It is not necessarily a matter of rejecting particular goals; it is rather that certain people lack the necessary life historical basis and the relevant linguistic syntactical means which make it possible for them to articulate certain goal configurations. The personal experience just isn't there, and the needed concepts and words are not part of the person's repertoire that would permit formulation of these goal statements.

Thus, while each person's course of life is unique, class forces are important determinants of concepts with which he is likely to become familiar. If boundaries between classes are difficult to cross and if classes are internally homogeneous, there will be notable differences in the goal vocabularies and personal lives which will evolve in the different strata. Our Open Society obscures distinctions but such variables as occupation, amount and source of income, educational level, and community status importantly delimit major aspects of the person's existence. They affect, for instance, where an individual will live, what his home will be like, with whom he will associate at work and at leisure, and his "world of property"—the cars, books, furniture, and other objects which constitute his immediate physical environment. These tangible aspects of experience, no less than the socio-relational ones, give rise to the specific concept learnings which establish the raw material for goal formulation.

To the extent to which language reflects class values, the language the child initially learns and which is modified in adulthood selectively draws his attention to objects and events that matter in these class environments. As Whorf (1956) has suggested, language becomes a specifically limiting mechanism, constraining significantly the kinds of thoughts that are "thinkable." As class environments influence the nuances of language structure and the jargons employed, class acts directly in preselecting the linguistic matrix within which the person states his conscious goals. The nature of these language structure nuances becomes apparent when one studies the literature dealing with slang, argot, cant, and the like, often relating to language patterns in delimited subcultures, but illustrating the same issues which pertain to class and institutional conditions (Wentworth and Flexner, 1960).

Conscious and Unconscious Goal Interplay

As Buhler has noted in her discussion of the life cycle, goals also may be subconscious or unconscious. In that case the person's total social environment, affected by class-related factors, establishes a context which, as though by osmosis, serves to determine in important measure the character of his goal vocabulary.

This interplay of forces—be they conscious, unconscious, or fantasy—is illustrated by a quotation from Oscar Lewis' *La Vida* (1965). In this particular passage, Felicita, one of the daughters of a poverty-stricken Puerto Rican family, reflects on her life goals:

> Now that I was a *senorita,* I would say to myself, "I have grown out of my childhood and soon I'll be able to get married." I always thought of getting married in a veil and crown. But I was never able to do it because of my stepmother's mean character. I thought of having a home, and of wearing a wedding ring on my finger like other girls. I wanted a pretty gown and a cake with a lot of layers. I wanted to marry a boy from the *Army,* not a civilian, because civilians only cut sugar cane. That was the thing that occupied my mind. I would say, "I'm going to marry a general."

> I wanted to have a bedroom set like my stepmother, a living room set, and things of good quality. And I wanted to learn to drive so I could buy a car and take out my family. I dreamed that I was going to the opera all the time, not to the movies, only to fancy places. I imagined how I would look in pretty dresses.

The statement itself, of course, represents conscious articulation. Still, its analysis reveals the operation of unconscious forces. Forays into fantasy prevail, and one may speculate as to the unconscious dynamics of Felicita's desire to equal her stepmother's living patterns. Undoubtedly many of Felicita's contemporaries are guided by similar goals, but although Felicita succeeds in finding words for her dreams, they, most likely, experience their dreams at a totally nonconscious level or perceive them but dimly.

Goals and Basic Tendencies

The effect of class on a person's goal probability frame and goal vocabulary assumes further meaning when related to Buhler's four basic tendencies of life. As Mills (1956) has observed, class significantly influences the level of power a person possesses. This power in turn is translatable into need satisfactions, as suggested by Buhler's first tendency. High class placement yields more power and therefore increases the probability that the person will be able to increase need satisfactions (comfort, release from disturbing conditions, happiness, etc.). The attainment of need satisfaction, in turn, enhances the opportunity for further need satisfaction; each time a need is satisfied it symbolizes the possibility of additional opportunities for satisfaction. This widens the person's scope of what he may conceivably accomplish. More and more related, though not necessarily identical, opportunities for satisfaction beckon, and that which previously had not been considered relevant now becomes relevant and potentially reachable. In this sense, upward social mobility reflects an expansion in the conception of the possible. It places a wider variety of significant goals within the goal probability frame and broadens the goal vocabulary.

On the other hand, Buhler's second tendency, self-limiting adaption or the search for security and "fitting in," serves to keep within bounds the goals to which an individual aspires. To the extent to which the person seeks to behave normatively, he expresses intents in line with standards of behavior explicitly or implicitly indicated by class structure. He restrains himself from wishing for the moon if it appears inappropriate to do so. Now, the number and kind of goals in the goal probability frame is restricted and the goal vocabulary becomes limited.

The third tendency, creative expansion, by definition involves affirmative confrontation of the world by productive acts resulting in productive outcomes. The very process of such expansion is differentially encouraged or discouraged by various class settings. Individual creativity, for example, once was deemed unsuitable for members of serf and tenant classes and reserved exclusively for the ruling elite and nobility. The present American concern with adult education and self-realization represents an effort to provide opportunities for creative expansion ostensibly independent of prevailing class lines. Still, the effect of social stratification is felt; one notes the predominant middle- and upper-middle-class character in much of the university extension enrollment, in the various "experiments in creative living," and in the self-improvement activities so popular in California in the 1960's.

Creative expansion implies qualitative and quantitative differences in goal probability frame and goal vocabulary. Goals of reaching out, of active use of potentialities, of a positive shaping of the environment appear frequently. When this tendency is lacking, goal frame and the derivative vocabulary remain relatively narrow and barren.

Upholding the internal order, the fourth tendency, appears to be complexly related to concepts of class consciousness and institutional loyalty. This tendency subsumes various processes of order-striving and self-integration. Membership in a given class often requires some self-justification, and to the extent to which class or institutional membership is a potent force in the person's life, the process of internal order maintenance has to play its part. Exhortations to a lathe operator by his union steward to attend union meetings and to affirm his belief in the importance of the United Auto Workers, or the yell of a cheerleader to spur on the rooting section, may be regarded as efforts to uphold internal order among participants in particular institutional contexts.

Historically, there are numerous instances of the powerful influence of appeals for class loyalty and of the significance of ideologies of class consciousness. Marxist-Leninist thought is undoubtedly the best known example of explicit class-ideological impact on goal setting in large, distinguishable social strata.

Some Goal Dimensions

Implicit in the operation of forces expanding or delimiting goals in goal probability frame and goal vocabulary are a number of distinct and measurable dimensions. One of them is orientation in time, especially orientation toward the future. If boundaries separating distinct classes are regarded as becoming permeable soon, however objectively unrealistic this perception may be, the range of goals deemed relevant may become larger than suggested by the actual current class placement. In other words, the poor boy who is confident that, by luck and pluck, he can rise to an executive level and eventually become president of the company, is more likely to formulate a set of ambitious personal objectives than another boy, somewhat less poor, who is convinced that he is doomed to remain always in the confines of a modest calling.

The interaction of intrafamilial and psychodynamic factors with class and institutional forces in orienting goals toward the future has been demonstrated by Henry's work (1949) on executive role and personality. He notes that the "sense of the *perpetually* unattained" (ital. mine) is an integral part of an executive personality, especially among younger managers. Here, orientation to the future is conceptualized as one goal following on the heels of another; the nature of more distant goals may not be fully specified, but it appears certain that meaningful future goals will make their appearance as soon as prior goals have been attained.

Another fundamental aspect of goal probability frame and goal vocabulary is diversity—how many different goals or, perhaps more properly expressed, what variety of goals is present and worth thinking about? At the lower level, in the tightly constricted class structure where the paths of life are neatly circumscribed and invariant, it is clear that the goal probability frame will tend to have limited content and the goal vocabulary will be relatively impoverished. There is little to aspire to and that which is to be sought is precisely specified.

At the higher level of most class structures the goal vocabulary becomes increasingly diversified. While goals that are important to persons at lower class levels may be irrelevant to those on the higher rungs of the structure, the capacity for doing different things associated with increased financial and personal power expands the scope of relevant goals. For some individuals, however, the capacity to reach most any tangible goal may reduce motivation so that in fact few goals are purposefully formulated. The world-weary playboy is one example.

Then there is the boundary of ambition: what is the most ambitious goal that the person states at a given time? Is it to make a million dollars? To own a Rolls Royce? To write the great American novel? To achieve nirvana? Or is it a matter of paying next week's rent, or buying a steak, or of having a dry place under a bridge in the rainstorm?

What about the level of realism in the person's goals? Given the individual's personality and available resources, what are his chances for attaining his objective? It is apparent that class structure, for the influence that it vests and the room for personal movement that it permits, is of crucial importance in specifying the realism level. Cinderella may become a princess, but it is improbable that her counterparts in the realm will emulate her success.

Finally, there is the matter of explicitness of goals. In a class structure that permits little freedom of movement, goals may be so sharply delineated that there remains little ambiguity as to what the individual is to aspire, and he may, therefore, be able to state his goals explicitly. Persons aided by a high level of self-awareness also may know what they must do to optimally realize their potentials. In fluid class structures, however, goals often remain vague and indistinct, and the person has to draw on individual experience and unique family and peer influence to assist him in defining his personal goals.

An Illustrative Case Note

The operation of basic tendencies and of several goal dimensions may be illustrated by some excerpts from a case history of a young woman, here known as Carol Leeds. Twenty-year-old Carol comes from a childhood environment that is best described as rural lower class. Her father, living in Minnesota with her mother, is a handyman, a combination ranch hand and automobile mechanic, who has little formal schooling but possesses rough-and-ready manual skills. Carol left Minnesota for Los Angeles when she was seventeen. She is now a part-time model; she is intellectually capable and has fair clerical skills. Here are some descriptive vignettes from Carol's life.

Need satisfaction:

> . . . it was rough till I met Larry . . . he is Hawaiian Japanese, you know . . . he doesn't do much now . . . he's waiting for the Army to get him . . . but he is nice . . . groovy . . . we do talk and do things together . . . he's been living with me for a couple of months . . . when he gets his mother's car, we ride around . . . but really he is a biker (a motorcycle rider). We do have fun together.
>
> . . . modeling is sort of a drag . . . I don't like those kooks I work with . . . at least most of them are kooks . . . I don't get much fun out of showing my body . . . I'm still a little too fat . . . but I'm eating less . . . mainly I drink milk . . . so I'm losing a little weight and I plan to get rid of another eight pounds . . .

Self-limiting adaptation:

> I really have to get a dress . . . you know, usually I just wear Levis and this old black shirt . . . but in some ways I guess you've got to conform if you want a job . . . so maybe when I go to that interview (for a clerical job) I'll put on a dress. Maybe some chick will loan me one . . . or should I buy one? I better not buy one yet; I've got to save a little money, anyway . . .

Creative expansion:

> . . . I write poetry . . . it's about all kinds of things . . . mainly about life . . . and about being alone. You know we never did have much money, and I don't have much now . . . so when I write poetry it's sort of telling myself . . . "sure, you can have dreams" . . . it's got castles in it, and love . . . and people who do exciting things . . . maybe I'll do some of those things . . . I really want to learn more, and do more . . . not like my Dad . . . I want to read and get better in lots of ways all the time . . .

Upholding the internal order:

> . . . Stuff in church was always bugging me . . . They were always telling us it was a sin not to go, but frankly, I didn't give a damn. Especially out in the country, when I was in the forest and in the fields, that meant a lot more to me. It was my sort of church, but that other bit just left me cold . . .
>
> But, about that bikers club (the Hell's Angels) . . . they're a good bunch most of them . . . I know there are some bad ones, too, mainly the young ones. But the others they're really loyal and they really help each other. If anybody "finks" on somebody else, though, then things get rough . . .

It is apparent that class factors enter into establishing a general pattern in which Carol defines her life. Her need satisfactions unfold within boundaries in part linked to class . . . chances are that she would not have met Larry at the Hillview Country Club, and—unless it were a matter of direct revolt—her modeling job is less likely to have been spawned by an upper-middle-class environment.

In self-limiting adaptation, getting one single dress is not likely to be an aspiration even of the typical middle-class girl . . . *more* dresses, or the ubiquitous mink, may be more likely goals. But for Carol, the one dress represents a step in the direction of general conformity, a compromise perhaps but a necessary one to adapt to present realities.

The use of poetry by adolescents and postadolescents, as an approach to creative expansion, whatever its intrinsic merit, is rather widespread. Yet, we have here some class-related uniqueness: poetry as a means for "dreaming" across class-linked constraints. And finally, in upholding the internal order, the special class and institutional environment in which Carol now moves leaves its mark, witness the internal institutional pressures of the Hell's Angels and the rejection of the bland pressures of the conventional church.

Carol's goals are oriented to the future in a moderate degree; there is the matter of losing a little more weight, some thought of saving money and a general view toward "getting better in lots of ways. . . . " Her goal world is not particularly diversified nor is the boundary of her ambition unusually lofty; rather she appears to blend a measure of day-by-day realism (making the best of modeling, looking for a clerical job) with some aware flights of fantasy (poetry, you can have dreams). Her class environment is fairly ambiguous in its goal formulations; she has much leeway in specifying her particular goals, and she manages to be quite explicit in most statements, though she does not probe deeply beyond the initial assertions. After a few sentences, her particular goal vocabulary becomes sparse, and one surmises that there are ample sets of unconscious aims that cannot be readily elicited in conventional conversation and interview.

While we have dealt only briefly with Carol's testimony concerning her goals, it is possible to design more carefully constructed inquiries, systematically probing, for instance, the prominence of each of the basic tendencies in a person's goal configuration. Preliminary factor analysis of the Buhler-Coleman Life Goals Inventory reveal further subdimensions. Need satisfaction appears to relate to life pleasure, family, love and sex satisfaction, self-limiting adaptation to caution, submissiveness, acceptance of limitations, and avoidance of hardships. Creative expansion seems linked to the desire for self-development, to strivings for fame, power, and public role, while upholding the internal order is related to success and to moral and social values.

Quantitative measures can be developed for dimensions such as time orientation, diversity, boundary of ambition, realism, and explicitness of goal expression. Both analytic and clinical procedures are in order to explore the person's goal world and its relationships to class and institutional environment.

It is significant that class and institution exert their influence in subtle but powerful ways. The broad social matrix acts directly and indirectly, inspiring certain kinds of goals, creating special languages, defining one or another set of expectations and aspirations, and buttresses other factors that coact in establishing the goals that guide the course of human life.

References

Berelson, B., and Steiner, G. A. *Human behavior: an inventory of findings.* New York: Harcourt, Brace and World, 1964, 453-491.

Bradburn, N. M., and Caplovitz, D. *Reports on happiness.* Chicago: Aldine, 1965, 9.

Broom, L., and Glenn, N. D. *Transformation of the Negro American.* New York: Harper & Row, 1965.

Centers, R. *The psychology of social classes.* Princeton, N. J.: Princeton University Press, 1949.

Cole, G. D. H. *Studies in class structure.* London: Routledge and Kegan Paul, 1955.

Douvan, E. Social status and success strivings, *J. Abnormal and Social Psychology,* 1956, *52*:2, 222.

Gans, H. J. *The urban villagers.* New York: Free Press, 1962, 229-262.

Henry, W. E. The business executive: the psychodynamics of a social role, *Amer. J. Sociology,* January, 1949, *54,* 286-291.

Lees, H. Making of a Negro middle class, *The Reporter,* October 8, 1964, *31,* 41-44.

Lewis, O. *La vida.* New York: Random House, 1965.

Lipset, S. M., and Bendix, R. *Social mobility in industrial society.* Berkeley and Los Angeles, Calif.: University of California Press, 1960, 11-75.

Lundberg, G. A. Occupation and "class" alignments in the United States, 1870-1950, *Social forces,* 1955, *34*:2, 130.

Mills, C. W. *The power elite.* New York: Oxford University Press, 1956.

Myrdal, G. *An American dilemma.* New York: Harper and Bros., 1944.

Pettigrew, T. F. *A profile of the Negro American.* Princeton, N.J.: Van Nostrand, 1964.

Reissman, L. Levels of aspiration and social class, *American Sociological Review,* 1953, *18*:3, 233ff.

Rose, A. M. Class differences among the elderly: a research report, *Sociology and Social Research,* 1966, *50*:3, 356.

Schneider, L. In Julius Gould and William L. Kolb (eds.). *A dictionary of the social sciences.* New York: Free Press, 1964, 338.

Schumpeter, J. *Imperialism and social class.* New York: Meridian, 1955, 126.

Strodtbeck, F. L. Family interaction, values and achievement. In *Talent and society.* New York: Van Nostrand, 1958, 188.

Warner, L. W. *et al. Social class in America.* New York: Harper Torchbooks, 1960.

Wentworth, H., and Flexner, S. B. (eds.). *Dictionary of American slang.* New York: Crowell, 1960.

Whorf, B. L. In John B. Carroll (ed.), *Language, thought and reality.* New York: John Wiley & Sons, and Cambridge, Mass.: Technology Press, M.I.T., 1956.

Chapter 18

Cultural Traditions as Codeterminants of Goal Setting

Jean Livermore Sanville

In a clinical interview with a very intellectual mother and her rebelling adolescent daughter, Norma, the former asserted in exasperation, "We *have* to pass on to you those values which we have found to be important in our lives, and which our families for generations before us found good." To which the daughter replied, "I don't *want* your values or those of the past. I want to find my own way."

Of course, whether one wants it matters not, for no individual finds his way altogether anew. Norma has received a cultural heritage which is really quite rich and, although for the most part she is unaware of it as such, it is influencing and will continue to influence her in the goals which she sets and the methods she will use to attain them. Paradoxically enough, this bright girl is critical of her parents and of her older brothers precisely because they seem to be settling for a value scheme which might indeed be regarded as a departure from some of the traditional ways of the Jewish people. She sees her parents as having arrived, after considerable struggle, at a comfortable middle class status, devoting their brains and energies to acquisition of material possessions, and abandoning the fight for liberal causes, except to write checks for organizations in whose work they profess to believe. She, meanwhile, quite consistently lives out a dedication to a liberal ethic. She plans college, in spite of a somewhat jaundiced view of the educational system. She refuses to compete, by way of dress, make-up or automobiles, with the "social girls." Her interests are music, art, and literature. Her friends are similarly interested. They are drawn from a left-wing youth organization; they are full of moral indignation and believe it their task to show up the hypocrisies of the adult world and to create a better one.

Norma is in the second of those five phases of self-determination which Charlotte Buhler has delineated as existing successively throughout life. She is giving real consideration to the total scheme of things in a preliminary attempt to define some of her own goals in relation to the whole of life. She is singularly devoted to maintaining genuineness to the extent of some sacrifice of adaptive maneuvers, such as "going along with" her mother and the majority of her peers, which she recognizes make life easier. She is not yet certain of what her own authentic self consists, but she is conducting an ardent search, and is reluctant to specify her own intents until she has found what she calls "the core of me." Meanwhile, she is leary of anything that might demand limiting that budding self, including those dubious values of the past. One might predict, on the basis of her present attitudes and behavior, that Norma in her later years will most likely choose fulfillment goals more in terms of accomplishment than of comfort, and that, with her keen awareness of herself and the world around her, she may have a good chance to become what she wants to be, to do what she wants to do. Yet there are many adolescents who manifest this fierce insistence on being themselves who, with passing years, succumb to the pressures of society and end up with severe constriction and even regression to the level of need satisfaction (the earliest of C. Buhler's four basic tendencies).

This chapter concerns itself with the role of cultural tradition as one factor in goal setting, and its interrelatedness with other factors, biological, psychological, and social. The central question examines the part tradition plays in either enabling or blocking an individual in the ultimate attainment of what Charlotte Buhler calls fulfillment: "happiness" that his essential needs have been met, "self-realization" in creative accomplishments, and "peace of mind" in the resultant internal order (4).

There would seem to be vast differences in the traditions passed on to children. By their very definition these traditions consist of beliefs, customs, and practices handed down from the past. Whether or not these inherited ways are suitable guides for the present attitudes and behavior of an individual living in contemporary society is an important question. In a rapidly changing world hangovers from the past can be actually maladaptive. Today one can observe countries, newly emerged from a colonial past, eager to utilize their new freedoms, but grossly handicapped by the persistence of child-rearing methods which do not produce adult citizens capable of the creative endeavor necessary to forge new nations. On the other hand, there are peoples with inherited value schemes which seem to facilitate the setting of currently esteemed goals and which enable their bearers to utilize quite fully the opportunities open to them. What happens to the individual in either instance? How great are his frustrations when there are conflicts between his cultural heritage and the demands and outlets of the existing milieu, or between that heritage and his own basic nature? Is he assured of fulfillment when there is congruence between his inherited values and those of his present society? Or can there be a further problem when there is disharmony between those values and something in his own makeup?

C. Buhler believes that a biologically determined, predominant tendency either toward need satisfaction or creative expansion plays a major role in the individual's concept of fulfillment. She sees his main choice, that between comfort and accomplishment, not as primarily developmentally conditioned but rather as a consequence of this innate structure. I agree that there are inherent differences between one individual and another, but tend to think that environment and culture play proportionately perhaps greater roles. Were this not so, there would be no way of understanding why societies differ so in the degree to which people strive for accomplishment. There are many societies in which, despite a natural environment rich in potential resources, people content themselves with meeting their basic needs, without striving for goals beyond the immediate ones of securing food, clothing, shelter, and perhaps a few simple pleasures. There are others in which, in spite of a natural environment quite sparse and unyielding, people exert such aggressive endeavor as to wrest from it a great abundance, and endow their lives with all sorts of creative products, intellectual and artistic. The enlightened no longer subscribe to the belief in inherent differences between groups of peoples, but presume somwhat the same scatter of predominant basic tendencies in each group. Explanations of differences may be found in the cultural heritages of these diverse societies: their methods of child-rearing, the educational system, the models held up to children by percept and precept.

Tradition-Dominated Vs. Changing Societies

It may be useful at this point to examine some of the ways in which cultural tradition acts as codeterminant of human choice.

There are tradition-dominated societies in which man is born to a given status. The position ascribed at birth is one he must occupy throughout his life. A few persons, by dint of special innate endowment or exceptional luck with environmental opportunities, may break out, strive for, and even reach goals which were not included in the originally ascribed status.

There are changing societies in which cultural tradition still exerts a powerful influence on human goals. Frequently a racial or ethnic group chooses to cling to its past as a defense against some of the disorganization attendant upon change or as a bulwark against some of the hostilities of other groups. An example of this would be the East Indians in Guyana who at one time in history were beginning to be assimilated to a remarkable degree, but who, following the racial disturbances which attended political changes, have rather self-consciously returned to the ways of their past, insisting that their children learn Hindi or Arabic, study the Hindu or the Moslem religions, and avoid unnecessary contacts with other ethnic groups. It is likely that more persons will break out of the pattern here but still at a great cost to themselves, because there are no approved institutional ways to modify the patterns. For instance, it is part of the cultural tradition that parents arrange marriages for their children. Now, however, because of exposure to another major segment of the society in which it is not so, the African, and also because of the influence of films from Europe and America, the goal of marrying for love has come into being. This creates a conflict between generations, and, particularly if youth's choice of marital partner is someone of another ethnic group, parental opposition is intense. Since there is no acceptable mode for children to assert themselves against the will of their parents, there is a tendency to take certain drastic actions. Currently there is a wave of suicide attempts, particularly on the part of young East Indian women in their late teens. They swallow malathion, an insect poison which is easily available in their agricultural society. If a woman manages to survive this gesture, she is frequently successful in communicating to the parents the intensity of her wish to do what her own feelings tell her. Permission for the marriage is then granted by the parents who no longer threaten to ostracize their child. Interestingly enough, these young persons who solve their problems thus do not appear to have psychiatric disabilities in the usual sense. They select a desperate mode of protest, for it is the only one available.

The individual in this modern world is usually the product not of one culture but of two or more. When there is a certain congruence between these cultures things may go smoothly. When, however, there is a clash between the values of one culture and another, there is created within the individual a conflict which complicates goal setting. In one sense the possible choices may be broader, and if the individual successfully resolves the dilemma he may have a greater opportunity for self-realization than had he been limited to a single heritage. Many persons cannot work out the dual pulls so well and instead of being enriched, bog down. This state of affairs may lead to a search for psychological help, when this is available and at least partially acceptable to the value scheme of the individual involved (26, 27).

Liberating Influence of Awareness

The less awareness an individual has of being influenced by cultural tradition the more it affects his goals, without his even having the possibility of a choice. He does not question whether his goal represents something for which he is suited, or whether he would like to be or do what it indicates. An example of this is a patient, a Jewish man in his middle forties. He has always had the conscious goal that one day he would set himself up in some private enterprise. He would be the owner-manager, sitting behind a big walnut desk, directing others. In actuality, he works for someone else in a capacity for which he was specially trained, and he is quite good at his profession. He is, in fact, a somewhat easy-going individual who enjoys the sensual pleasures of life, rarely stirs himself to meet unnecessary challenges, follows passive pursuits in his spare time. He had been living with a pervasive sense of guilt and inadequacy for years, and it was intensified each time an opportunity came up for him to go into business for himself. There was always some reason why this particular venture was not quite the right one. Never, until therapy, did he question whether the goal he cherished was in truth for him.

Sometimes the individual's fight against the persons who would foist onto him cultural values inimical to his own nature creates other types of problems. I know, for instance, an artistically talented youngster who has been battling for her right to develop her talent in her own mode; she is constantly fending off the many teachers and classes which her family wants to inflict on her. Actually, as she has come to see in her therapy, she sometimes declines even that degree of tutoring which would help her to develop her own skills better and more rapidly, because she is so afraid of someone taking over and dictating to her how she should express herself. Sadly enough, her mother, who is the main pressure, is herself a most unfulfilled woman, in work and in love, who went along with all the dictates of her family, achieving high standards scholastically and marrying "the right sort of man."

Sometimes, of course, there is a fortuitous blending of cultural tradition with the natural inclinations of the individual and with environmental factors. Even without much awareness of these determinants, the individual may choose goals that are quite suitable to his nature, quite pleasing to his parents, and quite satisfactory to his society. Such a person is fortunate in that he does not need to spend energy fighting for the right to be himself.

There are probably many persons in whom cultural heritage plays a rather minimal role: those with a high degree of awareness of themselves as unique individuals, of the environmental influences which shaped them, and of the cultures into which they have been born and in which they function. Such persons have the maximum opportunity for true freedom in their choice of goals. Knowing fully these various codeterminants, one might come to validate the ways of one's ancestors, embrace them as suitable to one's self and times. One might accept certain values while rejecting others. One also might conclude that there was little of worth in that past, and that one must strike out anew, possibly borrowing from other cultures. This latter route is not for the passive, nor for those dominated by a tendency to need satisfaction, nor those given primarily to self-limitation. It requires a great deal of energy and creativity, and a considerable ability to synthesize if the internal psychic order is to be upheld.

Some anthropologists have of late been bemoaning the probability that cultural traditions as they have known them in the past may well be dying out. There are indeed many forces which tend to make for a blending of cultures: industrialization, urbanization, education, ease of travel, mass communications. However, we are a long time away from a universal culture, and studies such as that of Glazer and Moynihan (11) remind us of the tenaciousness of traditional ways.

Developmental View

To understand how cultural traditions become part and parcel of the human psyche we must regard the individual's endowments as he enters the world, and the manner in which he is shaped by and shapes the environment around him.

Our developmental outlook starts with the assumption that human beings the world over have something in common at the time they are born. They share a biological heritage which is not limited to the innate, nor even to the invariant traits of the species. It includes a maturational potential, which is not identical in each person, but which ordinarily involves a regular sequence of development, a timetable of growth. This *anlage* in the newborn infant requires interaction with environmental factors for its unfolding. Culture, therefore, in the true biological sense, is the nutrient medium necessary for the formation of man. The richer that medium, the more completely can man evolve the possibilities inherent in his make-up; the poorer that medium, the less will his possibilities be actualized in ways useful to himself or his society.

Anthropologists have leaned toward concepts like "basic personality type" (16) or "national character" (1; 22). They observe that child-rearing techniques tend to be somewhat alike throughout a given society, and reason that similar experiences in early life tend to produce similar personality configurations. The data from which they draw their conclusions are mainly behavioral. Since the bulk of the members in a society share many traits, there is an assumption that the value-attitude systems are also shared.

Clinicians, on the other hand, are more impressed with their observations that similar experiences in childhood tend to produce the most varied results. The data at which we look deal with the subjective aspects of individual functioning. For example, we see mothers applying the popular permissive type of upbringing to their children, and, although the surface behavior would seem the same, the motives behind it can be most diverse. One mother can be quite relaxed, comfortable with that mode; it suits her temperament. Another applies it because Dr. Spock says it is the "right way"; she actually is tense and unhappy with it. Still a third gains libidinous gratification from the impulsive behavior of her children. Since the "meanings" to the mothers are different, the meanings to the children will also be different, although their observable behavior may seem pretty much alike on the surface. It would seem that cultural modes are the instrumentalities through which individuals can come to express idiosyncratic motives.

Simple, relatively homogeneous societies may not have so great a divergence in parental character structure, and a more certain correspondence between overt behavior and the motivations behind it may therefore be expected. Moreover, there would be less self-conscious modes of child-rearing; the ways would be prescribed and not open to question. In America parents are frequently uncertain, for they see about them other parents doing things differently. This makes them ready consumers of the formulas which child psychologists and educators have been purveying for several decades. These formulas have undergone and probably must continue to undergo radical changes. Some of these changes have been due to discoveries which indicated that human nature was not what we had assumed it to be, and, to the extent that scientific investigations can clarify this basic matter, we may expect some stabilizing of theories. However, societies and cultures will continue to be altered, and we cannot as yet predict the full impact of such alterations on human raw material. One of the challenges of today is to devise modes of child-rearing which will protect and promote what is unique in each individual, while at the same time insuring that he will set for himself goals suitable to the world of tomorrow and possible of attainment for him.

Innate differences in infants

Much recent research into the beginnings of life has shown that there is a greater difference between one infant and another than we had previously thought (8). This has made it still clearer why the same techniques of child-rearing have different results when applied to different children. One baby will tend to adjust autoplastically, while another from the start is inclined to alloplastic measures, although, of course, each may resort to the alternate mode. These findings lend tremendous support to C. Buhler's thesis that self-limiting tendencies and those toward creative expansion are inherent in the baby's biological equipment (3). These differences between infants elicit different mothering responses, and these in turn affect the infant's development. Thus human material is not simply clay to be molded but exerts its own influence, which increases as the potential evolves.

R. Spitz (30) sees a brief initial period when the baby experiences "unpleasure" at any state of excitation. Shortly, however, he is not only acted upon but is active, striving toward the mother with increasing directedness. Spitz declares that "experiences and *intentional* actions are probably *the* most important single influence in the development of the various sectors of the infant's personality" (italics mine). Thus these forerunners of goals are vital to the infant's character-to-be. Learning begins when the baby experiences "success"; he repeats success-specific actions and abandons those which lead regularly to failure. Since the mother's own ideals, conscious and unconscious, impel her to discourage in her child certain tendencies of which she disapproves and to encourage those she approves, she will tend to reinforce those strivings which are culturally valued and to oppose those less acceptable. Since communications during this period of the infant's life take place on an affective-conative level, it becomes quite comprehensible that much of our social legacy is deposited in the deepest layers of the unconscious. Moreover, in the years to follow, there will be other events which are absorbed without conscious awareness, to some extent precisely because they fit so well with what has already been laid down. This is not to say that they are necessarily "repressed" but rather that they are unquestioned, unchallenged.

Conscience formation

In his concept of the superego, which he called "the vehicle of tradition and of all the age-long values," Freud gave us a useful conceptual tool to comprehend the link between the individual and his culture. He saw the superego as the repository of parental attitudes, prohibitions and commands, and thus as the representative of society within the individual's psyche. He described the superego as the heir of the Oedipus complex, which has been resolved through the devices of introjection and identification with certain aspects of the parents. Later psychoanalytic writers have disagreed with Freud, both as to the mode and to the timing of the formation of this structure. Melanie Klein believes that the superego can be tracked back to introjection in the earliest stages of infancy. She sees the child building up an "inner world" consisting of these internalized objects, and this "inner world" influences his perceptions of the external world in a way that is decisive for his development (17). Her theory would seem to give more credence to the role of the infant's biological make-up in the shaping of these inner objects.

Charlotte Buhler, from her nonanalytic viewpoint, sees a self-limiting tendency as basic to conscience formation. Certainly clinical evidence, as well as the infant research previously mentioned, indicates that children differ tremendously in their self-limiting inclinations. Most of us who work mainly with analytic concepts have endeavored to explain these differences on the bases of problems of identification, but have found it necessary to include certain innate tendencies as contributing to those problems. Children who have few inner controls are said to be "impulse ridden." In their goal structure they are mainly preoccupied with what Buhler calls "need satisfaction." As one patient described it, the attitude is "I want what I want when I want it—which is now!" Thus deficient superego development would predispose the individual to strive for immediate gratification rather than for any long-term aims. There are, on the other hand, children who are unusually constricted, whose parents may or may not have dealt with them in a harsh or excessively punitive fashion. Such children are so defeated by each felt failure, and so apprehensive over any possible shortcoming, that they withdraw effort, and limit severely the goals toward which they will strive. Considering once more the question of what role cultural tradition plays in this matter, it would seem that groups with a rather meager heritage contribute disproportionately to the number of delinquents and criminals in society, and of those who relinquish all hope of ever developing their creative potential. Since we cannot conclude that these groups are inherently lacking the ability to form conscience, we must cede to culture a role of considerable importance.

The superego alone, however, does not suffice as an explanation of the impact culture has on the individual. First, the superego is assumed to be fully formed and not essentially subject to change after the Oedipal period. Second, it is presumed to exert its power over motivation largely by creating pain in the form of guilts which the individual suffers when he does not live up to moral standards. Hence this concept does not explain either the obvious fact that cultural influences continue throughout life (15) and can affect certain changes in motivation and behavior, or the fact that the individual experiences pleasure, self-approval, and even sheer joy in using his own capacities in the pursuit of ends deemed desirable in his society.

The Ego, Ego Ideal, Self, and Ideal Self

Freud utilized another concept, that of the ego-ideal "by which the ego measures itself, toward which it strives, and whose demands for ever increasing perfection it is always striving to fulfill" (10). He did not, however, distinguish this structure from superego. He saw its origins rooted in the child's ability to "hallucinate" the image of the mother who is gone, and thus in fantasy to reunite with her and to regain some of the narcissistic state which he lost when he realized his own impotence. He described this faculty as a developing one, so that as the child grows older he is able to take on the traits of the admired, loved, powerful persons, and thus to be pleased with himself.

Later writers have seen an advantage in regarding the ego-ideal as a separate structure, with functions involving standards of thoughts, feelings, and conduct acquired later than the Oedipal superego (23). Thus, although the ego-ideal is rooted in primitive identifications, it depends also on later significant persons, and has a "wish-fulfilling" function, contrary to the restricting and prohibiting functions of the superego (19;13).

Hartman (12) and others have seen the necessity to distinguish between ego and self, the former being a part of the psychic system, the latter being "the totality of self-representations as opposed to object representations within one mind" (28). This self-representation is built up through the child's experiences with his own body, through its interaction with the external world, and through identifications with his objects, both internal and external (25). These experiences are determined in part by the child's biological nature, in part by the patterns of child-rearing engaged in by his family, his particular culture, and in part by his exposure to other persons and possibly other cultures.

Not only does the child develop a sense of self, but he develops also an ideal self, against which he measures his self perception at any given time. This ideal self begins in early childhood through identifications with the admired aspects of the parents. It undergoes modifications as the child enters school and looks up to other authority figures. He also uses as models his age mates, national heroes—military, athletic, political—and even characters in the books he reads. In adolescence the peer groups are a powerful force in forming the image of how one ought to be (14). This emphasis on peers is a phenomenon of rapidly changing cultures. It allows the still flexible adolescent to develop ideals which may differ radically from those of his original cultural heritage, and hence diminish somewhat the latter's influence on his goal setting.

Charlotte Buhler believes the self-system to be a better guide than the ego, which she sees as frequently responsible for causing the individual to pursue false values, to lose touch with his own basic traits. She warns that culture and environment may at times bend and cripple the individual's basic tendencies and hamper his potential for ultimate fulfillment. Certainly his identifications with others may or may not facilitate his finding and being guided by his "true self." One sees in many adolescents a "trying on for size" of various identifications. When there is a good "fit," there is a marked "economic gain" because when the adolescent identifies with objects which he admires and loves, he has an increased amount of energy at his disposal. On the other hand, identifications which run counter to his nature and to his already established values tend to exact a toll from his energy. An illustration of this is a bright and capable 16-year-old girl who was brought to me by her parents because in high school she seemed to have dropped her previously high academic aspirations and had associated with a crowd bent only on fun. Her grades fell off and she was out of sorts with her family and with herself. In therapy she arrived at some honest self-representation and concluded, " I have not been acting myself." Gradually she found that she could once more concentrate on her studies and pick up her former goal of going to college with real interest and enthusiasm. This involved renewing some previously discarded identifications with the culturally derived values of her parents; the change was helped by the availability of models of the same values in the peer culture.

It is worth noting that the counterpart of the ideal self is the ideal object, the sort of friend or loved one it would be desirable to have. When the above mentioned patient "got back on the track," she broke a relationship with a ne'er-do-well boy, a dropout from school, and began to date boys who shared her own reaffirmed values and goals—an illustration of the direct connection between ideal self and object choice. When self-esteem is low, because one perceives that one is not living up to the ideal, one does not feel worthy of a relationship with persons who seem superior.

Although the ideal self undergoes many modifications throughout childhood and adolescence, a mature person eventually has a relatively stable self-concept and concept of "that which is desirable for me." The process of forming these concepts draws upon the individual's creative abilities as well as upon his capacity for synthesis. In some cultures his use of these tendencies, which Charlotte Buhler considers innate, may be hampered by a paucity of verbal expression, while in others the rich language available facilitates a consciousness of the inner and outer world that promotes maximum freedom in the choice of goals.

Charlotte Buhler, as well as many of the child psychologists, has long been interested in exploring the intricate interrelationships among the individual's biological endowment, including its maturational potential, the facilitating or restricting environment, and his unfolding psyche. Her work coordinating these factors has been both useful and an inspiration (6). She has made us discontent with current theories and has been influential in modifying them.

Eric Erikson (7) has indicated the requirements from infancy to maturity if the environment is to facilitate maximal development, and has also pointed out the crippling effects on the budding ego when the environment is constrictive or deficient. When the individual does not have the right experiences at the right times to accomplish the developmental task appropriate to his age, he will be unable to advance to the succeeding state without a degree of impediment. Conversely, success at earlier stages increases the probability of success at later ones. In his eight-stage chart, which sets the nuclear conflicts of each period of existence in proper order and in relationship to the individual's physiological growth and decline, we have a device that enables us to distinguish decisively among different cultures. Moreover, it allows us to be quite specific as to the stage of growth in which a given culture creates the greatest strains or offers the least supports.

Heinz Hartman (12) emphasizes that the ego grows, not only through conflicts, but also in so-called conflict-free spheres that occur in the development of perception, intention, object comprehension, thinking, language, recall phenomena, and productivity, as well as in the better-known phases of motor development and the learning processes. He points out that, beyond the assured gains, the exercise of functions that constitute the reality principle can be pleasurable in and of themselves. Furthermore, the ego will be strengthened by the pleasure gain from its own activities. For this to occur, the culture must provide conditions that promote the transformation of instinctual (both libidinal and aggressive) to neutralized energy, which will then be available to the ego for flexible disposition. In cultures where people must tie up energies in defensive maneuvers, the pleasure possibilities potential in developing ego functions will be minimized.

As previously mentioned, man does not come to terms with his environment anew in each generation but takes over from his ancestors many methods of problem solving. He adapts to an environment, a "reality," already molded by man; moreover, he is constantly creating and modifying the conditions to which he must adapt. In some tradition-dominated cultures he will not even have a choice of goals. His father's position will determine his own, and that of his children after him. Since the part played by his cultural legacy in such societies is all too clear, we will devote our attention to situations in which man has some option and will attempt to see how tradition influences, along with other factors, both his goal setting and his chances of success or fulfillment.

Case Studies

Several case studies will help to make more tangible some of the previous theoretical considerations. The first concerns an adolescent Negro boy from the rapidly changing Caribbean. He and his country are just beginning to emerge from a social order in which status has been ascribed, and closely correlated with race and color. Although his particular island is somewhat unique, both because its past did not include the domination by the white man that was the fate of most of the area, and because its present does not yet include the opportunities for social and economic betterment that loom in some of the surrounding islands, its people are nevertheless immensely affected by both.

Lance S.

I first met Lance while serving as a mental health consultant on the small island of St. Vincent in the eastern Caribbean. He had just had a "breakdown" and had been in the mental hospital for about a week. He was a handsome, medium-dark Negro of 18, intelligent and verbal, although constantly apologizing that he could not express himself well. He told me at once that he aspired to be a veterinarian but that he had to drop out of school temporarily. He hoped to be well enough to resume his studies in a few months. That was "the most important thing in the world" to him. He described the circumstances leading to his emotional collapse. He had been studying hard, reading a lot, worrying about whether he would make it in the secondary school which he was privileged to attend. It was a big expense to his mother to have him there; therefore he had to do well. The gang he ran around with were calling him "book worm." They were just out for a good time, spending their money on parties, on rum. They told him he was too serious. Lance believes that most of the people on the island just do not care to think, other than how to be clothed and fed. They do not read, except pulp magazines. He has a condemning attitude toward them; he wants something better for himself. He has a girl friend who also is an earnest student. Marriage is not even contemplated, as both first wish to complete their education. He could not explain his choice of career other than to say he has always loved animals. There is one veterinarian on the island and he has been kind to Lance. Lance must go to college in Canada, and the question of how he can afford it obsesses him. He does not know his father, who abandoned the family when Lance was quite small, going off to England to work. He may have the money to help, but there is just no connection with him. Lance and his stepfather, who came into his life a few years ago, do not get along at all well. It was largely for that reason that he has moved away from his mother's home and has been living with an adult friend while attending school. His mother is a nurse and helps him as she can, but her resources are limited. He is rather proud of his mother, who got her education in spite of her own parents' considering it unimportant and of little use. He feels his stepfather is beneath her because he comes from a poor background and is uneducated.

Another concern of Lance's is that his mother has often told him that when he was four he had whooping cough and that it "weakened his brain." Both he and his mother feared that this would make it difficult for him to concentrate and do well academically. For several years he has been engaging in body-building exercises, sending to the U.S. for equipment he saw advertised in a magazine.

Just before the break, his adult friend, seeing all of the boy's tensions, decided that he should try religion. Lance had been brought up as an Anglican, but now he began to accompany his friend to what are known as "Shaker" services, meetings which are characterized by the group working itself up to a wild fervor, to the point of screaming, wailing, fainting. After some sessions of this sort Lance found it increasingly difficult to come out of the "trances." He developed many bodily symptoms and "noises in the head." Then somehow he found himself in the hospital. He felt bad about having been locked up, and questioned me as to whether they had thought him violent. He was considerably frightened about what this episode would mean for his future, because above all else he wants to pursue his plans for a profession.

Following the schema outlined in the preceding pages, let us look first at this young man's developmental history. His birth and maturation were uneventful, as confirmed in subsequent interviews with his mother. Except for the episode of the whooping cough he was physically healthy and well coordinated. His mother, like most mothers in the Caribbean, brought her son up without benefit of a father. Since the union was a consensual one, it was easy for the man to walk out on his mate and offspring, as does nearly every man on this island who has a chance to go abroad to seek his fortune. However, unlike most mothers in this society, Lance's mother was ambitious and, following the birth of her baby, went into nurse's training. (Nursing was one of the few careers open to someone without secondary school education.) During that time Lance was cared for by his maternal grandmother but it was the mother again who urged that he attend public school. The teachers there are quite inferior, few having even secondary school education; they lack any ability to inspire. There is a paucity of opportunity even for those who do complete the six years of free schooling, with the consequence that the third elementary form is the average educational level of adults. For those who do finish grammar school there is a stiff competitive examination for admission to the one secondary school; the expense of books and tuition, however, keep many potentially apt students from entering. Nevertheless, Lance's mother, perceiving his good mind and alert to the possibilities which were opening up in nearby islands and in Venezuela, impressed upon him the value of education. By percept and precept she gave him a fantasy of something better, and a hope that he could attain it. One could say that she bucked the traditional culture almost singlehandedly.

What is the culture? The Negroes, who comprise the bulk of the population, have the heritage of slavery. Their family patterns were destroyed long ago, and there are no "age-long values" to guard and promote. If one analyses the dominant value orientations according to the topics suggested by Kluckhohn and Strodtbeck (18), one would say that human nature is deemed largely evil but not immutably so, since many of the religious rituals are to be understood as ways of exorcising the devil within. The relationship of man to nature is one of subjugation. Although the land is bounteous, hurricanes often destroy crops. There is still some belief in the supernatural, including witchcraft. As Lance says, most people lead a hand-to-mouth existence, and live in the present with no regard for tomorrow. "Being" is the mode of existence. Those who "do," like this boy and his mother, are in the minority and gain no great approval from their peers for their strivings. In fact, there is a degree of resentment of those who rise above the general level, and they do pay a price. Through press and radio (no TV as yet), which are available only to the literate and monied few, through contact with those who have migrated and returned, a dream of something better is beginning to develop. The individualistic orientation is minimal, however, and it is not without guilt that a Lance can pursue his own interests.

We see thus a young man whose work goals are derived from outside the tradition of his society, and who, therefore, grows up with a paucity of those experiences which might ease his way and strengthen his ego. At each subsequent stage of life the hurdles become higher and the necessary supports fewer. It is impossible for the boy not to experience hostility at the frustrating forces, not to feel self-doubts when the successes are so hard to come by and the rewards are so few—all of which diminishes the neutralized energy available for learning and coping with difficulties. Finally, when academic pressures are greatest and the much needed confirmation by others is not forthcoming, his psychic structure becomes shaky. He turns to a cultist religion but, instead of supporting his ego, it unleashes his sexual and aggressive impulses and he becomes psychotic.

Significantly, Lance exhibits minimal expectations from heterosexual relationships. His aspirations do not include becoming either husband or father. He has had no models for those roles, sees no source of satisfaction in them; they do not become part of his ideal self. His girl friend sees nothing worth striving for in the wife-mother role either. Neither conceives any possibility of realizing the ideal self through marriage or parenthood. In this regard, these two adolescents are similar to other secondary school students of their ethnic group in the Caribbean. Vera Rubin (24) quotes a 1957 study done in Trinidad in which students were asked to name the three things in life that give most satisfaction. Fifty percent of the Negroes and East Indians named "career" first; only 17 percent named "family." On the other hand, 40 percent of the white students named "family" first. The cultural heritage of the latter contains more adequate role models and more obvious rewards.

A final word should be said about the fact that in spite of all obstacles, internal and external, Lance has every intention of pursuing his career aim. He has committed himself to specific and definite goals, although he is not yet "well into his twenties," which Buhler estimates as the earliest probable age at which a person can make a sound self-determination. The obstacles and the deficiencies in his environment and culture are so great that they have interfered even with that degree of finding himself that is theoretically possible at 18. His ultimate fulfillment depends on whether his own strengths will prove great enough to overcome the many practical barriers in his path.

The indigenous cultural tradition in this case did not codetermine goals much, unless one thinks of it as a negative influence, motivating a wish to change things. There had to be some positive inspiration, and this came in the form of ideas, wafted in on the trade winds, so to speak, and eagerly supported by his mother. Lance's society needs the potential of young men like him. The crucial question is whether it can actualize that potential so as to draw upon it.

Joe

The second case is that of a man descended from a once-proud people, now largely demoralized, whose culture was debased by contact with that of their conquerors. We shall call this American Indian "Joe."

I first met Joe in his teepee in the middle of a national forest. Clad in a buckskin costume of his own making, and with a full-feathered headdress, he was busy instructing some young boys in the art of making Indian arrowheads. The ranger had told us of this half-Cherokee who was attempting to live the life of his forebears, existing solely on the foods provided by nature, making his own tools and equipment, even creating his own garments. He had dedicated himself to the task of perpetuating what he feared might be a dying culture. Not at all asocial, he welcomed visitors to his dwelling place and gave generously of his time and considerable teaching skills, refusing recompense because one of his wishes was to avoid the money culture which he saw as corrupting present-day America.

Several years later, Joe, then about 37 (no birth certificate), turned to me with some personal problems, precipitated by the fact that in the eyes of the law he had incurred certain obligations which had to be met in financial terms; it was then that I learned more about him and also obtained his permission to tell his story.

Joe was born of a full-blooded Cherokee father and a white mother. The family lived in abject poverty, with both parents employed as itinerant farm laborers, following the crops and living from hand to mouth. It was evidently difficult for them to care for their infant son, and he was, therefore, given to the paternal grandfather to keep. Except for brief periods when he sojourned with his parents, Joe spent the years until he was 12 living alone with his grandfather in the forests of the Northwest.

The latter had set out a trapping area and took his young grandson with him on the shorter trap lines, teaching him the tricks of the trade. They survived by selling pelts and dried meats, and by living from game, fish, and vegetation. This is where Joe learned the survival techniques necessary to his present existence. He remembers his grandfather with fondness as a kind man who entertained him with a great storehouse of Indian tales. He taught him Cherokee, which unfortunately he remembers hardly at all, but the lore and legends are vivid to him still.

Quite contrasting are Joe's memories of the periods spent with his father and mother. They lived mainly in tents, occasionally moving into a packing house when the tent roof leaked. The staples in the diet were cornbread and suet, with beans when they could pick them up from the trails the wagons left. He recalls once finding wild asparagus and rhubarb, and his parents not knowing how to use them. In depression times, driven by hunger, the family robbed Japanese gardens.

Joe's father was "obsessed with liquor." (Joe himself will not drink at all, and has a firm belief that Indians cannot handle alcohol.) When the father was drunk there were frightful scenes. One involved the patient's sister, Betty, then an infant; ordering everyone out of the house, and brandishing his shotgun, the father threatened to "blow Betty's head off." Joe's maternal uncle instructed Joe, "Run with your sister," and as he did so, he heard the hammer on empty chambers. The father was arrested after this fracas, and his guns were taken away from him. When the patient was 12, his father committed suicide by connecting the exhaust pipe of his Model T Ford to the interior of the car. The patient's reactions to this were minimal because his relationship to his father had not been very meaningful to him. He recalls his father's appearance as decidedly Indian, with high cheekbones, dark complexion. The father, however, rejected his Indian heritage; he took on a rather English-sounding name and never alluded to his cultural background. The patient knew him to be ashamed of it. In fact, ten of his father's eleven siblings rejected what their parents had to offer; one became a hobo and drew upon his knowledge of survival out of necessity.

Joe's mother, he "thinks," was of Swedish descent. Her parents, who died shortly after his father did, did not figure prominently in his life. Joe has little information about them. Interestingly enough, Joe's appearance is not at all what we consider Indian, for he is fair-skinned with light brown hair. He does have somewhat high cheekbones, and is slender and lithe. When in costume he wears a long, braided, black wig, and with his skin tanned by exposure to the elements, passes well for the aborigine he wishes to be.

Following the husband's death, Joe's mother went on public assistance. There were many moves, and the patient found it hard to make the necessary adjustments. He suffered a pervading feeling of shame, associated with his family's poverty and with his ineptness socially. He was never able to find much comfort in the companionship of his peers, and felt rejected by the girls who were attractive to him. His shame was increased by rumors that his mother was keeping company with service men.

Perhaps eager to leave this situation, he volunteered for military service when he was 15. To get out of an unpleasant situation was not consciously his motivation; rather, he says, he did not want to be drafted as "it is an Indian attitude to volunteer."

Following a brief naval career he was discharged and, under the GI bill, studied to be a sign painter. He was not strongly motivated for this, and when a partner with whom he had unwisely teamed up turned out to be crooked, he decided to "get lost." He returned to the Navy, signed up for Pacific duty and served during the Korean war. The most memorable part of this experience for Joe was living on a small island, where he was enchanted with the people whom he perceived of as "the original Hawaiians." There was an enormous appeal to him in their simple way of life, and he felt more acceptance with them than he had had in the cities of America.

After his discharge, Joe again turned to studying, this time for work as an elevator mechanic. He was bright and learned quickly and well, but once more associated with persons of dubious ethics. He seems to have been so hungry for approbation that what little judgment he had, he disregarded. This was particularly evident in his marrying the one girl who was receptive to his advances, only to discover that she had had a long career in prostitution which she was not about to give up because of him. Humiliated by her, and pushed by his boss to be increasingly dishonest, he finally decided that it was ridiculous to continue such an existence. His wife by now had a child, but he strongly suspected that he was not its father. Therefore, he simply "took off," not bothering with divorce proceedings, caring only to escape what had become intolerable.

Now Joe began his return to nature. He went to the Southwest and, with the help of the Indians there, brushed up on information he had previously obtained from his grandfather and "filled in the gaps." In the spring he went north, obtaining material for a teepee such as his grandfather had taught him to make. He was proud of his bow made from a wagon tongue, and with it shot a deer and dried the meat. Supplementing this with donations from other hunters and with fish and greens, he managed quite well while the weather was warm. In the fall he once more made his way to the Southwest, again adding to his store of knowledge, both by conversing with other Indians and by reading. He has followed this pattern for some years. Occasionally he works in the lodges in the national forests to buy the few necessities nature cannot provide. Otherwise, he shows considerable reluctance to earn money.

Joe was born into several cultures, none congruous with the others, and had no opportunity to absorb any of them fully. His earliest exposure was to his parents' way of life, a life characterized by profound physical, emotional, and spiritual deprivations. The migrant farm laborer's existence, with its crowded living quarters, its violence and alcoholism, and its lack of those stable and persistent qualities which mark settled communities, might well be called a "culture of poverty," as described by Oscar Lewis (20). There are few ways of life to be passed on from generation to generation when the composition of the group is in a constant state of flux and change. The positive aspects sometimes claimed for the life of the poor held true in Joe's family only in the most minimal way. There was no preservation of an ethnic tradition which sometimes strengthens the people of poverty. There was little of the cooperation or mutual aid that can mark the extended family; these were a displaced people with few meaningful ties. There was a paucity of the conscious, critical attitudes toward some of the values and institutions of the dominant classes which can be utilized in political movements against the existing social order. It is only recently that some of these attitudes have been mobilized sufficiently to permit the formation of an agricultural union. In Joe's time there was just a hopeless submission to exploitation.

Some researchers (notably of the Montessori school) have noted a proclivity toward independence and self-education in the poor and have attributed it to the fact that children are less often taught by parents and teachers (the tradition bearers) than by their peers. Even this does not seem to have held true in the agricultural camps; children were, for the most part, laboring in the fields with their parents. Joe has almost no memories of games, play, or of toys. Altogether he remembers the periods he spent with his parents as unhappy ones.

Life with his paternal grandfather, on the other hand, was full of positive meanings for the boy. This aged Cherokee had had only marginal contact with whites and he lived according to the traditional ways. His rather undemonstrative emotionality was a welcome relief to Joe after the turmoil of his parents' existence; Joe felt him to be kind. The grandfather was generous in sharing material things and folklore, and Joe learned to value the qualities of bravery, courage, and self-reliance. The Indian's philosophy was that man must live in harmony with nature and not take more than he requires for his needs. Although it took a lot of "doing" to obtain these necessities, there seems to have been time for contemplation, too. He emphasized the concrete realities of the present and the need to learn the skills necessary for survival, skills which the boy took pride in learning. He paid little attention to long term goals, other than to store up enough dried meats to tide him over the winter season.

Joe was not equipped by these early experiences for the demands of life in the city with his mother which began at the onset of his adolescence. His formal education was sparse, his language skills meager, his social aptitudes almost nonexistent. The life of poverty now became even more painful because it contrasted with that of most of his schoolmates. He felt keen humiliation at being on relief, always a source of shame in a culture which believes in the individual's responsibility for his own fate. Moreover, he was agonizingly aware of the community's censure of his mother's sexual episodes.

Again we see Joe in a period of life when demands and pressures are increased and supports removed. He coped by running away, a mode previously rewarding. Twice later, when he was disappointed by his business partner and disillusioned with both his wife and his work associates, he ran away from his problems. It was the only defense of which he was capable, and it was an acceptable one to him.

It is obvious that Joe was almost totally lacking in judgment of people and had great interpersonal difficulty in all his contacts with the white world. His only happy memories of the Navy were while living on a Pacific island, where he felt some approbation from the natives. This experience probably reinforced for him the conviction that he could best fulfill his own values by living away from the cities, away from urban people.

He is what the Spindlers (29) would call the "reaffirmative native type." He has rebounded to the traditions of his grandfather because of blocks in adaptation to the major culture. He is not without doubts about Indian culture either; in fact he knows so little about it that he reads books written for children to inform himself. There is thus a compensatory, self-conscious quality to his adjustment, but it is not without rewards to him. He gains superiority over the white man, who would probably perish if he were returned to nature and left to his own devices, and the status of a teacher in the eyes of those who care to learn what he knows of Indian skills and lore. What kind of contributions a man like Joe can make to society must remain unanswered at this time.

Mr. K.

Our third case is that of a man born into a society in transition. He solved his problem by leaving his country and trying to make his way in the new world. His story illustrates how the values a person derives from his own cultural tradition can be applied to new circumstances.

This patient is a 43-year-old Turkish man, employed in a top level managerial position. He is physically large and dark complexioned. His manner is polished; he is very bright and highly articulate. At the time I began to see him he had been married for three years to a woman who had a little girl, then 10, from a previous marriage.

This couple had lived together for some years prior to their marriage but had delayed legalizing their relationship because of his violent temper. To overcome this, Mr. K. underwent five years of psychoanalysis, and both he and his wife agreed that his angers had become milder and less destructive. However, he sought further help for his almost total lack of sexual desire in a marriage that was otherwise entirely happy, and for the periodic depressions which beset him. He performed well in his work but had many questions as to whether it was fulfilling for him. His secret aspirations are to be a writer. He has published several novels but the demands of his job are such that there is little time or energy left to do what he really wants. To complicate matters, his wife spends most of her time writing, and although his love for her is great, he does not regard her talent highly.

The patient, born in Turkey, is of noble birth. His ancestors were descendants of the Ottomans, and had consciously emphasized their history and their importance to the empire. They had always been statesmen and soldiers and had never been involved in business or commerce. These latter fields of endeavor were regarded as unworthy of their high status and were left to the Greeks. Mr. K., Sr., fought in the war for independence, but wished for a constitutional monarchy. He was not sympathetic to Ataturk, but the latter had to use him in a diplomatic capacity because there were few educated people who were able to represent the country. The patient's formative years, therefore, were partially spent in the various capitals of Europe. He regarded his father as a gentle, lovely man, and regretted the frequent separations which ensued when the family was not allowed to join the father on his assigned posts. During such periods the mother and her three children (the patient had two sisters) remained with the paternal grandfather.

This old patriarch maintained an island retreat which he had converted into a miniature Ottoman empire with all the pomp and formality of the past. He regaled the patient and his boy cousin, who frequently resided there too, with glorious tales of past heroism. Stimulated by these, the boys engaged in games of war, organizing the few children on this island into enemy camps, creating some actually fairly dangerous situations, and then, through daring and leadership, proved their ability to defend themselves. This cousin, the patient's agemate, was his closest friend during these years. It was a relationship based both on kinship and on intellectual companionship. There was no sex play between them. The patient explains that, according to Moslem religion, a man must not be seen naked from his knees to above his genitals; the children took this interdict seriously.

Mr. K. regarded his mother as a neurotic, hysterical woman, whose frequent emotional scenes were very distasteful to him. She was the only person in his surroundings who was uncontrolled in her angers. Her behavior was the opposite of the "glass-smooth" surface, so valued culturally. The patient often wished, as he grew older, to ask his father why he stayed married to his wife, but that kind of intimacy was somehow adroitly avoided.

Between the ages of 2 and 6 the patient suffered severe amoebic dysentery for which there was no cure, and from which he nearly died. He was often bedridden, and when he was able to venture forth there were sometimes "accidents," loss of bowel control which rendered him embarrassed and ashamed. People did uncomfortable things to him against his will. He frequently felt excluded from the mainstream of events; the sounds which he would hear from his bedroom gave hints of goings-on at which he could only guess. Although Mr. K. overcame his disease, he still has bouts of diarrhea when under severe stress.

When the patient enrolled at a university abroad, he assumed he was headed for a military or diplomatic career, and only as he neared the end of his studies did he decide that this was not for him. His father in the meantime was forced more and more frequently to compromise his principles to serve a regime in which he did not believe, and his dissatisfaction with his work became increasingly evident. He did not, therefore, offer much resistance when his son confessed his inclination to give up his former aspirations and to accept an opportunity to be trained in an industry in the United States.

The patient worked for a number of years for the same firm and because of his brilliance and creativity advanced rapidly. Yet he was not very happy with his job; "It was no action, just theory," he says, and although his ideas were implemented he did not feel he was given recognition. He was therefore receptive to the offer of his present position, where he has more opportunity to exercise his imagination, and where there is much acclaim for his accomplishments. He puts enormous energy into his projects, and when he has carried one through to completion is often exhausted. But this does not seem sufficient to account for the depression which can accompany his greatest successes.

One theme which emerged as he searched for causes of his discontent was that for him there is something wrong with having to *prove* superiority; as a member of the nobility he simply *is* superior. Sometimes, when he is interrogated by a man who ranks higher on the table of organization than he, he thinks, "Who are you to question me?" Once he became quite disconsolate when his office was changed to a location in the building that seemed less prestigious; he nevertheless dealt with it overtly in a polite, courteous fashion.

He finds it difficult to deal with that part of his job which involves haggling over money. "To talk of money is bad taste." It is particularly frustrating for him to ask for a raise for one of his subordinates. A sort of "noblesse oblige" pertains; yet the matter is not truly in his hands—the power of acceding or denying resides in another person. He can recognize these vestiges of his upbringing and see their inappropriateness to his present situations; he makes great efforts to counteract these residuals in himself. Yet the feelings of alienation are occasionally almost unbearable. He wonders what he is to others at the plant: "Just a strange Turk going in and out! Who would care if I died?" In that connection he has recently felt and expressed a longing to be buried in Turkey.

Mr. K.'s ambition to be top man has caused him some conflict, particularly when there seemed real likelihood that he could attain his goal. He recalled then his adolescent fantasy that he would become commander-in-chief of the armed forces and would install his father as prime minister. He had never permitted himself to dream that he himself might occupy that position.

In regard to his sexual disinclinations, Mr. K. reported that his pattern had been to be sexually powerful in the early stages of his relationships with the important women in his life. He had never been promiscuous, but had had a number of fairly lasting relationships, including a previous marriage. As it becomes evident that the woman is "conquered," he loses interest in sex (although he is well able to develop intellectual and cultural ties to his loved one); it becomes for him a "chore and childish." He then senses the anxiety in the woman, and grows anxious himself with the feeling of "my God, I have to perform." That this feeling has its origins in his infantile experiences of illness and being under the control of others is clear. But there were also many early fantasies of conquerors in wars whose spoils included the women. Their wives were, he imagined, to keep the home fires burning, but were hardly important as sexual objects.

Mr. K. comes from a land rich in history. Constantinople, once the "holy city of Byzantium" (Yeats), had been a crossroads of civilizations, and been not only a political capital, but a religious, intellectual, and artistic center as well. From the mid-15th century it had been in the hands of the Ottoman Turks. Eager to prove to the Greeks that they had a culture of their own, they had built mosques, libraries, hospitals, fountains, and the city had developed a cosmopolitan character. Renamed Istanbul under Ataturk, it began to grow into an industrial metropolis, strongly influenced by the West but with its roots still in Islam. Mr. K.'s family had been intimately involved in that history, and he grew up greatly conscious of their involvement.

It will be useful to reconstruct some of the developmental phases of this man's life, to reflect on how the interactions of the biological, psychological, and cultural aspects codetermined the course and directions he has taken. Erikson (7) states that a traditional system of child care is a factor making for trust. It is quite probable that Mr. K.'s parents, with their aristocratic background and their religious faith, were not lacking in conviction about their ways of guiding, at least while the boy was small. One may also speculate that in the stage of life where the patient's developing autonomy was jeopardized by dysentery, his parents' sense of autonomy and initiative was being jeopardized by political and social changes. In the stage of his conscience development, the dysentery continued, preventing normal locomotion and motor exploration. C. Buhler may, however, use his story to illustrate what she sees as a basic positive response to reality (5). It is clear that through his intelligence, excellent language skills, and imagination, the patient did reach out to apprehend pleasurably the world around him. His mental explorations were, of course, valued and nourished by his family, so that he seems to have been unhandicapped in his development of an "unlimited radius of goals." The remnants from these periods would seem to be a special effort to avoid the inner loss of control which could lead to guilt and shame, plus a particular sensitivity to external situations which would threaten to constrict him. Subsequent developments have been such that these defensive attitudes were not altogether disadvantageous but in many ways adaptive. But one unfortunate attitude did persist from this time; a hatred for the mother whom he saw as given to the very explosiveness that he had to bottle up within himself. Combined with a tendency of his culture to devalue women, this problem was to form the nucleus of later conflicts which, however, because of other strengths were not insoluble.

It is hard to imagine a greater contrast than that between Mr. K. and the two previous patients when it comes to education. It was taken for granted in Turkey that the children of the aristocracy obtained schooling through the university level, not for the purpose of upward mobility, but to enable them to take their predetermined places in society. Mr. K. had many models in his family and their associates, all of whom represented a high level of intellectual attainment, combined with an ideal of service. His peers, like him, never doubted the value of school. There were many good teachers who recognized his gifts and fostered them. In addition to basking in the assured status of his parents, he developed a real sense of his own adequacy and even a feeling of superiority. This latter was, of course, in part compensatory for past inferiorities, but was also firmly based on his ability to excel, and the discovery of his considerable creative capacities.

The task of integrating childhood introjects with later identification was facilitated by numerous opportunities to know others who were easy to idealize. Mr. K. did not suffer in late adolescence the identity crisis so common in America. There were no really conflicting choices; he "knew" he would become a diplomat or military officer. His way of life had been clearly defined and included, he then felt, a chance to dedicate himself to his country as his forebears had done. He envisioned himself as a leader, as he was clearly one of the best qualified in the land.

There was by then some restiveness in his father, which grew during Mr. K.'s college years, some dissatisfaction with his own social role in his country's transition to a democracy. This deeply affected the young man, and together with a certain crystallizing of feelings within himself, was influential in his rather radical shift in goals. People of his father's political inclinations were less assured of occupying the particular positions they wanted. There was no longer the degree of autonomy they had previously enjoyed, and this was of utmost importance to the young Mr. K. He had been exposed to other young persons of different backgrounds and goals, and began to question his own, formerly taken for granted. With supreme confidence in his own abilities he then formulated the goal of working in America. As nearly always for the favored of this world, along with aspiration came opportunity.

How is it that Mr. K. has been so "successful" in a venture representing seemingly such a departure from earlier directions? Unlike the Jewish migrants to the United States, he came with no business and professional tradition, and unlike them, he did not set his sights on a small business of his own. From the beginning he became part of a large corporation where his capabilities in mapping out strategy and tactics, derived from his long familiarity with military and diplomatic affairs, made him an esteemed man. In the war games of his childhood, in listening and talking to military figures, in his education and reading, he had learned that one needed foresight and the ability to anticipate the moves of the adversary in order to plan when to attack and when to retreat. In diplomacy, too, one had to be able to predict in order to plan one's approach, when to push for what one wanted, when to give in, when to compromise. And big business required these traits in its management councils, because a company that does not look ahead in this era of rapid change and plan its activities with a view to future eventualities, is likely to find itself squeezed out.

Why then the recurrent depressions in this successful man? One reason is obviously that there are distasteful aspects for Mr. K. in being an "organization man." He does not always take to the democratic process that presumably governs interrelationships between colleagues. At times it would be easier for him to be autocratic. It is particularly painful to him to have to submit to criticism from persons he deems inferior. These difficulties represent "hangovers" from earlier identifications that are not so adaptive here.

Another cause for occasional gloom is the fact that he puts so much energy into his work and is so productive in this area that his capacity for being a sexually loving person is sometimes lost. When his wife responds to this situation by demanding her rights, he experiences again the loss of autonomy, so unbearable to him. Yet his own desire for intimacy is great, and this part of his problem he is now surmounting. He is actually a very good father and enjoys that role.

There is another and even more significant source of Mr. K.'s depressive moods, and that is his pressing wish to create, in his own way, not just for the corporation but for humanity. He feels constricted in this in two interconnected ways: his own perfectionism prevents his releasing any product of himself that he does not consider excellent; and to create a work of which he can be proud takes time and energy, both of which tend to be used up in his daily occupation.

We have examined the intersection of history with the lives of three men from three diverse societies, and have attempted to show how the cultural tradition of each exerted its influence on goal setting and its execution. In each of these individuals there is a persistence through time of certain personality characteristics, fostered by the cultural tradition and closely connected to value-attitude systems. However, the vicissitudes of these traits depended also on subsequent experiences with other cultures. If they are largely maladaptive, as in the boy from the Caribbean isle, they will conflict with the new values necessary in a new setting. Much human energy will be expended in this conflict, to the detriment of the individual and his society. If the old ways of life offer more compensations than the new, there can be a retreat to tradition as we saw in the half-Cherokee. The individual may be happier but society may be the loser. If, as with our Turk, tradition has been rich enough to endow the person with values and traits that can be adapted to new circumstances, both the individual and society will be rewarded.

Glazer and Moynahan (11) have observed in New York City's immigrant groups much of what we have noticed in these three individuals. The authors show the tenacity with which people cling to cultural tradition. Although their ways do change under the impact of the dominant culture, they change in directions which are very much determined by what they have been in the past. Each ethnic group thus maintains its own identity, differing from the others, and the melting pot never really occurs. Groups whose value orientations contained elements congruent with the new culture made the best adaptation as measured by their progress on the socio-economic scale and their contributions to the new society. This was particularly true of the Jews whose value system closely resembled the Protestant ethic. Groups whose value orientations did not agree with those of the major culture have done worst. Tragic in this regard are the Negroes, who, like Lance of St. Vincent, are still disadvantaged by the heritage of slavery.

It has been said that in this rapidly changing world elasticity is a quality of great survival value, but sometimes this seems to mean that it is best not to think too much about one's ethics lest one note discrepancies. Certainly those people in our society who attain the upper rungs of the socio-economic ladder must manifest a considerable flexibility during the climb. They must take the values which they were verbally taught as children more lightly in order to compete in an adult world where hardheadedness and shrewdness count a great deal. The adolescent girl with whose story I began this chapter is in a stage of life where she still takes seriously the ideals her parents once passed on to her, and she bitterly accuses them of a hypocrisy of which they are but dimly aware, so great is the human capacity for rationalization. There is indeed some valid question as to what gets left behind or blocked out when material gain becomes a person's goal.

The offices of psychotherapists are full of patients whose problems center around vague feelings of unfulfillment, even though these individuals consider themselves "successful" in terms of the conscious goals that they have set themselves. Having become what they thought they wanted to be, they are yet haunted by an uneasiness that there was something more they *should* have become. Charlotte Buhler has called attention to the fact that all peoples have, throughout time, seen fulfillment partly in terms of some "law," some universal meaningfulness of existence. Modern man frequently utters a disclaimer to such belief, declaring that rationality is a sufficient guide to behavior. However, deep within him he still contains the echoes of those moral codes which were laid down in the earliest years, codes derived from cultural tradition as inculcated by his parents. Something like the golden rule is frequently the core value, a quality which C. Buhler defines as "consideration of other men." In the pursuit of comforts and accomplishments this value, which includes everything from how a person deals with family and friends to a concern for mankind, is often brushed aside, if it is not actually unconscious. And it is the neglect of this value that becomes the source of a person's feeling unfulfilled.

Mr. K. is a man given to self-assessment, and he is keenly conscious of the sources of his frustration, his "need" to do something for humanity, but he has not enough hours left in the day nor vitality after the demands of his office to do it. Eventually he will give himself the necessary freedom and make use of it.

For many others, however, it is not simply a question of time and energy. Man is often so molded by his daily pursuits that, like the hermit crab when it is removed from its foster shell, he finds himself distorted in form and movement; when he is suddenly released from pressure, he cannot enjoy his liberation. I think of one surgeon, who, because there was little financial help from his large, working class family with a low educational level, had to earn much of his own way. It was a source of pride to him and his family when he became "Doctor." He has a fine training and is highly regarded by his colleagues and patients. Yet he wakens miserable each morning and comes home to his wife and children at night so gloomy that the home is a welter of tensions. Neither his early upbringing nor his professional education provided him with a world view which could give him the perspective on himself and his situation that he needs. Technically expert but humanistically ignorant, he rants against those social changes, like Medicare, that he sees threatening the high income which has become necessary for him to maintain the lavish home and estate which he recently purchased. He is, in terms of our society, a man of achievement, and there is no doubt that in his professional capacity his contributions are great. But how can one weigh his accomplishments against his lending himself to all reactionary causes, his stifling influence on his family's pleasures and on their chances of self-realization? Our culture has sown the seeds of many persons like him and will have to reap the harvest.

There seem to be certain parallels between current theories dealing with the development of life on this planet (2), and those dealing with the interrelationship between man and his culture. Evolution is now interpreted as a complex interaction between the level of oxygen *generated by living organisms* (italics mine) and the way in which that level produces new opportunities for evolution. From time to time, it is said, such stages in the formation of oxygen were reached that vast opportunities were afforded and seized upon by physiological responses of organisms. This notion is helpful in explaining the vast leaps, both in terms of speed and of complexity, in the production of life forms.

Just as organisms created oxygen which then became the fuel through which they grew and diversified, and by their flourishing created further sources of power, so human societies seem to have generated cultures in the processes of group existence, cultures which then nourish psychologically the individuals within them and cause them to display patterns of great variety and richness. These individuals in turn are the generators of further cultural improvement. It is possible, though, that just as phylogenetic development slows down during periods of relative scarcity of sources of energy, the evolution of the human species slows down or halts when societies fail to provide the value orientations that elicit from man his potential flowering.

References

1 Benedict, T. *The chrysanthemum and the sword.* Boston: Houghton Mifflin, 1940.
2 Berkner, L. V., and Marshall, L. C. The role of oxygen, *Saturday Review of Literature,* May 7, 1966.

3 Buhler, C. Basic tendencies of human life, theoretical and clinical considerations. In R. Wisser, (ed.), *Sein und Sinn.*
4 Buhler, C. Theoretical observations about life's basic tendencies, *Amer. J. Psychother.*, 1959, *13*:3, 561-581.
5 Buhler, C. The reality principle, *Amer. J. Psychother.*, 1954, 8:4, 626-647.
6 Buhler, C. *Values in psychotherapy.* New York: Free Press, 1962.
7 Erikson, E. *Childhood and society,* 2nd ed. New York: W. W. Norton, 1963.
8 Escalona, S. *Emotional development in the first year of life.* New York: Josiah Macy Foundation, 1953.
9 Erikson, E. Growth and crises of the healthy personality. In C. Kluckhohn, H. A. Murray, and D. Schneider (eds.), *Personality in nature, society and culture.* New York: Knopf, 1962.
10 Freud, S. *New introductory lectures.* London: Hogarth Press, 1933.
11 Glazer, N., and Moynihan, D. P. *Beyond the melting pot.* Cambridge, Mass.: M.I.T. Press, 1963.
12 Hartman, H. *Essays on ego psychology.* New York: International Universities Press, 1964.
13 Hartmann, H., and Loewenstein, R. M. Notes on the superego. *The psychoanalytic study of the child, XVIII.* New York: International Universities Press, 1963.
14 Havighurst, R. J., Robinson, M. Z., and Dorr, M. The development of the ideal self in childhood and adolescence, *J. Educ. Research, 40,* 241-257.
15 Horney, K. *Neurotic personality of our time.* New York: W. W. Norton, 1937.
16 Kardiner, A. and Associates. *The psychological frontiers of society.* New York: Columbia University Press, 1950.
17 Klein, M. On identification. In M. Klein, Heimann, and Money-Kryle (eds.), *New directions in psychoanalysis.* New York: Basic Books, 1955.
18 Kluckhohn, F., and Strodtbeck, F. *Variations in value orientations.* Evanston, Ill.: Roe, Peterson, 1961.
19 Lampl-de Groot, J. Ego ideal and superego. *The psychoanalytic study of the child, XVII.* New York: International Universities Press, 1962.
20 Lewis, O. *The children of Sanchez.* New York: Random House, 1961.
21 Livermore, J. Some identification problems in adopted children. Unpublished. Presented at American Orthopsychiatric Association, 1961.
22 Mead, M. National character. In A. L. Kroeber (ed.), *Anthropology today.* Chicago: University of Chicago Press, 1962.
23 Novey, S. The role of the super-ego and ego ideal in character formation, *Int. J. Psychoanal.*, 1955, *26.*
24 Rubin, V. The adolescent: his expectations and his society. In *The adolescent in the changing Caribbean.* Kingston: The Herald Lts., Printers, 1961.
25 Sandler, J., Holder, A., and Meers, D. The ego ideal and the ideal self, *The Psychoanalytic study of the child, XVIII.* New York: International Universities Press, 1963.
26 Seward, G. *Clinical studies in culture conflict.* New York: Ronald Press, 1958.
27 Seward, G. *Psychotherapy and culture conflict.* New York: Ronald Press, 1956.
28 Spiegel, L. A. The self, the sense of self and perception, *The Psychoanalytic study of the child, XLV.* New York: International Universities Press, 1959.
29 Spindler, G. D., and Spindler, L. S. American Indian personality types and their sociocultural roots, *Annals of The American Academy of Political and Social Science,* 1957, *12.*
30 Spitz, R. A. *The first year of life,* New York: International Universities Press, 1965, 123.

V The Individual's Integration of Goal-Determining Influences

In Part V, Chapter 19, Charlotte Buhler discusses the problem of how the individual integrates the different goal-determining influences.

She raises these questions: how the process of integration is to be understood, how it progresses during the individual's development, what the determining factors are, under what aspects integration takes place, and how the integrating system may be conceived of. A final point is how a reorientation of daily integration goal setting can take place through psychotherapy.

The process of integration seems to manifest itself early in the infant's observable behavior with individuals showing different degrees of "integrative capacity" (T. French).

Integrating procedures may be observed developmentally in "spontaneous" activities, selective perception, contact formation, will and identify formation, realization of mastery or lack of it, constructive or destructive goal setting, achievement goals, orientation in the direction of beliefs and values, personal commitments, attempts at Weltanschauung, awareness of purpose and meaning, fulfillment and failure experiences. Tentative and experimental life goals follow these steps which build up goal setting in the first phase of life. The integration takes place with adequate or inadequate considerations of present, past, and future.

The integration problems encountered in these five phases of life are considered next. They are seen in premature or immature integrations, in disappointments, problem- and conflict-resolving difficulties, failures, and in the experience of unfulfillment.

Buhler then turns to the factors determining integration and finds that integration takes place on different levels, with respect to different needs and values. Goals are shown to be more or less effective and more or less comprehensive in regard to time or areas of life.

Four main contributing factors—the genetic, emotional dynamic, cultural-ideological, and the structural age and maturation factors—were discussed in the previous parts of the book. Here the question is raised of how in individual cases one or the other of these factors plays a dominant role in the individual's integration.

A further problem is the aspect under which integration takes place. The author doubts that a simple hierarchy of values can ever be established. Fulfillment may be seen in what she defines as happiness, participation, accomplishment, and dedication.

Finally the question of how the *integrating system* may be conceived is raised. The author sees the individual's intentionality located in the self rather than in the ego. The core system is conceived of as the existential reality of the individual's being in the sense of Heidegger's conceptualization.

In Chapter 20, E. Shostrom investigates time as an integrating factor, mostly as related to the results of his Personal Orientation Inventory studies. He finds his hypothesis confirmed that the self-actualizing person lives fully in the present, and that he is able to tie the past and the future to the present in meaningful continuity. He demonstrates with examples the time orientation of self-actualizing persons in contrast to pathologically past- or future-oriented individuals.

In Chapter 21, E. Weisskopf-Joelson investigates meaning as an integrative factor. She starts out by discussing meaning as integration of private and public worlds, following Leites' analysis of the hero of Camus' *The Stranger*. This alienated man is inauthentic, a way of living which the author describes in Jungian terms. She then discusses certain sociological, individual, and ontological factors that keep a person from relating to both worlds. She finds that, from a sociological viewpoint, the stress on industry and commerce contributes to the loss of relatedness. Among individual factors, she also emphasizes that the relationship with the mother is the most decisive experience causing an individual's relatedness or estrangement. Ontologically, she agrees with Tillich and holds the split between subjectivity and objectivity responsible for the separation between inner and outer world which may be overcome by certain integrating behaviors. Most important among these is the creating of meaning by integrative explanations of life. With V. Frankl, the author considers the pursuit of meaningful goals as the ultimately most integrating attitude and behavior.

In Chapter 22, J. F. T. Bugental examines the function of values as seen in the existential perspective. All values, in this author's opinion, have to do ultimately with being and nonbeing. They are choices, made in the moment of action, with which we respond in ways that either affirm or deny existential values, such as wholeness, rootedness, identity, meaningfulness, and relatedness. They are expressions of a person's being authentic in his own living.

In Chapter 23, Fred Massarik suggests that in normal living, each person's sense of *today's* events gives substance and meaning to his goal setting. His approach to the day's opportunities, his agenda of daily activities, his continuous response to them, and his assessment of the day's accomplishments translate long-term aspirations into experiential realities.

In Chapter 24, Charlotte Buhler discusses the experiences of results of life, which may, in extreme cases, be described as experiences of fulfillment or failure. Usually, the results are experienced as either partial or essential fulfillment, or as compensatory fulfillment or resignation.

Fulfillment seems to depend on the degree to which a person has found self-realization in sex, love, and/or accomplishment; the integration in family and society is another essential factor.

In her concluding observations the author summarizes the main ideas of the book and emphasizes again that human beings live, consciously or unconsciously, their lives as a whole.

Chapter 19

The Integrating Self

Charlotte Bühler

Gordon Allport (1961) has given considerable thought to the concept of integration and finds that it "is best understood by referring to the cell theory in biology" (p. 98). Physiologically defined, integration is the interaction of different cellular and nervous processes in such a way as to assure maximum unity in the performance of bodily functions. "Separate nerve cells function together in such a way as to lose their independence. The simplest possible integration would be of two nerve cells (one sensory and one motor) functioning together as a simple reflex arc. Whether or not there are any reflexes involving as few as two neurones is not known." (C. S. Sherrington, the physiologist who above all others is responsible for the concept of integration, regards this example as a "convenient though improbable abstraction.") "Similarly," continues Allport, "at the opposite extreme, the completely integrated personality is also a convenient though improbable abstraction" (p. 99).

But how the integrated personality may be understood in its structural and dynamic build-up and its development is still an unresolved problem. Allport suggests that a hierarchical organizing takes place in time; he thinks of personality in terms of a progressive, although never complete, integration of all systems.

Among the major questions still awaiting answers are how the integration process is to be understood, how it progresses during the individual's development, what the determining factors are, under what aspects integration takes place, and how the integrating system may be conceived of. The hypothetical observations that follow are presented in the hope that they may stimulate further research.

The Process of Integration

The observer of a very young infant will notice not only his many uncoordinated movements, but also some pre-conscious biologically conditioned coordinated movements that occur during the intake of food or in sensory reactions as well as conscious attempts at coordinated activities. The best example is the playful finger movements which Preyer calls "spontaneous" because they are neither responses to outer stimuli nor do they seem to serve any homeostatic purpose. Even before he is 1 month old, the alert infant watches his fingers.

While this constitutes an easily observable behavior, representing a kind of attempt at organizing, we do not know how this action and subsequent more complex activities relate to or are directed by some central system.

I said that an alert infant watches his fingers. This alert baby also may do other things which appear to be spontaneous, i.e., watching a person's mouth and imitating the sounds coming from it (see Piaget, 1951), responding with a smile and gurgle to a smiling person, grabbing for a rattle, or looking searchingly for the origin of a noise.

A baby who is curious and active thus reveals from the start certain consistent characteristics (see A. Thomas, et al., 1962) which may be interpreted as his modes of operation, originating from a central system. Although the implications of this statement are largely speculative, it is fairly accurate to say that such a baby is genetically endowed with curiosity and lives in an environment which not only allows him to use his endowment but also encourages its development.

Curiosity, then, is one integrating trait. But when we try to discover how it interacts with other traits, what role it plays in the total intellectual behavior of an individual and ultimately his personality, we confront a mass of processes of extreme complexity.

One point, however, should be emphasized. We usually think of curiosity and a turning toward objects as primarily directive behavior that inaugurates integration, whereas we consider conditioned reflexes, habits, and other learned behavior as something acquired and then secondarily to be utilized within the frame of reference of whatever an individual wants to do. In other words, we think of a person's goals as a decisive integrating factor.

As mentioned in the introductory chapters of this book, these goals originate in a central core system called the self. Evidence of the establishment and effectiveness of the self generally can be found in the 2- to 4-year-old child's self-assertive behavior. This self-assertion, this at first hesitant and later more determined manner in which a 2- to 4-year-old speaks of himself as "I" and says "I want" or "I don't want," seems to indicate some centralization and unification of direction.

But we know very little about the preceding stages. The experienced observer of infants may note that even in the second half year of life some children seem to concentrate on certain of their pursuits. They may watch and manipulate a toy, grab for their bottle, coo, or move toward a person in what appears to be a determined manner. They seem at such moments to act with a unifying intent.

There are, however, infants who never appear to be concentrating. They seem distracted and dispersed and seem not to focus on anything for longer than a few seconds. They seem to have little of what T. French (1952) calls "integrative capacity."

This defect often manifests itself at the 2- to 4-year period. I observed brain-injured children of this age level trying desperately to set up a tower of blocks and being unable to coordinate their movements sufficiently to succeed. Often, they just gave up, threw the blocks, got up and ran around.

Children with childhood schizophrenia, as observed by L. Bender, A. Weil, and B. Fish, displayed a lack of integration in their total behavior.

A. Weil (1956), who specializes in the study of childhood schizophrenia, believes that the unevenness of these children's maturational patterning, apart from their peculiarities, is the reason why their development lacks integration at all times. In this she sees their basic pathology. And, indeed, the inability of integration seems to be part of the basic pathology of schizophrenics at any age.

The self, we hypothesized, is oriented toward the individual's fulfillment of life by means of maximal potential self-realization. This is implemented by the operations of the four basic tendencies. While the intentionality with which the individual pursues his life goals is often an unconscious one, studies of old people have proved its persistent workings. Take, for example, the general habit old people have of looking back over their lives and evaluating them in terms of fulfillment or failure. An anticipating expectancy must thus have been in operation all along.

The Development of the Individual's Integrating Processes

Chapter 2 as well as two other, more detailed, studies (Buhler, 1967, and in prep.) contain a tentative listing of the stages of intentionality development throughout the life cycle.

The stages are: 1) the spontaneous activity with which the new-born takes hold of the world around him; 2) the selective perception with which the young infant begins to build his own individual world; 3) the contact which, again from infancy on, the individual establishes with those who take care of him; 4) the beginning of will, identity formation, and conscience with which the 2- to 4-year-old child begins to find some direction of his own; 5) those experiences of "I can" and "I cannot," which give the baby his first inklings of mastery; 6) more complex and in the form of a more comprehensive reaction to the experience of the outside world, an attitude of predominant constructiveness or destructiveness which the older child demonstrates by going along with his environment or going against it; 7) a more generally and gradually consistent attitude toward achievement as a goal; 8) an increasingly established set of beliefs and values which allows the older child to handle matters with conviction; 9) the adolescent's first commitments of love, friendship, and other more permanent relationships; 10) the adolescent's struggles to integrate all he knows and wants in a first Weltanschauung; 11) the adolescent's first attempts to find direction, purpose, and meaning for his life, and 12) the adolescent's first concept of the different kinds of fulfillment life may offer. With these last three categories we have arrived at the second phase of life.

In the second phase, schematically the period between 15 and 25, life goals are conceived tentatively and experimentally. There is a first grasp of the idea that life represents a time unit with a beginning and an end. For the first time, the youth thinks of his life as something which belongs to him. He begins to show an interest in how it began. He throws a lasso, as it were, back to his beginning and forward to his end and, if he is a thoughful person, even may write his first autobiography.

Thus the second phase is conceived of as one in which life goals are tentatively and experimentally set, while in the following phase, the period between 25 and 45 or 50, they are set in a more specified and definitive way. People between the ages of 45 and 65 are assumed to concern themselves with the assessment of their lives in terms of fulfillment and failure.

These phases, which I have hypothetically called normative motivational stages, occur in different patterns. Depending on how problematic or even neurotic a person's development, he either favors or hinders progression to the next phase.

My hypothesis consists of two parts: the manner in which a person experiences the present, and the manner in which he handles the past and future. All three are interrelated. The manner in which a person experiences his present depends greatly on the kind of past he has had. His outlook on the future, though, is mainly determined by the way he lives his present.

The past, as we know from psychoanalysis, is apt to intrude on a person's present life to the extent that it can be emotionally disturbing and damaging. Certain neurotics are so preoccupied with their past that they handle their present lives poorly and thus are prevented from leading a healthy, self-realizing existence.

A healthy person lives predominantly in the present, and handles the future by tying it up with the present and forging a meaningful continuity, as Shostrom (1964) recently demonstrated.

At close inspection one may distinguish between an immediate, intermediate, and distant future. The immediate future is continuously intertwined with a person's present, in that it requires constant forethought and preparation. The intermediate and distant future may be planned more or less tentatively, clearly, definitely, flexibly, or rigidly. Hope or fear prevails, depending on the successes and failures of the present and past.

Integration Problems Encountered in the Five Phases

A person's progressive integration seems beset by constantly new problems. In other words, his ability to pull himself together and to function in a unified manner seems endangered by new problems as well as by the aftereffects of old ones.

The first problem arises in conjunction with the maturational progress in time and is reminiscent of the role that an infant's irregular maturational patterns play in his integration, except that the origin of these later developmental irregularities is not physiological but psychological. For a number of reasons people may, in certain areas, develop slower or faster than the norm. Sometimes both processes take place simultaneously and may not progress according to the goals of a certain phase. For example, a person may be intellectually mature but emotionally immature. Such a person cannot integrate himself properly because his knowledge and his feelings operate on different levels and cannot be unified. His goal setting, therefore, may be partly or totally immature, a condition which can have serious repercussions for the rest of his development.

A second problem may be created by a person's having selected what turns out to be a disappointing rather than a satisfactory goal.

A young man, for instance, who drops out of college and takes a job that requires less education and offers more immediate rewards, may, a few years later, not only regret his earlier decision but also find himself hampered in his personality development. He may find that his choice of goal was wrong with respect to his potentialities and that his new commitments, perhaps to the family he has started, prevent him from changing his course.

Third, a person may find himself incapable of handling certain problems or conflicts because of developmental failures in the foregoing stages.

For example, a woman in her early thirties who has refused to marry may have done so because of sex fears and an unrealistic perfectionism regarding her relationship with a man. She cannot progress in her development because she feels there is something wrong with her and her life, and unless she learns to clarify and resolve her problem, she will not be able to get on with her life.

This arrest of her development may well give her the feeling of failure, which is the fourth point of importance. The experience of success or failure is connected with a person's concept of the results of life. People often assess the results of their lives, but such assessment becomes a particularly dominant feature in the climacteric age, which I have called the fourth phase of life. Persons in their forties, fifties, and sixties are apt to review their lives and evaluate them as to their original intentions as well as potentialities. They may feel that they have fulfilled or failed them and themselves, and this is the fifth point that I want to make. A person may experience fulfillment or unfulfillment, even despair, in an existential awareness of the totality of his life, at a moment when he experiences his life as a whole, as related to his intentionality to the world at large, and to the universe.

As Erikson (1959) pointed out, there are many critical turning points in the course of an individual's life, and several appear to be particularly crucial.

The first of these is that stage in late childhood or early puberty when an individual decides for himself whether he wants to live his life in what I have called a constructive or destructive manner. These decisions usually are preceded by long preparations, as illustrated by the two cases below.

I define (Chapter 2) an essentially constructive person as one who handles himself and his social relationships in a way that benefits him and others, and an essentially destructive person as one who is full of hostilities and determined to damage others or even himself.

In introducing these concepts I think of them as complex motivational patterns. Constructiveness is not a simple entity, such as activity, but rather a complicated unit, more akin to achievement. Both contain the instinctual element of building. But constructiveness and destructiveness, as understood here, are developed under the influence of a person's interaction with his environment. Most people have constructive as well as destructive attitudes. But, similar to the achievement attitude, constructiveness or destructiveness may under certain circumstances be all pervasive.

Studies on this aspect of constructiveness or destructiveness are not as yet available. Fritz Redl and David Wineman (1951), in *Children who Hate*, come closest to it in describing and analyzing an all-pervasive destructiveness of a group of preadolescent youngsters.

The term constructiveness denotes the basic orientation of a person who tries to work things out for himself and others in a way that assures beneficial results. A result is beneficial when it gives pleasure or educates or contributes to any kind of growth and development. The opposite tendency, destructiveness, is the basic orientation of persons who harbor much hostility and try to damage others or themselves. Such damage may be consciously or unconsciously inflicted and may range from preventing others or oneself from happiness and success to actually attempting to injure, ruin, and eliminate people.

Harmful aggression with a destructive intent can be observed even in nursery school children. As a basal attitude of malevolence, it begins to dominate a child from about 8 to 10 or 12 years on, the age in which some of the conflicts between children and their parents culminate.

Criminal adolescents and adults often have a predominant orientation toward destructiveness.

Typical of the conflicts youngsters may face and the decisions they make is the development of Jeffrey and Ben, details of which were revealed during psychotheraphy, which Jeffrey entered at 32 and Ben at 50.

Particularly interesting is that while both, as little boys, felt unappreciated by their parents and made certain self-destructive decisions, their development during puberty proceeded in opposite directions. Jeffrey revoked his earlier self-destructiveness and assumed a constructive behavior, while Ben reaffirmed his self-destructiveness and even intensified it.

> Jeffrey's father was a brilliant surgeon whom the boy admired and whose recognition he avidly sought. The father was undemonstrative and showed his interest in his son only by continually correcting and criticizing him. Jeffrey, who now believes his father loved him, remembers how rejected he felt, as early as age 3, when his father told him that this or that could have been done better. Being unusually skillful and handy himself, the doctor impressed on his son that he was slow and clumsy. He also was quick to punish the boy for little misdemeanors.

"I remember," says Jeffrey, "that every time when I cried—for example, when I had my teeth pulled when I was between 5 and 7—father would slap me and tell me not to cry. I could have killed him. When I was 7 I told him: 'I hate you and wish you were dead.' I was sent to my room with deprivals. At 8, I thought of getting a hammer and killing him."

Jeffrey hated his father, was afraid of him, and yet worshipped him. His mother, whom he now remembers as detached and self-centered, was of no help to him. He became a sickly and whining child.

A dream that Jeffrey has had repeatedly since he was about 5 years old reveals much of what he felt. In this dream Jeffrey climbs up a stairway. There is no banister; only clouds and fog. He gets to the top and falls off. "I wanted to climb up these stairs and hit my father. I got to the top but there was nothing. I went over; I could not stop myself, I felt pushed over—I felt terrified up there—I had agoraphobia, was afraid of heights, don't like mountain roads—feel my mother pushed me off—I feel she just did not want me. I fell in a spiral, down and down." He cries. This dream occurred two or three times a year till Jeffrey was about 10.

"At four," he says at another time, "I began turning people off. I did not know how to act, how to get along with the kids—I turned them off because I did not know what to do with them. I made a decision in kindergarten. I had painted a tree, underneath the ground—life growing the other way, dying, hiding, and the kids thought what I painted was silly. I felt 'you don't understand me, you don't like me and I don't like you. I will not have anything to do with you.' Even the teacher laughed that time, but when I cried, she consoled me. It was a color paint, a purple tree growing into the black ground. It was then that I decided to give them hell, the parents and the children. I decided to fight."

In elementary school, Jeffrey resolved "to become independent, to give up on people. I became a permanently angry, hostile brat." He started to read a lot and to live a self-centered, lonely life.

Then came the great change, and Jeffrey, not even 12, reversed his earlier childhood decision. He abandoned his negative, self-destructive way of living and accepted a constructive outlook on life and himself. The reasons for this move were manifold.

One thing that helped him were some favorable experiences with the Cub Scouts, which he had joined when he was about 10. They did things together, and for the first time in his life he was part of a group. The Den Mother, too, seemed sweet and kind. "They were," he says, "kids I could play with." There was a friendly parental figure, and he also accomplished something. "I won badges.

"For the first time, my father showed an interest." Jeffrey remembers how on a Wednesday, Scout day, his father sat at home reading. He stopped Jeffrey and asked him about his badges. "I told him I would not be a crybaby any more. He said, 'That's good,' and smiled."

Then came the times when Jeffrey's father would take him along on calls on Saturdays. "I was very happy; I wanted this man so much to love me. I loved this man." At about that time, says Jeffrey, he discovered the wonderful world of books and his grades, too, began to improve.

To top it all, he got a newspaper job and proved to be most efficient. He earned the respect of his mother and sister and felt encouraged to make friends.

It is important to note that all this could not undo the harm done in the first years of Jeffrey's life because, when he entered psychotherapy, he still felt himself to be an unworthy person, to be too self-centered, and, deep inside, to be "no good." But at least he had adopted, since he was about 12, a predominantly constructive attitude and had worked toward positive solutions of life for himself and others.

This positive trend persisted and was reaffirmed in his twenties, when he went to college to study for a teaching career. He loved college and pursued his studies with great enthusiasm. But neither his teaching career nor his successful marriage could hide the personality problems of his earlier childhood, and he decided to seek help in psychotherapy.

Ben's problem began when he was 3. His very strict grandmother, in whose home he and his family lived at the time, forced him to eat things he did not like and punished him when he disobeyed. For revenge, he decided not to talk.

Ben's father continued the grandmother's strictness after the family moved away, and he punished Ben severely for violating any rules. Ben obeyed but was afraid of his father. Like Jeffrey, Ben had a mother whom he characterizes as "detached." This trait of hers increased during the years since besides several more children, she also had to take care of two uncles who lived with the family.

When Ben was 4, a baby brother arrived and Ben was no longer the center of attention. Instead of affection, his father now showered demands on him. His father also had a habit of being sarcastic and ridiculing Ben by comparing him unfavorably with his cousins. "I felt," says Ben, "that he did not like me as much any more. I felt I had disappointed him; he gave me the feeling I was not worthwhile; why did I not do better when I entered school, since I was intelligent? I felt I had deserved it. But," he continues, "during all that time I never adopted an attitude of belligerence, hostility, or protest against my parents. Father had me cowed; he wanted to be feared. I am inclined to think I am a weak person.

"Then, somewhere between 5 and 7, something happened inside of me, and I made a decision which I have never revoked: to drift away. I must have told myself something like, 'my father does not believe in me, OK; so I won't be anybody.' I began to roam around; I drifted away by walking around for hours, fantasizing."

Ben found no consolation among his peers, since he was not good at games. "I could not play ball as well as the others. The only thing I was good at was reading. I read a lot and thought up fabulous stories for myself." He was very aware of the conflict he had in wanting to be like his father and yet not liking many of his father's characteristics. Ben admits that he "never felt like a worthwhile person when I was with him, and most of the time I felt I was in the doghouse. My father made me feel inadequate," he reiterates, and continues: "I felt he was right; even when he was disparaging, even if friends protested on my behalf, he was right."

Gradually Ben hardened in his decision not to try and not to care. In his early teens he resolved never to cry again. Years later, at his father's funeral, was unable to cry. When he was about 12 years old, Ben began to enjoy his food, to look forward to the meals, and to grow rapidly. His skin broke out, and his father ridiculed him. Ben's hatred of his father grew, and he often wished his parents dead.

At 14 he quit school against the wishes of his parents, his reason being that he wanted to be independent. He now realizes that he wanted to hurt and disappoint his father. He was the oldest and, undoubtedly, most gifted son, and his father had wanted him to study law. He himself would have liked to be educated and perhaps to become a historian, a physician, or a writer. He dreamed of all this, and he admired learned people. But instead of pursuing any of these goals, he allowed spite to determine his actions. He took a clerical job, was dissatisfied and quit, changed jobs a few times, suddenly went to night school to take business courses, did a minimum of work, and spent his free time day-dreaming.

The turn Ben's development took was more or less determined when he was between 12 and 14. If there was an integrating principle at all, it was spite and the desire to get away from parental pressures and to be left alone. His negative and self-destructive motives were so strong that his positive directives could never take hold.

Later, in his early twenties, Ben tried to retrace his steps. Persuaded by one of his brothers with whom he was particularly friendly, he accepted financial help from his father, finished high school and graduated from law school. After his father's early death, he took over the latter's business. But this proved to be a mistake. His old feelings returned, and in no time at all he had ruined the business. He just is not a business man, he says. But he realizes now that feelings of revenge toward his father were at the bottom of this failure. After selling out Ben tried a few enterprises of his own, but his attempts were halfhearted at best and his guilt feelings prevented him from functioning appropriately. His pre-occupation with himself was so great that it interfered with his human relationships. He was married twice and divorced twice. He never really loved anybody.

When at age 50 he came into therapy, he was able to recognize the negative and destructive trends of his motivation. For the first time in his life he opened up sufficiently to fall in love and to have a mutually satisfactory affair with a divorced woman his own age. He also tried

> to find himself in the one occupation he always had felt was his and which he had attempted, off and on, quite successfully, that is, short story writing. But unfortunately he was by now too disturbed and distracted to concentrate for any length of time.
>
> It is very probable that the accident which resulted in his death at 52 was more or less suicidal.

The decisions Jeffrey and Ben made in their early teens integrated their goal setting in opposite directions, although their earlier childhoods had run rather parallel courses. They both had first decided on roles of opposition. Then one reversed his course while the other reaffirmed it, and finally in their later twenties, both reaffirmed the courses their lives had begun to take when they were in their teens.

I have cited these cases because they demonstrate the development of constructive and destructive integrative procedures. They also show how self-evaluation works in the direction of the fulfillment potential, which Jeffrey determined to develop and Ben to give up.

The Problem of Determining Factors

In trying to decide which factors determine integration, we must remember that integration takes place on different levels, with different degrees of comprehensiveness, and in relation to different needs and values.

To say that integration takes place on different levels means that simultaneous integrative processes are taking place in different subsystems of the personality. In a well integrated person, these subsystems function in a more or less hierarchical organization.

A well integrated person, such as Mr. X, for example, might wake up in the morning when his alarm clock rings. His whole system being under adequate control, he has slept well, feels rested, and is ready to begin the new day with a habitual ritual of bodily functions and a more or less flexible ritual of breakfast, most likely with his family.

The partly automized processes which organize his biological and behavioral procedures toward the pursuit of the day's program, however, leave Mr. X enough inner freedom to reflect on other things. He may, for instance, contemplate an episode of the previous day or a problem facing him; he may be cheered by the fleeting memory of a pleasant event or consider a conflict that needs to be resolved.

By comparison, a poorly integrated Mr. Y may get up late because he overslept or forgot to set his alarm. He may awaken tired after a late night out or because of some disturbing dreams. He dreads the day ahead because he does not have matters well in hand, nor do they interest him. He probably lacks well-established biological habits and regularity of functions. Having arisen too late to have breakfast, he is irritated by his family. In his preoccupation with his problems, he is apt to leave the house without the one document he needs for his meeting, and so on.

Let us assume that the integrating principle for Mr. X and Mr. Y is the proper pursuit of the coming day's chores and pleasures. It becomes quickly apparent that while Mr. X prepares for this goal with an all-inclusive hold over the subsystems involved in this process, Mr. Y has no such overall organization. He falls apart in the process of preparation, and at no point is he unified in his effort to pursue his goal.

The situation would be worse if there were no goal to pursue. A drifting or completely unorganized person like Mr. Z, for example, may not even get up, have any regular functions or habits, and may only vaguely know what to do with himself during the coming day.

Integration in these three examples is accomplished by an effective goal, the pursuit of a daily program. The effectiveness of this pursuit is enhanced, as in the case of Mr. X, by the integrated functioning of subsystems. The goals that are being pursued by the subfunctions—wanting to be fresh in the morning, to have clean teeth, to have time for a chat with the family—may vary greatly. But their common denominator is to intensify a person's functioning under the aspect of certain goals.

The different comprehensiveness with which integration takes place applies also to the time factor. A person can be integrated with respect to a momentary decision, an immediate action, a short-or-long-range term, or to the whole of his life. There may be flexibility or rigidity in the way the intervals of present, past, and future are held together.

Integration also may be more or less comprehensive with respect to the areas of life in which a person becomes interested and involved. In a therapy group discussion two patients, Mark and Martin, found out that they were each integrated in one and not in another area of life. Martin was extremely well-integrated in his professional life, while his personal life was undeveloped and unintegrated. The opposite was true of Mark.

Ideally, a healthy person is fully integrated in the important areas of life. In other words, his concerns and pursuits in the different areas of life are hierarchically organized as regards the time allotted, the energy spent, and the preference given them. There is also a consistency of efforts and continuity of concerns, which brings me to the most important and central determinants, i.e., the needs and values which act as the forces behind and the directives toward the integration process.

The question of how needs and values intertwine in propelling and directing the goal-setting process is the central theme of this book. In this chapter I would like to examine the impact these forces and directives have on an individual's integration.

Needs and values, as we all know, can pull an individual into opposing directions. As a matter of fact, this is a conflict that is basic to many neuroses. And as long as this conflict remains unresolved, the individual remains unintegrated. He is either split in his goal setting or he is stymied, inconsistent, and confused in his directives. He also is apt to make arbitrary decisions and to force one or another issue.

In the preceding parts of this book we have discussed the four main contributing factors to goal setting. The simultaneous impact of the genetic, dynamic, cultural-ideological and structural age as well as of the maturation factors is so complex that one wonders how integrated goal setting can ever be accomplished. Another question whose answer still eludes us is what causes one impact to dominate another.

Why should a man like Clarence Darrow, for instance (see Chapter 4), be so strongly determined by the ideology of his father? Possibly he loved both his parents but, in addition, admired his father so that he accepted his father's thinking as fully as he accepted the man. As Darrow himself says: "My father had directed my thought and reading. He had taught me to question rather than accept. He never thought that the fear of God was the beginning of wisdom. I have always felt that doubt was the beginning of wisdom, and the fear of God was the end of wisdom (p. 58)."

Strangely enough, this seemingly ideal background produced a person who, in a way, neglected his personal development over that of his objective goals. Not only was Clarence Darrow's first marriage at 21 poorly motivated and immature, but his parenthood, too, would seem to be rather inadequate. There is a strange contrast between the passion with which he dedicated himself to the defense of the criminal youths, Loeb and Leopold, and the apparent detachment with which he speaks in his autobiography about his son.

"Soon after I was twenty-one years old," he writes, "while I was living in Ashtabula, Ohio, I married Miss Jessie Ohl, whose parents were neighbors and friends of our family. Of this marriage my son Paul was born. Later in life we were divorced—in 1897. This was done without contest or disagreement and without any bitterness on either side, and our son has always been attached to both of us, and she and I have always had full confidence and respect toward each other" (p. 33).

Jean Livermore Sanville describes a case where the ideological factor overshadows the emotional dynamics in the selection of goal-determining values (see Chapter 18).

Possibly one could argue that Joe, the American of semi-Indian descent, was emotionally closer to his grandfather, to whose Indian culture pattern he ultimately returned, than to his parents. This cannot be said of Mr. K. The Turkish born Mr. K. also had a grandfather who was more emotionally satisfying to him in his childhood than his parents. Mr. K., however, ultimately decided against identifying with his grandfather's cultural ideology and tried to integrate himself into the American cultural pattern. His decision was based on the fact that he did not believe in the traditional ideology in which he had been raised. But since he also disagreed with certain aspects of the American cultural pattern, his choice caused him considerable difficulties. It must not be overlooked, however, that in addition to his ideological problems, he also had personal ones.

Livermore Sanville's third case, that of Lance, shows a less conflicted situation. Growing up in the cultural poverty of his Caribbean Negro surroundings, Lance receives his only emotional support from his mother, a staunch advocate of Western education. The final convictions he develops, therefore, do not clash with his emotional preferences.

As a last example, I would like to mention the case of Bill Roberts, whose biography I used as the prototype for the build-up of human life (Chapter 3). Roberts represents a healthy, average existence in our American culture. He comes from parents whom he loved. When, at 14, he lost his mother and his father married a woman with whom Bill did not feel close, he left home and supported himself with some help of out-of-town relatives with whom he stayed. His choice was based on the conviction that he wanted to stand on his own two feet. He feels that this streak of independence runs in his family, and is not bitter about his fate.

Another conviction, derived from Bill's cultural background, prevented him, a Presbyterian, from marrying a Catholic girl who demanded his conversion.

While emotionally well-rooted in his background, Bill did not identify with his family's goals and values, except for the idea of having a stable family of his own. He participated in the American upward movement by getting a job which gave him a better education than his parents had had and which allowed him to move around and see other places. Coming from the farm, he ended up as a city dweller. He remained faithful to his religious background but chose the opposite political party.

He enriched his life by a number of new social and cultural interests.

This emotionally well-balanced person, then, comes closer than any of the others to achieving an integrated attachment to and freedom from his emotional past, as well as an integrated loyalty to old and new values. It seems symbolic to me that what Bill cherishes most and considers his and his family's greatest experience is the trip they all took together through the United States.

In discussing the predominance of genetic over age factors, brief mention must be made of Van Cliburn, whose eminent musical talent and interest started him, when he was only 3, on his career and his predominant goal. As his biography (A. Chasins, 1959) shows, his was the unusually happy incidence of a favorable concurrence of all factors. Not only did he have loving parents, and a happy home life, but he also had a musically gifted and performing mother who became his teacher, at his request. His family did not exactly encourage his ideas about his future, but neither did they put any hindrance in his way. His case proves that an ingenious development does not necessarily have to be preceded by conflicts.

Other more complicated examples of the gradual goal determination of the genetic factor are contained in A. Horner's discussion of the "Genetic Aspects of Creativity." (See Chapter 8.)

Aspects under Which Integration Takes Place

The aspects under which integration takes place are determined by the ultimate intent a person pursues. People generally believe that the realization of this intent will result in fulfilled goals and a worthwhile life.

In younger people these intents usually are clouded and vague. They may speak of happiness, success, fame, and wanting to help mankind, without being too sure what they really want and can do. Many people, of course, never think in these terms; they live with short-range goals and are only vaguely aware of a far-away future and life's inevitable ending. Older people usually are much more aware of the fact that their lives have had certain directives, even though they may not always have been conscious of their interests.

Intents are usually manifold, i.e., the aspects under which people integrate themselves are numerous and defy a simple hierarchy of values. If we were to name a top goal, it would have to be something as general as fulfillment. The goal of self-realization, which has been favored recently, can only then be identified with fulfillment if self-realization includes living for others, doing right, etc.

The four main areas of attainment which give people a sense of fulfillment correspond to the relatively successful pursuits of the four basic tendencies that we outlined previously (see Chapter 6).

The statements about fulfillment, failure, and the in-between kind of resignation that patients and those over 55 make when they are asked what they have achieved in life, can be grouped under the aspects of happiness, participation, accomplishment and, for lack of a better word, dedication.

The aspect and intent of happiness is perhaps the most general of all. It corresponds to the tendency of need satisfaction. People try to integrate themselves with a view to attaining happiness. Love and possessions are probably the most widely pursued objectives of people who strive for happiness. Most persons admit that luck has played a role in what they have achieved in this area.

The aspect and intent of participation is part of an individual's need to belong, to be part of the group, to feel secure, and to be accepted and wanted. Success in this area means to be integrated into society and mankind and requires an adequate self-limiting adaptation to given situations. Here, too, opportunity plays a role in that some people feel they were given a chance appropriate to their potentialities, while others feel that circumstances prevented them from fulfilling their potential.

The aspect and intent of accomplishment is related to the tendency of creative expansion. I have found that most people feel strongly about accomplishment. They think that their lives should amount to something, bear fruit, and represent an accomplishment of some kind. (There should be "something to show for it.") Whether or not they attain this accomplishment greatly influences their sense of satisfaction or dissatisfaction with their lives. It is possible that this value is more important in our Western civilization than in others.

The aspect and intent of dedication, as I have called it for lack of a better word, results from the tendency to uphold the internal order. This internal order is established by beliefs, which may be anything and do not necessarily have to be moral. Some people conceive of success in terms of worldly recognition and possessions. The knowledge of having done right in terms of moral, religious, or other convictions also is usually experienced as a satisfying result. There are, furthermore, people who have dedicated themselves to causes, and a few whose pathological dedication to destruction dominates their constructive intents.

Fulfillment seems to result primarily from a constructive and thoughtful way of living; constructive in that even major tragedies and great misfortunes are overcome and used beneficially; thoughtful in that even mediocre potentialities are used for accomplishments and meaningful self-dedication; thoughtful also in the attempt to review and project one's existence and to assess it in whatever terms one believes in.

The aspects under which a person integrates himself can also be seen under a different perspective, as J. Bugental shows in Chapter 22. His emphasis on existential authenticity is an important consideration and one that is complementary to my discussion.

A special word, however, should be said about the aspect and intent of meaningfulness of life as a fundamentally integrative factor. Some people want their lives to have meaning. Meaning is what makes their lives seem worthwhile; they do not care about a life without a meaning.

This concept, to which we referred briefly in the first chapter, has undergone about eight different definitions since Brentano and Husserl, Dilthey, Spranger and Heidegger introduced it into modern philosophy and psychology. As these phenomenologists defined it, it characterizes the transcendence of human existence, an important aspect which was rediscovered recently by V. E. Frankl, A. Maslow, and F. W. Matson, among others. The most thorough discussion of this term can be found in *Sinn und Sein* (Meaning and Being), an anniversary volume dedicated to F. J. von Rintelen and edited by R. Wisser (1960).

Meaning in the existential sense has a cognitive as well as volitional connotation. It supposes that human existence relates to something beyond itself, presumably in the universe, and that it is intended to be lived in relation to that something. K. Buhler's (1929) previously mentioned definition of something being meaningful if it is a contributory constituent to a teleological whole is broad enough to allow for the existential context and purpose of human existence.

One who assumes that his life has significance within the framework of the universe considers this meaningfulness the basic integrating factor, and the one that provides the foundation for his order-upholding tendency. The relatedness to the universe is an essential constituent to his life. There are persons who do not need this at all. They experience meaningfulness in the dedication to their fellow men, without metaphysical convictions.

The fact that an individual feels his life is meaningful often manifests itself in his moral and religious convictions, which, under certain circumstances, are a naive expression of these philosophical thoughts. It also manifests itself in the way he conducts his life, as E. Weisskopf-

Joelson points out when she describes the cathexis to the outer, the public, world as a part of meaningful living.

Thus meaningfulness may be called the basic order-upholding, integrative principle of our existence.

Aspects of Reorientation through Psychotherapy

The complexity of the individual's own tendencies and the multiplicity of the factors which influence him almost necessarily lead to faulty goal setting. Nearly everybody—at least this is the prevalent impression—has one or the other neurotic hang-up, and psychotherapy with increasing frequency is becoming a modern adjunct to education. In that instance, psychotherapy is not used exclusively, as formerly, to cure the mentally sick, but rather as a uniquely helpful procedure to assist people to find themselves.

The reason for this development is a growing awareness on the part of many people that they are lost when it comes to establishing satisfactory goals.

First, they feel lost because of the multiplicity of goal-determining facts, the integration of which represents a major task at best. And second, they feel lost because the fluctuating value system of our time has caused them to question the validity of authorities and of their previously uncontested beliefs. While the profusion of goal-determining factors is confusing, the generally increasing doubt of the value of authority throws the individual back on himself. Furthermore, our educational system has not taught us how to find an honest and adequate answer to the problem of value orientation.

A brief example illustrates the problem:

> *Gladys,* an unmarried woman in her early thirties who lives with her mother, is a clerk in an accounting office. Her mother, whose husband left her in the first years of their marriage, holds on to Gladys, her only daughter, as a companion, household helper, and partial supporter.
>
> Gladys would like to be married but her mother has so far been most successful in keeping her from involvements with men, particularly by criticizing the friends Gladys brought home and by making her fearful of the sexual troubles in which all men would involve her. "That" was what all that men wanted, she had told her daughter, and it was "dirty."
>
> Gladys had normal desires for sex and even more for love, and her frustration and doubts as to what to do increased as the years went by.

Off and on she talked with other girls who tried to dissuade her from submitting to her mother and her mother's ideas and principles. They told her that in this day and age it was not unusual to have an affair, and that there was nothing wrong with sex. But Gladys' dependency was also enhanced by her own fear of sex and of society's disapproval should she "make a mistake," by becoming pregnant, for instance. Her church, too—she was Catholic—confirmed her mother's strict views about premarital sex. Although she obeyed her mother, Gladys was somehow aware of the fact that her mother's restrictions and demands went much further than the demands of her church. There was something wrong, something unjustifiable in the way her mother prevented her from living a life of her own. Her confusion and frustration brought her close to a breakdown; her despair brought her into psychotherapy.

In therapy, while working through her dependency relationship with her mother, Gladys gradually realized that she had been so submissive not only because she believed in parental and church authority, but mostly because she was afraid of accepting any responsibilities. One of these early responsibilities, for example, would have been to find out for herself about the different boy-girl relationships. She finally understood that her complete lack of confidence in her ability to act on her own was the real problem in the situation. Even if she wanted to refute the values of those who rebelled against the principles she wanted to hold on to, she should have been able to do so within the frame of reference of actual human relationships which, however, she avoided.

In relating this case to the problems of integrated goal setting which we mentioned earlier, we come to the following conclusion:

First, Gladys was never herself. The core self, from which self-determination proceeds in a preliminary way beginning in early childhood, had been prevented from developing by an overpowering, domineering mother. The patient's neurotic submissiveness to her mother and her inability to develop a self of her own had kept her in bondage, and her eventual discovery of the discrepancy in values further confused and incapacitated her. There was, on one hand, the moral code of her church which seemed to agree with her mother's principles; on the other hand, there were the many persons who did not accept these principles and had completely different convictions.

In this kind of confusion, occasioned by the modern conflict in value orientation, as well as in neurotic entanglements, psychotherapy seems to be the appropriate method. This procedure, then, of assisting a conflicted person to achieve an integrated goal orientation embraces a number of aspects.

The first is that a person learns to understand and think through his own motives. An honest interpretation of them under the therapist's guidance is perhaps the most important initial step the patient takes in developing an ability to choose values freely.

A second essential point is that a person is encouraged to feel his own feelings, an experience from which neurotics frequently cut themselves off. Third, in understanding his motives and experiencing his feelings, a person learns to discover his own self. He learns to face himself as he is and as he functions in reality.

By seeing himself more objectively, he may, and this is the fourth aspect, gain a clearer appreciation of his own potentialities. He may see for himself what his life amounts to in the present, what it has meant in the past, and what lies ahead; in other words, he may be able to see his life as a whole.

This then brings us to the fifth aspect. An individual is now able to assess his goals and decide what he wants to live for, and, with a clearer image of himself as a person, to take responsible action in the choice of his goals and values.

The Integrating System

As indicated in the Introduction and in the first chapter, we believe that integration is being accomplished by the self, which we assume to be the core system of the personality. We consider the ego, to which modern ego psychologists ascribe the role of integrator, as primarily a conscious, organizing agency within the realm of reality.

The self, however, appears to us to be a subconscious system which stores the individual's potentialities and their immanent directives. It represents and develops his intentionality toward ultimate fulfillment, a stage he is expected to reach by realizing his potential, modified as it may be by external influences.

Individuals vary in the extent to which they are able to remain themselves and to evolve in the face of external influences that threaten to overpower them. We have discussed the factors that codetermine an individual's ultimate goal setting in theory and through examples; aside from the role that creativity plays, we still know very little about the part the core system plays in an individual's development.

The so-called ego strength does not necessarily enhance the true self's plight. As was mentioned before, under certain circumstances the ego may fortify goals that are alien to the true self, a fact that was first pointed out by K. Horney (1945).

We do not know whether it is weakness, deficiency, poor inner organization, or a lack of coherence which causes the core system to be ineffective and create confused, torn, and split personality developments.

In the theory presented here, the core system is thought of as the existential reality of the individual's being, a concept which Heidegger developed in modification of Fichte's theories about the I.

Answers to the question of how the individual's intentionality materializes and integrates with experience are still ambiguous. A. Diemer (1960) discusses, in an enlightening article in *Sinn und Sein,* several ideas concerning the primary process of human experience. Husserl holds that it is the perceptive-theoretical method that is the *Urerfahrungsweise*—the first and primary manner of experiencing something—while Scheler sees it in the emotional response and Heidegger in the forming and mastering will. A determination in terms of science and psychology is thus far impossible.

In addition, the argument for the existence and actual functioning of the core system admittedly is still quite speculative. Those interested in the phenomenological and ontological studies assembled in *Sinn und Sein* will find there further arguments against the theory that the ego or the I represent the individual's core.

References

Allport, G. *Pattern and growth in personality.* New York: Harper, 1961.

Buhler, C. Human life goals in the humanistic perspective, *J. Humanistic Psychology,* Spring, 1967, 7.

Buhler, C. *Intentionality and fulfillment.* San Francisco: Jossey-Bass, in preparation.

Buhler, K. *Die Krise der Psychologie.* Jena: G. Fischer, 1927.

Chasins, A. *The Van Cliburn legend.* New York: Doubleday, 1959.

Diemer, A. Vom Sinn ontologischen Fragens (The meaning of ontological questioning). In R. Wisser, *Sinn und Sein (Meaning and being).* Tübingen: M. Niemeyer, 1960.

Erikson, E. *Identity and the life cycle.* New York: International Universities Press, 1959.

French, T. The integration of behavior. Chicago: University of Chicago Press, 1952, 1954, 1956 (3 vols.).

Horney, K. *Our inner conflicts.* New York: W. W. Norton, 1945.

Piaget, J. *Dreams and imitation in childhood.* New York: W. W. Norton, 1951.

Redl, F., and Wineman, D. *Children who hate, the disorganization and breakdown of behavior controls.* Glencoe, Ill.: Free Press of of Glencoe, 1951.

Shostrom, E. *Personal orientation inventory.* San Diego: Educational and Industrial Test Service, 1963.

Thomas, A. *Behavioral individuality in early childhood.* New York: New York University Press, 1963.

Weil, A. Some evidences of deviational development in infancy and early childhood, *11, Psychoanalytic study of the child.* New York: International Universities Press, 1956.

Chapter 20

Time as an Integrating Factor

Everett L. Shostrom

Time is one of the important integrating factors with respect to our goal setting. Time is used differently by different individuals and even by different cultures. This is a specific study on time as it relates to self-actualization within the frame of reference of our time and culture.

In 1962, I began the development of a test for the measurement of self-actualization. The Personal Orientation Inventory (POI) items were chosen from significant value judgment problems seen by therapists at the Institute of Therapeutic Psychology over a five-year span. They were based on observed value judgments of clinically troubled patients. Items were also derived from the research and theoretical formulations of many writers in humanistic, existential, or *Gestalt* therapy. The latter include Maslow's (1954, 1962) concept of self-actualization, Riesman's (1950) system of inner- and other-directedness, and May's (1958) and Perl's (1947, 1951) concepts of time orientation.

The recent work of Ellis (1962) suggests that psychotherapy can be viewed as a process of critically examining the irrational ideas and value orientations of the patient. Buhler (1962) suggests that value orientations are definite existential judgments. Following Kluckhohn, she states that these value orientations symbolize the fact that affective-cognitive (value) and strictly cognitive (orientation) elements are blended. A value orientation may be defined as a generalized and organized conception which influences behavior and is a conception of nature, of man's place in it, of man's relation to man, and of the desirable and nondesirable as they may relate to man-environment and interhuman relations.

It has been said that Freud's system of therapy focuses primarily on the past; that is, psychoanalysis sees the past experiences of an individual as primary in determining his present adjustment to life. Fenichel (1954) and Dollard and Miller (1950) reflect this emphasis.

The writings of Adler (1956), Buhler (1954, 1962), Allport (1955), and French (1952) all emphasize the future. Allport's "Becoming," French's "Hope," and Buhler's "Reality principle" are all illustrations of this emphasis.

In recent years, existential therapists have emphasized a here-and-now or "being" orientation to living, and stressed the here-and-now as the significant variable for therapeutic work (May et al., 1958). This emphasis has brought into focus the significance of the individual's approach to time as an important therapeutic variable.

THE TIME RATIO

The Personal Orientation Inventory contains items related to the time dimension. It was given to a group of "self-actualizing" people, to a group of "normal" people, and to a group of "nonself-actualizing" people to determine the differences between these three groups.

A ratio was developed to express the differences found between these groups. This ratio has become known as the time ratio, and is the ratio of time incompetence to time competence. By time incompetence is meant focusing primarily on the past or the future, and by time competence is meant focusing primarily on the present. The self-actualizing person appears to live more fully in the here-and-now. He is able to tie the past and the future to the present in meaningful continuity. He appears to be less burdened by guilts, regrets, and resentments from the past than the nonself-actualizing person, and his aspirations are tied meaningfully to present working goals. He has faith in the future without rigid or overidealistic goals. His use of time in a competent way is expressed in a time ratio score approximating 1 to 8, as compared to the nonself-actualizing time ratio of 1 to 3.

The ratio score is utilized to show that the nonself-actualizing person appears to be excessively concerned with the past or the future, as opposed to the present. He may be disoriented because he splits off the past or future from the present. His time ratio is 1 to 3 as opposed to 1 to 8 for the self-actualizing person.

When one begins to speculate on the meaning of these scores, the following conclusions may be warranted:

1. The pathologically past-oriented individual is characterized by guilt, regret, remorse, self-reproaches, and resentments. He is a person who is still suffering from the undigested memories of the past. He is the depressive who keeps remembering past hurts. Examples from statements made in therapy are: "I feel so bad about what happened to Father that life has no meaning for me now." "I feel so guilty that I didn't take better care of the house and children. Now I have nothing." "If my parents had only encouraged me to go to school, I'd be interested now. It's their fault I can't get started." "I resent that teacher. How do you expect me to do any good work for him?"

2. The pathologically future-oriented person is an individual who lives continually in terms of idealized goals, plans, expectations, predictions, and fears. He is the obsessive worrier who lives in the future. Examples are: "Someday I'll get going and return to school, but I've got too many responsibilities right now." "Next summer I plan to get the yard work done." "You wait and see—I'll be working here long after those guys are gone." "I'm so worried about what is going to happen, I just can't do anything right now."

3. The pathologically present-oriented person is the individual whose past does not contribute to the present in a meaningful way, and who has no future goals tied to his present activity. He is a person who engages in meaningless activity and unreflective concentration. He is the busybody who is always actively avoiding facing himself. Examples are: "I've got so many responsibilities right now I just don't have time to think." "I have three children and a husband to care for and I don't have time to think of myself." "Please love me—I've got so much on my mind." "I've made a list of all the things I'm doing today."

4. The self-actualizing person is an individual who is primarily time competent. He is concerned with living fully in the present, but uses the past and future to make the present more meaningful. He understands that memory and anticipation are acts in the present. His focus, therefore, is on the present, with the past and future providing the background. This is illustrated in Figure 1, which is a well-known

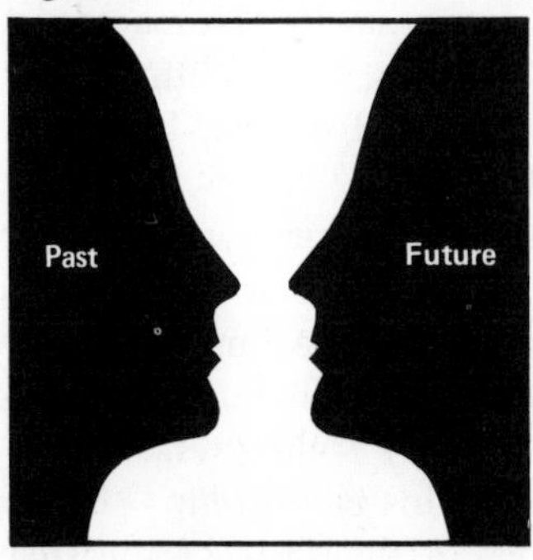

Figure 1. This example of the figure-ground phenomenon can be seen as either a white chalice on a black background or as two profile silhouettes.

textbook example of the figure-ground phenomenon. One sees a white chalice on a black background or, if the white area is taken as ground, the figure becomes two heads in profile silhouette. As one continues to study this ambiguous picture, he can switch from one way of looking at it to the other but he can never look at it both ways at once. If the chalice in the center becomes the primary focus, representing the present, the faces of the past and future become meaningfully related as background to the chalice. This symbolizes how the actualizing person relates the three dimensions of time. Examples of expression by a time-competent person are the following: "I am working on my term paper this weekend. I've been collecting materials since the beginning of the semester. I'll have it done by the deadline in three weeks." And, "I will finish my work for the Associate of Arts degree this semester. I've learned that if I do just a few units every semester, I'll get through. I plan eventually to get my B.A."

The Support Ratio

To understand the support ratio one needs first to understand the concepts of other-direction, inner-direction, and self-actualization. The material on inner- and other-direction leans heavily on the ideas of Riesman (1950). The material on self-actualization is primarily from Maslow (1954, 1962).

The inner-directed person appears to incorporate, early in life, a psychic "gyroscope" which is set in operation by parental influences and kept going by the influence of later authority figures. He goes through life apparently independent, yet obeying this internal piloting. The source of his inner-direction is developed early in life and later becomes generalized as an inner core of principles and character traits. The direction itself is guided by a small number of principles. One danger of excessive inner-directedness is that the individual becomes insensitive to the rights and feeling of others and feels that he can manipulate them authoritatively because of his own inner sense of "rightness." Examples are: "My feelings can be trusted." "Whatever I decide, I must make my own decision." "What I want is what I do."

The other-directed person, because of insecurity and doubt on the part of his parents as to how to bring him up, has been motivated to develop a radar system to receive signals from a far wider circle than just his parents. The boundary between the familial authority and other external authorities breaks down. His primary feeling tends to be fear of the fluctuating voices of "authorities" or of his peer group. The danger of other-directedness is that manipulation, in the form of pleasing others and insuring constant acceptance, becomes the person's primary method of relating. The original feeling of fear can thus be transformed into an obsessive, insatiable need for affection or reassurance of being loved. Examples are: "What will people think?" "Tell me what to do." "What is the right thing to do?"

The self-actualizing person tends to be less dependency- or deficiency-oriented than either the extreme inner- or other-directed person.

He can be characterized as having more of an autonomous, self-supportive, or "being" orientation. He is other-directed in that he is to be a degree sensitive to people's approval, affection, and good will, but the source of his actions is essentially inner-directed. While being somewhat inner-directed, his freedom is not gained by being a rebel or by pushing others around and fighting them. He transcends complete inner-directedness by critical assimilation and creative expansion of his earlier principles of living. He has discovered an inner mode of living which gives him confidence. Examples are: "I check with those who love me and then make my own decisions." "I gather as much data as possible on the problems and consequences, and then trust my deepest feelings for the decision." "I am free from their pressure but I still am interested in what they think."

In the validating group, the ratio between his other-directedness and his inner-directedness was approximately 1 to 3. This ratio is in contrast to the nonself-actualizing group ratio of approximately 1 to 1.

The Relation between Present Orientation and Self-support

Research on the Personal Orientation Inventory suggests that there is a moderately high correlation (r=.49) between time competence and inner-directedness. The question may be asked, "Why does this correlation exist?" It is suggested that the reason for this correlation lies in the fact that a self-actualizing person, living in the present, trusts more his own self-support and self-expressiveness than does the person who lives more in the past or in the future. In other words, an individual cannot depend on anything but freely experiencing life and himself when he lives with a here-and-now orientation to life.

Maslow (1962) describes the qualities of such freedom as follows: "I have tried to express this as a contrast between *living fully* and *preparing* to live fully, between *growing up* and *being grown*" (1961, p. 30).

The person who lives in the future is one who relies on goals to motivate him. In the developmental perspective Buhler suggests that in young people such long-range aspirations, when tied to immediate goals, make for productivity in the present. When it comes to middle-aged individuals, on the other hand, the author agrees with Perls (1947) that the future goals can simply become the means whereby the need for affection, appreciation, and admiration is being gratified. The neurotic person gratifies his vanity by picturing himself in terms of his goals. These invented goals are developed because he is incapable of accepting himself as he is in the here-and-now. Having lost the awareness of his biological being, he invents a meaning for life to justify his existence. By striving for the goal of future perfection, the individual turns his own life into a living hell and achieves the opposite of his intentions. He arrests his own natural development and promotes inferiority feelings in himself.

In a similar vein, the individual who lives in the past relies on blaming others as a substitute for self-support. Our problems exist in the here-and-now, and their solutions must be found in the present. For quite literally, the only time we can possibly live in is the present. We can remember the past, we can anticipate the future, but we can live only in the present. Even when we reexperience the past, we have not reversed time. We have, in effect, moved the past up to the present. So, if psychotherapy is to help us solve our problems it must help us to live in the present.

Alternative Views

Recognition must be given to those who suggest alternatives. Buhler (1962) states that self-actualization requires that the individual must also come to a realization of a desirable hierarchical order of goals to pursue for the future. "Values need not always be actual goals, but they always represent potential goals. As potential goals, values may become problematic to an individual. One may ask himself whether a certain value is worth attaining, worth striving for, worth consideration" (p. 121). And, as she adds later: "To me it seems doubtful that any human being can ever be satisfied with just 'functioning' and 'coping' with difficulties as they arise. A person cannot live for long without goals and without hope and be happy or even content. He needs a *future* to look forward to, to believe in, to build on. In my opinion merely coping with current problems is no goal, and adjustment is not enough" (p. 174).

Although Buhler emphasizes the future, she recognizes the need to tie present and future meaningfully together. On the other hand, psychoanalysts have traditionally emphasized the importance of the past in psychotherapy. As Fenichel (1945) remarks*:

> It is the aim of analysis to demonstrate to the patient the disturbing residues of the past in his present feelings and reactions —to connect the present with the past. . . . The patient misunderstands the present in terms of the past; and then instead of re-

* Modern ego analysts place a greater emphasis on present behavior than does the classical analyst.

> membering the past, he strives, without recognizing the nature of his action, to relive the past and to live it more satisfactorily than he did in his childhood. He "transfers" past attitudes to the present (pp. 28, 29).

A Therapeutic Reconciliation

Fenichel (1945) presents a partial therapeutic solution to our dilemma of whether the stress should be placed primarily on the *past* or the *present.*

> Thus a certain form of resistance consists in the patient's talking only about the present and refusing to see the past; in the converse form of resistance the patient talks only about childhood memories and refuses to see their representations in present reality . . . Freud once said that when the patient talks only of his present reality, the analyst must speak of his childhood; and the analyst must bring in present reality when the patient relates only childhood reminiscences. Theorizing about childhood relates only to a past that is not connected with present reality, whereas "acting out" is present reality, without its rootedness in the past becoming evident (pp. 28, 571).

The above suggests a solution to the other half of the dilemma presented in this paper: if a patient talks only of his future, the therapist must bring him back to the present reality. If he talks only about the present, the therapist must help him to tie the present into realistic future plans. The therapist must attempt, in effect, to bring the patient to a time competent orientation which ties him to the present, with past memories serving as significant learning experiences and future goals tied to here-and-now activity. Buhler* also agrees with this position.

A Theoretical Resolution

It is important to stress again that memory (from the past) and anticipation (toward the future) are acts in the present. Perls suggests that one may experimentally get this idea if one says, "Now, here I am remembering so and so and notice the difference from merely wandering off into memory; and so, now, here I am planning or expecting so and so" (1958, p. 290).

Furthermore, it should be remembered that a person given to reminiscences of the past or planning for the future is not refreshed but feels empty and exhausted. Such behavior is not active but passive. As Perls

* Personal communication.

implies, one's worthiness cannot be conveyed by explanations of the past or by promises for the future. Again, Buhler suggests that it is the right of the old person to reminisce about the past, especially his achievements. But for the neurotic such reference to the past is a rationalization. Perls points out that "The feeling of worthiness is given only by one's adequacy in an activity that is going on or in the relaxation after a completed situation. To explain or to promise is always felt as a lie, either consoling or self-punishing. But to do something and be oneself is a proof; is self-justifying" (1958, pp. 290-291). Examples of such self-actualizing present behavior are: "I feel so good, so alive, working in the yard today." "Gee, it's fun just running, jumping, and being free." "I feel like a good sleep—I've really got a lot done today." "I feel like a duck on top of the water. I'm really doing what I am capable of, fully!"

In summary, the healthy individual is one who lives primarily in the present. The reason is that living fully in the moment, or the present, does not require concern for support or sustenance. To say "I am adequate now," rather than "I was adequate once," or "I will be adequate again," is self-validating and self-justifying. Being in the moment, being an active process, is an end in itself; it is self-validating and self-justifying. Being has its own reward—a feeling of self-support.

References

1 Allport, G. W. *Becoming.* New Haven: Yale University Press, 1955.
2 Ansbacher, H., and Ansbacher, R. *The individual psychology of Alfred Adler.* New York: Basic Books, 1956.
3 Buhler, C. The reality principle, *Amer. J. Psychother.*, 1954, *8*:4, 626-647.
4 Buhler, C. *Values in psychotherapy.* New York: Free Press, 1962.
5 Dollard, J., and Miller, N. *Personality and psychotherapy.* New York: McGraw-Hill, 1950.
6 Ellis, A. *Reason and emotion in psychotherapy.* New York: Lyle Stuart, 1962.
7 Fenichel, O. *The psychoanalytic theory of neurosis.* New York: W. W. Norton, 1945.
8 French, T. *The integration of behavior, 1.* Chicago: University of Chicago Press, 1952.
9 Maslow, A. *Motivation and personality.* New York: Harper, 1954.
10 Maslow, A. Innocent cognition (as an aspect of B-cognition), *Notes on B-psychology.* La Jolla, Calif.: Western Behavior Sciences Institute, Aug. 31, 1961.
11 Maslow, A. *Toward a psychology of being.* Princeton, N. J.: Van Nostrand, 1962.
12 May, R., Angel, E., and Ellenberger, H. *Existence.* New York: Basic Books, 1958.
13 Perls, F. *Ego, hunger and aggression.* London: Allen & Unwin, 1947.
14 Perls, F., Hefferline, R., and Goodman, P. *Gestalt therapy.* New York: Julian Press, 1958.
15 Riesman, D., Glazer, N., and Denney, R. *The lonely crowd.* New York: Doubleday, 1950.
16 Shostrom, E. An inventory for the measurement of self-actualization, *Educational and Psychological Measurement,* 1964, *24*:2, 207-218.

17 Shostrom, E. *Personal orientation inventory, test and manual.* San Diego, Calif.: Educational and Industrial Testing Service, 1963.
18 Shostrom, E. *Therapeutic psychology, fundamentals of actualization counseling and psychotheraphy,* 2nd ed. (with L. M. Brammer). New York: Prentice-Hall, 1968.

Chapter 21

Meaning as an Integrating Factor

Edith Weisskopf-Joelson

We do not tend to give much thought to the air surrounding us. Only when the access to air is reduced or completely discontinued, as it is in suffocation, do we become acutely aware of air and our need for it. In this respect there is a similarity between air and "the meaning" of life. As long as life is meaningful, people tend to think and speak relatively little about its meaning. But as soon as there is a lack or absence of meaning, the problem of meaning plays an important role in a person's awareness and expression.

What do we mean by the meaning of life? Perhaps it would be best not to assign an arbitrary definition to this expression but instead to question the people who declare that "their life is meaningless," and to help them clarify what *they* mean when they say so.

Precisely this is the task which confronts the contemporary psychotherapist, because many patients enter psychotherapy with the complaint that their life is meaningless. The more specific complaints, such as obsessional or hysterical symptoms, which were so prominent at the time when Freud developed his theories, have diminished in frequency to be replaced by vaguer and more general ailments. I hope it will become clear in this article why the *Zeitgeist* causes or enhances such ailments.

It is by no means true that all patients mean the same thing when they speak of their life as meaningless. Meaning and meaninglessness mean different things to different people. It has been my experience that the meanings of "meaning" cluster mainly around three definitions, though there are others. Thus, three kinds of meaning will be discussed in this chapter. First, meaning as an integration of the private world and the public world, and lack of meaning as a separation of these two worlds. Second, meaning as an explanation or interpretation of life. And third, meaning as a purpose or task in life. Since the first definition of meaning is more basic than the other two, more space will be devoted to it.

Meaning as an Integration of Private and Public World (26)

When people who report that their lives seem meaningless are asked what they mean by this statement, their responses often show that the world of their thoughts, wishes, and daydreams is partially or completely separated from the world of outer reality. Thus, outer reality becomes meaningless, i.e., it is not cathected with interest or inner participation. But the inner world becomes meaningless too, i.e., it is not reflected in, not interacting with, and not reinforced or shared by, outer events.

Fromm (10, p. 120–151) has called this condition "alienation." A person is alienated when the separation between the outer and inner world has not been bridged, i.e., material and psychic reality have not been integrated. The individual has not achieved relatedness to the world, and this lack of relatedness gives rise to the feeling of meaninglessness. In the context of this volume it is important to stress that only the individual who is related to the world can engage in goal setting or in commitment. For goal setting is a process where inner guidelines lead to planned actions in the outer world, and it cannot take place when the inner and outer world are separated.

What is the phenomenology of alienation? The alienated person is surrounded by a world of people and objects like any other individual. He also has a world of thoughts, fantasies, and wishes. But his inner life is not connected with the real world of people and objects. There is nothing in reality around which he can spin his dreams. He cannot produce the mixture between fantasy and reality that makes life meaningful for others. He cannot make fantasies come true or, as Milner (20, p. 119–120) says, he cannot "change fables into history."

Translated into the terminology of this study, he is incapable of goal setting or commitment, since his inner guidelines do not extend into the outer world. "What he wants cannot be described in terms of anything that exists" (20, p. 119).

The alienated man, who lacks the integration of a meaningful life, resembles the hero of Camus' (4) novel, *The Stranger.* In his analysis of the hero, Leites (17) mentions, among others, five characteristics which are related to goal setting. Leites' analysis has been paraphrased and somewhat modified.

1. The stranger is indifferent, detached, and aloof with regard to the outer world.

2. He experiences the world as unintelligible.

3. The stranger cannot make any spontaneous value judgments. Values are not self-evident to him.

4. Choices which would seem crucial to others seem indifferent to the stranger. It does not make any difference to him whether he will become a physician or a bricklayer, or whether he will marry Jill or Betty.

5. Negative motivation by far exceeds positive motivation. What the stranger does is not done for its own sake but because there is nothing better to do. When asked why he engaged in an activity he tends to reply "why not?"

It is evident that indifference toward the world, experiencing the world as unintelligible, lack of spontaneous values, lack of concern with regard to choices, and predominantly negative motivation make a healthy setting of goals impossible.

Leites' analysis and clinical observation suggests that the separation between outer and inner world may be the beginning of a progressive change. When not cathected by involvement the outer world may gradually cease to be fully experienced; it may become unreal, like a shadow —or a far-away memory. Similarly, the inner world may lose its vividness when it ceases to be supported and validated by external events. Thoughts, wishes, and fantasies may gradually lose their inner glow and finally dry up completely. Then the individual is left empty.

But there are other ways in which alienation can manifest itself. The atrophy described above may take place in only one of the two worlds, either in the objective or the subjective world. In the former case the individual possesses a vivid inner life which is disconnected from outer reality. This lack of connection may result in psychosis. In the latter case the focus is on the external world and the inner world is ignored or neglected. This manifestation is especially frequent among "normal" contemporary men. Such people may become overly active in the pursuit of external goals. Like marionettes they are pulled by the strings of conformity. Their actions are inauthentic since they are dissociated from inner guidelines. They wear a mask not only in relation to others but also in their relationship to themselves. The aspects of their lives that do not fit their role have been repressed. This lack of authenticity, or integration, is perhaps the major cause of the experience of meaninglessness among modern men. In Charlotte Buhler's terms (3), these people are motivated by only one of the four basic tendencies of life, namely, self-limiting adaptation, while the other three, need satisfaction, creative expansion, and upholding the internal order, are severed from the mainstream of life. A life of this kind is an antithesis to self-realization.

The concept of authenticity and its lack has been mentioned frequently in the literature. Freud and his disciples implied it when they spoke about the dangers of repression, i.e., of dissociating a part of the personality so that it is not at the disposal of the individual.

Jung (14, p. 122–123)* describes the inauthentic man, who lives exclusively in the external world, as follows:

> A common instance of this is identity with the persona, which is the individual's system of adaptation to, or the manner he assumes in dealing with, the world. Every calling or profession, for example, has its own characteristic persona. It is easy to study these things nowadays, when the photographs of public personalities so frequently appear in the press. A certain kind of behavior is forced on them by the world, and professional people endeavor to come up to these expectations. Only, the danger is that they become identical with their personas—the professor with his text-book, the tenor with his voice. Then the damage is done; henceforth he lives exclusively against the background of his own biography. For by that time it is written; " . . . then he went to such and such a place and said this or that," etc. The garment of Deianeira has grown fast to his skin, and a desperate decision like that of Hercules is needed if he is to tear this Nessus shirt from his body and step into the consuming fire of the flame of immortality, in order to transform himself into what he really is. One could say, with a little exaggeration, that the persona is that which in reality one is not, but which oneself as well as others think one is. In any case the temptation to be what one seems to be is great, because the persona is usually rewarded in cash.

Similarly, Frances Wickes (27, p. 289-290)† describes the struggle for authenticity in Jungian terms as follows:

---

* Reprinted with permission. *Collected Works of C. J. Jung* (Bollingen Series XX), Vol. 9.1, "Archetypes and the Collective Unconscious," Trans. by R. F. C. Hull (copyright by the Bollingen Foundation, New York).

† Reprinted with permission. Frances G. Wickes. *The Inner World of Choice*. New York: Harper & Row, 1963.

> [The ego] may disregard the demands of the Self, leaving behind the early visions, the promptings of the heart, the simple human claims, and forget that the soul is the one who acts as interpreter of the creative images that arise from the depth of our being. For a long time the loss of soul may go unnoticed, activities increase, acquisitions multiply, yet underneath the achievement nothing satisfies, nothing nourishes; there is only emptiness. To stop and look into the depth would reveal, not that nothingness of the void out of which all unborn things come into creation, but the bottomless void of meaninglessness. Still the ego presses on—one more step and the goal that consciousness has set will be reached and the restless ego can rest satisfied, then will come plenty of time for enjoyment, for relatedness to his fellow men, for self-reflection, for inwardness, for the discovery of meaning. But instead, moments of depression increase, life slips away like sand through Time's hourglass and the man secretly fears that death may come before the moment of achievement when one may really begin to live. Questions arise. Who am I? What am I seeking? What dreams of the morning are now lost in the dusk of oncoming night? How can I find that sense of life that my youth once knew? Perhaps in spite of the ego's disregard of all except its own efforts to pull itself out of the slough by its own bootstraps, these restless questions may penetrate below the surface. . . .

The cleavage between the objective and subjective aspects of life is not limited to a selected few. Meaninglessness or alienation has become a prevalent feature in the life of western man of the twentieth century. When writing *The Stranger,* Camus (4) did not intend to describe an individual neurosis; instead, he meant to paint a picture of cultural psychopathology. With this in mind we might ask questions regarding the etiology of meaninglessness. What causes people to be incapable of relatedness to the world? The following discussion will center on three kinds of etiological factors contributing to a lack of relatedness or integration: 1) Sociological factors, i.e., factors pertaining to the society in which the alienated individual lives; 2) individual factors, i.e., factors which occur in the lives of only some individuals within the society, and which are part of the individual's life history; and 3) ontological factors, i.e., factors which are universal since they are inherent in the nature of man.

1. Sociological factors

We might imagine that a member of a small, primitive, and tradition-bound tribe would visit this country, and become a house guest in a "typical" American family. His attention would be attracted by many objects which he encounters, for example, by the family television set. He might wish to meet the person who made this fascinating and intricate object. To his amazement he would be told that it is not one person who built the television set but an entire "clan," called Westinghouse. He would also be told that, for a variety of reasons, it is unrealistic to expect to meet the manufacturers. The fact that some of them, for instance, the people in the assembly line, might not even know what they are manufacturing would be completely beyond his understanding. He would soon find out that in this country the relationship between the owner of an object and its manufacturer is an entirely impersonal one. It is quite different from this kind of relationship in his own society. Most objects he owns are made by people who are his friends. He is also closely related to the materials from which his possessions are made. For example, he remembers the tree which gave the wood for his table and knows the man who owned the tree.

The above is an example to show that the complexity and high degree of industrialization in a society tends to create a relative lack of relatedness or integration between man and the objects which surround him. His possessions are less meaningful to a member of such a society than they are to a member of a primitive tribe.

In a complex and highly industrialized society there is a similar lack of relatedness or integration between man and social institutions. For example, many people invest their money in various enterprises without being acquainted with their executive officers. A more personal way of investing would be to select a company whose president is a trusted friend of the investor. The play *The Solid Gold Cadillac* (16) represents a wishfulfilling fantasy where this lack of meaningful relationship between company and investor is overcome. The play shows an elderly woman who holds a position in a large business enterprise. She decides to write rather personal and somewhat chatty letters to the stockholders, especially to the female ones. Thus counteracting alienation she becomes so popular among the stockholders that she receives the majority of votes by proxy and gains control of the company. If alienation is a painful symptom which plagues western man of the twentieth century, the prediction could be made, to be tested by research, that there are more such wishfulfilling fantasies counteracting alienation in contemporary novels, plays, and other media than could be accounted for by chance.

The complexity and large size of a society may be responsible not only for lack of relatedness between man and objects, but also for lack of integration between man and the knowledge he possesses. Much knowledge becomes meaningless, because it is not possible in a large and complex society to participate directly in all ongoing events. Mass media, for example, make man conscious of happenings in which he has no direct participation, and in such a society, man then has to engage in what Fromm (10, p. 110–120) calls abstractification. This is knowledge that is stripped of concrete details and, especially, of emotional connotations. We may read about a war in the Far East, but if we have never been in combat and have never been in the Far East, the information may lack "the feel of the fact" (18, p. 45). Thus, in a large and complex society man knows, and is required to know, many things which he does not know in the true sense of the word "knowing." Our fictitious observer, the member of a small and primitive society, may feel that abstract knowledge without personal participation is a cold experience indeed, especially if he contrasts it with the only kind of knowledge he possesses. This kind of knowledge could be compared with the "here-and-now" stories read to American preschool children, where the hero of the story is described awaking in the morning, getting dressed, eating his breakfast, and doing, in the course of a day, the same kinds of things the little reader does. The primitive man may hear of an unsuccessful hunting expedition which has returned from the forest with empty hands. He knows what this means in the true sense of the word "knowing." He himself is a hunter, he has experienced lack of success, and he knows the persons who have taken part in the expedition. His knowledge is meaningful.

Man in large and complex societies tends to experience relatively little integration between himself, the objects which surround him, and the knowledge he possesses. This lack of integration makes his life less meaningful, according to our present definition of meaning.

The current stress on the quantitative sciences represents another factor leading to abstractification. Men in our society are more frequently required to perceive the world which surrounds them in terms of height, width, volume, price, and the like than in terms of emotional connotations which bestow meaning. For example, except within the realm of art, man of the twentieth century will rarely think of a river as a "rauschender Freund" (a murmuring friend) which is the way it is described in one of Schubert's songs. Instead, he will more likely describe a river in terms of location, depth, and commercial significance.

During preschool age the child tends to see the world in terms of emotional connotations. But when he enters school he gradually becomes accustomed to engage in abstract concepts. Two and two is four, no matter how he feels about it. The old trunk of a tree ceases to be seen as a secret meeting place for witches. Instead, the child may be led to count the rings on the trunk, and thus to determine the age of the tree.

Quantification leads to impersonal knowledge, and thus to lack of relatedness, or integration of man and his world. It is this lack of integration which is experienced as meaninglessness.

The above illustrations exemplify man's separation from objects, from institutions, and from knowledge, but western man of the twentieth century is also separated from himself and from his fellow men. Fromm (9, p. 72–73)* shows that such separation can result from excessive emphasis on commerce in what he calls the "marketing personality."

> As we shall see later, the mature and productive individual derives his feeling of identity from the experience of himself as the agent who is one with his powers; this feeling of self can be briefly expressed as meaning "I am what I do." In the marketing orientation man encounters his own powers as commodities alienated from him. He is not one with them but they are masked from him because what matters is not his self-realization in the process of using them but his success in the process of selling them. Both his powers and what they create become estranged, something different from himself, something for others to judge and to use; thus his feeling of identity becomes as shaky as his self-esteem; it is constituted by the sum total of roles one can play: "I am as you desire me."
>
> The fact that in order to have success it is not sufficient to have the skill and equipment for performing a given task but that one must be able to "put across" one's personality in competition with many others shapes the attitude towards oneself. If it were enough for the purpose of making a living to rely on what one knows and what one can do, one's self-esteem would be in proportion to one's capacities . . . but since success depends largely on how one sells one's personality, one experiences oneself as a commodity or rather simultaneously as the

* From *Man for Himself* by Erich Fromm. Copyright 1947 by Erich Fromm. Reprinted by permission of Holt, Rinehart and Winston, Inc.

> seller and the commodity to be sold. A person is not concerned with his life and happiness, but with becoming salable. This feeling might be compared to that of a commodity, of handbags on a counter for instance, could they feel and think. Each handbag would try to make itself as "attractive" as possible in order to attract customers and to look as expensive as possible in order to obtain a higher price than its rivals. The handbag sold for the highest price would feel elated, since that would mean it was the most "valuable" one; the one which was not sold would feel sad and convinced of its own worthlessness. This fate might befall a bag which, though excellent in appearance and usefulness, had the bad luck to be out of date because of a change in fashion (9, p. 70–71).

More generally speaking, in a society which stresses industry and commerce to a high degree, the aspects of man that do not serve the purposes of industry and commerce will be repressed. Thus, man sacrifices the integration of his total personality, loses the relatedness of inner and outer world and becomes the kind of inauthentic man who was described earlier in this chapter. He then experiences his life as meaningless.

2. Individual factors

The mother is probably the most important factor in the individual's life history, determining the degree of integration with the world, and thus of meaning, which he will achieve.

The mother can create relatedness between the public and private world firstly because she is a member of both worlds. From his relationship with her the child learns how he can spin his fantasies around "real" objects, namely, around her. Secondly, the child can integrate with the outer world because it is the mother's world, and he may learn that sharing a world with his mother leads to rewarding experiences. Thirdly, the mother may communicate to him that she wishes him to partake in the external world, and he has learned that fulfilling the mother's wishes leads to rewards. However, none of the above effects can be expected to take place if the mother is distant and impersonal. As Milner (20, p. 138) says: "Being at home in the world is something that we have to achieve . . . we do only achieve it by willingness of someone in our original environment of persons, in the actual home of our infancy, to fit in with our dreams. . . . [This shows] our original utter dependency on someone who would temper the implacable otherness of externality to fit our needs, temper it for us until such time as the external did come to grow happily significant."

Space does not permit me to discuss the many other variables in the life history of the individual which may contribute to the determination of meaning or a lack of it.

3. Ontological factors

Not to be totally integrated with the world is an inherent aspect of being human. Weisskopf (22, p. 108) describes Tillich's view on this condition as follows:

> The basic split or antinomy is derived from the dichotomy of subject and object, of "myself" and the world. Whatever we experience is split into two: a subject which experiences, and an object which is experienced. This applies not only to thought, but to all human remembering, imagining, feeling, willing, and acting.
>
> The basic source of the split in human existence is *consciousness.* Man can *transcend* any given situation because he is aware of it. Man "is" and, at the same time, he is conscious of his being. This establishes a cleavage between himself as conscious subject and the objective situation of which he is conscious.

According to the above, man cannot completely shed his aloofness from the objective world, even if he is a member of a primitive, simple, small, and non-industrialized society, and if his life history is free of trauma. He is not completely a part of nature, since he is able to reflect upon, and thus to transcend, nature. Were he to experience the meaning of his life only in terms of integration of private and public world, no human life could ever be experienced as completely meaningful. But there are other kinds of meaning which can fill the gap created by man's separation from nature.

Let us now consider the meaningful life, where the separation between outer and inner world has been bridged, and an integration has been established between psychic and material reality. In other words, the individual has achieved relatedness to the world, and this relatedness gives rise to the feeling that life is meaningful.

There are various endeavors in human lives which bring about or enhance an integration of private and public world. These endeavors combine the subjective and the objective aspects of life. Elsewhere (26, p. 275-282) I have called them "half-way houses." The original meaning of a "half-way house" is a home for patients who have been discharged from a mental hospital but who are not quite ready to live in a community under normal conditions. The half-way house fulfills their subjective needs, caused by their unusually heavy psychic burden, and simultaneously permits them to meet the objective demands of the outer world. But here I am using the term "half-way house" in a metaphorical rather than in a literal sense. A metaphorical half-way house is an enterprise which is a part of the external world and at the same time a part of the individual's inner life. It enables man to combine fantasy and reality, since it is an incarnation of fantasy within the real world. Thus, like the literal half-way house, it takes its position between the subjective and the objective goal of being. It makes life meaningful by giving the individual the possibility to set inner goals with reference to the outer world. (The term "half-way house" and some of the thoughts presented in this chapter are borrowed from Milner's book, *On Not Being Able To Paint* (20, p. 133), and have been discussed elsewhere (26).

Friendship and love, art, Weltanschauung, myth, hope, and creativity are examples of metaphorical half-way houses.

1. *Friendship and love.* We become friends or lovers by discovering a mutuality of experience. We discover that another person's inner life is similar to our own. As Dilthey says, we discover "the I in the Thou" (19, p. 251). By doing so we build a half-way house, because the shared experience is a part of our inner life and at the same time a part of the other person and, thus, of the external world. Friendship, by integrating the inner and outer world, makes life meaningful.

2. *Art.* Sometimes one's friends are fictitious rather than real. For example, they may be figures in a novel. They become friends if their experiences are described in such a way that they seem similar to our own. Thus, we may discover the I in the fictitious Thou. The shared experience belongs to our subjective world and simultaneously to the objective world represented by a novel, or by any other artistic production. This is how art, especially in the form of literature, may become a metaphorical half-way house or a bridge between inner and outer world. It results in integration, and, thus, in meaning.

3. *Weltanschauung.* Why do we embrace one philosophy of life rather than another? Most likely because the chosen philosophy is congenial to our thinking, i.e., it views the world in a manner similar to the one in which we view it. When we adopt a philosophy we discover, as it were, the I in a theory. Again, the outer and the inner world become integrated by such adoption, since the philosophy of life partakes in outer as well as in inner reality. Once again, life has become meaningful.

4. *Myth.* Webster's New World dictionary (12, p. 495) defines "myth" as "a traditional story of unknown authorship, serving usually to explain some phenomenon of nature, the origin of men, or the customs, institutions, etc., of a people. . . ."

The stories which comprise a myth are a part of the external world, regardless of whether they have a determinable basis of fact or a natural explanation, or whether they are purely fictitious. This is the case because they are shared, transmitted by oral or written communication, or acted out; all these aspects pertain to the objective world. At the same time they are related to the inner world of man. Were they not, they would not be believed, or transmitted, or experienced as important: thus, they are half-way houses as defined above.

The life of Christ is a part of the external world, either because it actually happened as it is told, or because it has been transmitted by written and oral communications and enacted in many kinds of rituals. But the fact that the myth of Christ has been believed by millions of people for nearly two thousand years suggests that it mirrors many aspects of man's inner life, for example, his knowledge that suffering is meaningful, and that one must die in order to be reborn. This time the I is being discovered in a faith. The gap between the individual and his world has been bridged, separation has yielded to integration and meaning.

5. *Hope.* Hope is a belief that something which is hitherto only a fantasy will someday become a reality. Thus, it is a link between fantasy and reality and it contains elements of both. Therefore, it is a half-way house and leads to the bestowal of meaning.

It is the integration between man's objective world and his subjective world which makes hope at times more comforting than present fulfillment. As Hoffer says, " 'Things which are not' are indeed mightier than 'things that are.' In all ages men have fought most desperately for beautiful cities yet to be built and gardens yet to be planted. Satan did not digress to tell all he knew when he said: 'All that a man hath will he give for his life.' All he hath—yes. But he sooner dies than yield aught of that which he hath not yet" (13, p. 76).

Hope may cease to be a half-way house, and lose its comforting quality when the hopeful fantasy becomes reality. For then it may lose its membership in the internal world and become altogether a part of the external world. Then life is meaningless again until a new hope is never be fulfilled during man's lifetime, namely, the hope for a here-embraced. Many religions give the believer a kind of hope which can never be fulfilled during a man's lifetime, namely the hope for a hereafter. Such hope remains comforting until death for it can never be fulfilled on this earth.

6. *Creativity.* When man is creative he achieves an integration between his two worlds in a manner that is somewhat different from those discussed above. Instead of *discovering* the I in the world he *puts* it into the world. When being creative man puts, as it were, incarnations of his fantasy into public reality. The creative product is a half-way house, because it pertains to the public reality as well as the private one. A world which contains man's own creations, be it his children, his artistic products, or his scientific theories, is more meaningful than a world without these creations. For meaning as discussed in this section is relatedness to the world or integration with the world; and the creator can relate to at least one aspect of the world, his own creations.

The metaphorical half-way houses described above are, so to speak, incarnations of our inner life in the outerworld. Thus, they are closely related to a concept which is discussed frequently in the field of humanistic psychology, namely, self-realization or self-actualization. "Realizing oneself" means being engaged in an endeavor which combines "the real," i.e., the objective world, and "the self," i.e., the subjective world. Thus, the half-way houses which I have described are special avenues through which self-realization can be achieved.

Meaning as Explanation or Interpretation of Life

When patients in psychotherapy report that they experience their lives as meaningless, their comments on this condition frequently suggest that what they experience as meaninglessness is often a lack of an explanation or interpretation of their lives. Such an explanation, in order to relieve the feeling of meaninglessness, has to be comprehensive, i.e., it has to embrace many, or all, aspects of life. It has to be an interpretation of the internal as well as of the external world. Not any interpretation will do; only an interpretation which is plausible, or congenial, to the individual will be viewed as endowing life with meaning. But an interpretation of life can be viewed as congenial only if it resembles the individual's own image of life, even if the latter is hardly conscious, vague, and unverbalized. Since such an explanation, if expressed and shared, is a public image which resembles a private image, it creates an integration of public and private world and, thus, gives meaning also according to our first definition. Thus, every public and congenial interpretation is at the same time an integration of public and private world, but every integration of public and private world is not necessarily an interpretation. This shows that the first definition of meaning is the broader one; therefore, more space has been dedicated to it than will be given to the present definition.

Meaning as interpretation of life, however, is integrative also in that many diverse aspects of life are brought together to form a whole. Only an interpreted life can give rise to goal setting, since an interpretation is required to determine which goals are worth striving for.

People whose lives suffer from lack of meaning, as defined in this section, cannot accept the fact that their "life is a tale, told by an idiot . . . signifying nothing" (21, p. 1194). Instead, they seek an interpretation of life.

It can be expected that lack of this kind of meaning will occur with less frequency in totalitarian societies, since such societies tend to offer its members a consistent interpretation which integrates various aspects of life. On the other hand it seems implausible that *any* kind of interpretation will give meaning to an individual's life. Rather, it has to be the "right" interpretation, adapted to the individual's need, and such adaptation may frequently be lacking in totalitarian countries.

In contrast, the western world could be characterized by absence of any strong and comprehensive philosophy, and, thus, by absence of interpretations and integration. This condition my be responsible for the large number of people who experience their lives as meaningless. Religious faith, which in the past has furnished integrative explanations for all aspects of life, has become less prevalent, less strong, and less convincing during the modern era. Modern man can no longer explain everything he experiences by divine providence.

In contrast, life is meaningful, in the present sense of the term, for individuals who hold a strong religious belief. Bolgar (1) studied theosophists and other followers of religious and philosophical sects. Her subjects were characterized by strong, consistent, and comprehensive belief systems. Case histories, interviews, tests, and projective techniques were the instruments used to study these subjects. One of the findings was the fact that a large number of these people gave protocols indicative of severe neurosis or psychosis; however, in spite of this fact, they functioned on a satisfactory level, and felt reasonably comfortable. These findings suggest that a strong, integrative, and comprehensive philosophy of life might help people with severe emotional disorders.

Creating meaning by integrative explanations of life is consistent with the recent emphasis on the psychology of the ego.

The above suggests that many therapeutic schools may be effective for reasons entirely different from the ones which are officially recognized. They may be effective because they make a convert out of the patient. They lead to cognitive structuring of the patient's view of life. He now has a belief system by which life is explained by an integrative principle and is thus meaningful. He may learn to interpret his experiences in terms of superego, ego, id, the oral, anal, genital phase, and the like, as Freud did. Or he may adapt Adler's concepts of inferiority feeling, drive for power, and *Gemeinschaftsgefühl.* If he is treated by a Jungian therapist he may view his life in terms of animus and anima, collective unconscious, and individuation; the interpretation of his dreams may give new meaning to his life.

Hypothetical constructs, as those mentioned in the previous paragraph, are sufficiently generalized to integrate various aspects of life into a whole, and, thus, to bestow meaning.

Moreover, the patient may become acquainted with other people who are, or have been, treated by the same therapist, or by a follower of the same school as their therapist. Such people may develop a mutual interest in each other because they hold the same philosophy of life. They might speak to each other in the language of the theory on which their therapy was based. A group of this kind can be compared to a religious parish. It represents a further step in integration, and thus in the bestowal of meaning.

The observation that methods of therapy which are not based on any acceptable scientific rationale may lead to improvement supports the hypothesis that improvement may be due to explanation per se, i.e., to the enhancement of meaning by structuring the patient's cognitive image of himself and the world and thus integrating his isolated experiences. While, according to traditional views, interpretation is therapeutic because it counteracts defenses and reveals "the truth," the above discussion asserts that interpretation is therapeutic because the patient perceives it as giving structure and integration to his life.

If the *alleged* sources of improvement in psychotherapy are different from the actual sources this discrepancy would be an important topic to study, since such study would make it possible to omit incidental aspects of therapy and to strengthen pertinent aspects. If interpretations are therapeutic per se, but if all interpretations are not therapeutic to all people, it becomes important to determine which views of life have a healing effect on people. It is quite possible that people of different age, sex, socio-economic class, or personality structure, need different philosophies to make life meaningful. I have devised a series of tests and projective techniques to help predict the kind of philosophy which will be most satisfying to the individual. Since beliefs can only be disseminated by people who hold the belief, patients would, after having undergone diagnosis of this kind, have to be referred to therapists with a congenial view of life.

Finally, I want to discuss a pathological aspect of the search for meaning in the sense of interpretation. The paranoiac, for example, can be viewed as a person with an excessive need for explanation. His need for meaning is so strong that he arrives at interpretations by a short-cut, ignoring the limitations set by reality. Systematized delusions represent an integration of realistically isolated experiences into a grandiose whole which bestows illusory meaning. Nothing remains unexplained.

> A man suffering from paranoia, for instance, believed that everything which happened in his surroundings was connected with the Bible. His delusion started when, one day, he felt that people had mentioned "milk" more often than could be accounted for by chance. A woman said her doctor had recommended she should drink a pint of milk a day; a child was scolded for spilling milk, and so forth. The paranoiac looked for the word "milk" in the concordance of his Bible, and found a reference to "As newborn babes, desire the sincere milk of the word, that ye may grow thereby (1 Peter 2:2)." Now he was certain that the people who had mentioned "milk" were speaking about "the milk of the word."
>
> From then on he looked in the concordance for other words which were connected with events in his immediate environment. Usually he found the word listed, with at least one reference. Soon he began to believe that this was not coincidence, but that people made allusions to the Bible in his presence because they wanted him to read it.
>
> The janitor gave him a key to a new lock: he was doubtlessly alluding to the key to the Kingdom of Heaven. Someone who was planning to move from the country to the city said she hated to leave the yard with the apple trees: it was obvious that she was alluding to Adam and Eve being expelled from the Garden of Eden. When someone spoke about a savings account it seems to the paranoid person that he meant the saving of souls rather than the saving of money. A friend of his pretended to be worried about her brother, but he felt she wanted to remind him "to be his brother's keeper." A boy who enjoyed showing how well he could imitate the sound of a sheep was suspected of wanting to remind him of the Parable of the Good Shepherd. People going barefoot brought to mind Christ's washing of his disciples' feet, and nails became a symbol of the crucifixion. He felt sure that he saw an unusually large number of cripples and people suffering from palsy on the street; it was clear to him that they were only pretending to be cripples in order to remind him of Jesus, the healer.
>
> Although this person had been depressed for many years before he developed the delusions, he now wrote into his diary, "I am happy. My

life has become meaningful." His life was now an integrated whole, since everything he experienced seemed to be related to the Bible.

One can only marvel at man's urge to integrate the isolated factors in his life and thus to find meaning; this urge can become so strong that it may force man to disregard reality and to construct an illusory belief system.

Perhaps such a belief system is supportive not only because it gives a structuring explanation of life, but also because it makes life more significant and less banal. A life where every event is related to the Bible, even though on an illusory basis, has certainly more splendor than most "normal" lives. A "realistic" view of life can hardly compete with such a delusion. Thus, May writes, as an introduction to an article by Gudeman (11, p. 196-197):*

> What gripped me vividly was the demonstration that people take on neurosis and psychosis because their normal lives are so banal. It seemed to me that we have to reconstruct our whole definitions of mental health and illness. . . . In our fields of psychiatry and psychology, we have been in the strange position of deducing our image of the normal healthy man from sickness and neurosis. Since we know neurosis (and many forms of psychosis) only by virtue of the fact that the sufferers therefrom cannot fit into our society, and since we understand illness by virtue of our techniques, we are bound to end up with a view of man which is a mirror of our culture and our techniques. This inevitably results in a *progressively empty* view of man. Health becomes the vacuum which is left when the so-called neurosis is cured; or on the psychosis level, if a man can stay out of jail and support himself, we call that vacuum health. This empty view of health (filled only by some vague biological assumptions about "growth," "satisfactions of libido," and so forth) has had much to do with the general tendencies in our day toward ennui, passionlessness, emotional and spiritual emptiness. The empty view of health often puts psychiatry and psychology on the side of making life increasingly more possible and longer at the price of making existence more boring. From this point of view we can understand why our patients often show a strange lack of zest for getting better, for they may not be so irrational in suspecting that neurosis is more interesting

* Reprinted from *Review of Existential Psychology and Psychiatry*, 1966, 6, 196-210.

than health, and that health may be the corridor to apathy.

It seemed to me that psychosis can, and needs to be, seen as a struggle for significance. The hypothesis struck me that the problem of identity in our society has evolved into a new form, namely the longing for significance. The problem is no longer "Who am I?" but rather "Even if I know who I am, can I have any influence, any significant impact on the world and people around me?" If we could see the positive side of the struggle in mental disturbances, we might better be able to draw out the genuine potentialities of health of our patients. To free psychology and psychiatry from their tendency to add to the emptiness and banality of modern life would indeed be a tremendous boon.

Viewing the etiology of paranoia in this manner represents an antithesis to Freud's view that repressed homosexuality is the cause of paranoia. Perhaps both etiological factors may be causative in producing systematic delusions. The interpretation of paranoia as an abortive search for meaning puts this disease into the class of "noogenic" disturbances, a term used by Frankl (25, p. 197) to designate disturbances which are caused by lack of a meaningful life.

Meaning as a Purpose or Goal in Life

The comments of some patients in psychotherapy who complain that they lead meaningless lives indicate that what they call meaningless is a lack of a task, a purpose, or a goal. Such comments suggest a third definition of meaning. This definition is less broad than the definition of meaning as an interpretation: the presence of a purpose of life presupposes at least a minimal amount of interpretation. Since I have shown before that the definition of meaning as an interpretation is less broad than the definition as an integration of the subjective and objective world, it follows that the present definition is the least broad among the three.

Man pursues many goals during his life, but a goal which should give meaning to life must be a long-term goal embracing large parts of life, or life as a whole.

While studying the psychological aspects of human lives through biographies, autobiographies, diaries, letters, and other sources, Charlotte Buhler (2) has described a great variety of characteristics of such long-term or lifelong goals. Her first finding is that such goals exist, that man is indeed capable of committing his life, or long periods of his life, to a single purpose. Thus, the actress Eleonora Duse said: "When I will have reached my goal, when youth will have gone and when I shall put the finis under all my successes—then I shall make an end and find shelter in quietude. Then I shall be able to say, full of blissful conviction: I have put my whole soul into art. . . ." (2, p. 182).* Similar dedication can be found in less famous lives. For example, many mothers give their entire lives to their children.

Other statements indicate that if a comprehensive goal of life is not present, man may consciously seek it. As the philosopher Kierkegaard stated: "It is important for me to understand my mission, to see what God really wants me to do; it is important to find a truth, which is true for me, to find the idea for which I want to live and to die" (2, p. 107).

Statements made by patients during psychotherapy indicate that also less "unusual" people than Kierkegaard seek a purpose in life, or suffer if such a purpose is not experienced. "I have a husband and a son, a home, and many friends, and my husband tells me that he loves me and needs me. Yet I have the feeling that I am nothing and that I do not know what I live for" (3, p. 37). Or: "Now, when I have my factory, and my mother is taken care of, I am asking myself what is all this for? What do I really live for?" (3, p. 37).

The title of this chapter is "Meaning as an Integrative Factor." Meaning as defined by comprehensive goals in life is indeed integrative since it results in a view of life, or of long periods of life, as a whole. On the other hand, the setting of comprehensive goals presupposes a certain amount of integration. Thus, there is an interaction between goal setting and integration whereby integration can be a cause or an effect of goal setting.

According to Charlotte Buhler's (2, p. 132-146) earlier findings, which have been replaced by newer formulations, a "change of dominance" tends to occur sometimes during man's third decade, i.e., goals begin to be determined by objective requirements to a larger degree than by subjective needs. The composer Franz Liszt once remarked: "I started as the master of my art, but I finish as its servant" (p. 143). Else Frenkel and Edith Weisskopf (8), when interviewing Viennese middle-class subjects of various age groups, found that the words "tasks" or "duties" began to be mentioned with higher frequency than "needs" or "wishes" around the age of 35.

Leading the reader through a fascinating array of life histories, Charlotte Buhler (2) shows in her early studies that striving toward a comprehensive goal can lead to an expansion of one's personal existence,

* All quotations from references 2 and 3 have been translated by the author.

or it can displace this existence, and even damage it in self-sacrifice. The writer Romain Rolland, regarding his fight against corruption and aggression which resulted in a boycott of his works in France, once said: "I do not need approval to hope, and I do not need success to persist" (2, p. 71). The attempt to reach a comprehensive goal can consist in developing and shaping one's own personality. The diplomat and scientist Wilhelm von Humboldt believed that: "The enobling of one's whole being, the greatest possible heightening and broadening of the mind, is a task which man has to fulfill, as well as the integrity of his actions" (2, p. 79). It can work for a cause which transcends the self; it can be experienced as a passive yielding to an inner calling." Eleanora Duse asked: "What shall I find at the end of my long journey? Perhaps the sweet secret that I have been true to my fate. Perhaps . . ." (2, p. 181). It can be the product of an active decision to dedicate one's life to one of many possible causes and, finally, it can be focused upon life on earth or on an eternal life hereafter.

In the references just quoted Charlotte Buhler has studied mainly the lives of famous people. If these lives are viewed as the highest possibilities rather than as modes of life, this should not discredit her findings. In her later writings (3) she focuses on less unusual life histories.

Meaning, the topic of this chapter, brings to mind another student of human life—Frankl (5, 6, 7, 24. 25). The concept "meaning" is central to his teachings: whereas Freud emphasizes man's will to pleasure, and Adler man's will to power, Frankl focuses upon man's will to meaning. His writings suggest that he uses the term "meaning" in the sense in which it is discussed in this section, that is, synonymously with purpose, goal, or task.

Frankl's experiences as a prisoner in German concentration camps (7), for example, corroborate his belief in a will to meaning. Prisoners who had a purpose in life, such as returning to a beloved relative or finishing a book, could shoulder the extreme burdens of the camps better than prisoners whose life was devoid of meaning. Thus, Frankl is fond of quoting Nietzsche, who commented: "Whoever has a reason for living endures almost any mode of life" (5, p. 54).

But it is predominantly the phenomenological analyses of his patients which gave rise to his focus on meaning. There is a kind of emotional disturbance, prevalent in the modern age, says Frankl, which is caused by lack of a meaningful, or purposeful, life. He calls this disturbance a noogenic neurosis (25, p. 197).

According to Frankl, even some of the classic neurotic symptoms may be at least partially caused by lack of meaning. The anxiety neurotic may displace his fear about not facing his relevant responsibilities onto irrelevant stimuli such as open or closed places, and the like. This permits him to engage in "metaphysical frivolity," as Scheler says (5, p. 179), and to remain free of guilt.

"The obsessional neurotic mails a letter or locks his door with the same gravity and care that a normal man might employ in choosing his profession or his wife" (5, p. 190-191). Meticulousness regarding relevant goals has been replaced by meticulousness regarding irrelevant ones.

Sunday is the day when noogenic neurotics suffer agonies because they cannot drown their sense of meaninglessness in work (5, p. 127-128); thus Sunday may be the saddest day in the week for them. There are also certain periods during the course of life where the quest for meaning comes to the foreground. One, for instance, is the climacterium in women, when one task, the bearing and rearing of children, is usually accomplished, and the search for another purpose may leave life temporarily meaningless.

Frankl goes beyond empirical data and becomes a philosopher when writing about the meaning of life. He conceives of meaning as the fulfillment of responsibilities through actualizing values. These values are not a part of man but they transcend man; they exist in a world above us. Thus, the actualization of values is not merely self-actualization but goes beyond the boundaries of man.

According to Frankl there are three kinds of values to be actualized: 1) creative values, i.e., values which are actualized by the creation of a product which benefits society; 2) experiential values, i.e., values which are actualized by experiences such as love, joy, curiosity, admiration of the beauty of nature or art, and the like; 3) attitudinal values, i.e., values which are actualized by courageous shouldering of unavoidable suffering.

In a country like the United States, where activity and its products are valued highly, the inclusion of more passive values which do not yield any material results, such as experiential and attitudinal values, can be expected to have a compensatory and, therefore, a therapeutic effect.

To elevate suffering to the status of a positive value is especially compensatory in view of a prevalent attitude which Martha Wolfenstein (28) calls "fun morality," a moral obligation to have fun and to be happy. Even from a hedonistic point of view such an attitude would not be desirable, for unhappiness is an unavoidable part of life; fun morality adds to this unhappiness since people are not only unhappy, but they are unhappy about being unhappy. Moreover, happiness may be a goal which is more easily reached as a by-product than as an intended goal. as Kierkegaard says: "The door to happiness opens outward" (5, p. 40).

Frankl's writings suggest that his transcending of empiricism and venturing into philosophy was not an arbitrary decision on his part. Instead, it is the modern patient who "forces" the therapist to concern himself with philosophical issues by confronting him with questions regarding the what-for and the where-to of life, questions that formerly were the domain of philosophers and religionists. Frankl (5, p. 269) quotes Paracelsus as saying: "It is a lame creature who calleth himself a physician and he be void of philosophy and know her not." Frankl's concept of meaning is thus integrative in a new sense: it integrates the realm of transcendent values with the realm of human lives.

His notion that human lives can be meaningless for a period of time until a situation arises which offers new meaning may be comforting to people who are suffering from a temporary lack of purpose. Similarly, his statement that every human being is unique insofar as nobody else can shape the world in exactly the same way as he does may be therapeutic for people who have lost their pride in their search for meaning.

Frankl is the founder of a psychotherapeutic school called logotherapy, based on the theories discussed above. He helps his patients find meaning in their lives, i.e., he helps them to set goals within the three kinds of values which have been described. This kind of therapy is applicable whenever a patient's life lacks meaning and when he is suffering from a noogenic neurosis; it can often also be applied in conjunction with more conventional forms of therapy.

The patient suffering from a conventional form of neurosis can be compared to a man with a broken leg, while the patient with a noogenic neurosis is like a man with two healthy legs who does not know in which direction to walk. To carry this comparison one step further, conventional therapy, as it were, fixes the patient's broken leg while logotherapy helps him find the right direction in which to walk.

I have previously pointed out that "psychoanalytically oriented therapists might argue that no real improvement can be achieved with methods such as logotherapy, since the pathology in 'deeper' layers remains untouched, while the therapist limits himself to the strengthening or erecting of defenses" (25, p. 201). But I believe that

> Such conclusions . . . may keep us from the awareness of major sources of mental health because these sources do not fit into a specific theoretical framework. We must not forget that such

concepts as "defenses," "deeper layers," and "adequate function on a superficial level with underlying pathology" are theoretical concepts rather than empirical observations. It might be argued that there is an operationally definable difference between a person who "functions adequately on a superficial level, but shows pathology on a deeper level," and a person who is "healthy" according to depth-psychological standards; that, for example, the former will maintain normal functioning only by great expenditure of energy; or that the former's seeming balance will break down when conditions change, especially when stresses increase. But, to my knowledge, it has never been empirically established that such differences actually exist. However, it would be possible to test experimentally the hypothesis that of two groups of equally adequate individuals, so far as the functioning level is concerned, the ones who show underlying pathology as measured by projective and other devices show less resistance to stress. Before such differences are established, we must, in Kardiner's terms, beware of permitting "the tail [theory] to wag the dog [observation] (15, p. 14), (23, p. 602).

In summary, meaning as an integrative factor has been discussed according to three definitions of the word "meaning":

1. Meaning as an integration of private and public world (26). Healthy goal setting is possible only if such an integration has been achieved. Failure to achieve it leads to the experience of meaninglessness, the phenomenology of which has been briefly considered. The causes of meaninglessness may be sociological, individual, and ontological. Friendship and love, art, creativity, myth, hope, and Weltanschauung can bestow meaning upon life by integrating its internal and external aspects.

2. Meaning as an interpretation. The integrative aspect of interpretation has been briefly discussed. Only an interpreted life can give rise to goal setting. Consistent philosophies of life may have therapeutic effects while their absence may be pathogenic. Psychotherapy has been viewed as a form of conversion. Paranoia has been interpreted as an attempt to achieve the experience of meaning by an integrative, though illusory, explanation of life.

3. Meaning as a purpose or goal. In her studies of the global aspects of human lives, Charlotte Buhler (2, 3) has shown how some people are capable of dedicating long periods of their lives, or their entire lives,

to a comprehensive goal. Such goals may then be the cause or effect of an integrative attitude toward life. Furthermore, she states that goals tend to become predominantly task-oriented during the middle period of life, a hypothesis which has been supported by the investigations of Else Frenkel and Edith Weisskopf (8).

Finally, Frankl's (5, 6, 7, 24, 25) school of thought has been discussed, in which meaning, defined as purpose, is the central concept. Phenomenological analyses suggest that man is motivated by a will to meaning. Failure to find such meaning may result in noogenic neurosis. Frankl erects a philosophical system on these findings; he holds that the meaning of life is the fulfillment of responsibilities, which, in turn, can be fulfilled by the actualization of values. These values are not within man but transcend him. There are three kinds of values, namely, creative, experiential, and attitudinal values. Frankl's therapeutic school, called logotherapy, is based on the philosophy outlined above. With the help of logotherapy an individual can be guided to find purpose in his life and to strive toward meaningful goals.

References

1 Bolgar, H. A study of the personality structure of members of religious minority groups. Paper read at the Ind. Psychol. Asso., Indianapolis, April, 1952.

2 Buhler, C. *Der menschliche Lebenslauf als psychologisches Problem.* Leipzig: S. Hirzel, 1933.

3 Buhler, C. *Der menschliche Lebenslauf als psychologisches Problem.* Göttingen: Hogrefe, 1959.

4 Camus, A. *The stranger.* New York: Knopf, 1946.

5 Frankl, V. E. *The doctor and the soul.* (2nd ed.). Knopf, 1965.

6 Frankl, V. E. Fragments from the logotherapeutic treatment of four cases. In A. Burton (ed.), *Modern psychotherapeutic practice.* Palo Alto: Science and Behavior Books, 1965, 361-379.

7 Frankl, V. E. *Man's search for meaning: an introduction to logotherapy.* Boston: Beacon Press, 1966.

8 Frenkel, E., and Weisskopf, E. *Wunsch und Pflicht im Auflau des menschlichen Lebens.* Wien: Gerold, 1937.

9 Fromm, E. *Man for himself.* New York: Rinehart, 1947.

10 Fromm, E. *The sane society.* New York: Rinehart, 1955.

11 Gudeman, H. E. The phenomenology of delusions, *Rev. exist. Psychol. Psychiat.,* 1966, *6,* 196-210.

12 Guralnik, D. B. (ed.). *Webster's new world dictionary.* New York: World Publishing Co., 1960.

13 Hoffer, E. *The true believer.* New York: Harper, 1951.

14 Jung, C. G. *Collected works,* 9:1. New York: Pantheon Books, 1959.

15 Kardiner, A. *The psychological frontiers of society.* New York: Columbia University Press, 1945.

16 Leichmann, H., and Kaufman, G. S. *The solid gold Cadillac.* New York: Dramatists Play Service, 1956.

17 Leites, N. The stranger. In W. Phillips (ed.), *Art and psychoanalysis.* New York: Criterion Books, 1957, 247-267.

18 MacLeish, A. The poet and the press, *Atlantic Monthly,* 1959, *203,* 40-46.
19 Matson, F. W. *The broken image.* New York: Braziller, 1964.
20 Milner, M. B. *On not being able to paint.* New York: International Universities Press, 1958.
21 Shakespeare, W. Macbeth, *The London Shakespeare.* New York: Simon and Schuster, 1957.
22 Weisskopf, W. A. Existence and values. In A. H. Maslow, *New knowledge in human values.* New York: Harper, 1959, 107-118.
23 Weisskopf-Joelson, E. Some suggestions concerning Weltanschauung and psychotherapy, *J. abnorm. soc. Psychol.,* 1953, *48,* 601-604.
24 Weisskopf-Joelson, E. Some comments on a Viennese school of psychiatry, *J. abnorm. soc. Psychol.,* 1955, *51,* 701-703.
25 Weisskopf-Joelson, E. Logotherapy and existential analysis, *Acta psychother., psychosom., orthopaed.,* 1958, *6,* 193-204.
26 Weisskopf-Joelson, E. An antidote against separation, *Rev. exist. Psychol. Psychiat.,* 1962, *2,* 265-283.
27 Wickes, F. G. *The inner world of choice.* New York: Harper, 1963.
28 Wolfenstein, M. The emergence of fun morality, *J. soc. Issues,* 1951, *7,* 15-25.

Chapter 22

Values and Existential Unity

James F. T. Bugental

SYNOPSIS

In this chapter I will propose that we recognize as the basic fact of human life the fact of existence itself. Existence is beyond words, but we need words to talk and think about our individual lives; therefore we invent-discover aspects of the unity which is existence. In this fashion, I will describe a way of thinking about the givens of our being and about the core dynamic sequence that leads either to our being authentic or to our losing our being in inauthenticity. These givens and the sequence that links them are heuristic conventions that are helpful to me as a psychotherapist as they aid me in thinking about the processes of being in my patients. With the help of this framework I will then examine the function of values as seen in this existential perspective. Briefly, I propose that that function is to restore the ontologic unity which our need (in terms of daily living) has fragmented.

Being is ultimately a unity, but I can only experience that unity wordlessly. As soon as I begin to think about being—and particularly when I begin to talk or write about—I must fragment the indivisible. Most conscious awareness (and all verbalizable awareness) about the incredible fact of being is, perforce, partial awareness. At any given moment we are aware only of aspects of what is most truly a unity. And it is through values that we try to reachieve that unity within or beyond the experienced diversity.

The I-Process and the Self

I will use two contrasting terms in referring to the person (Bugental, 1965, pp. 189-217). The *I-process* refers to the person as pure subject, pure process, without substantive qualities.[1] The *I-process* is awareness and choice or, better yet, being-aware-and-choosing. On the other hand the *Self* is the accumulated experience of the person and is purely object and exclusively substantive. So used, the *Self* has no awareness, makes no choices. What I call the *I-process* might also be termed the "Self-as-*doing*"; while my use of *Self* is the same as the often used phrase "Self-as-object."

Values and Beliefs

We must distinguish between values and beliefs if we are to have an appreciation for an important existential reality. In simplest terms, we may think of values as conditions of being which the *I-process* seeks to actualize. Beliefs, on the other hand, are associated with the *Self*. Thus my values are unspoken, directly intuited, and expressed in the choices I make. Beliefs are the things said about choices, whether implicitly or explicitly. We can have beliefs about values; we may value belief. Accordingly, we may use beliefs to try to give a consistent account of our lives. When we do so we evidence that we value consistency in belief. I can speak of beliefs or of your values, but in the latter instance I am expressing my perceptions—or even, my beliefs—about meanings in your actions. I never can see your values directly.[2]

Now this distinction between the locus of values being the choices of a person and the locus of beliefs being his account of himself is immediately a part of the existentially significant matter of the subject-object split within the individual. The alienated person may know

[1] This is a contrasting conception to that of Charlotte Buhler who postulates a "self" or "core system" with substantive properties. In simplest terms this is the contrast between a purely existential and an essentialist view. To understand the function of values as unifying agents this difference is probably not crucial.

[2] This manner of discriminating between values and beliefs is not general in the literature on these topics. I feel, however, that it has useful implications for our understanding of two related but contrasting aspects of our experience.

his beliefs in the sense that he can be articulate about what he perceives as important and unimportant, but he may be inconsistent and conflicted when it comes to his actual choices because of the confusion in his values.

Our values are expressed in the manner in which we confront the existential givens of being. The point of confrontation is the point at which value is created, is actualized. All authentic values can, ultimately, be traced back to these givens, I believe. Thus all values deal, ultimately, with courage and dread, with being and non-being, with life and death.

The Givens of Being

What, then, are the givens of being? (Bugental, 1965). As we have already seen, there is only one; the fact of existence itself. Each of us confronts this fact but partially, and each in his own way. As a psychotherapist I have found it helpful to recognize five attributes of the givenness of being:

1. We are embodied physically.
2. We are limited—in awareness, in strength, in life span, in all dimensions—within unlimitedness.
3. We can act and not act.
4. We can choose among the actions we will take.
5. We are apart from yet a part of others.

These aspects of the givenness of our being[3] are in themselves neutral or without subjective emotional significance; however, as we confront them in our lives and experience them subjectively, we find anxiety arising within us. This is existential or natural anxiety, natural in that it comes out of our very nature. Let us now examine how this comes about.

We are embodied physically

Because I am embodied, I am changing. As earlier chapters have already stated, the life of the individual is a constant evolution. It is in our bodies that we experience most acutely the fact of continual change. Recognizing this as a given of our being, we experience the existential anxiety of pain and destruction. This is to say that we are always in some measure subject to pain, concerned with avoiding or reducing it,

[3] To avoid unwieldy phraseology below I will not repeat the underlying recognition that these givens and the conceptual structure which is built upon them are heuristic conventions which I have developed to facilitate my thinking and communication about the wordless unity of the fact of existence. They are not true discoveries about the ultimate nature of the "out there."

and fearful of incurring or increasing it. Pain is a continuing form of our existential or natural anxiety. The pain itself is not the same as the anxiety of it, the sense of it as potential to our experience. Destruction, whether partial or complete, of our bodies is the ultimate form of the existential anxiety associated with confronting change. Destruction is not the same as death (see below) but is, rather, the threat of a change in one's being that is violent, reducing of our being, and irreversible.

We are finite

Because I am finite, I am confronted with contingency. I find that I can never know enough to ensure that which I want or to forestall with certainty that which I do not want in my life. I am not without ability to influence what ensues but I am always less than certain. Contingency means that my limitedness brings about the existential anxiety of fate and death.[4] The sense of being subject to fate is the awareness that what will happen is always in some measure unknowable, and it is the recognition that while many factors are involved in the determination of what will be actual, I can only control some of them. My best efforts and my most sincere intent may be unavailing at times, although often they may accomplish much. The threat of death, it will be seen, is the ultimate form of the sense of fate. What my death means and when it may come, I do not, cannot, know. Thus I must accept the existential anxiety of fate and death if I am to be authentic.

We can act or not act

While I cannot control all that will happen, I can take certain actions, and my actions do affect the flow of what becomes actual. I take part in the creation of reality. What I do and do not do contribute to what is. Thus I must confront responsibility. Responsibility is the subjective experience of making a difference. It brings with it the existential anxiety of guilt and condemnation. Guilt, as I am using it here, is not neurotic guilt nor does it carry an implication of moral failure. Existential guilt is the recognition that we are responsible and that in the exercise of our responsibility we always less than fully realize our potential. It is the recognition that our doing and not doing may result in consequences we would not have chosen had we been more fully aware that they would ensue. Condemnation is the ultimate form of this existential

[4] I am following Tillich's (1952) valuable observations in terming three of the forms of existential anxiety—fate and death, guilt and condemnation, and emptiness and meaninglessness—as he did. From the psychotherapist's perspective, our understanding is helped by adding two further forms: pain and destruction, and loneliness and isolation.

anxiety, and condemnation brings home to us the weight of our limitedness.

We have some choice as to how we will act

Man is not solely governed by instincts. At every point endless alternatives open to him. Man has choice. In vain man seeks signs and portents, knowledge and wisdom which will remove the terrible blessing of choice only to discover that he must confront his autonomy if he is to be authentic. This experience of autonomy is the root of the existential anxiety of emptiness and meaninglessness. The sense of emptiness arises from the recognition that the universe does not give answers, that the "right" and the "true," as well as the "beautiful," are always in the eye of the chooser. This is the continuing form of the existential anxiety whose ultimate form is the threat of meaninglessness. To the species-old cry, "Why am I here? What does it all mean?" the threat of meaninglessness provides only the haunting answer of silence.

We are each separate from but related to others

Each man is separate from each other man; yet always, unaccountably, each is somehow a part of the other. Confrontation of this paradoxical condition of apartness leads to the existential anxiety of loneliness and isolation. Loneliness is the relative condition which is always at least implicit in our lives and which reminds us of the ultimate threat of isolation from our fellow beings. Man is only human in a human context and requires that context of relationship as surely as he requires the atmospheric medium if he is to remain sane and realize his potential.

The Core Dynamic Sequence

The concepts presented in the foregoing paragraphs can be shown in a tabulation which will clarify their interrelation and some of the implications they have for our present study of the nature and function of values.

What is postulated here is a heuristic analysis of the existential fact of being. We need to make this analysis into the five aspects shown in Table 1 not because the existential fact is so divided (it is not), but because we cannot (at least at this point in human evolution) talk about the unity of existence. I have found that these five aspects help us to think and communicate about the unitary fact of being. They enable us to speculate on how our experience can be described in terms that are

Table 1. The Core Dynamic Sequence*

I discover world through awareness. I am in world. I am . . .				
EMBODIED	FINITE	ABLE TO ACT	ABLE TO CHOOSE	SEPARATE
These are the *existential givens.*				
Because I am so, I find I am subject to . . .				
PAIN	FATE	GUILT	EMPTINESS	LONELINESS
These are the forms of *existential anxiety.*				
I cannot escape existential anxiety. I can confront it. To confront it means to incorporate into my being-in-the-world . . .				
CHANGE	CONTINGENCY	RESPONSIBILITY	AUTONOMY	APARTNESS
These are the *existential confrontations.*				
If I find these too devastating to accept, I may seek to avoid the existential anxiety. Thus I will fall prey to feelings of . . .				
ILLNESS	POWERLESSNESS	BLAME	ABSURDITY	ESTRANGEMENT
These are the forms of *neurotic anxiety* or *dread.*				
On the other hand, if I do confront and incorporate existential anxiety, I am able to realize my being-in-the-world through . . .				
HEALTH	FAITH	COMMITMENT	CREATIVITY	LOVE
These are the forms of *authentic being* or *courage.*				
If I am authentic in my being-in-the-world, then I am able to realize . . .				
WHOLENESS	ROOTEDNESS	IDENTITY	MEANINGFULNESS	RELATEDNESS
These are the *existential needs* or *values.*				

*Adapted from Bugental, 1965, p. 287.

linked to them. These thoughts in turn lead us to conceive that we can respond to our being in a way that either flees from what is frightening in it—the response of dread or inauthentic living—or meets and accepts (incorporates) the frightening element and goes beyond it to a fuller accord with being. This we call the response of courage (Tillich's usage), and the characteristics that such living has may be thought of as existential values (our analysis here parallels that of Erich Fromm; *q.v.*, 1959). In this manner we have tried to integrate our concept of values with our analysis of the nature of being. The existential values we distinguish thus may be termed wholeness, rootedness, identity, meaningfulness, and relatedness.

VALUES ARE CREATED BY ACTION CHOICES

A human life is a continually evolving succession of answers that the individual gives to the questions put to him by the very fact of his being. Let me say this somewhat differently: I am constantly creating my life out of the stuff of my self and the ways in which I experience the givens of being. Each moment that I confront the limits of my knowingness, set against the unlimitedness of the potential, I bring my life into being anew. Thus at various stages in my life I give different answers to the questions put to me by my being.

Our study of the "core dynamic sequence" has shown that values have their locus in the moment of choice, the moment of action (whether overt or covert). Some choices are very peripheral to the existential confrontations while others are very central. However, to a greater or lesser degree every choice, every action, is ultimately a statement about one's living. Thus we may say that the confrontations ask us questions about our lives, and we respond in ways which either affirm or deny the existential values.

> Peter believed deeply in the importance of his family and home to his life. He was a devoted husband and a considerate father. Yet whenever his work called for him to be out of town, he found himself getting drunk or picking up a prostitute in a bar despite his conscious intentions not to do so. He came to fear, yet secretly look forward to, these trips on which he violated his own beliefs about himself.
>
> In Peter's therapy this compulsive misbehavior on his trips was found to be—as is almost always the case—multiply rooted (overdetermined). However, one clear line that emerged had to do with Peter's terrible dread of loneliness and isolation. As a boy he had been orphaned by an automobile accident that claimed the lives of his father, mother, and only sibling. He was raised by a succession of families, none of which really made him a part of its home. It became clear in the therapy that when Peter's business trips brought him to confront his essential apartness, he panicked at a deep level and had to drown out his anxiety with alcohol or deny it with a purchased simulation of intimacy.
>
> Further therapeutic work demonstrated that Peter feared any conflict with his wife. He also began to realize himself how he fluctuated between being too indulgent or too strict with his children. In brief, he was not able to be easy and natural with his family, which he valued so highly, because he used them as hedges against the dreaded confrontation with his apartness. Only as Peter came to recognize that essentially he had become estranged from his family by his use of them, could he begin to accept the fact of his ultimate aloneness and begin really to experience his love for his wife and children. The love had been there all along, of course, but had been diminished and blocked from full expression by the dread. Now it came through with great feelings of relief and joy for Peter. He came to value his relatedness to his wife and children for the relationships themselves and for these people who were so truly dear to him. Thus he actualized the value of relatedness

when he confronted his existential apartness and responded with the courage to love.

The therapeutic work with Peter involved a continual "peeling back" of his resistances (Bugental, 1965, pp. 88–151) by which he had kept himself from recognizing how much he lived in fear of being abandoned and in how many ways he had organized his life to avoid any test of his relationships with others. Therapy disclosed how he seldom gave orders or reprimands or otherwise acted "like a boss" with his subordinates at work, how he always made excuses for associates who seemed to treat him thoughtlessly, and how he usually left the room when his wife and children were in conflict.

The turning point—as much as any one event could be so described—came when Peter "broke through" his resistance of being "unable to think," i.e., when he finally recognized how often he used being "blank" as a way of avoiding confrontation. Shortly after achieving this insight in the therapeutic hour, Peter experienced a sharp sense of panic, great aching pangs of loss (particularly thinking of his wanting for a father), and a kind of desperation about his lifelong feeling of being phony and basically unlovable.

He had a brief and very angry dispute with his wife in which he spoke his feelings very candidly. Then they found they felt very close to each other, and Peter experienced his love for his wife with a newness that surprised him. When next he had occasion to travel, he told me later, he "somehow never got around to having more than a drink or two and didn't even think about picking up a girl."

Now the things to understand about Peter's experience are these: 1) His *beliefs* about family life were genuine and were not deceptions, although he was not able to live them out as those beliefs themselves would have dictated. 2) He was inauthentic in his being-in-the-world because he shrank from confronting his existential apartness and interposed many resistances born of his dread. 3) His living experience of his family (and his work and other aspects of his life as well) was incomplete and not fulfilling because of his inauthenticity. 4) When he reconfronted his anxiety about being separate and this time came to accept it, he was released to experience genuine love for his family in which he did not have to use them to hide from the reality of his being. 5) The basic value of life is authenticity; all other values are derived from this or are particularized interpretations of authenticity. Peter actualized his relatedness to his family when he confronted his aloneness and he argued with his wife, and when he went on a trip and accepted being alone without using drinking or sex to avoid that fact. The existential *value* we call relatedness was not something Peter verbalized to himself, nor is it something residing solely in our description of Peter's experience. The value is the implicit meaning Peter actualized at the choice points noted above; it is the way he experienced what it would mean to be authentic at those times.

This point is often difficult to grasp because our accustomed ways of thinking about such matters look for values as substantive patterns one consults in making decisions. The point I am trying to make here is that there is only one such guide that the person consults in actually choosing a course of action (as opposed to verbalizing about it), and that is authenticity (unless a flight from dread intrudes on the action-determination process and then it is *in*-authenticity which becomes the key). Perhaps the point can be made clearer if we imagine what Peter might have verbalized to himself had he been in touch with the processes of his awareness through which he made the decision to fight with his wife: "I just don't think she's right to say that. . . . I've usually ended the conversation at this point. . . . If we keep on, we'll fight. . . . If we don't keep on, it will be as if we weren't really important to each other. . . . I'm afraid to fight; I'm afraid she'll leave me like my parents did. . . . I can't be me or love her unless I tell her how I feel even if we do fight. . . . Well, here goes. . . ."

This, of course, is a completely hypothetical portrayal of what a person in Peter's situation might have gone through. Actually he reported no such internal conversation; the debate and decision were implicit in his "feel" of the situation, but they clearly had to do with his experience of being real in himself and his relation to his wife. What he might actually verbalize about his whole process would be his belief about it. In some instances the content of the belief might accord with the interpretation of the value actualized in his living but that does not equate the belief and the value.

This is a very important and much misunderstood point. I believe that value conflicts among authentic values do not occur when viewed in this way but belief conflicts do. Moreover I think that people often do not recognize that they have made value-actualizing decisions; Peter, for instance, did not speak of choice on the trip where he did not follow his compulsive patterns of many previous years. It is as though a person said, "Being who I am, I could do nothing else." "Being who I am," is being authentic. But when in flight, a person may very well do other things.

Let us pause to note that "being who I am," as I have used that phrase, is quite different from "being true to myself." If one seeks to be true to the *Self* as we have conceived it in this chapter, then he is being constrained by the past whether or not it is pertinent to authentic choice in the present moment. Such a choice is more a matter of beliefs about one's self than it is an actualizing of authenticity values. Perhaps we could phrase it this way: when a person experiences that he is expressing the underlying unity of his *I-process* in a choice, he is actualizing authenticity as a value. However, when a person is trying to build a consistent self-image by a choice, he is seldom acting authentically and is most likely responding through dread.

Some people may wonder how, if the *I-process* is conceived as fundamentally the process of awareness-and-choice, it can hold values? The answer lies in the conception of values we are here employing. They are not values of an objective nature (e.g., cleanliness, efficiency), nor do they constitute values in themselves (e.g., truth, justice). The values we have recognized—wholeness, rootedness, identity, meaningfulness, and relatedness—are merely ways of describing a person's being authentic in his own living, and are particular functional expressions of the basic value of authenticity. They are, then, the reactualization of the unity of the person, his existential oneness with his being and thus with all being.

References

Bugental, J. F. T. *The search for authenticity*. New York: Holt, Rinehart & Winston, 1965.

Fromm, E. Value, psychology, and human existence. In A. H. Maslow (ed.), *New knowledge in human values*. New York: Harper & Row, 1959, 151-164.

Tillich, P. *The courage to be*. New Haven: Yale University Press, 1952.

Chapter 23

"Today" as an Integrating Factor

Fred Massarik

However the course of human life may be defined, it is experienced in its entirety only on rare occasions. In the assessment of a life's work, in that specious moment when purportedly one's whole past flashes before one's eyes, we may note these exceptional instances. Even then, of course, it is the bygone stream of events that moves through our consciousness, though we may wish to view this historic aspect of our existence in the context of an anticipated future. But as an operational unit of goal setting, it is most often "today," *this* day, rather than any longer period, that gives substance to our aims and aspirations. Indeed, we may conceptualize the time dimension of goal setting, treated elsewhere by C. Buhler (Chapter 1) and E. L. Shostrom (Chapter 20), in terms of a series of complexly-overlapping "surfaces," each having specific saliency of its own at a given moment, and each in turn variously influenced by the others.

Among these interrelated surfaces, or time units, it would appear to be the *day* that provides the usual, natural element within which goal setting and, in fact, much of the essence of human experience derives concrete meaning.

Typically, "today" serves as the phenomenological focal point of the forces of the past, the arena of action for present events, and the base for orientation toward short- and long-range goals. Minor chores are defined and collated under the heading, "Things to do today"; long-term and complex objectives are subdivided into smaller, directly manageable tasks and finally allocated on a day-to-day basis. In the streams of events that constitute the course of life, it appears to be the day that thus emerges as most experientially salient in the study of goals, perhaps because it proves to be both long enough to contain diversified content and short enough to be conveniently grasped. It stands at the juncture, somehow, of the ineffable moment of fleeting experience—too brief for reflection—and of the "long haul" of weeks, months and years, often too remote and abstract to penetrate deeply into the fibers of consciousness and selfhood.

The above is not to imply any monolithic constancy in the day's significance for all people or all cultures, nor such constancy for one individual at all stages of his life. Some people do, of course, perceive *their* primary reality in longer time units, especially if they set for themselves (and ultimately live through) a series of extensive, well-preplanned goal events. Others lead their lives devoid of goal setting in any formal sense, responding on a continuous, *ad hoc* basis to circumstances as they evolve, so that their relevant unit of personal time becomes an ill-defined succession of "here-and-now's," each vaguely blending into the other. Stable cultures may extend the time unit, rapidly changing ones may contract it, and the child's day seems infinitely longer and more filled with a cornucopia of goals, attained or not, than that of the adult. A systematic inquiry into the nature and correlates of time units as variously relevant to people under varied circumstances seems needed. Without prejudging the outcome of this kind of investigation, this chapter considers the normal, often unspectacular day, *this* day, as a useful concept focusing many forces of the life-long goal setting process.

"Today" as an Integrating Concept

It has been said, poetically and in philosophic reflection, that each day—indeed each moment—represents the current joint outcome of the vast tangle of interlocking factors that shape our lives. There is, of course, nothing static about this "outcome"; it constitutes simply a convenient abstraction in a process of persistent change. Nor is it possible at the present stage of knowledge to provide a rigorous analytic dissection that would separate this often-mystifying knot into distinct strands, ultimately to demonstrate their differential levels of importance in affecting the human condition. This book notes the operation of *codeterminants* in goal setting, and the interaction of these codeterminants is revealed in some measure as we consider the person's objective situation and subjective sense of what his "today" is all about. We may apply this approach to concepts considered in this volume:

This is a new day. The person awakens. Though at the time he typically makes no effort to analyze his situation, he faces the day at a given stage in his life's course (Part I), heir to a complex past that incorporates the interplay of genetic factors (Part II), early emotional dynamics (Part III), and sociocultural Forces (Part IV). In a sense, his very "being" constitutes an ahistorical net result of the several co-determinants, as related not only to goal setting, but to human life in general.

Specifically, what has emerged from the crucible of the past, with its blending of intrapersonal and interpersonal dynamics, is the person's self-system. It comes to serve as the *modus operandi* of daily goal setting, expressing the thrust of C. Bühler's "basic tendencies," and predisposing toward relative soundness or pathology in goal choice.

Facing The Day

There is that ephemeral state—we may call it the *sense of awakening*—when sleep has not quite faded and when awareness of the new day's reality has not yet fully asserted itself. Even in this perceptual twilight of early morning, the context for the day's goals is established. At this point, the day's potential may appear as little more than an inchoate haze, but, all the same, within it is lodged the capacity for approach to or withdrawal from the tasks ahead. The person emerges from the psychophysiology of sleep which, partly through the vehicle of dreams, serves to express desires and needs that later are reformulated in terms of goals and objectives. One may jest about "getting up on the wrong side of the bed" and about "being no good until after that first cup of coffee." Still, the hypothesis that a significant relationship exists between the sense of awakening and subsequent morning "warm-up" on one hand, and response to the day on the other, may deserve systematic investigation. The relationship probably is complex rather than directly causal; for instance, persistent ill humor upon arising may not be a simple "cause" of negativism during the day, but both conditions may reflect an underlying hostile life style.

Eventually, the person evolves his *day's agenda*. Several dimensions in agenda formulation may be noted. First, *explicitness*. For some people, the process of daily agenda setting is explicit and specific, while for others it remains implicit and vague. In K. Lewin's terms (1936), one may consider various life spaces, some showing neatly separated, distinct goal regions, with clear boundaries, while others contain little if any indication of the presence of goals.

The process of explicitly specifying what today's goals are is, in Western (or Westernized) culture, implemented by any number of devices. These may include, for example, a person's hand-written entries in a pocket calendar, a secretary's appointment book, a well-defined mental image of projected activities, or a multitude of scribbled notes on the backs of a motley assortment of used envelopes. In a military setting, they may take the form of "orders of the day"; in a corporate situation they may relate to entries on a PERT chart, indicating the timing and sequential flow of subtasks—parts of a larger task system, required ultimately to yield a complex end product.

However, there are those for whom daily goal setting in any formal sense is anathema, or simply irrelevant. Two major polarities in personality structure may appear: (a) the spontaneous, and (b) the anomic.

The spontaneous, though lacking clear daily goals, face the unfolding of the day's events with immediate and intentional response, drawing, in the process, on a well-integrated repertoire of personal resources. While they make no effort to spell out what they will do *today*, they are guided by long-term, or even by life-long, goal patterns. These provide a stabilizing general framework, leaving room for considerable freedom and improvisation in dealing with the current exigencies of living.

The anomic are, like the spontaneous, devoid of daily goals, and perhaps make no intentional responses other than those concerned with direct need satisfactions. Their repertoire of personal resources is relatively impoverished, and to them no long-term or life-long configuration of goals is available to establish a broad context within which purposeful daily activity may plausibly occur. At the extreme, this personality structure includes the alienated and the drifter, for whom neither the day ahead nor the sweep of a lifetime has substantial meaning.

A second dimension of the day's agenda is its *complexity*. In some cases, the day is so arranged that the person perceives, either explicitly or implicitly, only a few distinguishable goals; "to read a book," for instance, may be a vacationer's sole goal on a particular day. For others and under other circumstances, there may be a whole jumble of goals, many ill-defined but all competing for attention. Perhaps more functionally, there may be elaborate, carefully-devised edifices of goals, with each goal level setting a firm base for the level to follow.

Finally, a third dimension of the day's agenda is its *rigidity*. This dimension—the capacity for reorienting goal patterns as necessary—is especially salient when such goal patterns are explicit and complex. It is tested as the pressures of events "upset the applecart" of plans well made. How does the person react when the unforeseen erodes, or annihilates, what he has set out to do this day? Is he capable of mobilizing an appropriate "back-up" agenda that in some measure will maintain movement in the direction initially intended? Is he able to switch to a spontaneous response mode, thereby dealing appropriately, though on an *ad hoc* basis, with changed conditions? Or else, does destruction of the initial agenda lead to an abandonment of all goal-directed behavior? The literature on frustration and its psychodynamic and sociopsychological consequences, though focused usually on longer time spans and on pathological states, is relevant to the study of goal rigidity in daily agenda formation.

Ending the Day

The concepts of integration (Part V) and of fulfillment and failure (Chapter 24) are applicable to the study of "today," particularly to the day's end. This terminal point is in part a reflection of the day's cyclical aspect. This cyclicity emerges as a point product of at least three interactive factors; (a) the prevalent succession of sunrise, daylight, sunset and night, (b) the processes of human physiology, especially as related to the organic requirements of nourishment and rest, and (c) the correlative social and psychological processes—for example, awareness of the necessity for nourishment and rest, and of the culturally-linked modes of their satisfaction. In turn, it provides a period, notably in the latter stages of the day, as one cycle moves to its conclusion and the next one looms ahead, that appears suitable for purposes of interim assessment.

Review of a lifetime's success or failure is a meaningful and weighty matter; it is necessarily abstract and speculative. In it the events of many years are treated synoptically, for it requires consideration of a multitude of part-remembered, part-forgotten, and often faded or distorted recollections. A life-long past is, in the words of poet-author John Updike, "... after all but a vast sheet of darkness in which a few moments, pricked apparently at random, shine. . . ." (1962). Much less so the day. With their relative recency, the day's events, in spite of the person's selective recall, at least carry an immediacy and specific impact lacking in reflection on longer time periods. Thus, an evening review of the afternoon's accomplishments is likely to generate more direct action *quickly* than a long-term retrospective self-assessment. The latter may have deeper roots and eventually may lead to more profound emotional changes, but it also requires greater persistence in a retracing of the vast cumulative canvas of personal and social experiencing. Pathologies, of course, may be diagnosed in which the day's concern with an apparently minor occurrence becomes as agonizing as though the person were confronting a fundamental existential crisis.

There now unfolds a process which is phenomenologically the reverse of the sense of awakening. Noting the day's fulfillment or failure and the gradations between these extremes may, of course, be a fully wakeful procedure, a rational, purposeful weighing of the positive and negative events that have just transpired. Or it may be a gentle, unplanned process, a drifting off into hypnagogic thought, where the day's occurrences are experienced vaguely, shrouded with a varied aura of pleasure or concern (Foulkes, 1966). In some way, the person responds to questions he himself poses: "What does it add up to?", "Is it all worth it?" In the course of these reflections, the person also may find that he is engaged in exploration of prospective goals, developing a basis for formulation of tomorrow's agenda.

"Today" as Research Topic

Throughout history, time and its significance in human life has been a favorite area for speculation and theorizing. In recent years it has become a moderately active field of empirical inquiry. Illustrative of the former are philosophic classics such as Martin Heidegger's *Being and Time* (1927, 1962), J. B. Priestley's eclectic and colorful *Man and Time* (1964), and curiosities such as the anonymous *Art of Employing Time to the Greatest Advantage, the True Source of Happiness* (1822). Examples of the latter include compilations such as Pitirim A. Sorokin and G. Q. Berger's *Time Budgets of Human Behavior* (1939), survey and diary approaches like Sebastian de Grazia and Nelson N. Foote's *Aging and Leisure* (1961), John Cohen's conceptual analysis in *Humanistic Psychology* (1958, 1962), Paul Fraisse's comprehensive *The Psychology of Time* (1963), and Robert Tannenbaum and Arthur Shedlin's sentence-completion and interview studies (1967).

Much of the published research reports quantitative analysis of time use, particularly differentiating various categories of people in their behaviors as consumers, their leisure preferences, and their work patterns. Beyond descriptive and relatively simple analytic treatments, the more deeply probing search for understanding of the personal meaning of time, whether for the course of life or for a single day, is sparse. The variability of the day's activities with the seasons of the year, for instance, has been recognized (Foote, 1961). But "today" as a topic for humanistic research, encompassing not only gross distinctions among broad rubrics, but focusing also on the existential subtleties of daily experiencing, has not yet come into its own. It is not a matter of either-or: comprehensive survey, diary, and observational methods, particularly for large representative samples and systematic typologies, need to establish broad frames, to be augmented by the phenomenology and inner exploring that has as its aim a fundamental grasp of what this day really seems to be about, especially as viewed by the protagonist himself.

Methodologies are required that will do justice to the interwoven sequential, simultaneous, and cumulative significance of a day's living. They will need to take into account the stream of other orientations, such as the past and the overlapping futures, ultimately extending to life as a whole, that establish the context of today's experiencing. Within this time-linked, uneven mélange of goal configurations, "today" with its unique relevance provides an opportune rallying point for philosopher and scientist in their joint quest for a more thorough understanding of human goal setting.

References

(Anon.) *The art of employing time to the greatest advantage, the true source of happiness,* London: Henry Colburn and Co., 1822.

Cohen, J. *Humanistic psychology,* New York: Collier Books, 1962, pp. 103-124; (reprinted from George Allen and Unwin Ltd., 1958).

De Grazia, S. "The uses of time," in Robert W. Kleemeier, ed., *Aging and leisure,* New York: Oxford University Press, 1961, pp. 113-154.

Foote, N. N. "Methods for study of meaning in use of time," in Robert W. Kleemeier, ed., *Aging and leisure,* New York: Oxford University Press, 1961, pp. 155-176, espec. p. 167.

Foulkes, D. *The psychology of sleep,* New York: Charles Scribner's Sons, 1966, espec. pp. 121-137.

Fraisse, P. *The psychology of time,* New York: Harper and Row, 1963.

Heidegger, M. *Being and time,* New York: Harper and Row, 1962, (first published, 1927).

Lewin, K. *Principles of topological psychology,* New York: McGraw Hill, 1936, espec. pp. 118-165.

Priestley, J. B. *Man and time,* Garden City, N.Y.: Doubleday, 1964.

Tannenbaum, R., and Shedlin, A. Unpublished reports, Graduate School of Business Administration, University of California, Los Angeles, 1967.

Updike, J. "The Astronomer," in *Pigeon feathers, and other stories,* New York: Penguin Books, 1962, p. 129.

Chapter 24

Fulfillment and Failure of Life

Charlotte Bühler

Concluding Experiences of Fulfillment and Failure

Few people's lives seem to be guided by an overall directive. Their pursuits often seem incoherent and incomplete. Yet, in the later phases of life, people tend to look back over their lives and to evaluate them in terms of total or partial fulfillment and/or failure. In thinking of their lives in these terms, they prove in a way that, although subconsciously, directives have been operative all along. Only this assumption would explain the fact that they view their lives in relation to certain results that should have been obtained or avoided. Strangely enough, people think of these results not only as something that they would have liked to accomplish, but beyond that as something that they "should" have accomplished, even though usually nobody told them so.

There are, of course, individuals who cannot admit their lives' failure to themselves. But psychotherapy can usually help a patient to see himself clearly in this respect and to make peace with himself after he has accepted the truth.

> For instance, a refugee woman, now 60 years of age, felt that the circumstances of her life were responsible for the fact that she was living alone and still had to work hard. Irina was sure that if she had not been forced to leave her native Poland in the middle of her twenties, when she was engaged and looking forward to a secure and happy life, she would not find herself in the situation she was in now.
>
> It is true that the loss of her fiancé, who stayed on as an officer of the Polish army and died in the war, was not her fault. But after she came to the States, she had settled quickly for a marriage with a man with whom she had very little in common, and whom she divorced after a few years. And furthermore, instead of pursuing during this marriage her great wish to prepare herself for a teaching career, she let herself be induced to try for a quick financial success in a real estate career. She was not particularly suited for the latter and consequently did not become successful enough to feel secure.

Her personal life led her through a number of affairs, one of which was a mutual love relationship. But her twice divorced partner did not wish to marry again. So Irina found herself at 60 without the husband and family she would have liked to have had, and without the interest or the security of a really desirable occupation. When she entered psychotherapy to find help for her unhappy and rather bitter feelings, she was convinced that the "waste" of her life was entirely due to the unfortunate circumstances she encountered in her youth. But gradually she realized that at several turning points her own decisions had prevented her from striving toward more satisfactory as well as self-realizing goals.

Self-Realization in Sex, Love, and Accomplishment

Sex, love, and accomplishment seem to be the areas of life in which people experience self-realization and subsequently fulfillment.

As psychoanalytic studies of half a century have shown, the pathway to healthy and successful sex-love relationships is full of perils. Warped desires, conflicting drives, excessive expectations, wrong choices of partners, and other neurotic behavioral patterns prevent all too frequently the development of satisfactory as well as lasting diadic relationships. Yet most people realize as they get on in years that the failure to have experienced the right sex-love relationship prevents them from ever feeling fulfilled.

A similar feeling of failure occurs in the area of accomplishment when a person has not been able to realize his full potentials. Thus Irina felt that no matter how difficult it would have been, she should have struggled to prepare herself for the professional career she wanted. She felt that even if she had been successful at the occupation she chose, it would not have brought her the fulfillment that she would have found in teaching.

Aside from cases like this, where lack of self-realization in the chosen work area is the reason for failure feelings often described as "waste," we encounter still another kind of disappointment in cases who complain of the "emptiness" of their existence when they begin to consider it retrospectively.

Integration in Family and Society

Lowell, 60, had been a hard-working businessman who was on the point of retirement. From very poor beginnings, he had developed a chain of stores in several communities and had made a considerable fortune for himself and his family. Instead of enjoying the fact that he had reached his original goal so fully, he fell prey to a depression and a feeling of emptiness that he could not explain to himself. He did not know what to do with his free time. He had no desire to travel as his wife wanted them to, he had no hobby, no interest, no commitment to occupy him. His interest in politics had been rather superficial and his study of the stock market had of late failed to stimulate him.

In examining Lowell's life history one finds that he lived in a satisfying marriage with an attractive but rather passive housewife-type of a woman, whom he said he loved, and their one, now grown-up, son. This boy, who had studied law and was about to establish himself in a practice and with a family of his own, had never been interested in his father's stores and had more or less moved out of his parents' lives. The relationship between all these people was friendly, though rather superficial. Lowell had always, he said, had his family in mind when he worked, and this commitment was obviously meaningful to him. Yet he did not really give of himself and was, in a way, a very isolated person. He had no close friends, and participated in organizational and community activities only in the most superficial ways. He belonged to a club, he gave money to charities, but he gave nothing of himself. Thus his integration in family and society was obviously not very deep. His feeling of "emptiness," therefore, must be interpreted as the result of his isolation within the pattern of superficial participation.

What is lacking in his life is a true dedication which, as we said before, makes life meaningful. Its absence seems to leave people with the feeling of emptiness or meaninglessness, even if they move within patterns of commitments.

Partial and Essential Fulfillments

On careful inspection one hardly ever finds a completely fulfilled life. Denials, losses, and failures seem unavoidable but many lives are at least partially, or even essentially, fulfilled.

An essentially fulfilled life is one in which the just mentioned basic requirements of fulfillment have been obtained. Several case histories show that people can overcome severe misfortunes, once they have had the chance to love truly and devote themselves to some objective. We speak of partial fulfillment if a person has found full satisfaction in only one of the two basic areas of life.

Compensatory Fulfillments and Resignations

Although we have no quantitative data as yet, a student of life histories gains the impression that compensatory fulfillments and resignations constitute the majority of any given sample, that is to say, that most people seem to make compromises when they enter marriages or careers. They may, depending on their adaptability as against their self-actualization needs, accept the life pattern that offers itself or harbor a resentment and disappointment without being able to do anything about it. These life histories end with semi-acceptance or a somewhat bitter resignation, subject to the amount of compensatory or frustrating experiences.

Concluding Observations

This book has had two major objectives. The first objective was to show the complexity of the process of goal setting. We have studied goal setting in human life and all through life as it develops under the impact of four major factors: the structural, genetic, emotional dynamic, and socio-cultural factor. The problems of integration with which the individual is faced were also examined.

The second objective of the book was to offer a new point of departure to the psychotherapist and possibly to the educator. In complementation to existentialism which holds that human beings are concerned with the whole of their existence, this book shows, from the point of view of humanistic psychology, that there are different degrees to which human beings experience the course of their life as a whole. They feel to different degrees responsible for this entity and expect from it certain results toward which they strive, often without being fully aware of it. But the fact that toward the end people are able, or even feel compelled to, size up the result of their lives indicates that they have followed a directive all the time or much of the time. We have shown it operative from the start of the individual's life, and have called it the human being's intentionality toward fulfillment.

Index

U

V

W

Y

Author Index

D

E

F

G

H